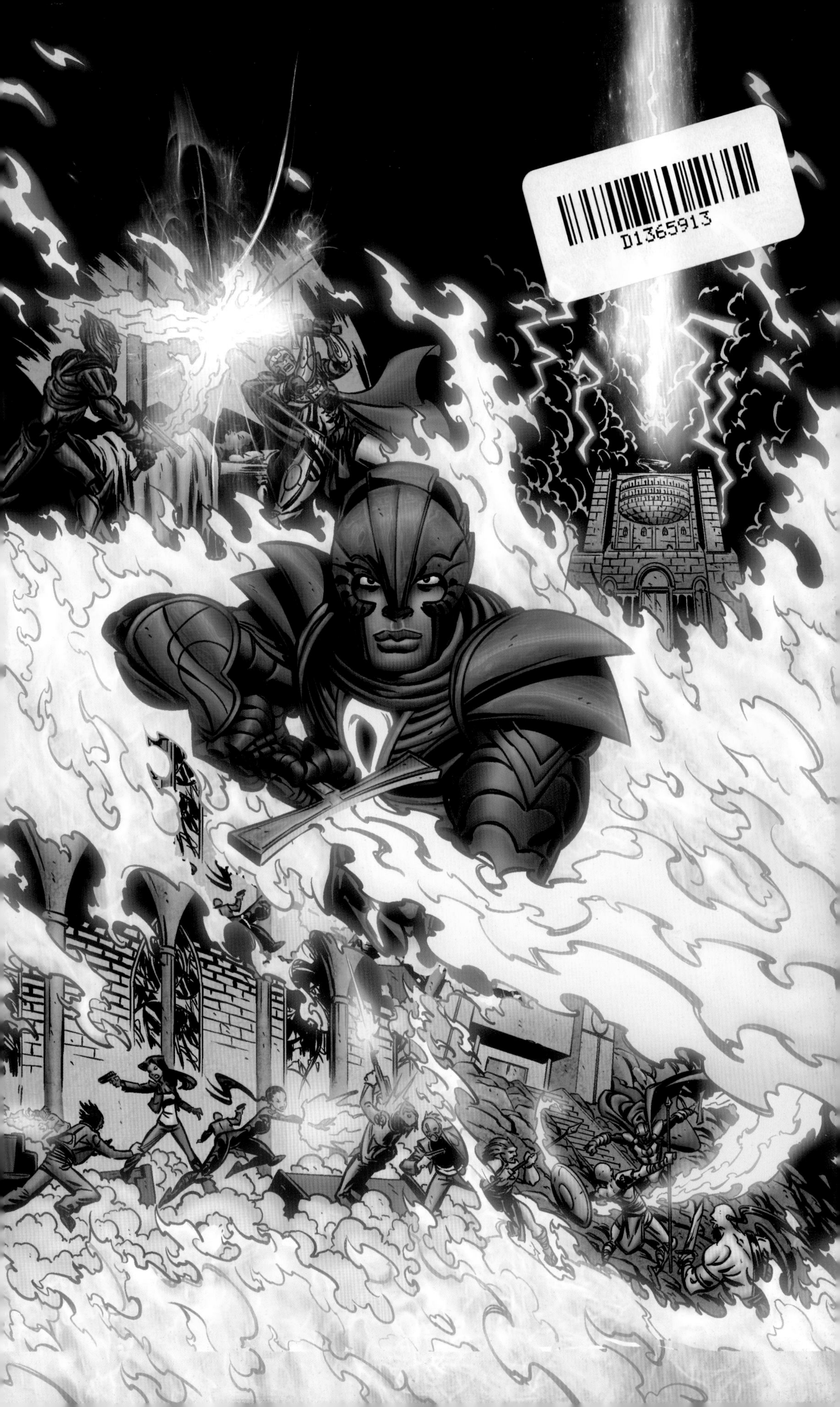

PREVIOUSLY IN…

—LEGEND OF THE—
MANTAMAJI™

Elijah Alexander, A.D.A. in New York, learned he was the last of a race of mystical knights called the Mantamaji. Motivated by revenge for the death of his mother Mariah at the hands of Sirach—a former Mantamaji turned evil—Elijah agreed to join Noah, an age old Mantamaji, to take down Sirach and his army of followers. The first step was to kill the Four Horsemen—disciples of Sirach whose deaths, it was said, would weaken their leader.

Elijah's girlfriend, Detective Sydney Sanchez, was pursuing the story behind Brother Hope (Sirach's public face), and started to piece together the history with the help of the last surviving Sanctuants-warrior women from the time of the Mantamaji.

Elijah and Noah defeated the first two Horsemen in a huge firefight at Unity Bank, where they learned that Sirach plans to open the gates of time and alter earth's history. They raced to the Cloisters, where Brother Hope/Sirach was about to lead a rally.

After faking his own kidnapping to elude Sydney and her police commander boss, Sirach set a trap for Noah and Elijah. Elijah killed the last two Horsemen—and learned that everything he thought he knew was a lie. Sirach was stronger than ever. Betrayed, beaten and helpless, Elijah was thrown off the cliff into the Hudson River and left for dead.

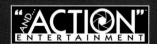

"AND..." ACTION" ENTERTAINMENT

"And... Action!" Entertainment © ™ All Eyes On E, Inc.
10061 Riverside Drive, Suite 296 Toluca Lake, California 91602

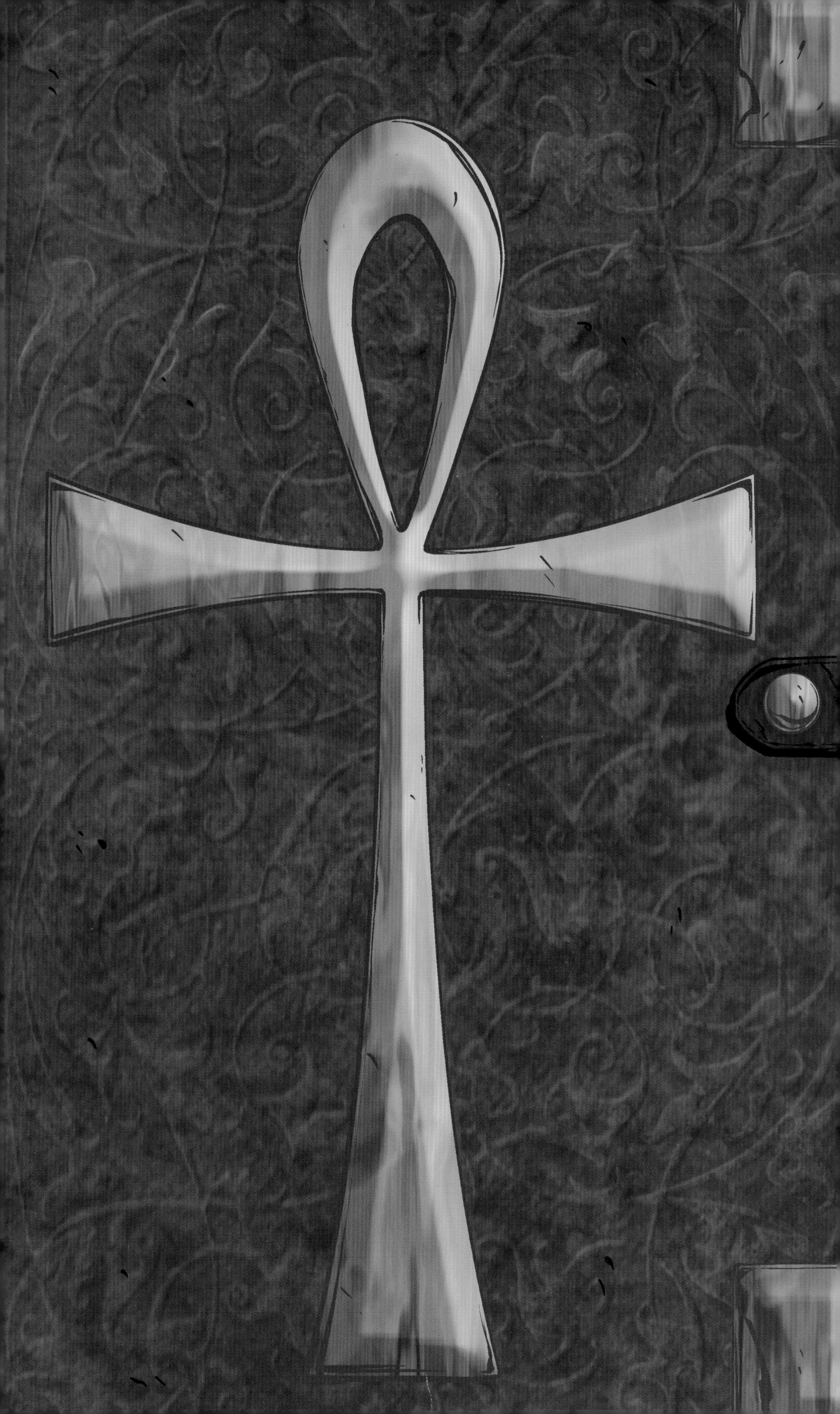

CHAPTER ⑫

My all-beautiful Son, I must tell you an ancient tale. It concerns a race of divine protectors, mystical defenders, who sacrificed their lives for their people's safety. Their appearance was always comforting, for they were noble and they were good. But it was also disturbing, for surely they would not appear unless something was very wrong...

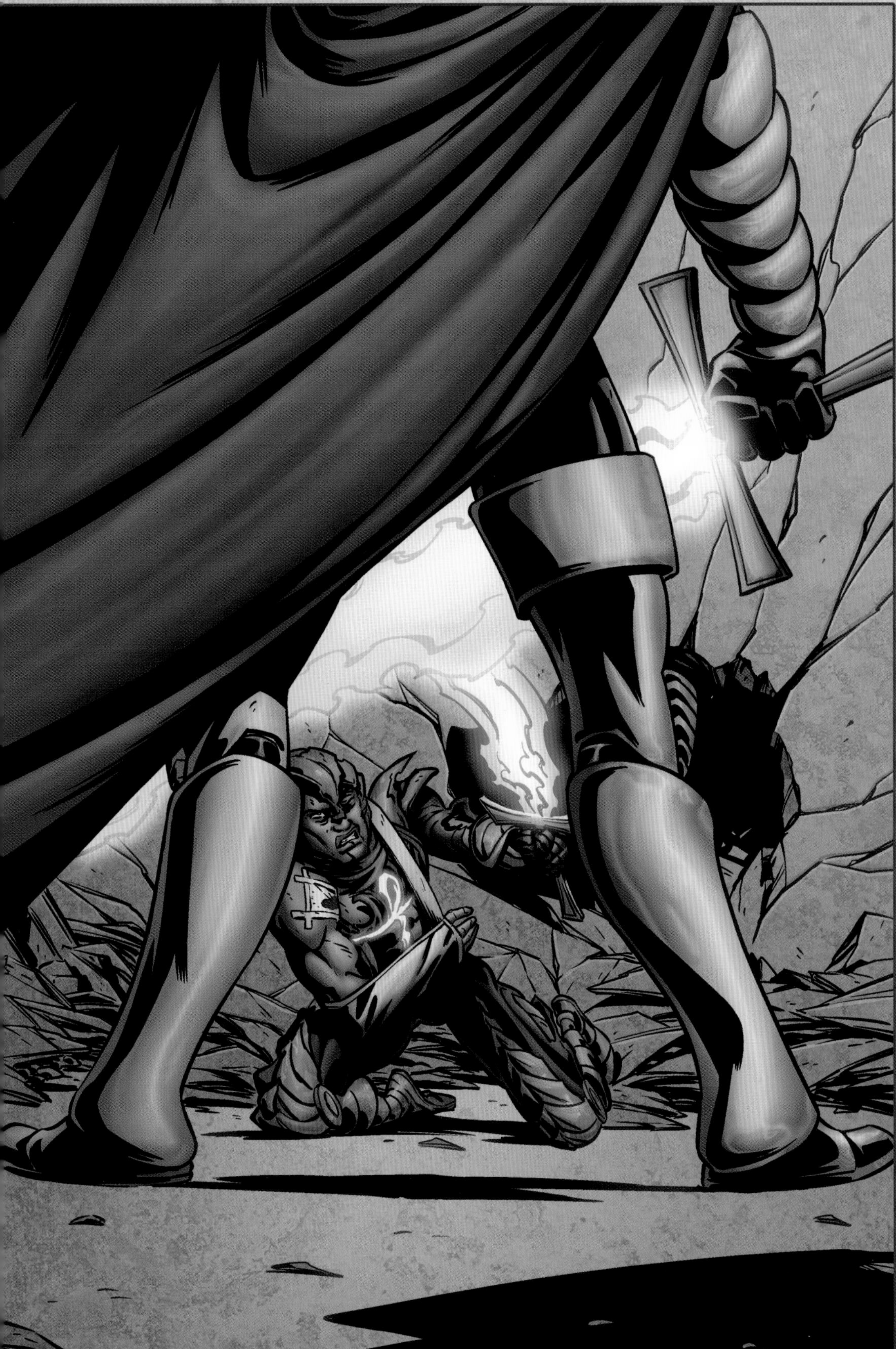

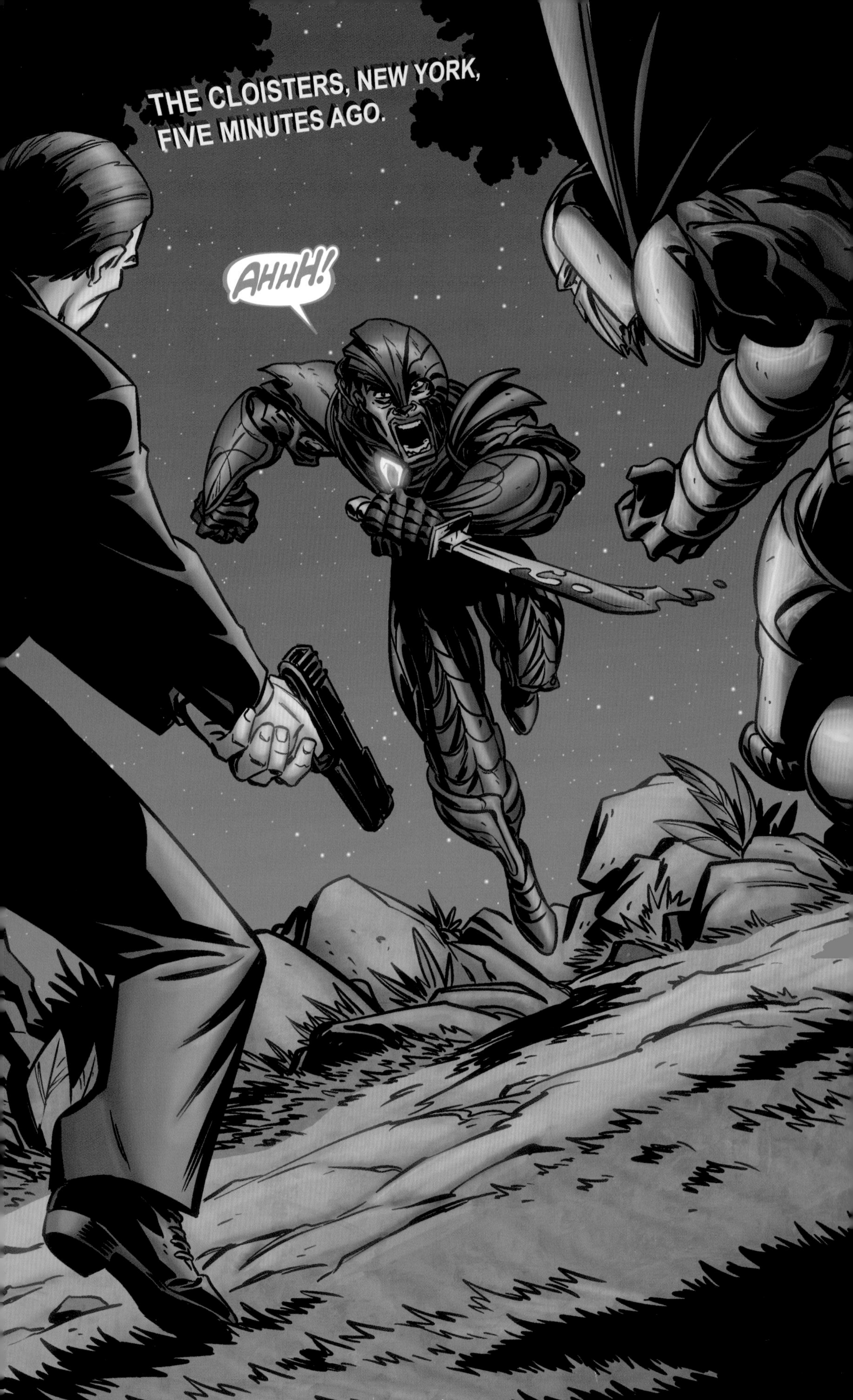
THE CLOISTERS, NEW YORK, FIVE MINUTES AGO.
AHHH!

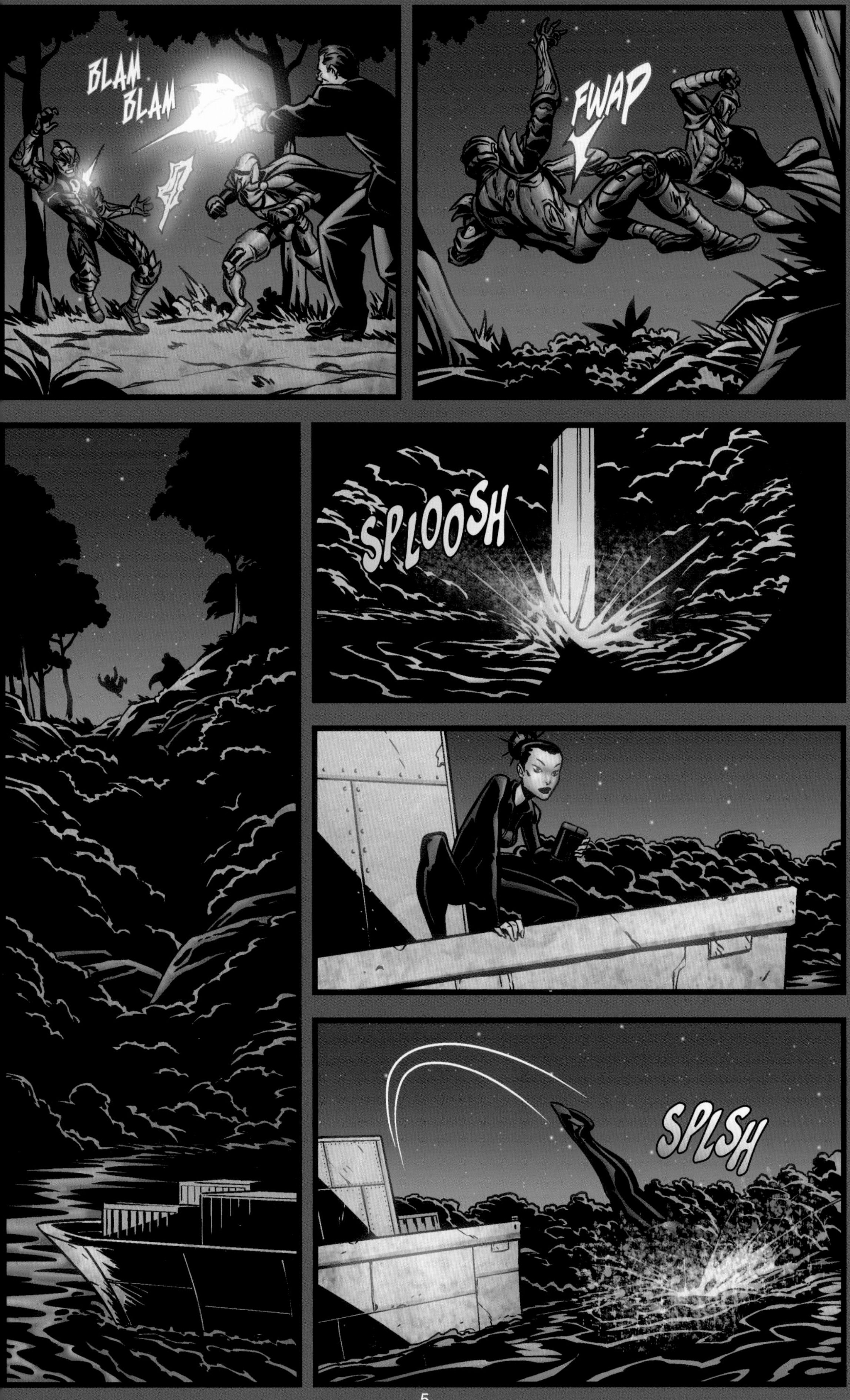
BLAM
BLAM
FWAP
SPLOOSH
SPLSH

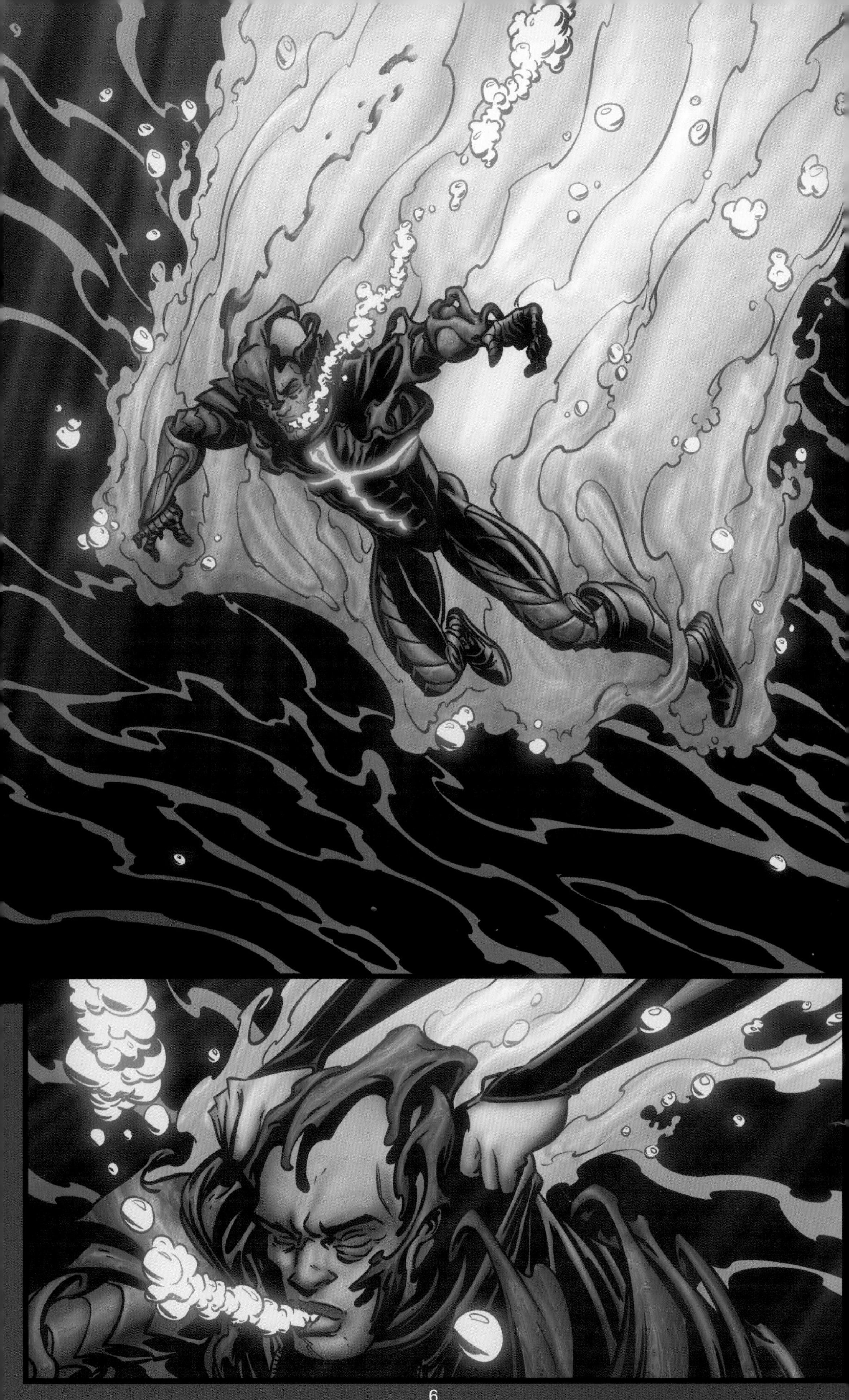

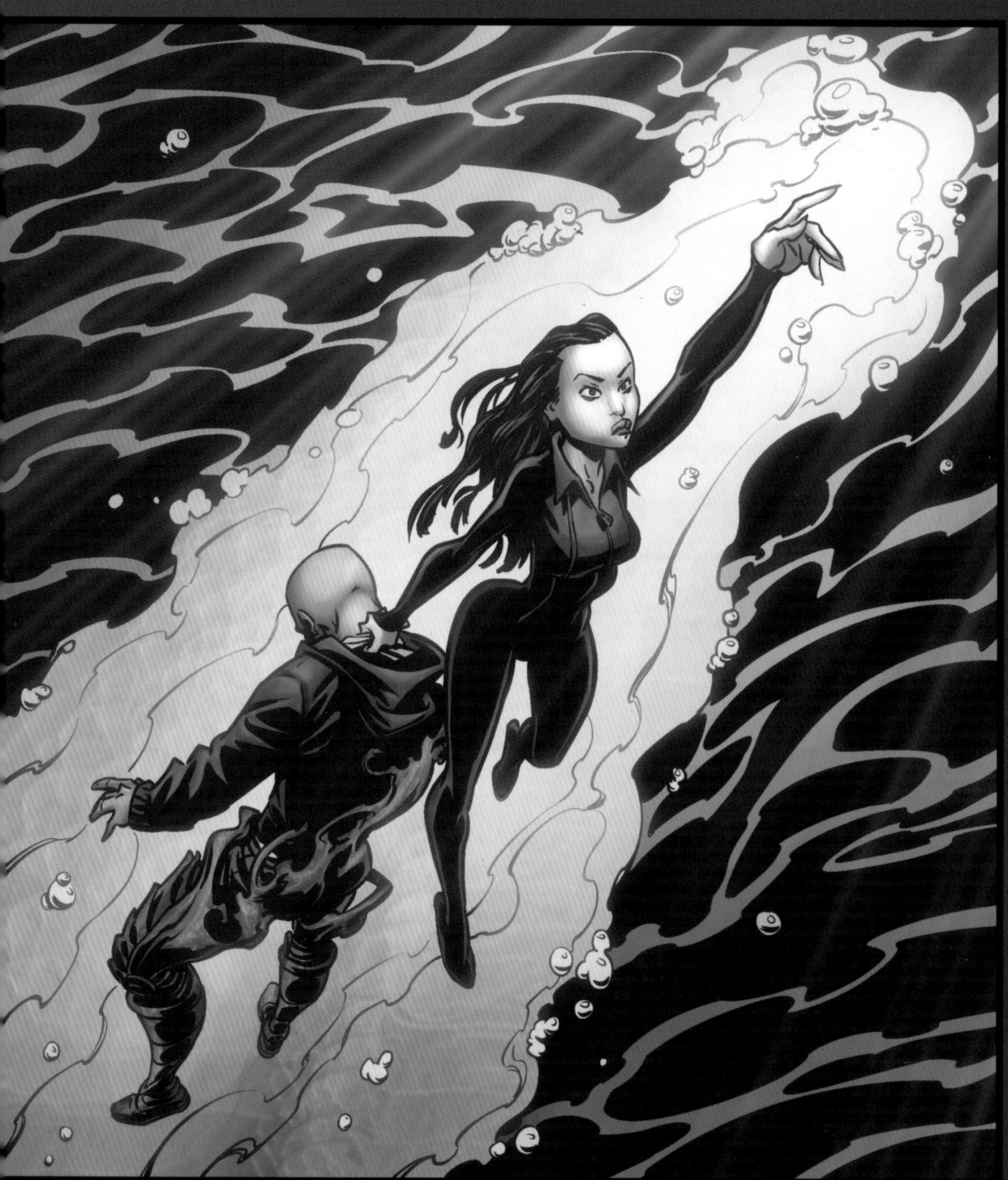

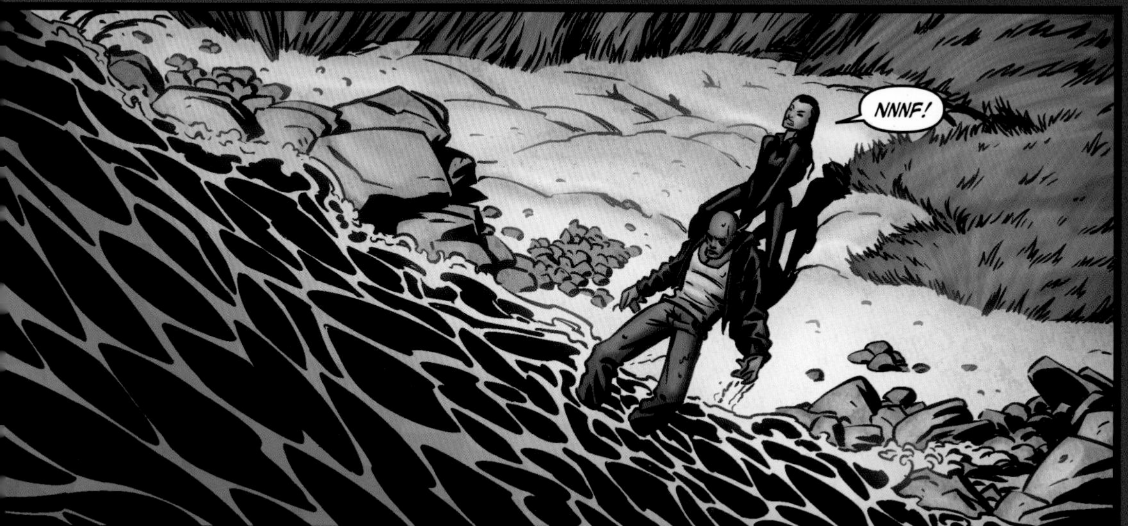
NNNF!

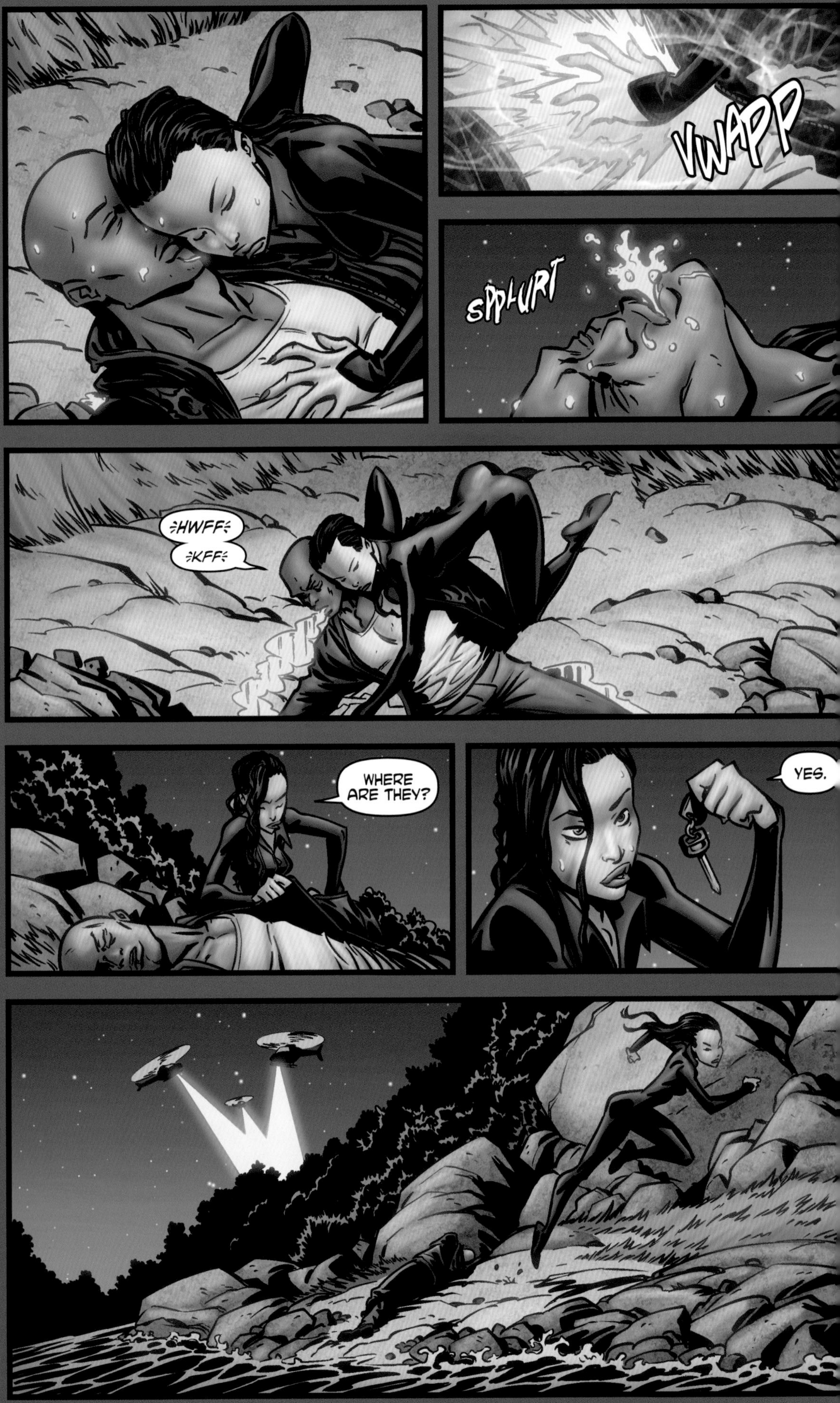
VWAPP
SPPLURT
HWFF
KFF
WHERE ARE THEY?
YES.

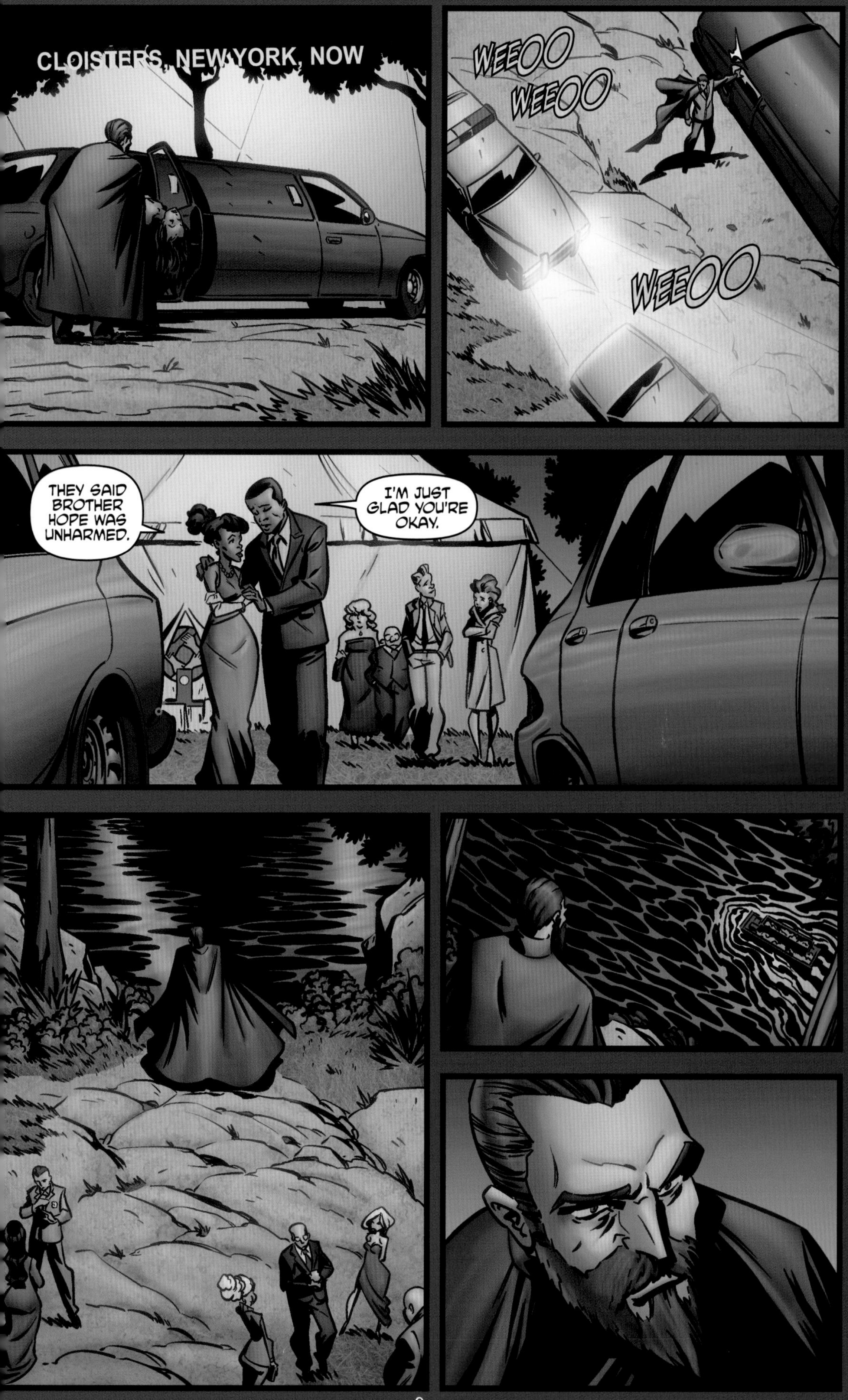
CLOISTERS, NEW YORK, NOW
WEEOO
WEEOO
WEEOO
THEY SAID BROTHER HOPE WAS UNHARMED.
I'M JUST GLAD YOU'RE OKAY.

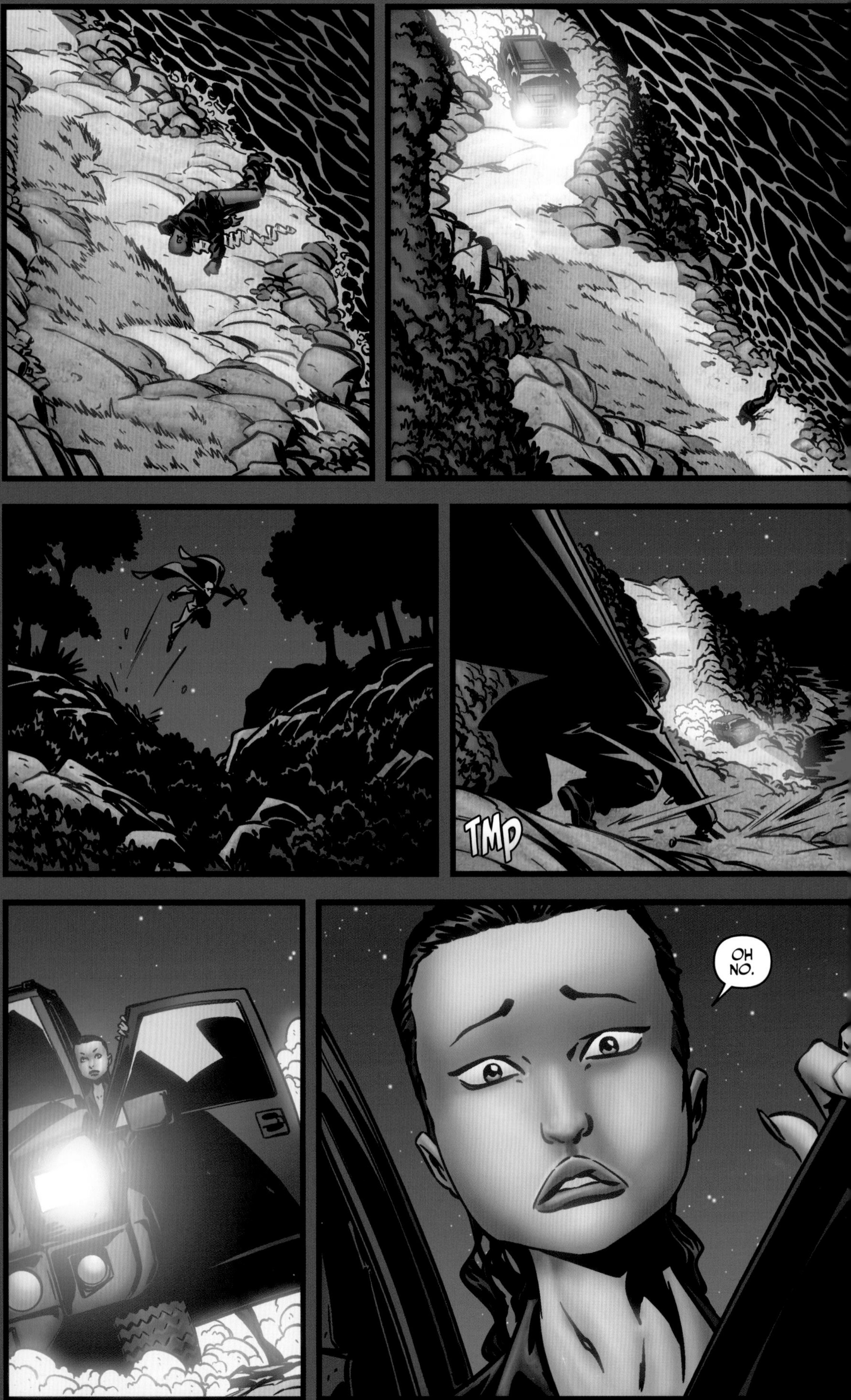
TMP
OH NO.

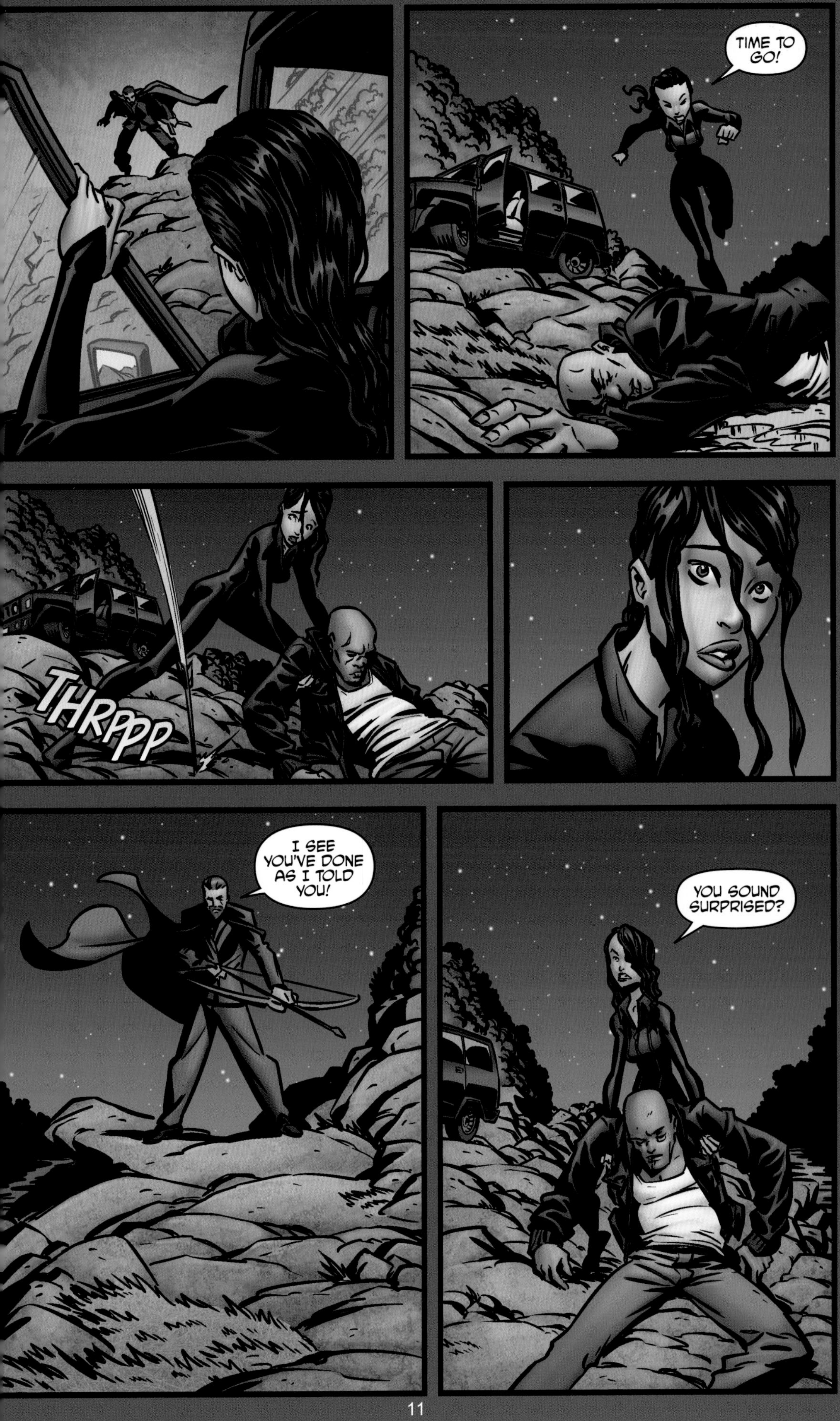
TIME TO GO!
THRPPP
I SEE YOU'VE DONE AS I TOLD YOU!
YOU SOUND SURPRISED?

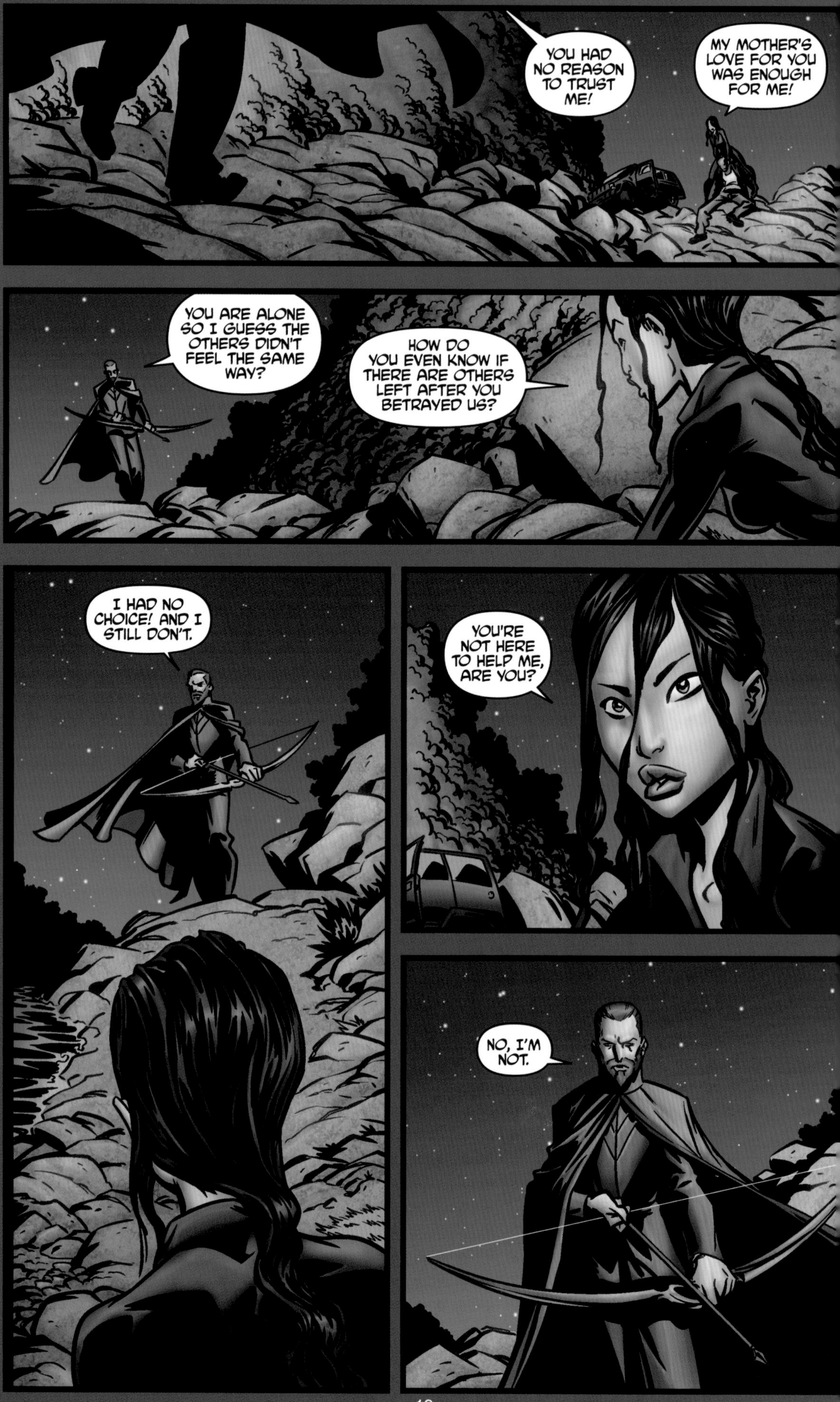
YOU HAD NO REASON TO TRUST ME!
MY MOTHER'S LOVE FOR YOU WAS ENOUGH FOR ME!
YOU ARE ALONE SO I GUESS THE OTHERS DIDN'T FEEL THE SAME WAY?
HOW DO YOU EVEN KNOW IF THERE ARE OTHERS LEFT AFTER YOU BETRAYED US?
I HAD NO CHOICE! AND I STILL DON'T.
YOU'RE NOT HERE TO HELP ME, ARE YOU?
NO, I'M NOT.

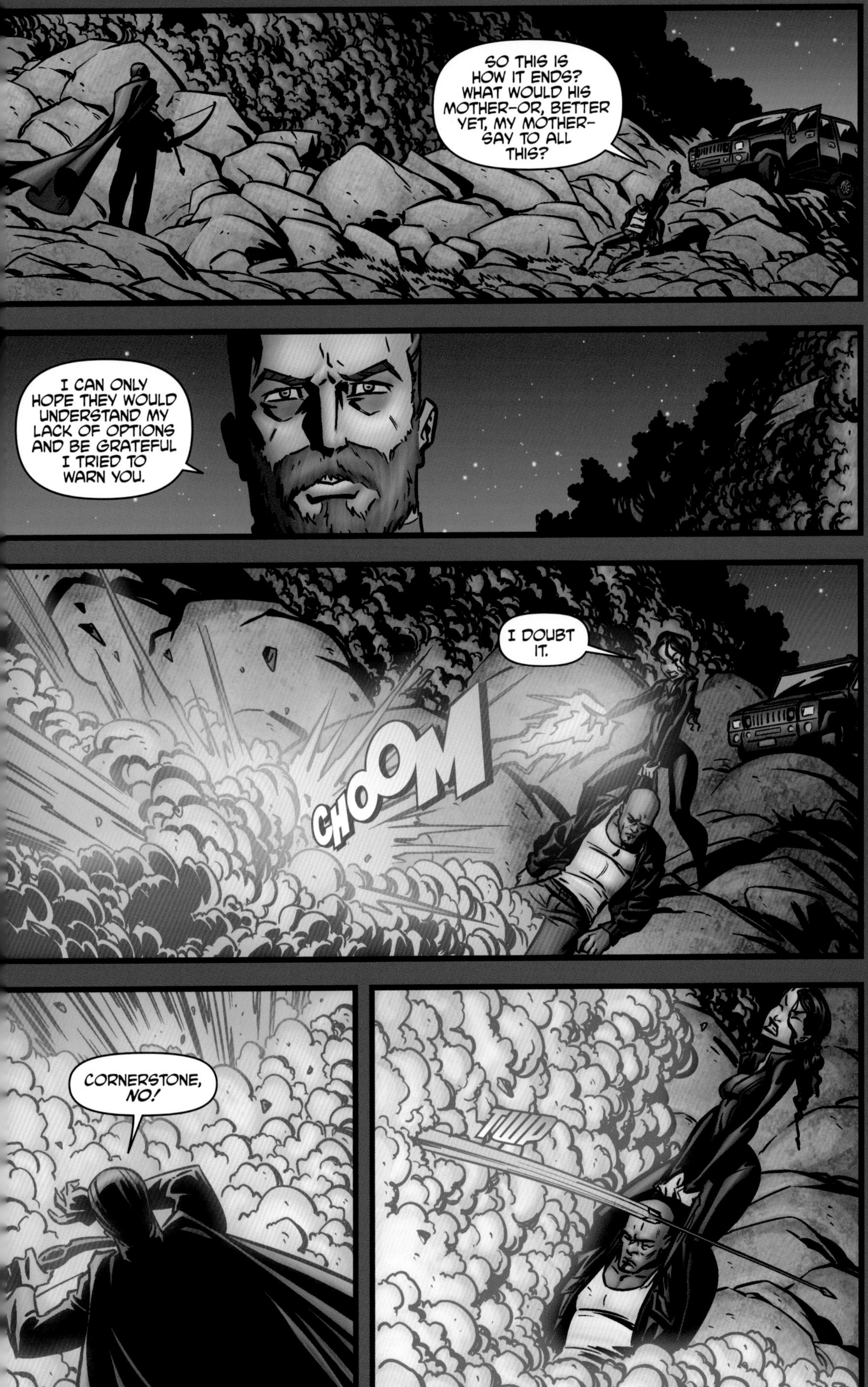
SO THIS IS HOW IT ENDS? WHAT WOULD HIS MOTHER—OR, BETTER YET, MY MOTHER—SAY TO ALL THIS?
I CAN ONLY HOPE THEY WOULD UNDERSTAND MY LACK OF OPTIONS AND BE GRATEFUL I TRIED TO WARN YOU.
I DOUBT IT.
CHOOM
CORNERSTONE, *NO!*
TWP

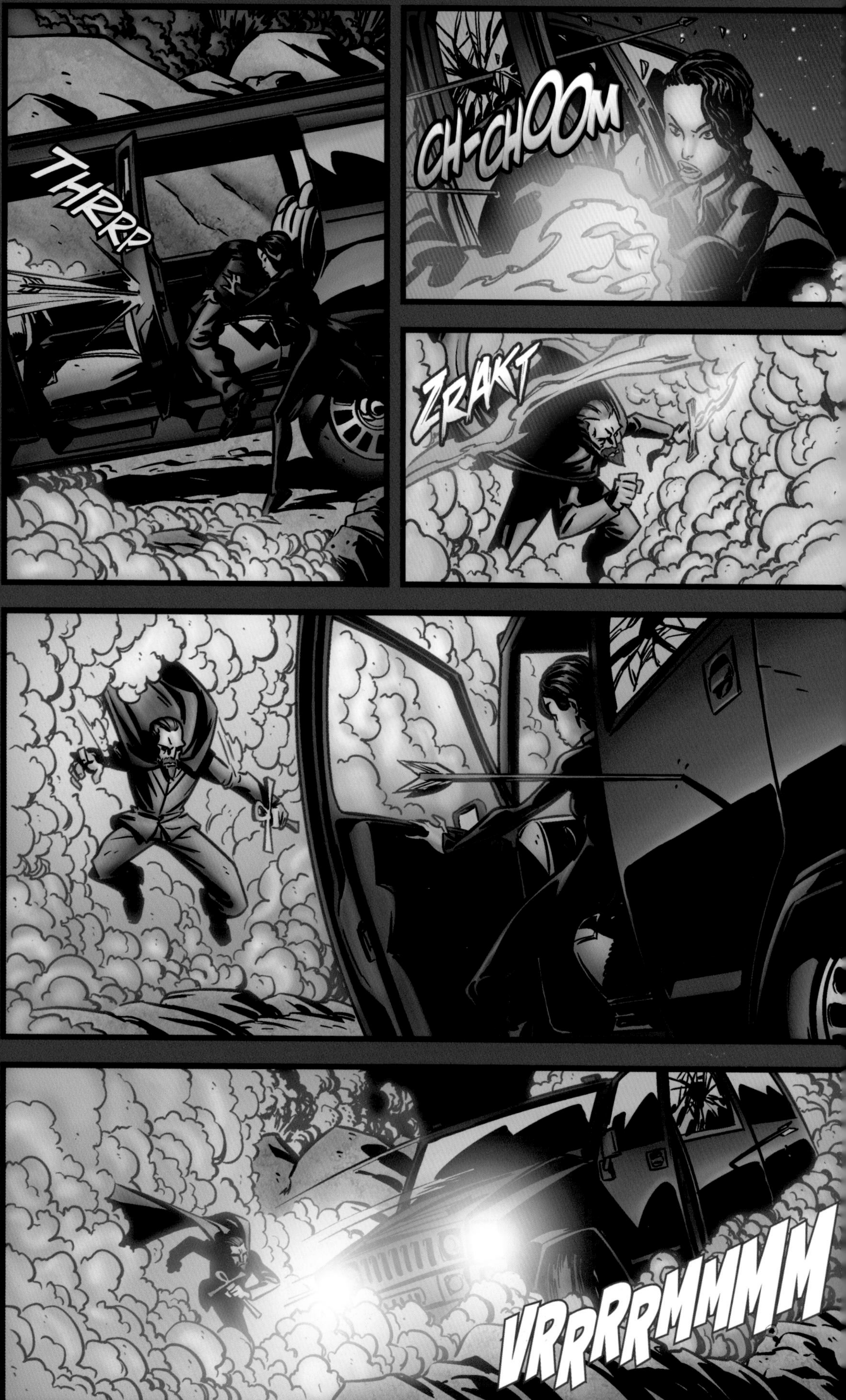
THRRP
CH-CHOOM
ZRÄKT
VRRRRMMMM

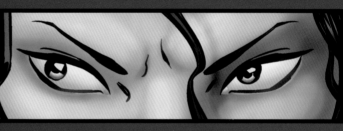

COME ON! JUMP, OLD MAN, JUMP!

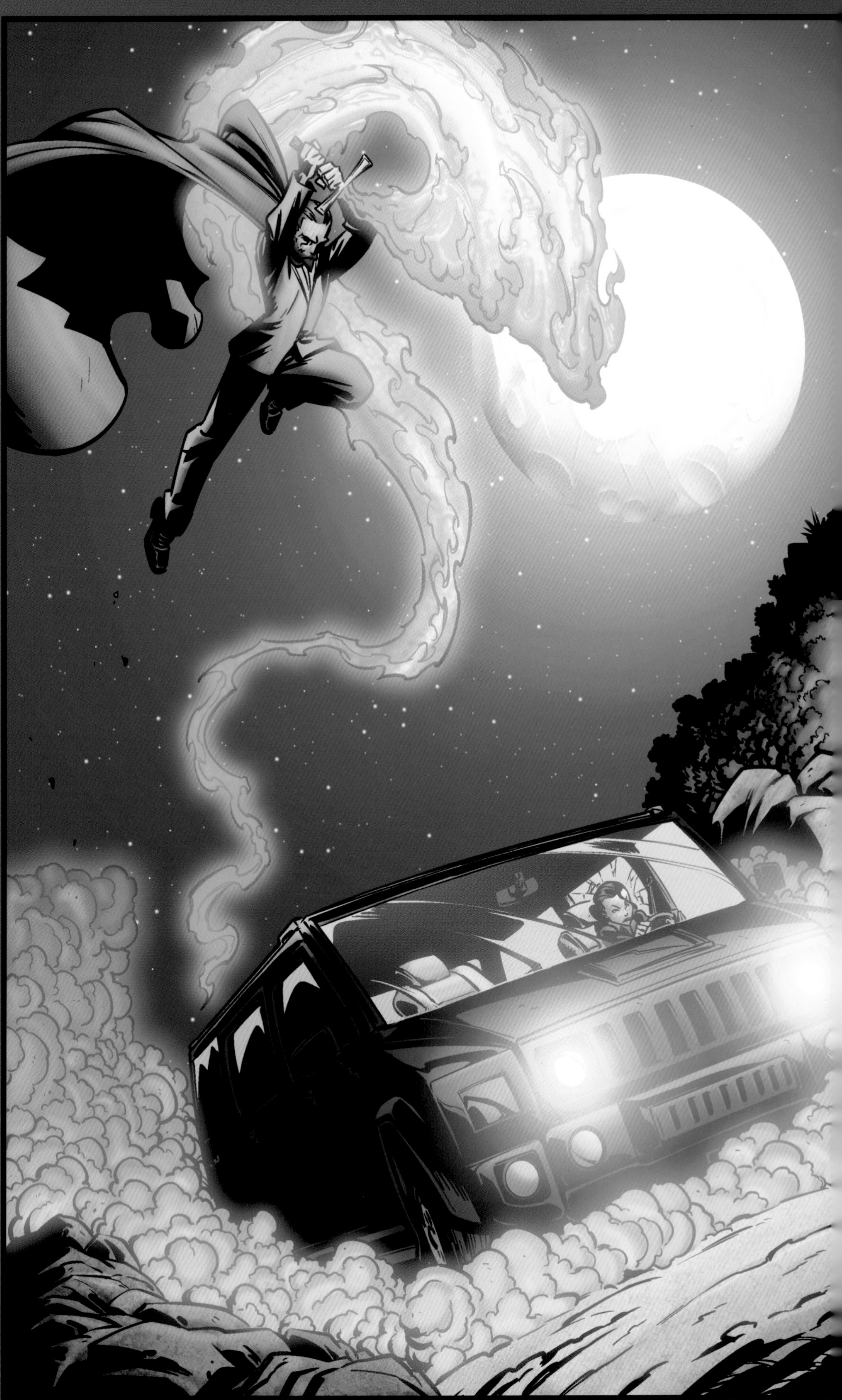

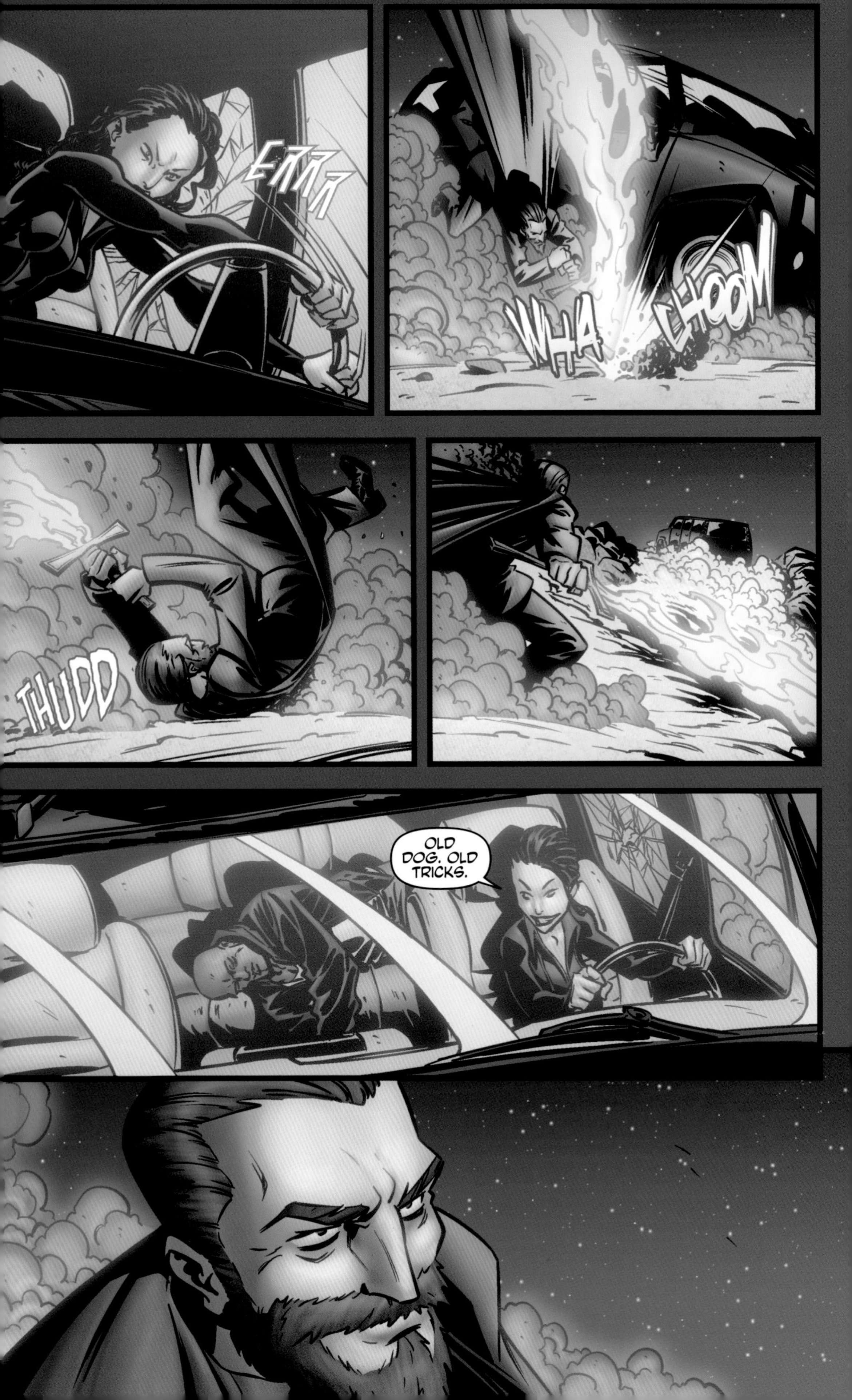

ERRRR
WHA CHOOM
THUDD
OLD DOG. OLD TRICKS.

LEGEND OF THE MANTAMAJI

CREATED AND WRITTEN BY
ERIC DEAN SEATON

ART BY
BRANDON PALAS

COLORS BY
ANDREW DALHOUSE

LETTERS BY
DERON BENNETT

EDITED BY
DAVID ELLIS DICKERSON

10061 Riverside Drive, Suite 296 Toluca Lake, California 91602. Legend of the Mantamaji and its related characters are ™ and © 2015 of Nighthawk Entertainment, Inc. All rights reserved. Published by "And... Action!" Entertainment © ™ All Eyes On E, Inc. Any similarities to persons living or dead is purely coincidental. None of the publication may be reprinted, copied or quoted without the written consent of Nighthawk Entertainment, Inc. Printed in Korea. ISBN 978-1-930315-56-3

CHINA TOWN, DAWN. 10 HOURS LATER

I CAN NOW REPORT THE RUMORS OF AN ARMORED ASSAILANT CALLED THE MANTAMAJI ARE TRUE.

THIS MANTAMAJI IS ALSO THE LEADER OF THE GANG KNOWN AS THE NEW WORLD KNIGHTS, WHO SEEK REVENGE AGAINST BROTHER HOPE.

NYPD CMDR. CARL COTTON

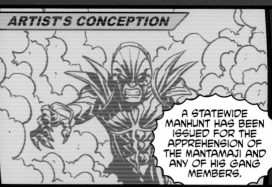

ARTIST'S CONCEPTION

A STATEWIDE MANHUNT HAS BEEN ISSUED FOR THE APPREHENSION OF THE MANTAMAJI AND ANY OF HIS GANG MEMBERS.

LAST NIGHT, IN A FAILED KIDNAPPING ATTEMPT, THE MANTAMAJI KILLED BUSINESSMAN ARGO YAMATO AND THE OWNER OF THIS NETWORK, LISA LEGARDI.

Argo Yamato   Lisa Legardi

IF ANYONE HAS ANY LEADS TO THEIR WHEREABOUTS, PLEASE CONTACT THE NEW YORK POLICE DEPAR--

CLICK

NICELY PLAYED, SCUMBAG.

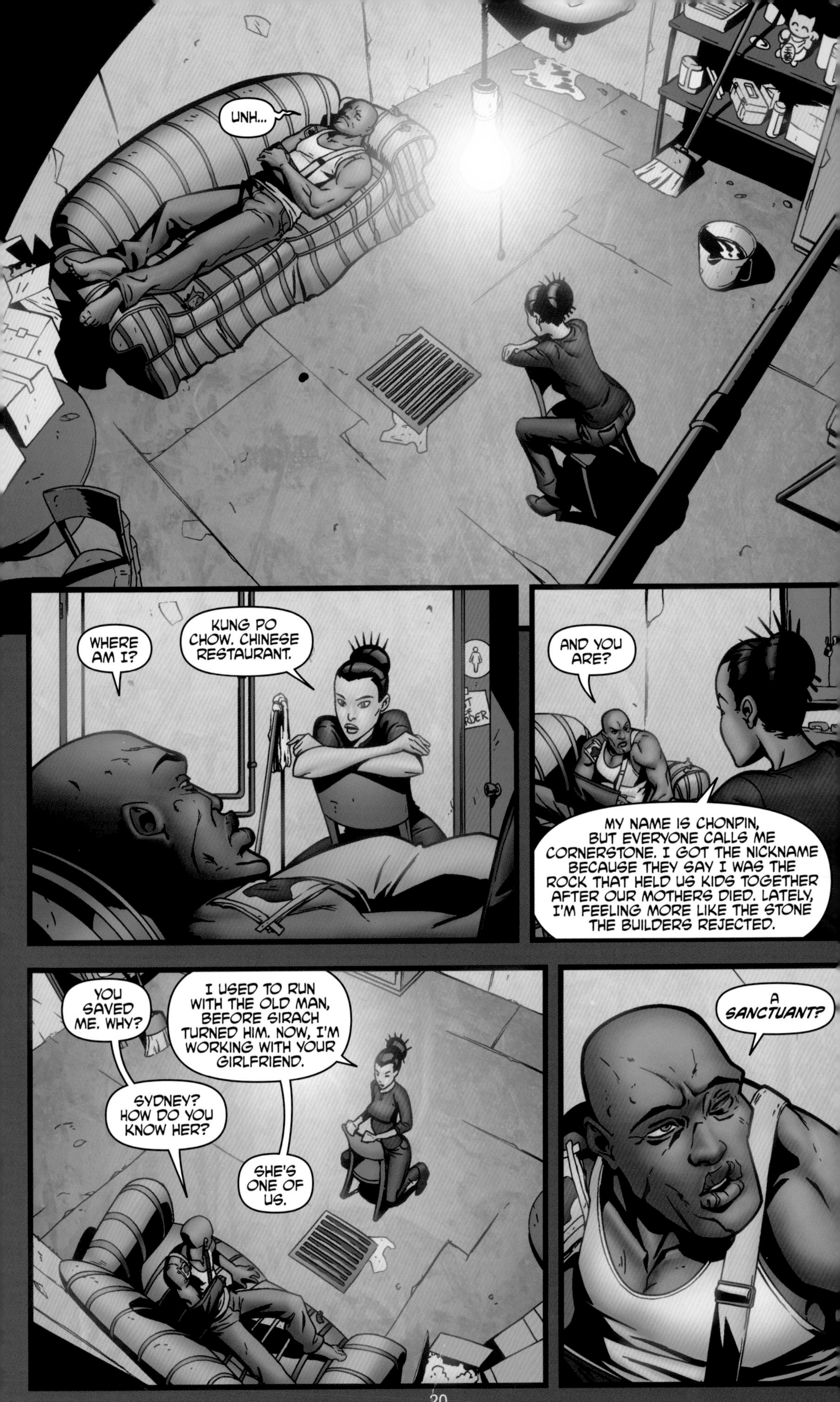
UNH...
WHERE AM I?
KUNG PO CHOW. CHINESE RESTAURANT.
AND YOU ARE?
MY NAME IS CHONPIN, BUT EVERYONE CALLS ME CORNERSTONE. I GOT THE NICKNAME BECAUSE THEY SAY I WAS THE ROCK THAT HELD US KIDS TOGETHER AFTER OUR MOTHERS DIED. LATELY, I'M FEELING MORE LIKE THE STONE THE BUILDERS REJECTED.
YOU SAVED ME. WHY?
I USED TO RUN WITH THE OLD MAN, BEFORE SIRACH TURNED HIM. NOW, I'M WORKING WITH YOUR GIRLFRIEND.
SYDNEY? HOW DO YOU KNOW HER?
SHE'S ONE OF US.
A SANCTUANT?

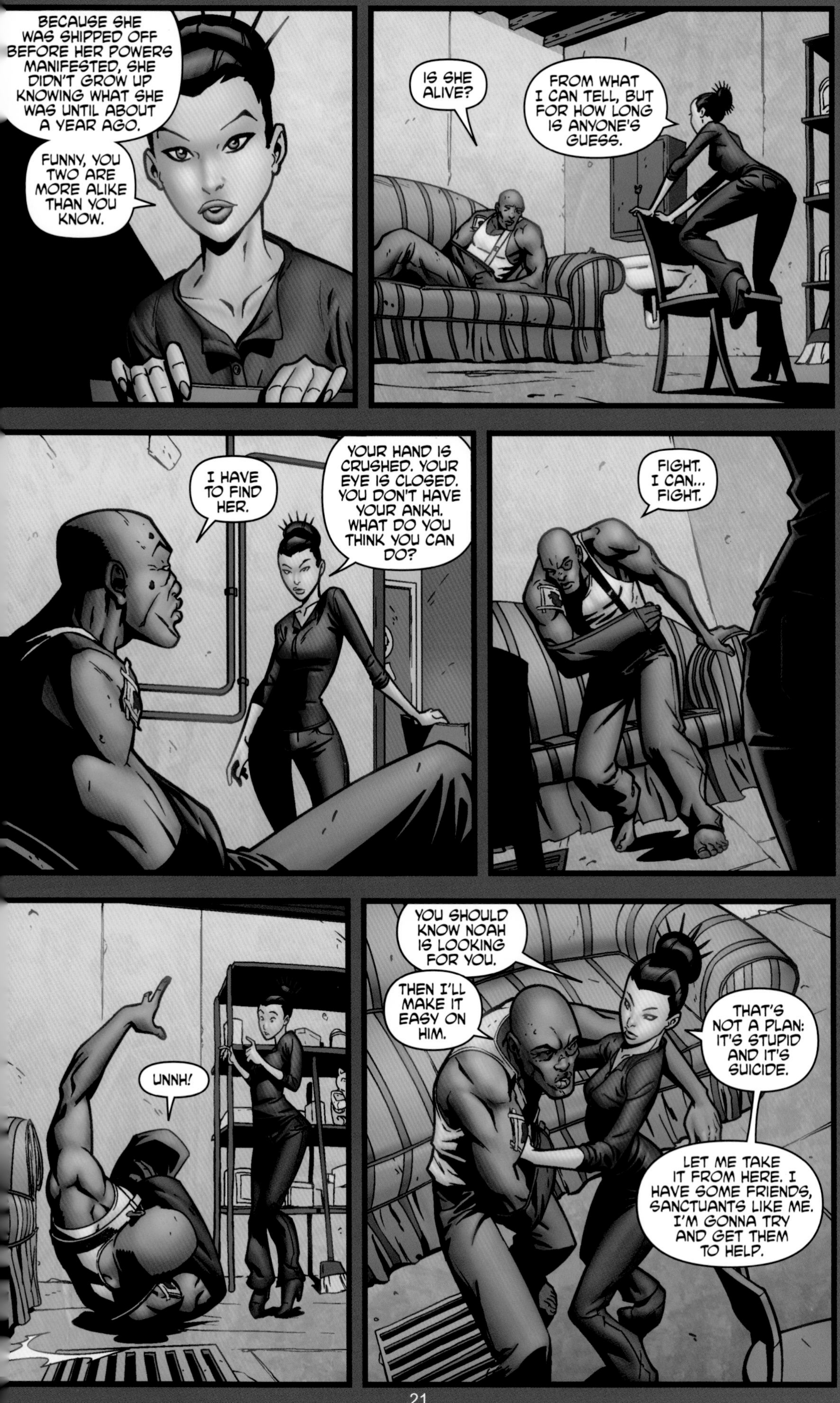
BECAUSE SHE WAS SHIPPED OFF BEFORE HER POWERS MANIFESTED, SHE DIDN'T GROW UP KNOWING WHAT SHE WAS UNTIL ABOUT A YEAR AGO.
FUNNY, YOU TWO ARE MORE ALIKE THAN YOU KNOW.
IS SHE ALIVE?
FROM WHAT I CAN TELL, BUT FOR HOW LONG IS ANYONE'S GUESS.
I HAVE TO FIND HER.
YOUR HAND IS CRUSHED. YOUR EYE IS CLOSED. YOU DON'T HAVE YOUR ANKH. WHAT DO YOU THINK YOU CAN DO?
FIGHT. I CAN... FIGHT.
UNNH!
YOU SHOULD KNOW NOAH IS LOOKING FOR YOU.
THEN I'LL MAKE IT EASY ON HIM.
THAT'S NOT A PLAN: IT'S STUPID AND IT'S SUICIDE.
LET ME TAKE IT FROM HERE. I HAVE SOME FRIENDS, SANCTUANTS LIKE ME. I'M GONNA TRY AND GET THEM TO HELP.

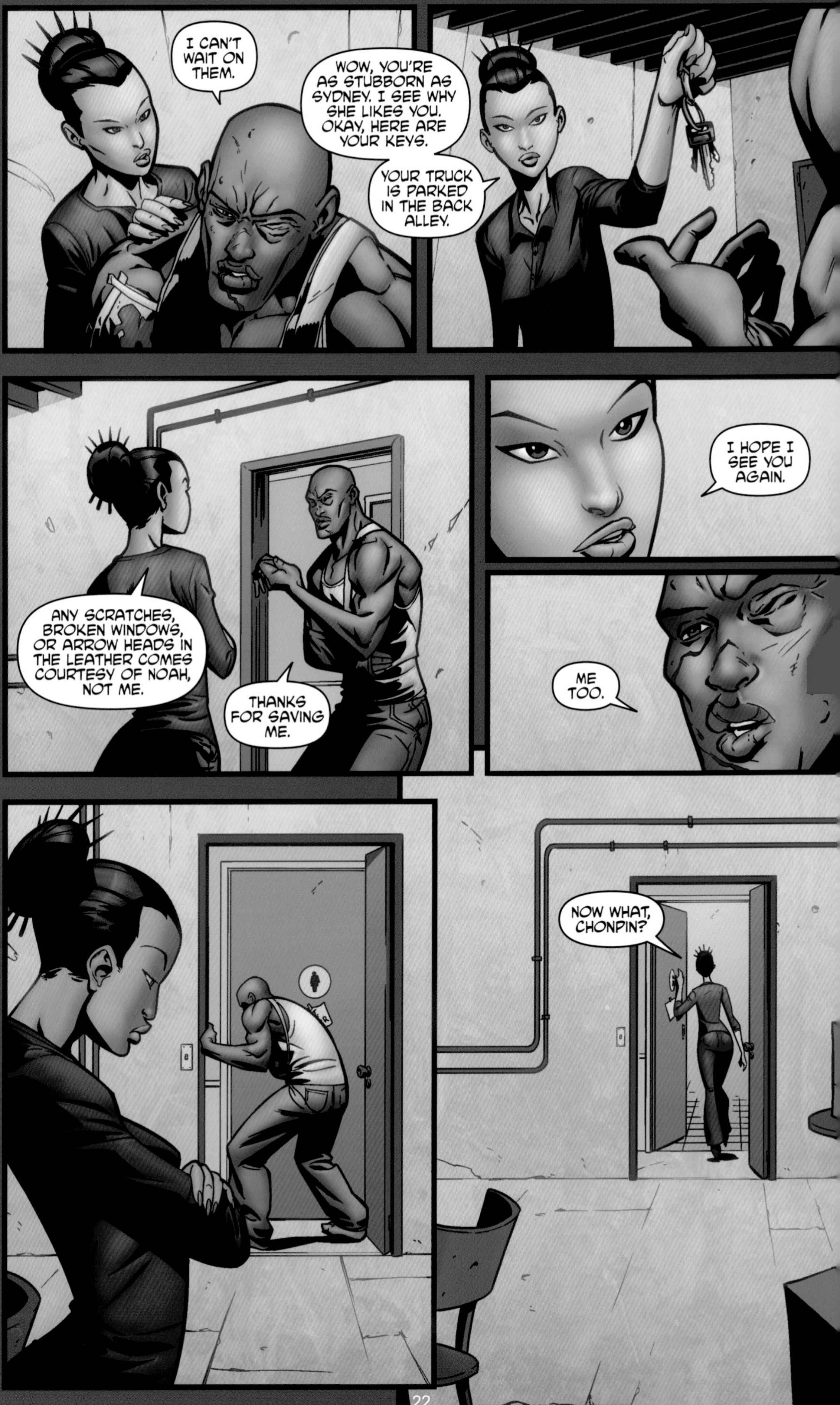

I CAN'T WAIT ON THEM.
WOW, YOU'RE AS STUBBORN AS SYDNEY. I SEE WHY SHE LIKES YOU. OKAY, HERE ARE YOUR KEYS.
YOUR TRUCK IS PARKED IN THE BACK ALLEY.
ANY SCRATCHES, BROKEN WINDOWS, OR ARROW HEADS IN THE LEATHER COMES COURTESY OF NOAH, NOT ME.
THANKS FOR SAVING ME.
I HOPE I SEE YOU AGAIN.
ME TOO.
NOW WHAT, CHONPIN?

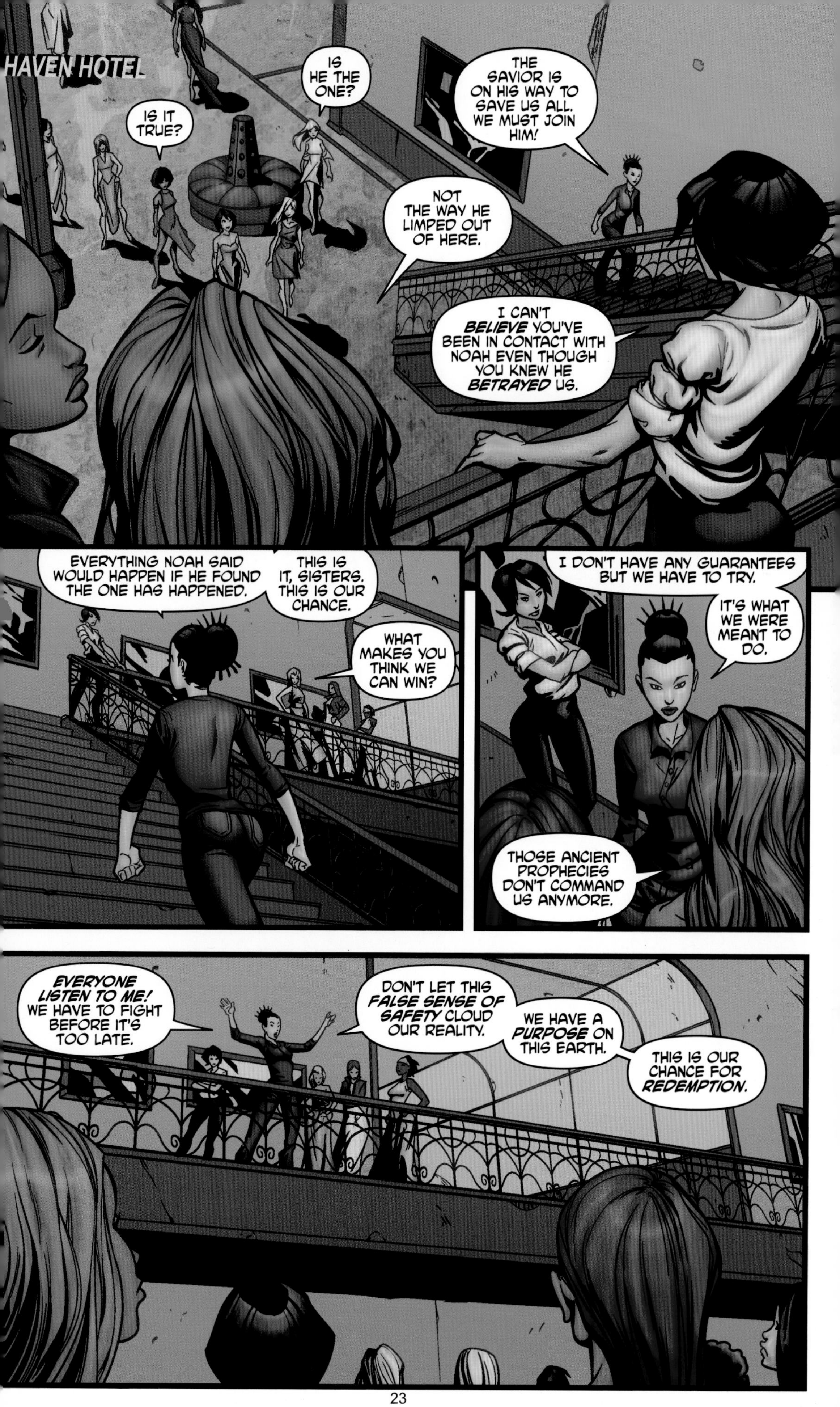
HAVEN HOTEL
IS IT TRUE?
IS HE THE ONE?
THE SAVIOR IS ON HIS WAY TO SAVE US ALL. WE MUST JOIN HIM!
NOT THE WAY HE LIMPED OUT OF HERE.
I CAN'T *BELIEVE* YOU'VE BEEN IN CONTACT WITH NOAH EVEN THOUGH YOU KNEW HE *BETRAYED* US.
EVERYTHING NOAH SAID WOULD HAPPEN IF HE FOUND THE ONE HAS HAPPENED.
THIS IS IT, SISTERS. THIS IS OUR CHANCE.
WHAT MAKES YOU THINK WE CAN WIN?
I DON'T HAVE ANY GUARANTEES BUT WE HAVE TO TRY.
IT'S WHAT WE WERE MEANT TO DO.
THOSE ANCIENT PROPHECIES DON'T COMMAND US ANYMORE.
EVERYONE LISTEN TO ME! WE HAVE TO FIGHT BEFORE IT'S TOO LATE.
DON'T LET THIS *FALSE SENSE OF SAFETY* CLOUD OUR REALITY.
WE HAVE A *PURPOSE* ON THIS EARTH.
THIS IS OUR CHANCE FOR *REDEMPTION*.

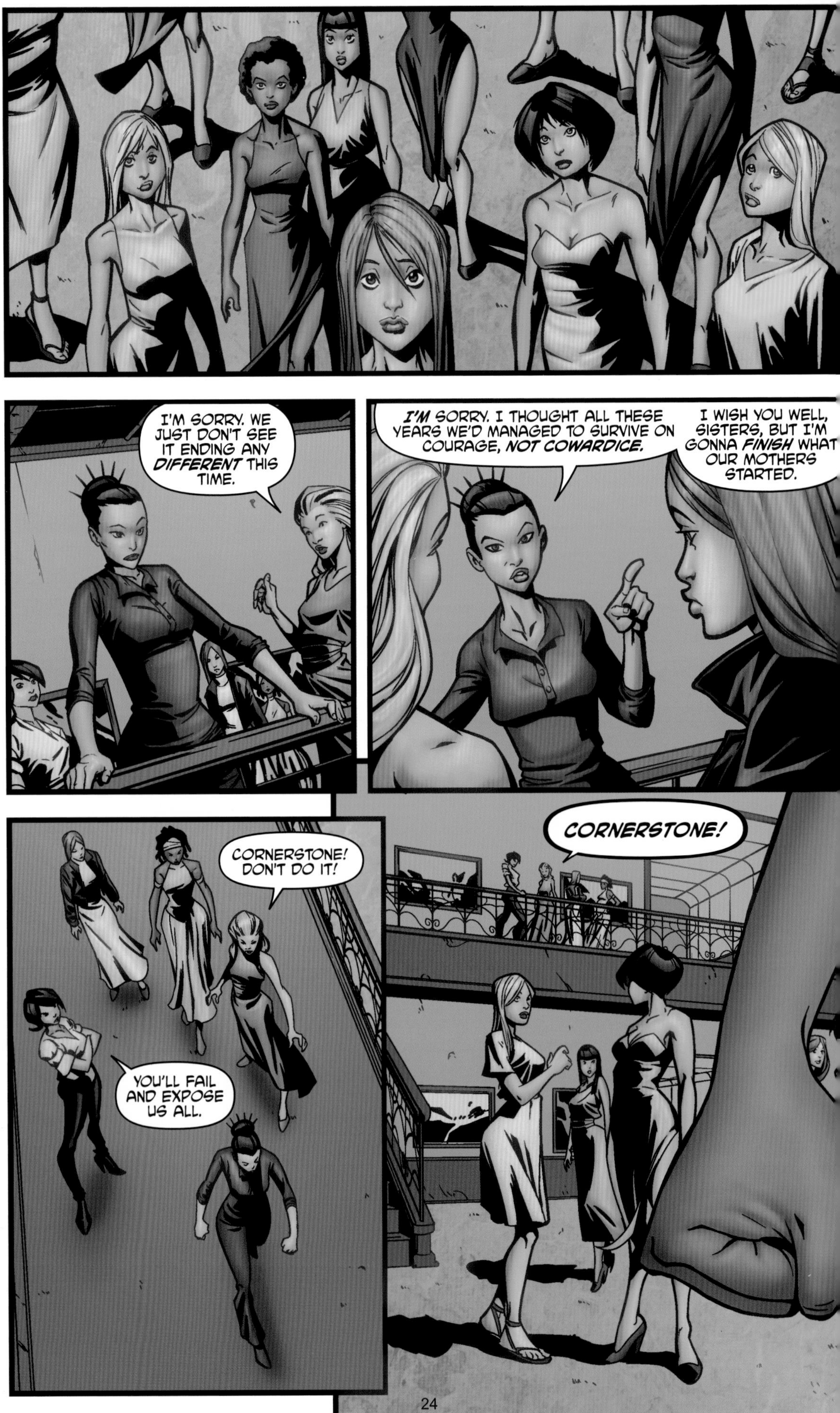
I'M SORRY. WE JUST DON'T SEE IT ENDING ANY *DIFFERENT* THIS TIME.
I'M SORRY. I THOUGHT ALL THESE YEARS WE'D MANAGED TO SURVIVE ON COURAGE, *NOT COWARDICE.*
I WISH YOU WELL, SISTERS, BUT I'M GONNA *FINISH* WHAT OUR MOTHERS STARTED.
CORNERSTONE! DON'T DO IT!
YOU'LL FAIL AND EXPOSE US ALL.
CORNERSTONE!

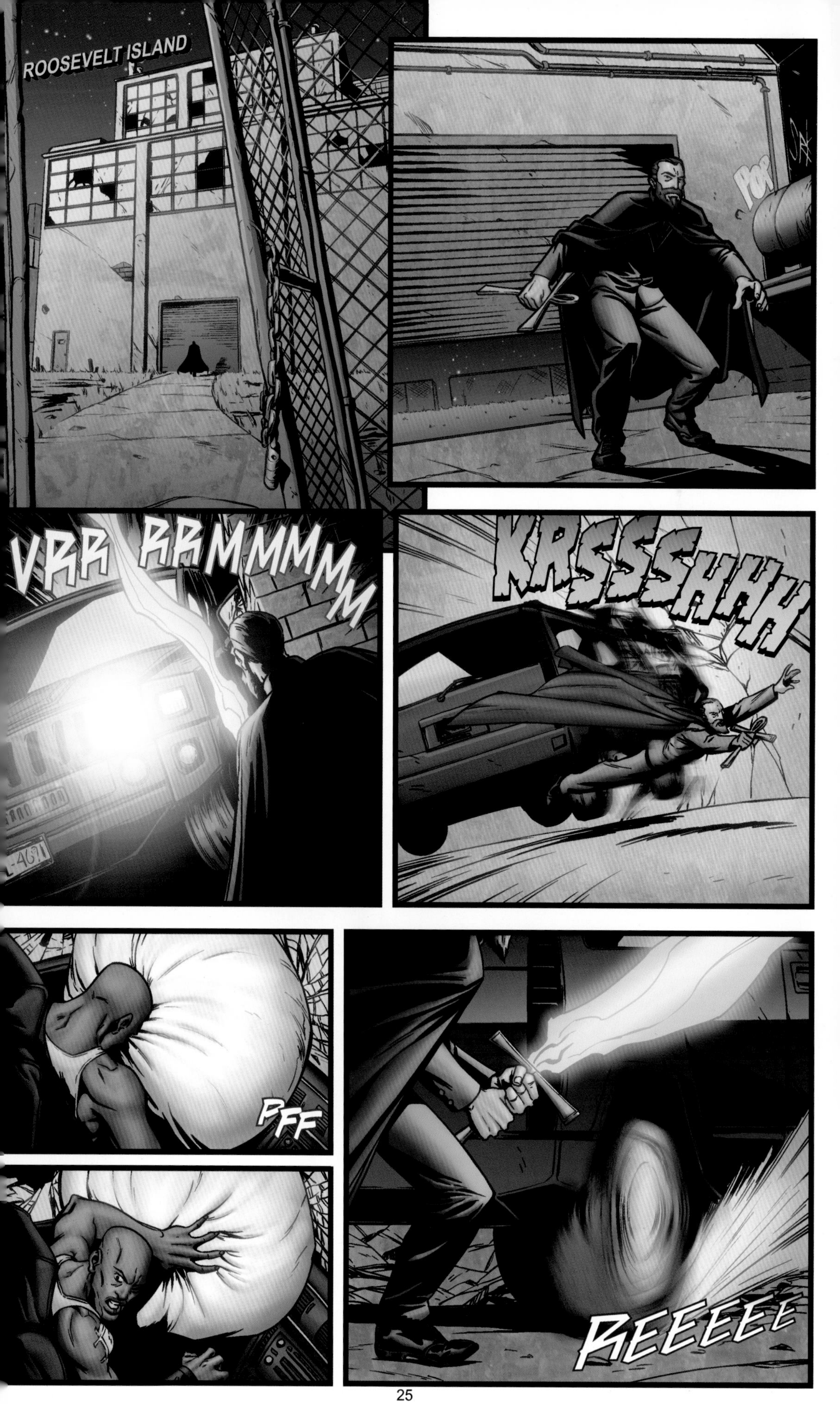
ROOSEVELT ISLAND
POP
VRR RRMMMMMM
KRSSSHHH
PFF
REEEEE

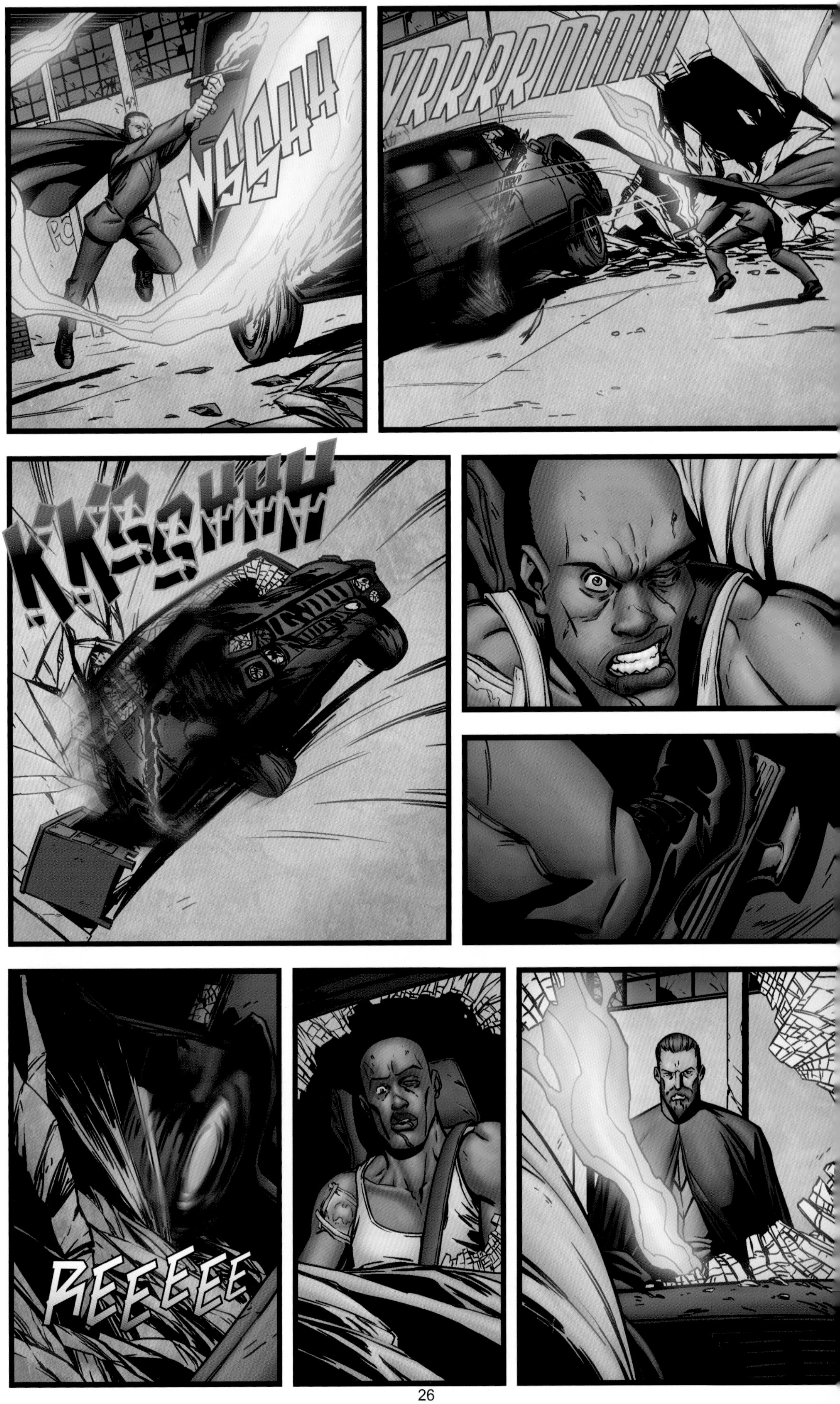
WSGHH
VRRRRMMM
KKSSHHH
REEEEE

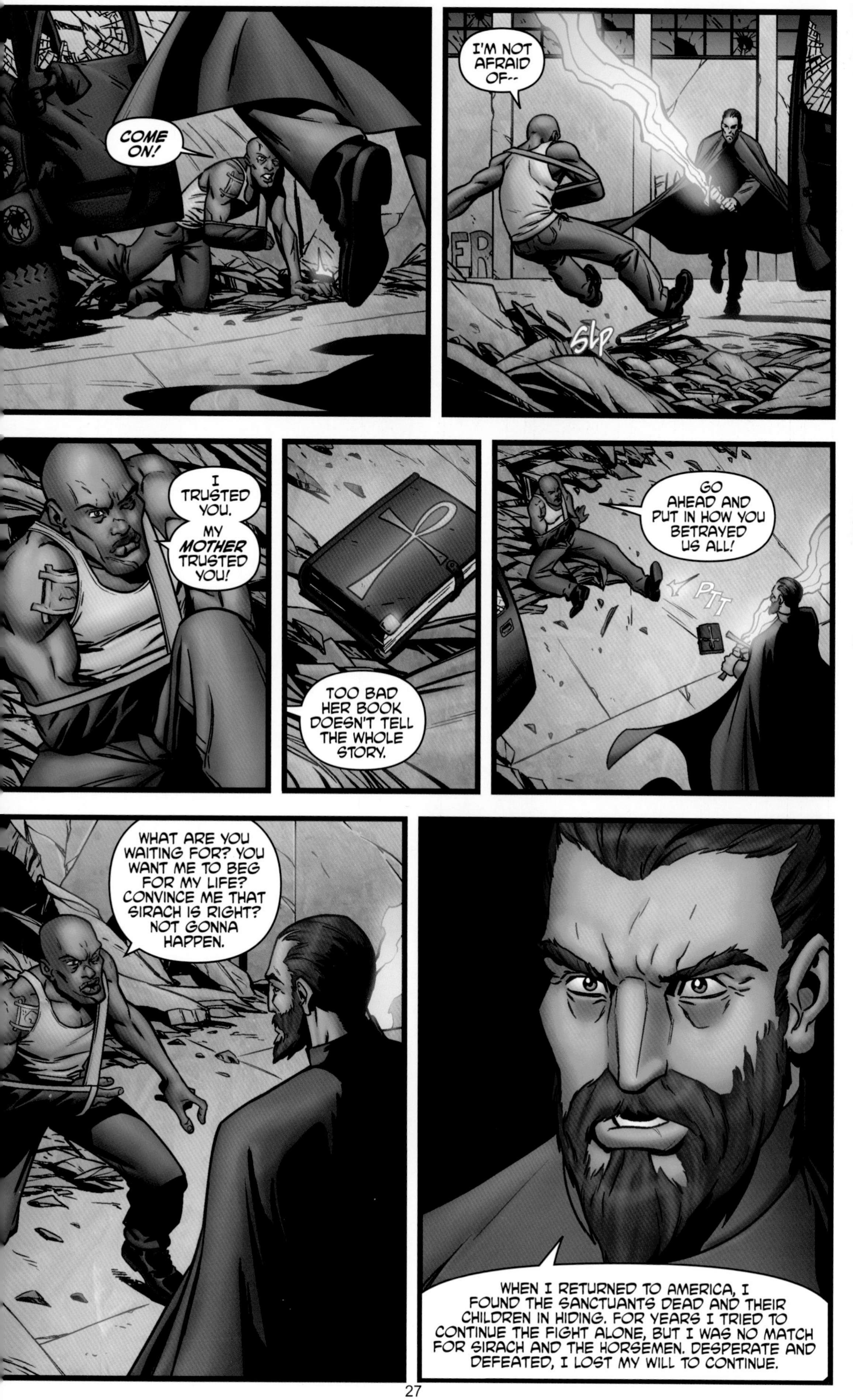
COME ON!
I'M NOT AFRAID OF--
SLP
I TRUSTED YOU.
MY MOTHER TRUSTED YOU!
TOO BAD HER BOOK DOESN'T TELL THE WHOLE STORY.
GO AHEAD AND PUT IN HOW YOU BETRAYED US ALL!
PTT
WHAT ARE YOU WAITING FOR? YOU WANT ME TO BEG FOR MY LIFE? CONVINCE ME THAT SIRACH IS RIGHT? NOT GONNA HAPPEN.
WHEN I RETURNED TO AMERICA, I FOUND THE SANCTUANTS DEAD AND THEIR CHILDREN IN HIDING. FOR YEARS I TRIED TO CONTINUE THE FIGHT ALONE, BUT I WAS NO MATCH FOR SIRACH AND THE HORSEMEN. DESPERATE AND DEFEATED, I LOST MY WILL TO CONTINUE.

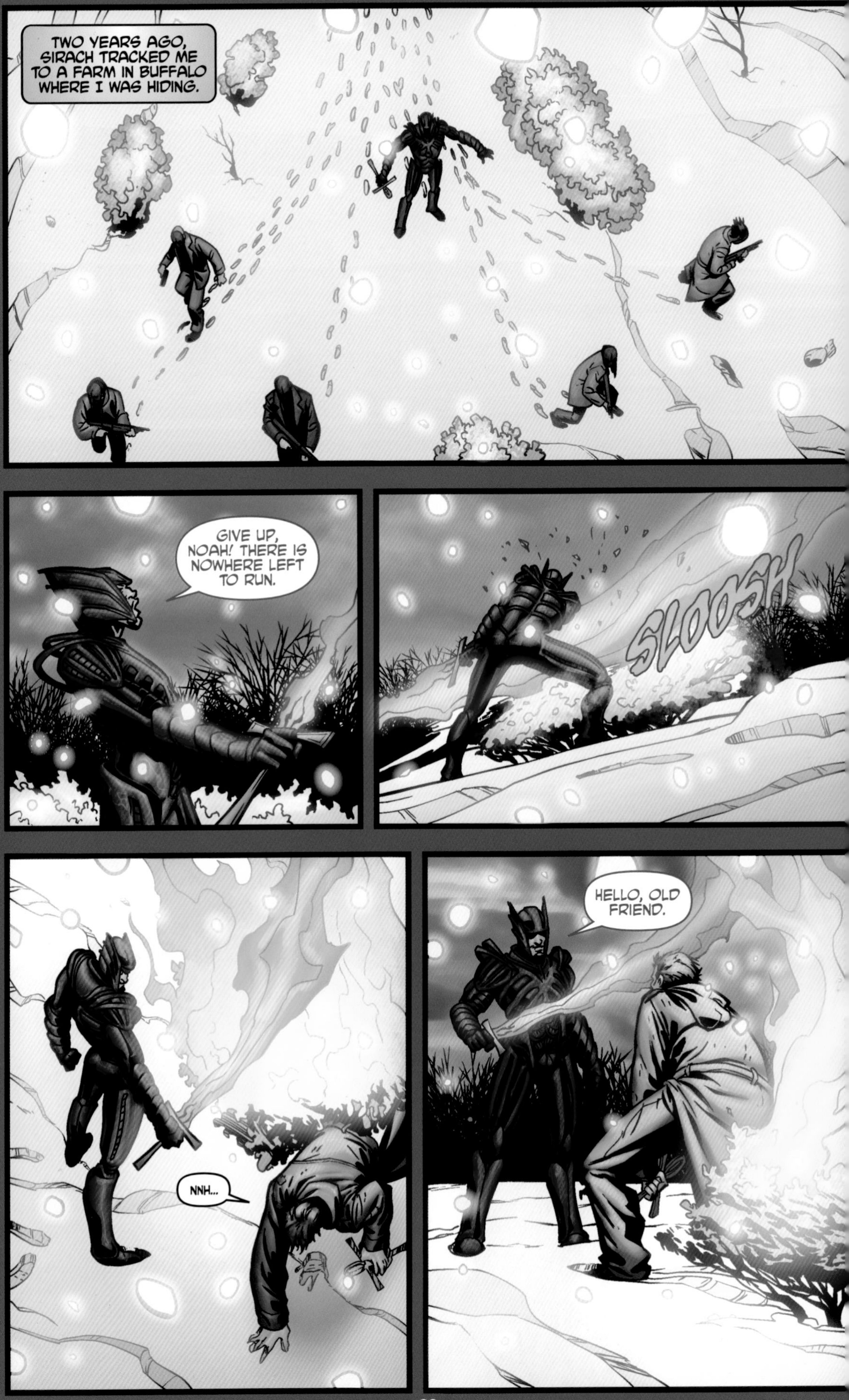
TWO YEARS AGO, SIRACH TRACKED ME TO A FARM IN BUFFALO WHERE I WAS HIDING.
GIVE UP, NOAH! THERE IS NOWHERE LEFT TO RUN.
SLOOSH
NNH...
HELLO, OLD FRIEND.

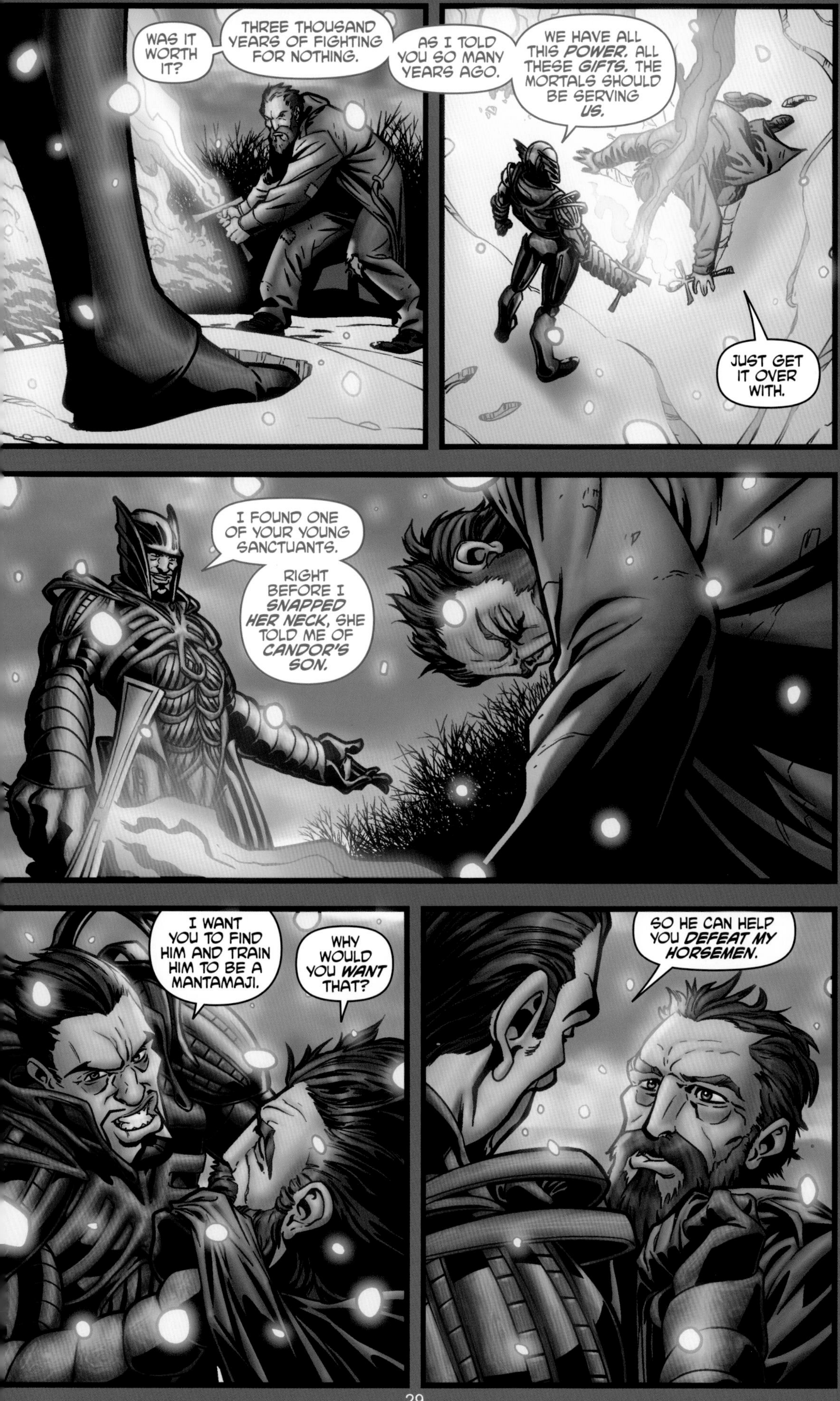
WAS IT WORTH IT?
THREE THOUSAND YEARS OF FIGHTING FOR NOTHING.
AS I TOLD YOU SO MANY YEARS AGO.
WE HAVE ALL THIS POWER. ALL THESE GIFTS. THE MORTALS SHOULD BE SERVING US.
JUST GET IT OVER WITH.
I FOUND ONE OF YOUR YOUNG SANCTUANTS.
RIGHT BEFORE I SNAPPED HER NECK, SHE TOLD ME OF CANDOR'S SON.
I WANT YOU TO FIND HIM AND TRAIN HIM TO BE A MANTAMAJI.
WHY WOULD YOU WANT THAT?
SO HE CAN HELP YOU DEFEAT MY HORSEMEN.

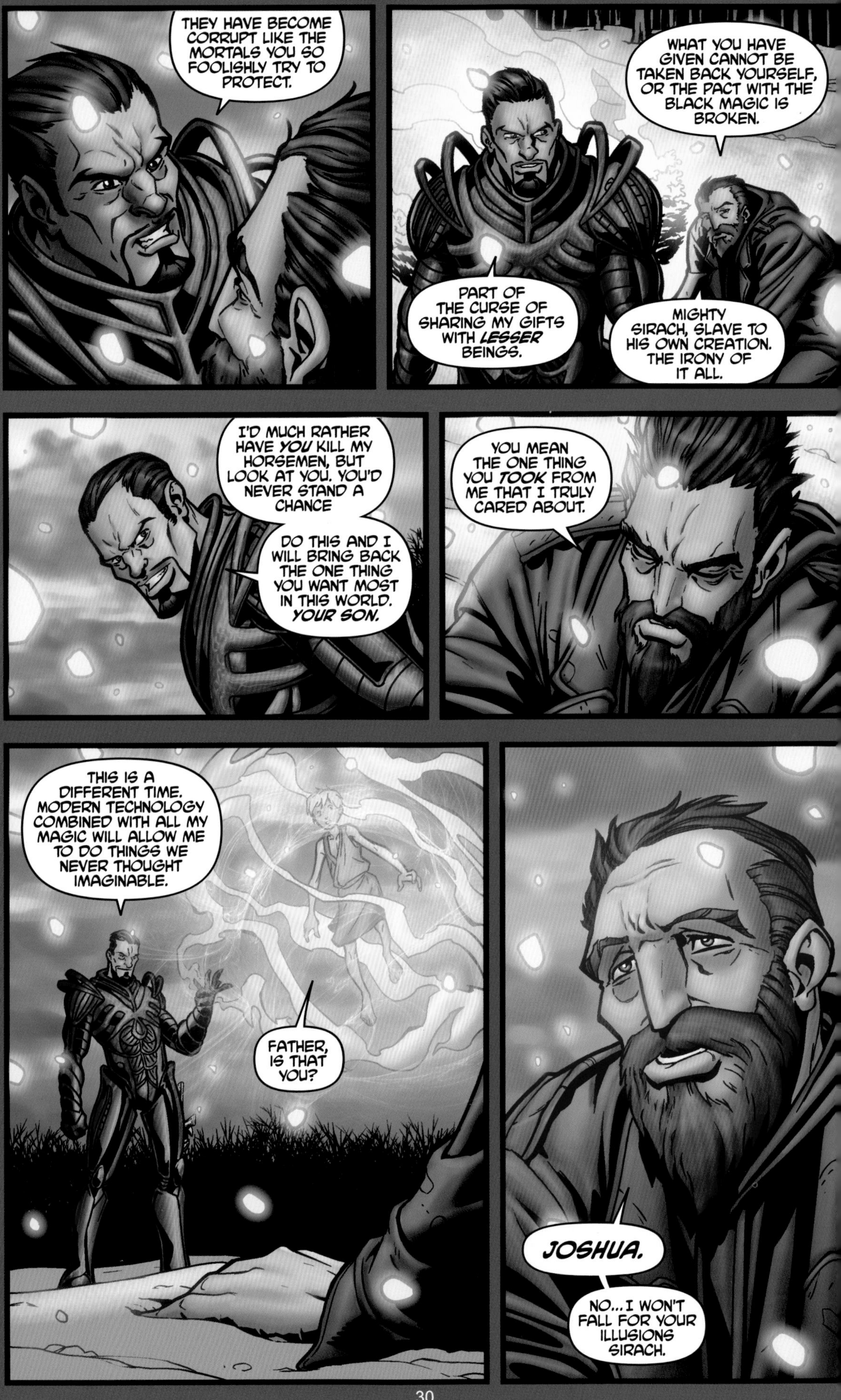
THEY HAVE BECOME CORRUPT LIKE THE MORTALS YOU SO FOOLISHLY TRY TO PROTECT.
WHAT YOU HAVE GIVEN CANNOT BE TAKEN BACK YOURSELF, OR THE PACT WITH THE BLACK MAGIC IS BROKEN.
PART OF THE CURSE OF SHARING MY GIFTS WITH *LESSER* BEINGS.
MIGHTY SIRACH, SLAVE TO HIS OWN CREATION. THE IRONY OF IT ALL.
I'D MUCH RATHER HAVE *YOU* KILL MY HORSEMEN, BUT LOOK AT YOU. YOU'D NEVER STAND A CHANCE
DO THIS AND I WILL BRING BACK THE ONE THING YOU WANT MOST IN THIS WORLD. ***YOUR SON.***
YOU MEAN THE ONE THING YOU *TOOK* FROM ME THAT I TRULY CARED ABOUT.
THIS IS A DIFFERENT TIME. MODERN TECHNOLOGY COMBINED WITH ALL MY MAGIC WILL ALLOW ME TO DO THINGS WE NEVER THOUGHT IMAGINABLE.
FATHER, IS THAT YOU?
JOSHUA.
NO... I WON'T FALL FOR YOUR ILLUSIONS SIRACH.

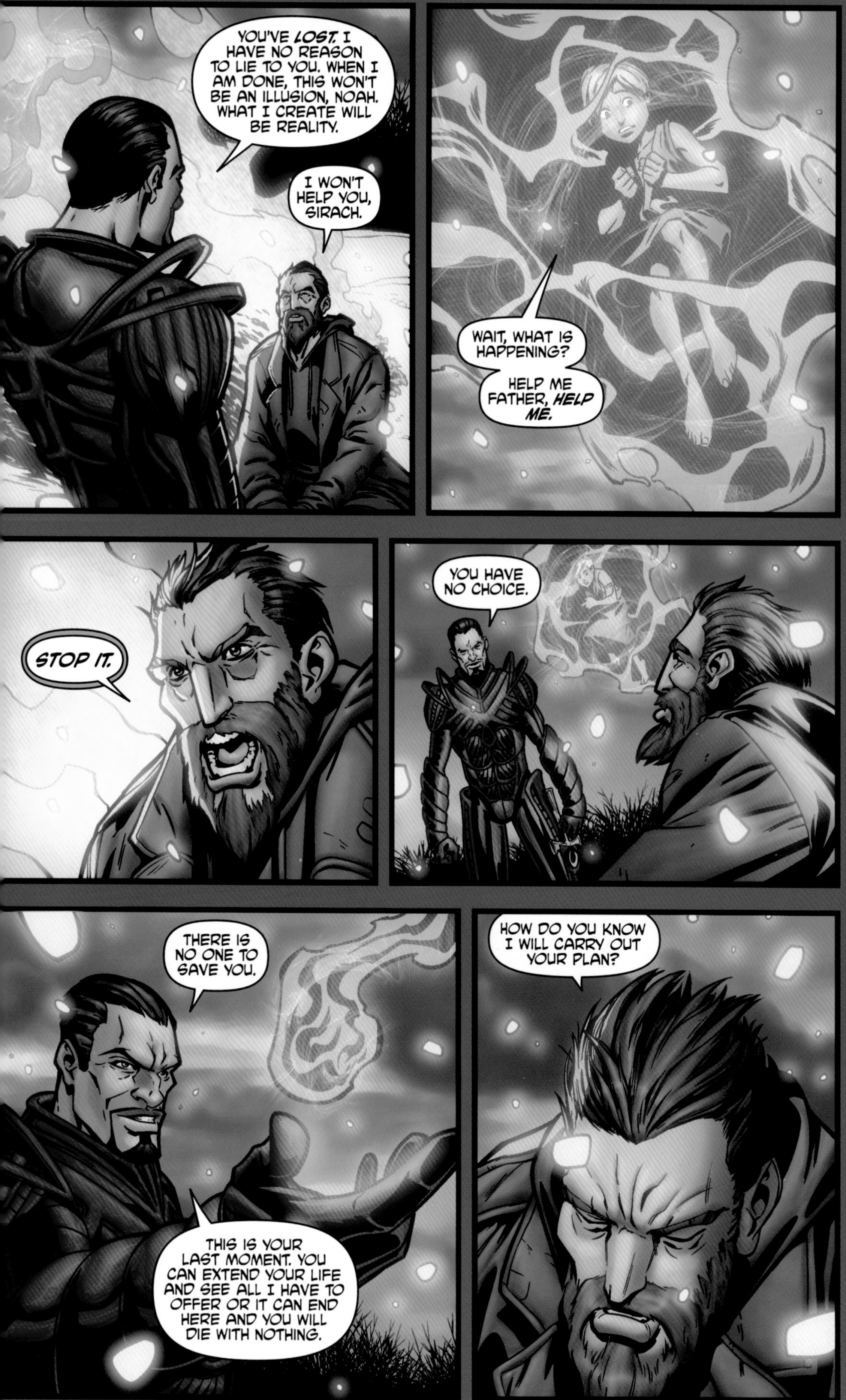
YOU'VE LOST. I HAVE NO REASON TO LIE TO YOU. WHEN I AM DONE, THIS WON'T BE AN ILLUSION, NOAH. WHAT I CREATE WILL BE REALITY.
I WON'T HELP YOU, SIRACH.
WAIT, WHAT IS HAPPENING?
HELP ME FATHER, HELP ME.
STOP IT.
YOU HAVE NO CHOICE.
THERE IS NO ONE TO SAVE YOU.
THIS IS YOUR LAST MOMENT. YOU CAN EXTEND YOUR LIFE AND SEE ALL I HAVE TO OFFER OR IT CAN END HERE AND YOU WILL DIE WITH NOTHING.
HOW DO YOU KNOW I WILL CARRY OUT YOUR PLAN?

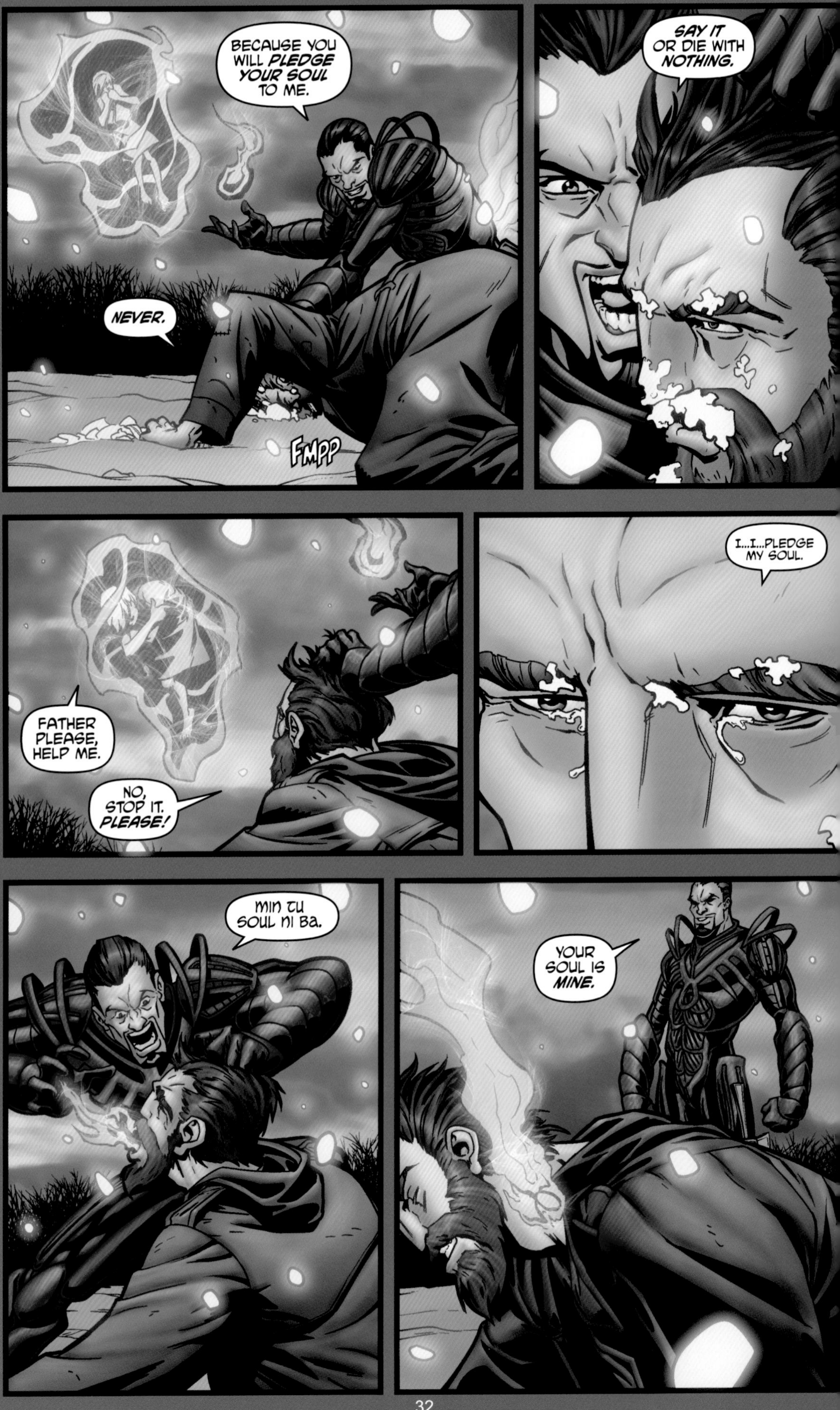
BECAUSE YOU WILL PLEDGE YOUR SOUL TO ME.
NEVER.
FMPP
SAY IT OR DIE WITH NOTHING.
FATHER PLEASE, HELP ME.
NO, STOP IT. PLEASE!
I...I...PLEDGE MY SOUL.
MIN TU SOUL NI BA.
YOUR SOUL IS MINE.

FOR TWO YEARS HE KEPT ALIVE THE LEGEND OF NOAH, HIS *GREATEST ADVERSARY,* WHILE I SEARCHED UNTIL I FINALLY FOUND YOU, RIGHT WHERE HE *NEEDED YOU,* WHEN IT *MATTERED MOST.*

NOW ALL THAT IS LEFT FOR ME TO DO IS GIVE YOU THE POWER TO DEFEAT SIRACH AND THE CIRCLE WILL BE COMPLETE.

WHAT DID YOU SAY?

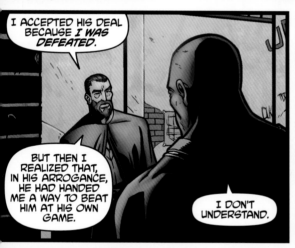

I ACCEPTED HIS DEAL BECAUSE *I WAS DEFEATED.*

BUT THEN I REALIZED THAT, IN HIS ARROGANCE, HE HAD HANDED ME A WAY TO BEAT HIM AT HIS OWN GAME.

I DON'T UNDERSTAND.

WE COULD NEVER DEFEAT SIRACH BECAUSE HE SHARED HIS SOUL WITH HIS HORSEMEN. WHAT IF WE DID THE SAME?

THE SOUL-PACT HAS NEVER BEEN MADE BETWEEN TWO *MANTAMAJI* BEFORE.

HOW MUCH MORE POWERFUL WOULD YOU BE? COULD YOUR WOUNDS HEAL? COULD YOU BE STRONGER, FASTER?

IS THIS SOME SORT OF *TRICK?* DO YOU AND SIRACH NEED MY POWERS TO CARRY OUT YOUR PLANS?

NO TRICK. JUST A CHANCE. A CHANCE WE MAY NEVER GET AGAIN.

SIRACH OWNS MY SOUL WHILE I AM ALIVE. BUT IF I DIE AND I PLEDGE MY ETERNAL SOUL-POWER TO YOU, MAKE IT PART OF YOURS, IT MAY GIVE YOU JUST ENOUGH OF AN EDGE TO WIN.

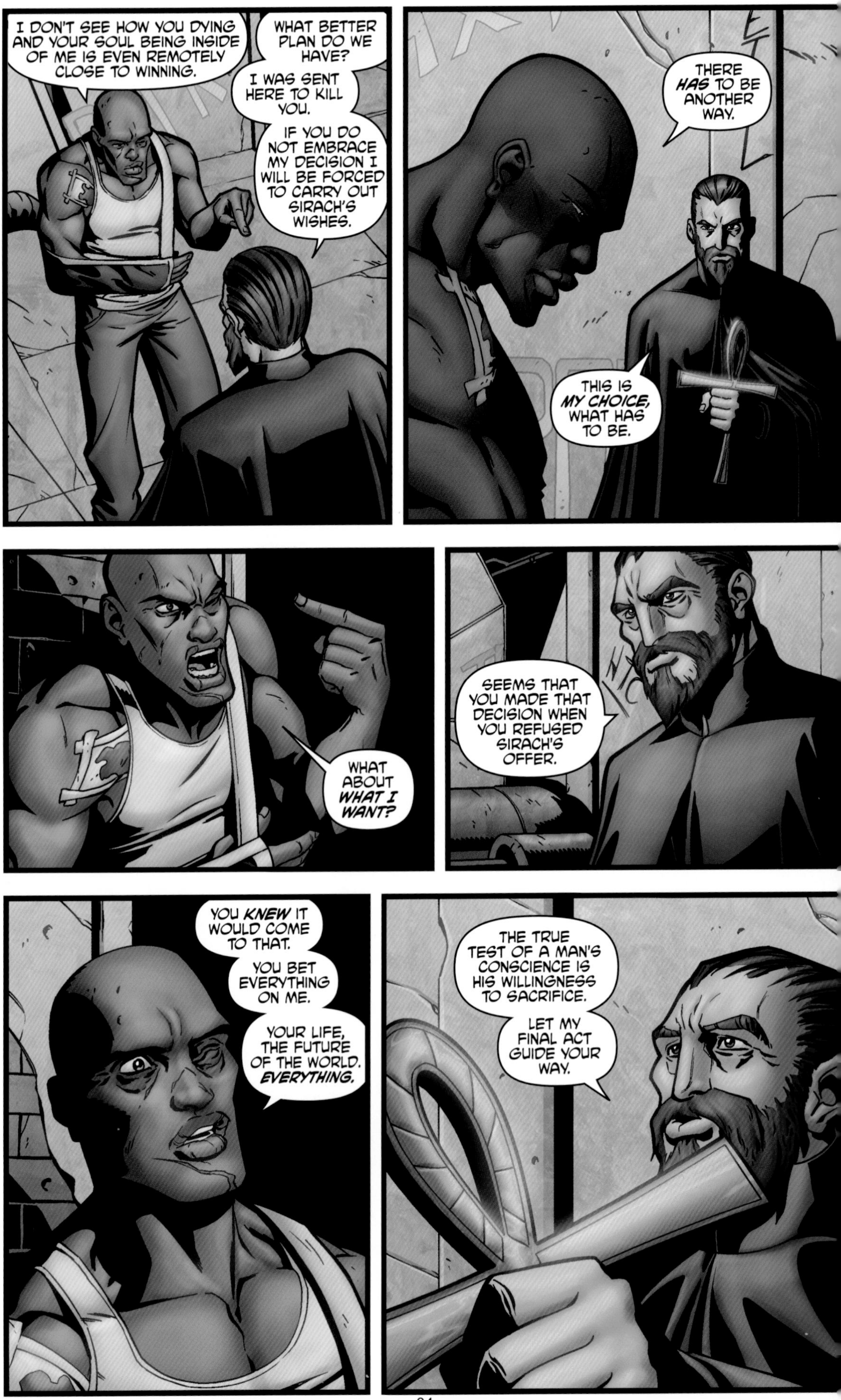

I DON'T SEE HOW YOU DYING AND YOUR SOUL BEING INSIDE OF ME IS EVEN REMOTELY CLOSE TO WINNING.
WHAT BETTER PLAN DO WE HAVE?
I WAS SENT HERE TO KILL YOU.
IF YOU DO NOT EMBRACE MY DECISION I WILL BE FORCED TO CARRY OUT SIRACH'S WISHES.
THERE *HAS* TO BE ANOTHER WAY.
THIS IS *MY CHOICE,* WHAT HAS TO BE.
WHAT ABOUT *WHAT I WANT?*
SEEMS THAT YOU MADE THAT DECISION WHEN YOU REFUSED SIRACH'S OFFER.
YOU *KNEW* IT WOULD COME TO THAT.
YOU BET EVERYTHING ON ME.
YOUR LIFE, THE FUTURE OF THE WORLD. *EVERYTHING.*
THE TRUE TEST OF A MAN'S CONSCIENCE IS HIS WILLINGNESS TO SACRIFICE.
LET MY FINAL ACT GUIDE YOUR WAY.

DID MY MOTHER KNOW OF YOUR PLAN?

NO. HER SACRIFICE WAS YET ANOTHER CASUALTY OF THIS WAR. FOR THAT I AM TRULY SORRY. DOES IT BRING YOU ANY PEACE TO KNOW THAT AT THIS MOMENT SHE WOULD BE VERY PROUD OF YOU?

YEAH, IT DOES.

I PLEDGE MY SOUL TO YOU, ELIJAH.

TAKE IT, SO I MAY JOIN MY SON IN ETERNITY.

ZSHH

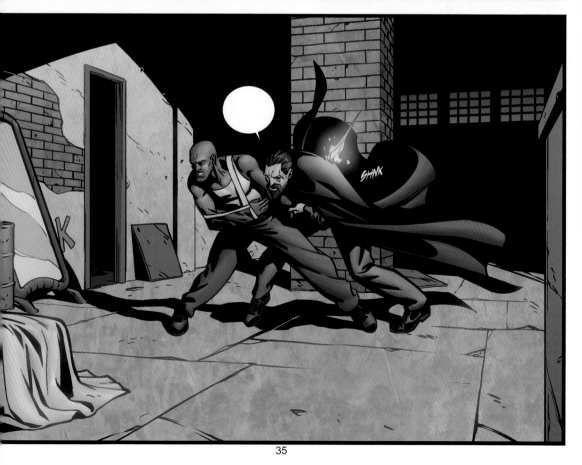

SHNK

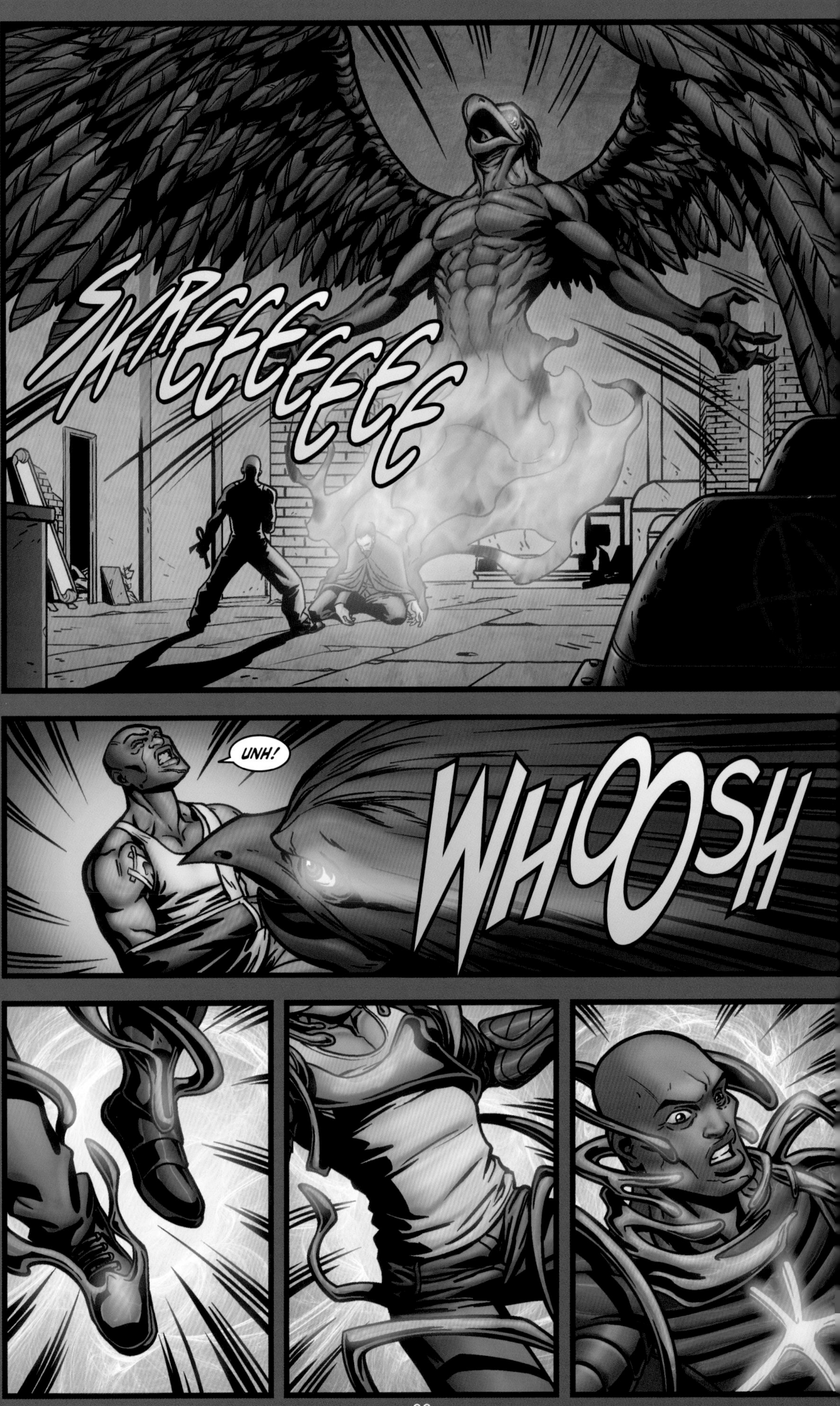
SKREEEEEEEE
UNH!
WHOOSH

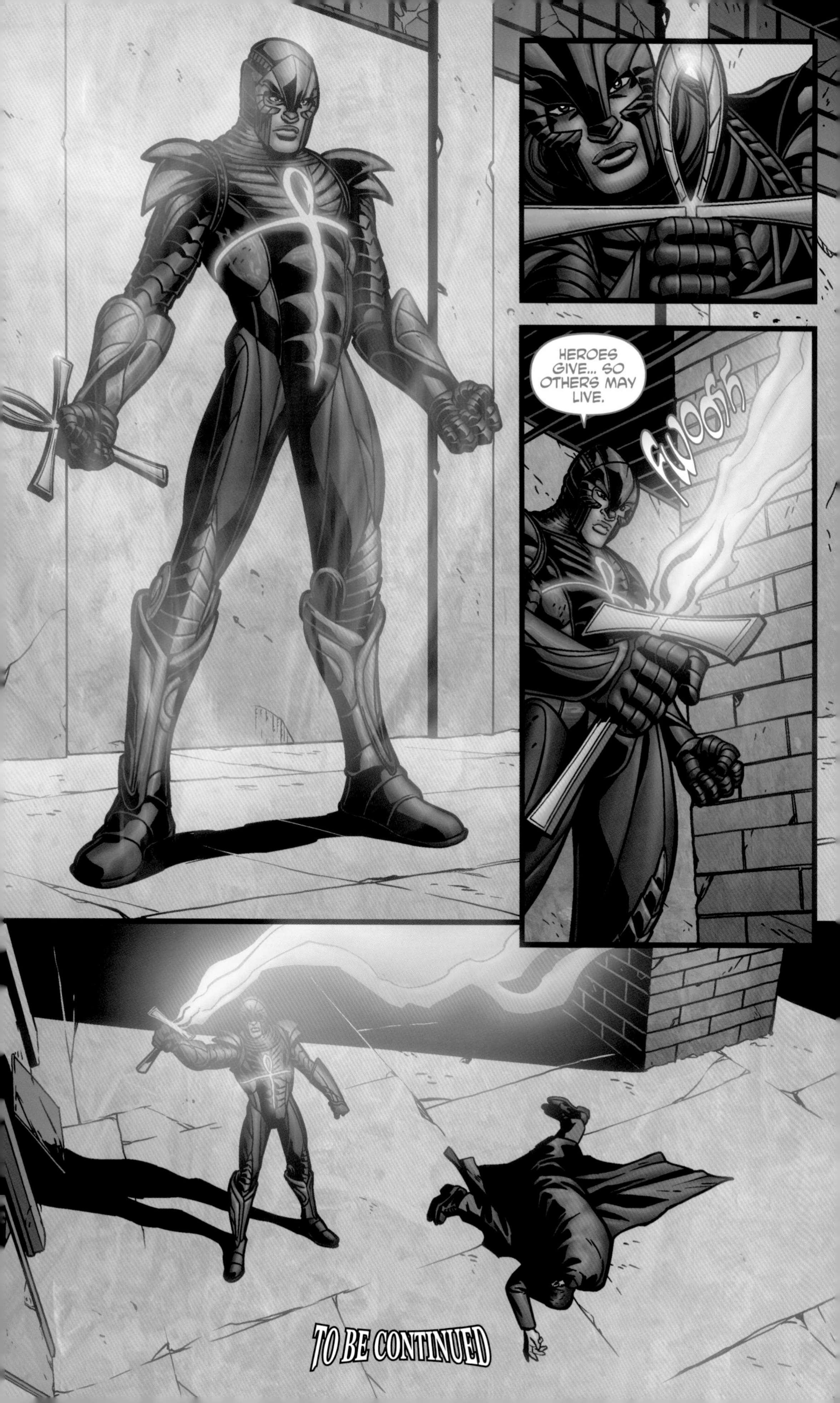
HEROES GIVE... SO OTHERS MAY LIVE.
FWOOSH
TO BE CONTINUED

CHAPTER 13

Before entering battle, the Mantamaji would exchange these final words: "When we meet again, let it be in victory." What started as a simple rallying cry gained deeper meaning over time. "Victory" became the Mantamaji's term for the place of soul-rest. Even if they did not win the battle, the Mantamaji would live on in Victory, a land beyond the farthest desert, where it is always cool as a twilight moon.

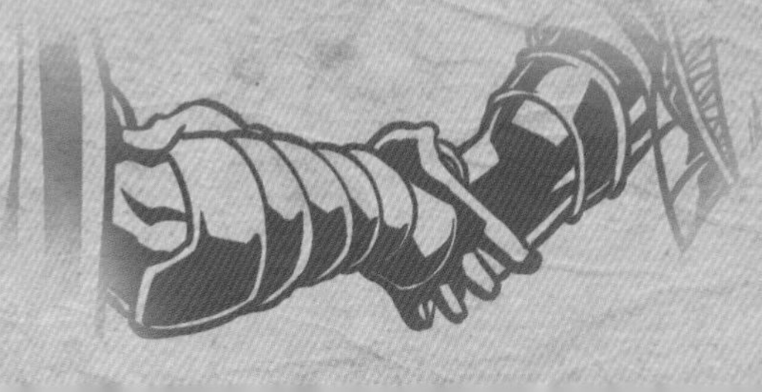

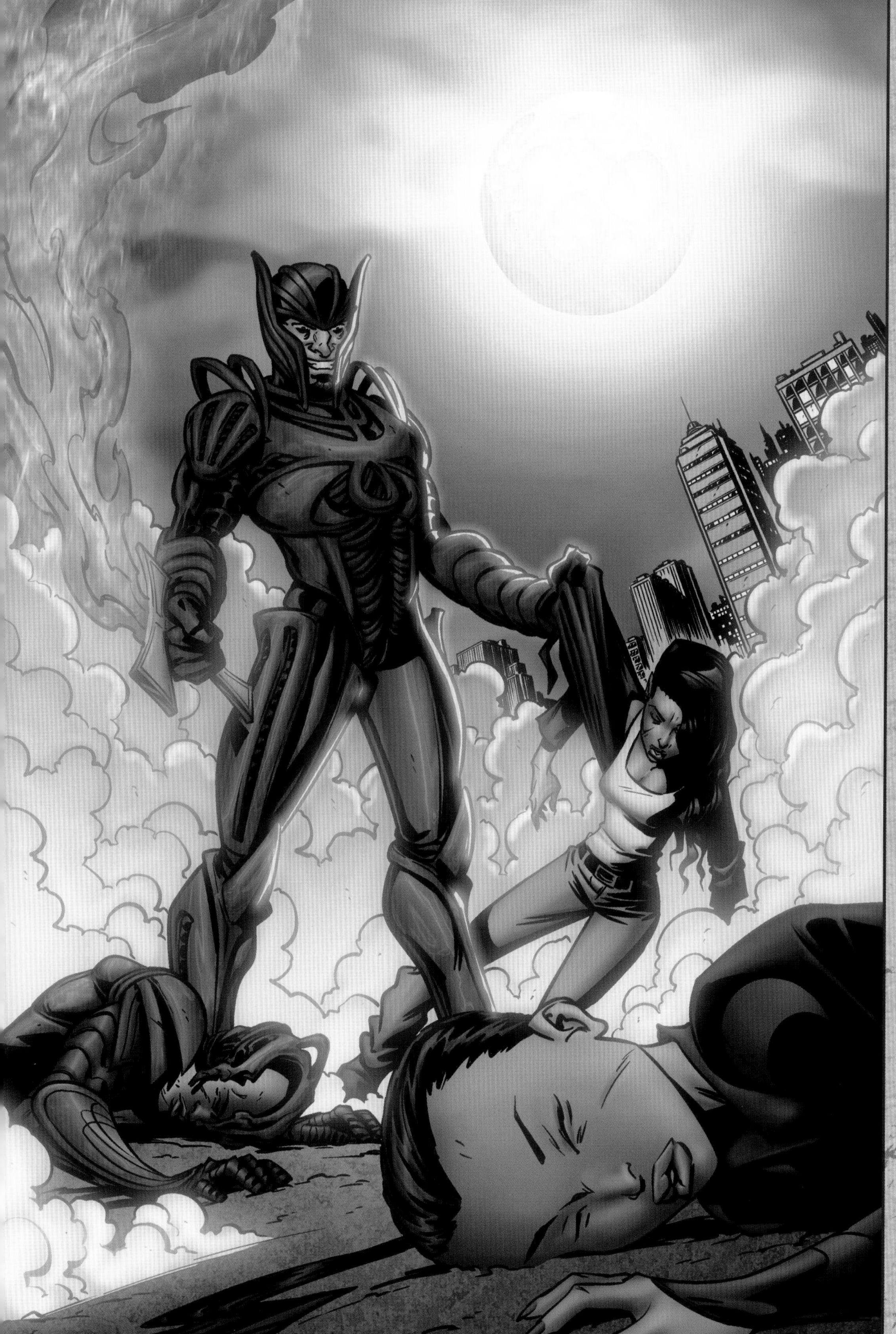

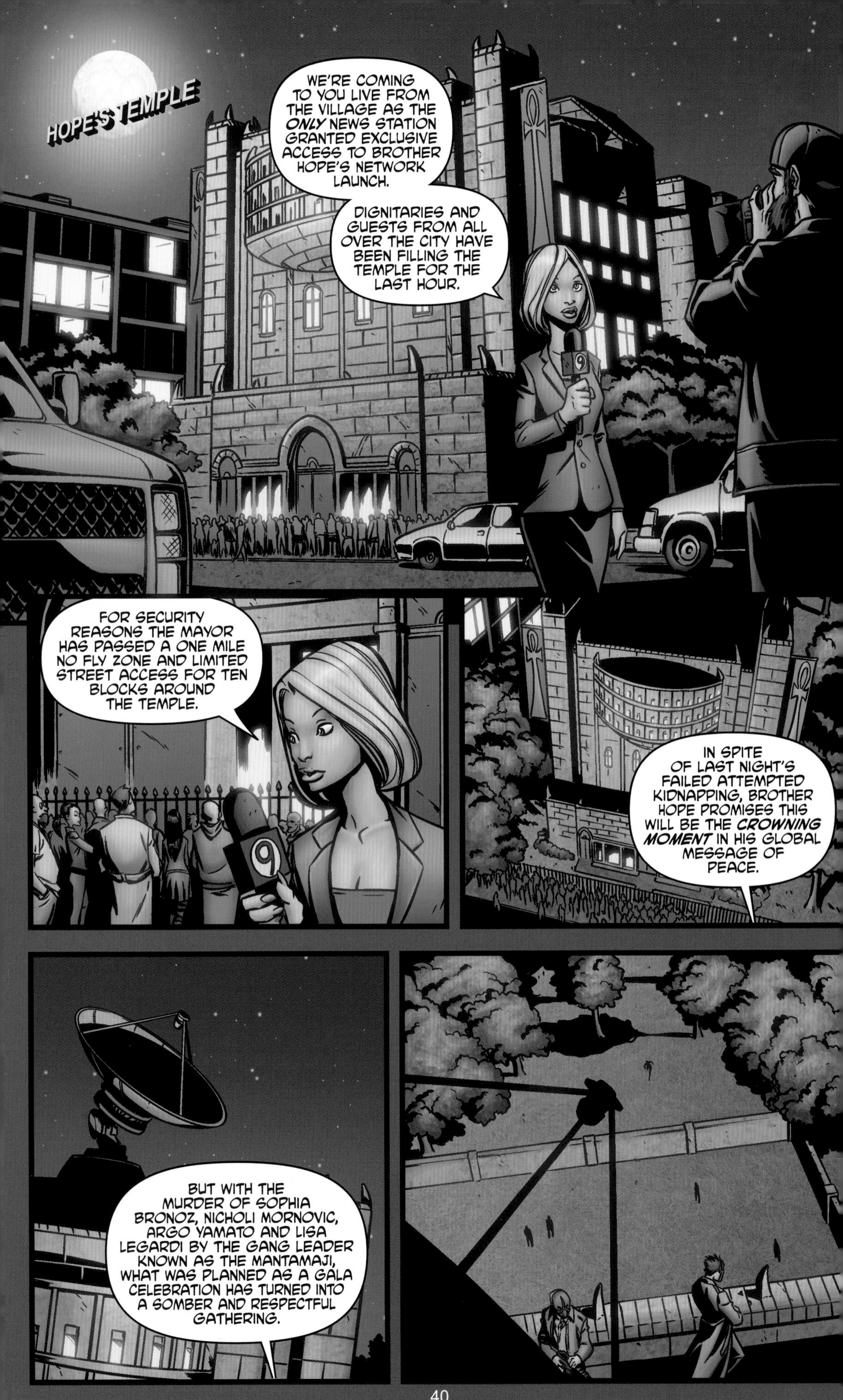
HOPE'S TEMPLE
WE'RE COMING TO YOU LIVE FROM THE VILLAGE AS THE *ONLY* NEWS STATION GRANTED EXCLUSIVE ACCESS TO BROTHER HOPE'S NETWORK LAUNCH.
DIGNITARIES AND GUESTS FROM ALL OVER THE CITY HAVE BEEN FILLING THE TEMPLE FOR THE LAST HOUR.
FOR SECURITY REASONS THE MAYOR HAS PASSED A ONE MILE NO FLY ZONE AND LIMITED STREET ACCESS FOR TEN BLOCKS AROUND THE TEMPLE.
IN SPITE OF LAST NIGHT'S FAILED ATTEMPTED KIDNAPPING, BROTHER HOPE PROMISES THIS WILL BE THE ***CROWNING MOMENT*** IN HIS GLOBAL MESSAGE OF PEACE.
BUT WITH THE MURDER OF SOPHIA BRONOZ, NICHOLI MORNOVIC, ARGO YAMATO AND LISA LEGARDI BY THE GANG LEADER KNOWN AS THE MANTAMAJI, WHAT WAS PLANNED AS A GALA CELEBRATION HAS TURNED INTO A SOMBER AND RESPECTFUL GATHERING.

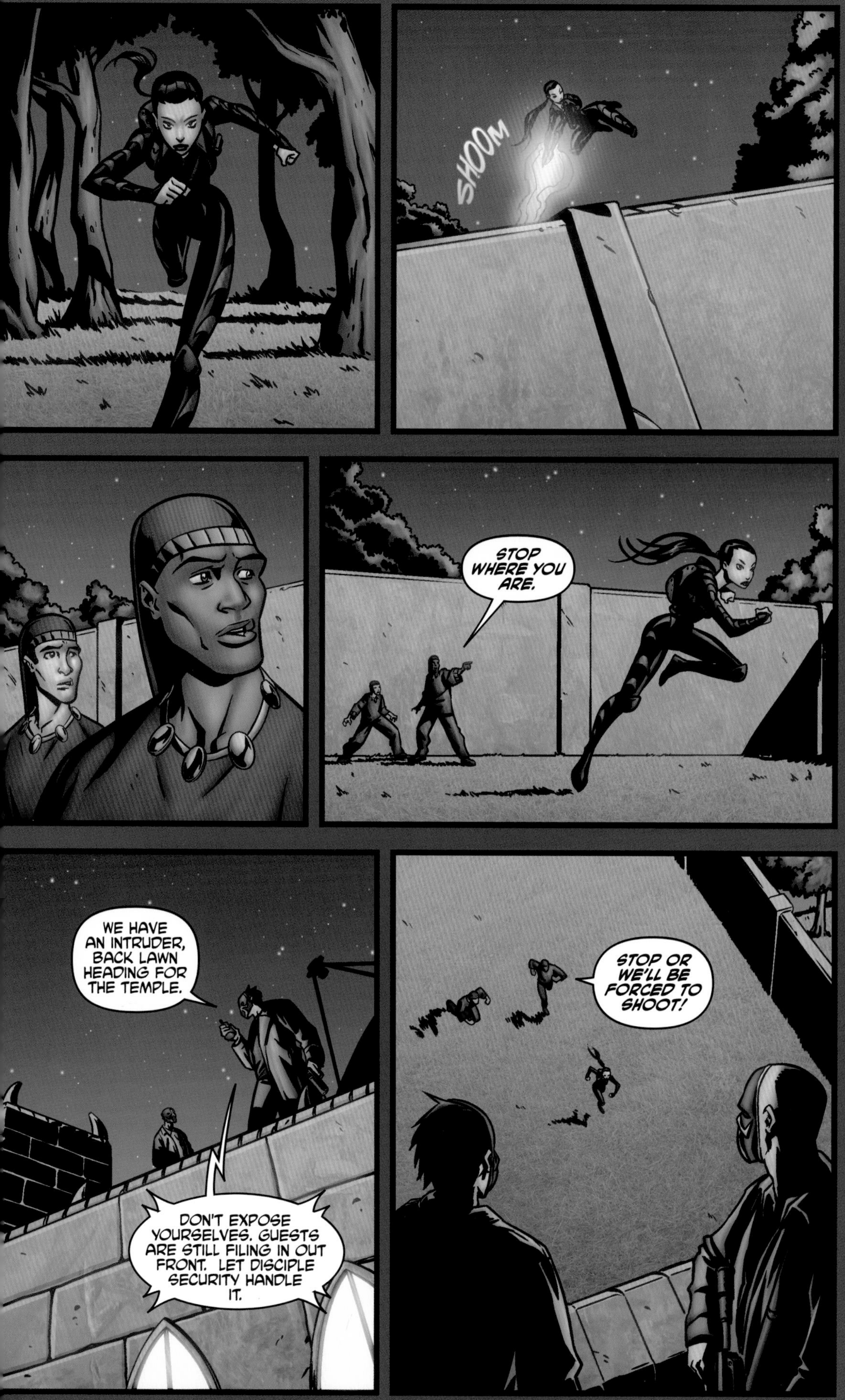
SHOOM
STOP WHERE YOU ARE.
WE HAVE AN INTRUDER, BACK LAWN HEADING FOR THE TEMPLE.
DON'T EXPOSE YOURSELVES. GUESTS ARE STILL FILING IN OUT FRONT. LET DISCIPLE SECURITY HANDLE IT.
STOP OR WE'LL BE FORCED TO SHOOT!

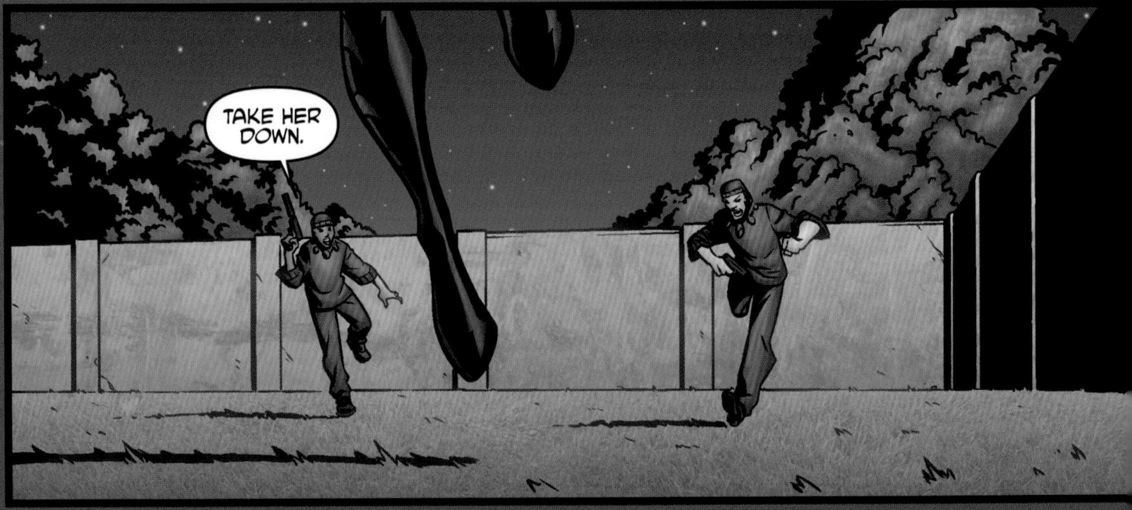
TAKE HER DOWN.

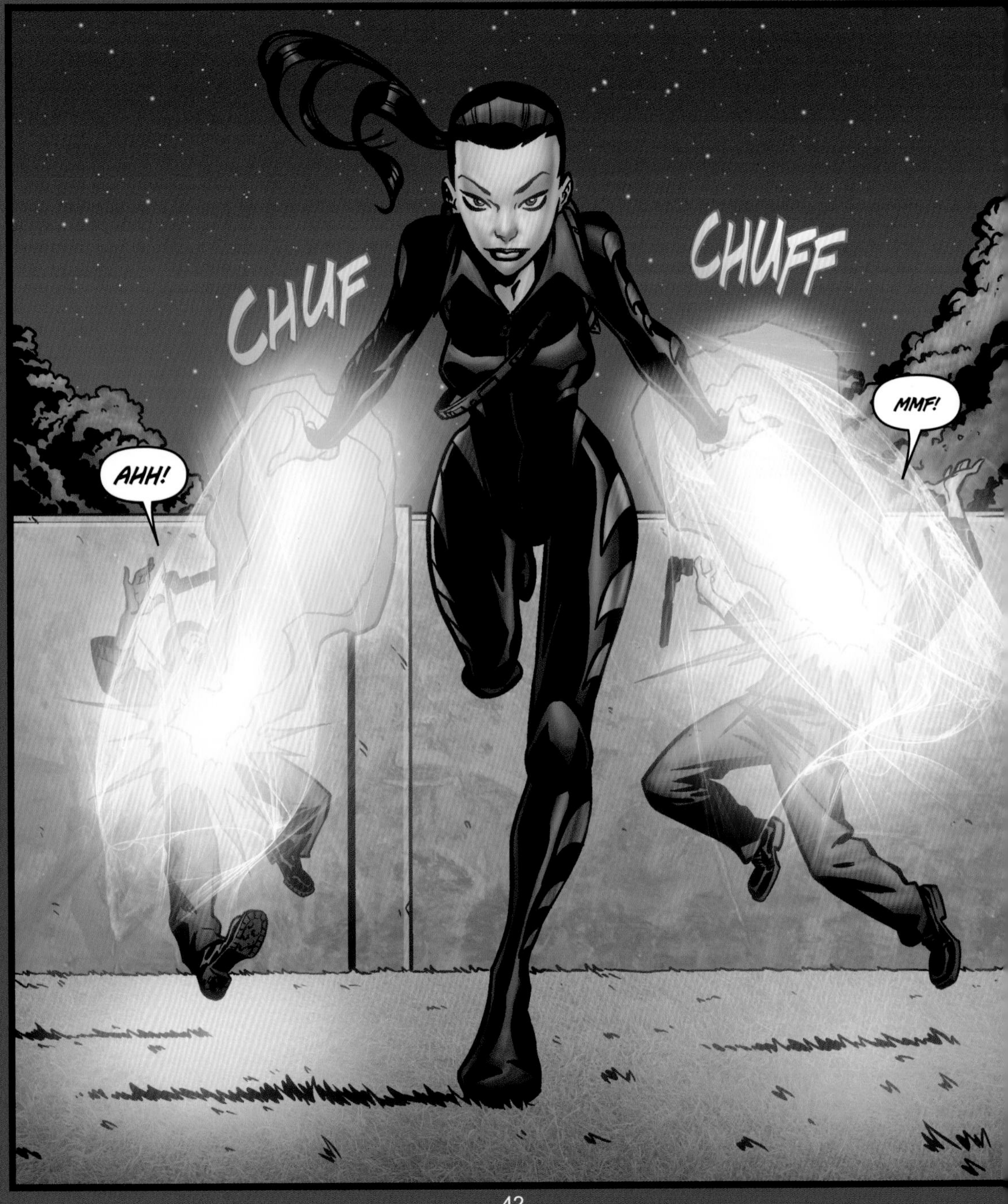
CHUF
CHUFF
AHH!
MMF!

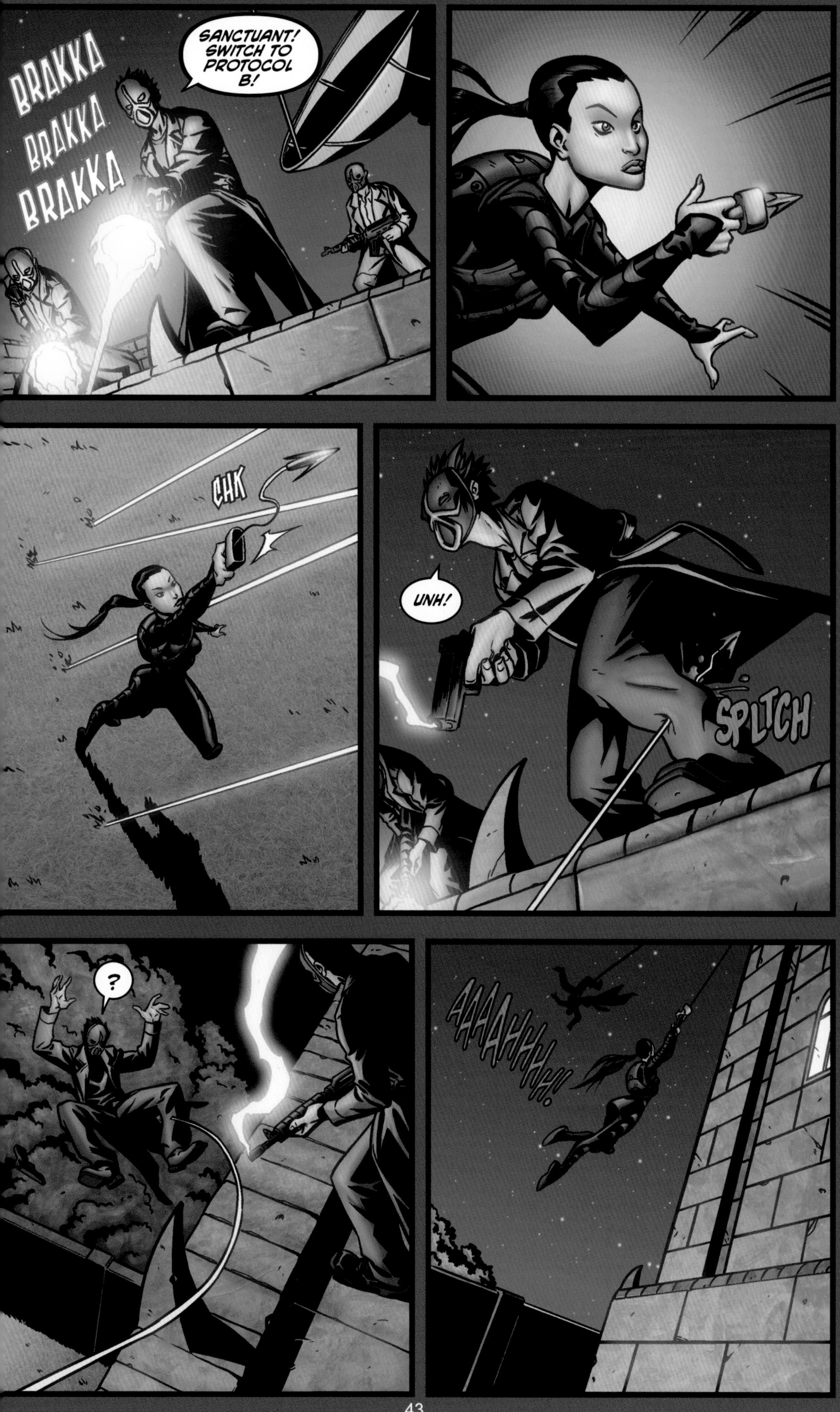
BRAKKA
BRAKKA
BRAKKA
SANCTUANT! SWITCH TO PROTOCOL B!
CHK
UNH!
SPLTCH
?
AAAAHHH!!

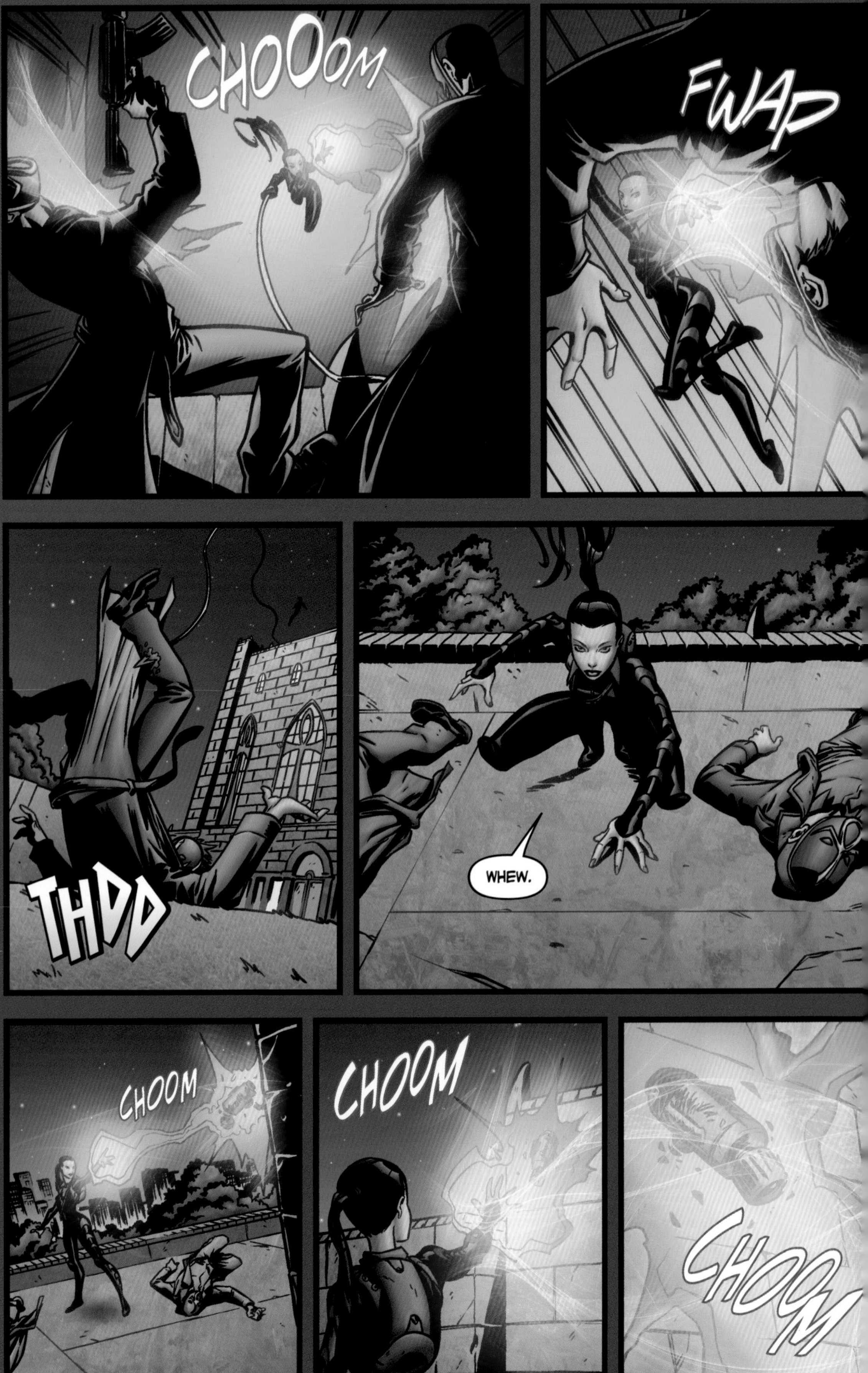
CHOOOM
FWAP
THDD
WHEW.
CHOOM
CHOOM
CHOOM

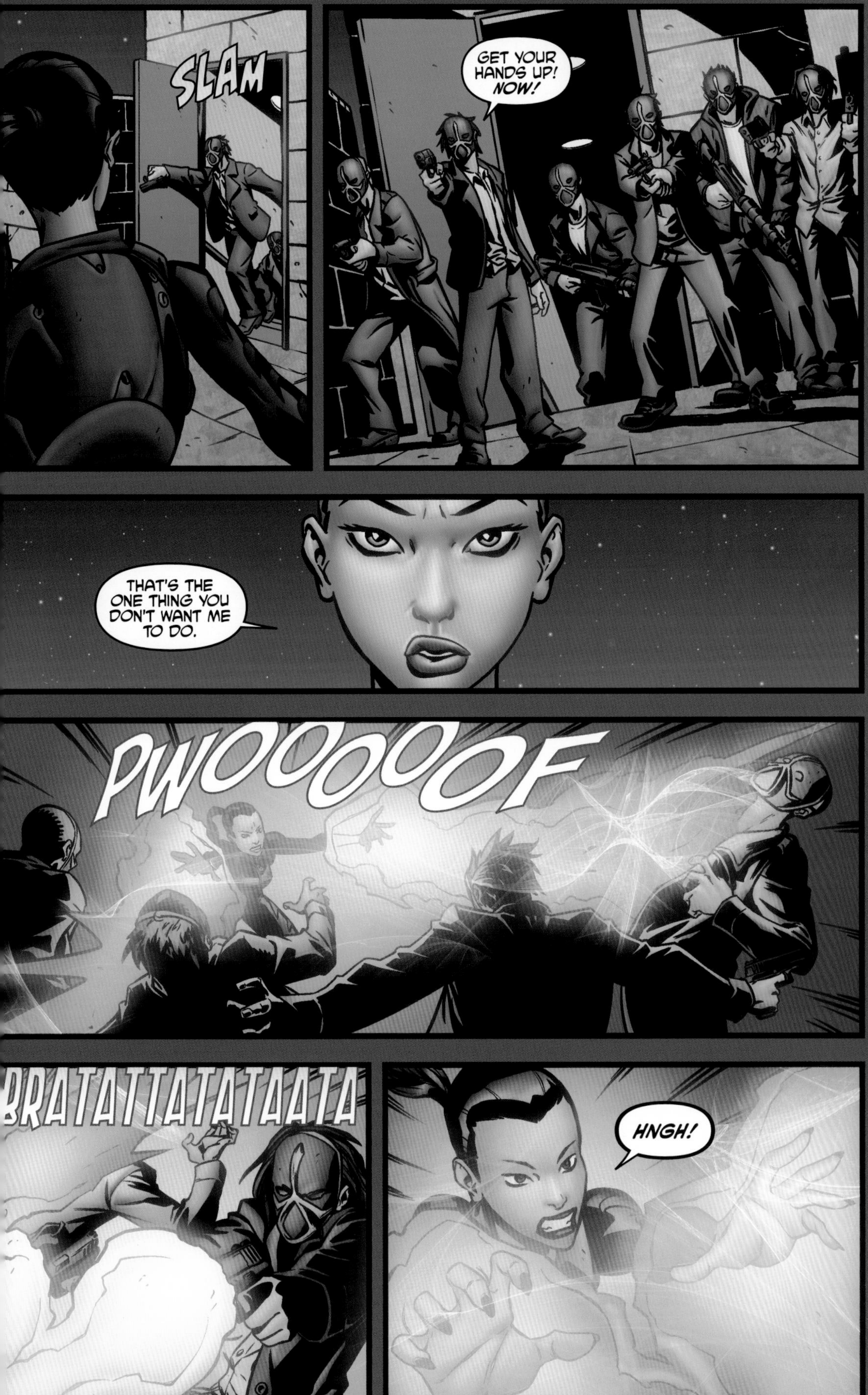
SLAM
GET YOUR HANDS UP! NOW!
THAT'S THE ONE THING YOU DON'T WANT ME TO DO.
PWOOOOOF
BRATATTATATAATA
HNGH!

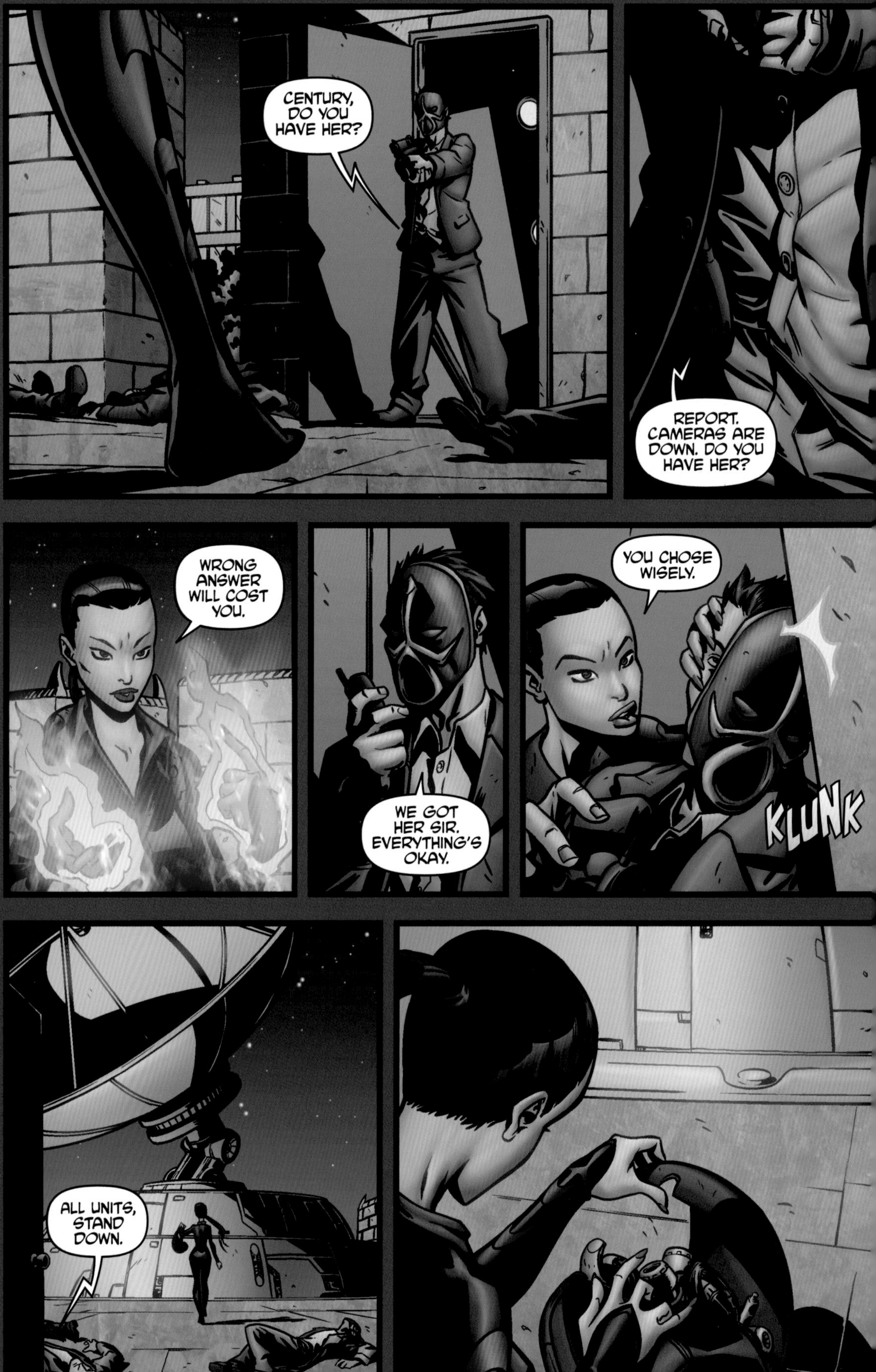

CENTURY, DO YOU HAVE HER?
REPORT. CAMERAS ARE DOWN. DO YOU HAVE HER?
WRONG ANSWER WILL COST YOU.
WE GOT HER SIR. EVERYTHING'S OKAY.
YOU CHOSE WISELY.
KLUNK
ALL UNITS, STAND DOWN.

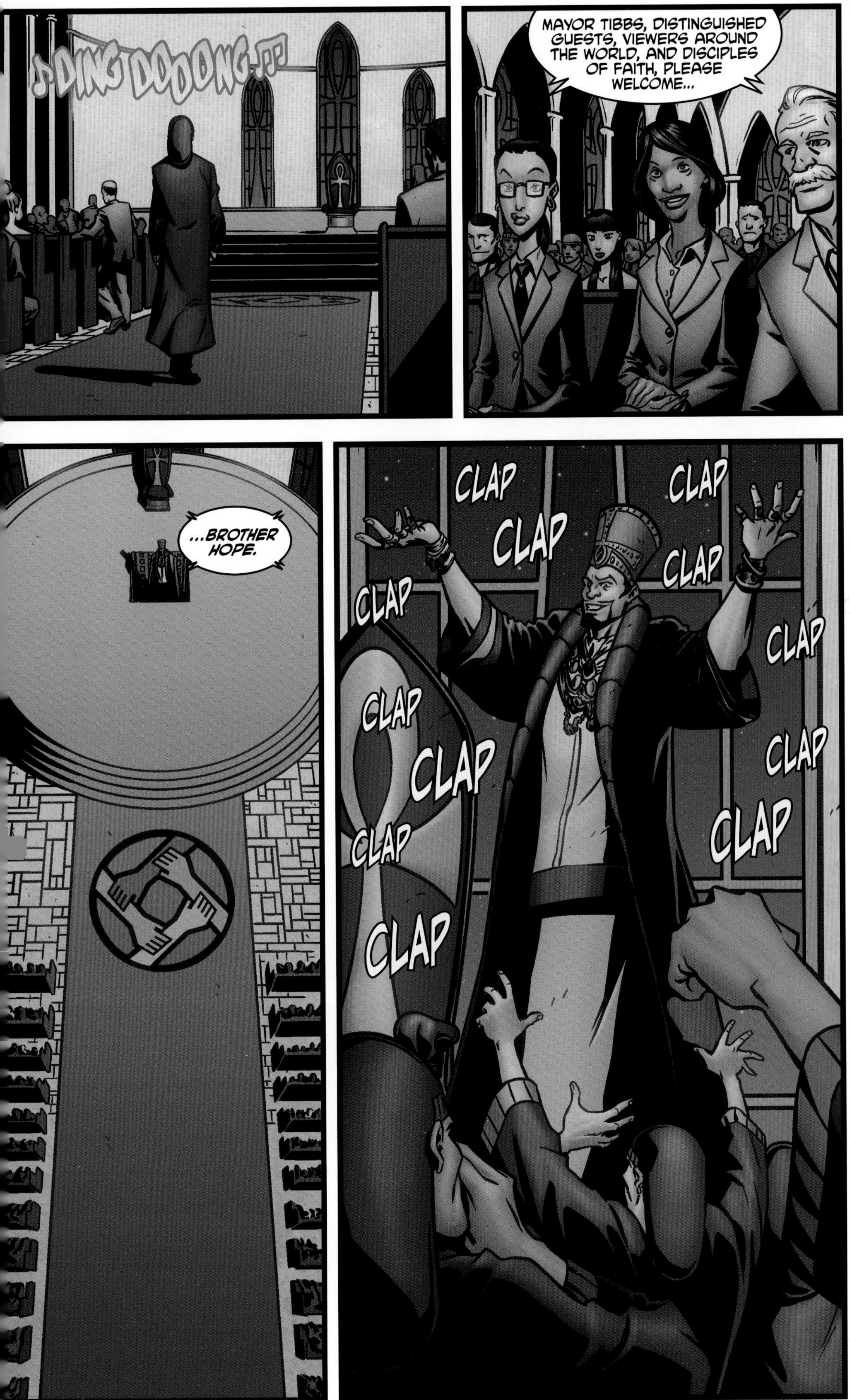

DING DOOONG
MAYOR TIBBS, DISTINGUISHED GUESTS, VIEWERS AROUND THE WORLD, AND DISCIPLES OF FAITH, PLEASE WELCOME...
...BROTHER HOPE.
CLAP CLAP CLAP CLAP CLAP CLAP CLAP CLAP CLAP CLAP CLAP CLAP CLAP

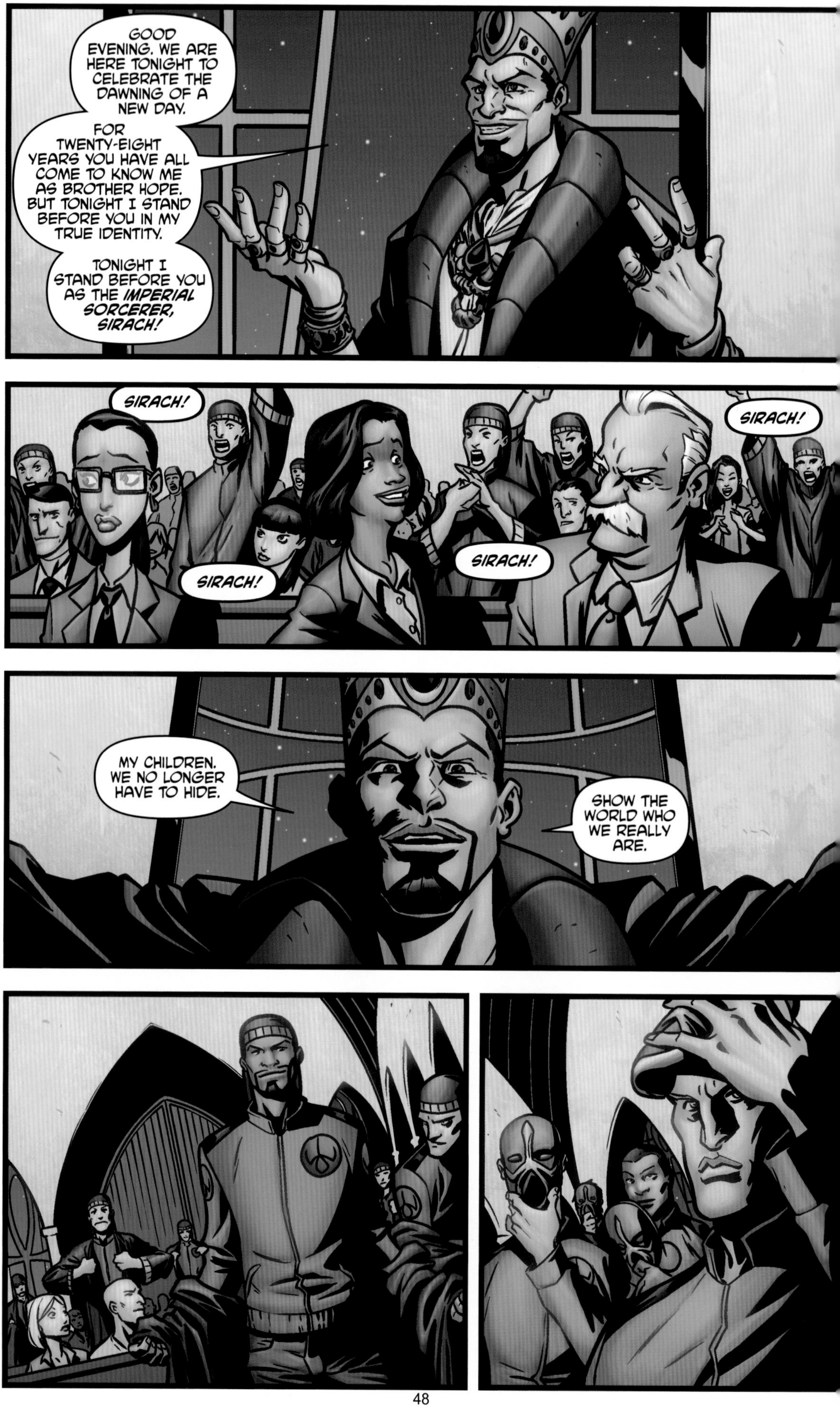
GOOD EVENING. WE ARE HERE TONIGHT TO CELEBRATE THE DAWNING OF A NEW DAY.
FOR TWENTY-EIGHT YEARS YOU HAVE ALL COME TO KNOW ME AS BROTHER HOPE. BUT TONIGHT I STAND BEFORE YOU IN MY TRUE IDENTITY.
TONIGHT I STAND BEFORE YOU AS THE *IMPERIAL SORCERER, SIRACH!*
SIRACH!
SIRACH!
SIRACH!
SIRACH!
MY CHILDREN. WE NO LONGER HAVE TO HIDE.
SHOW THE WORLD WHO WE REALLY ARE.

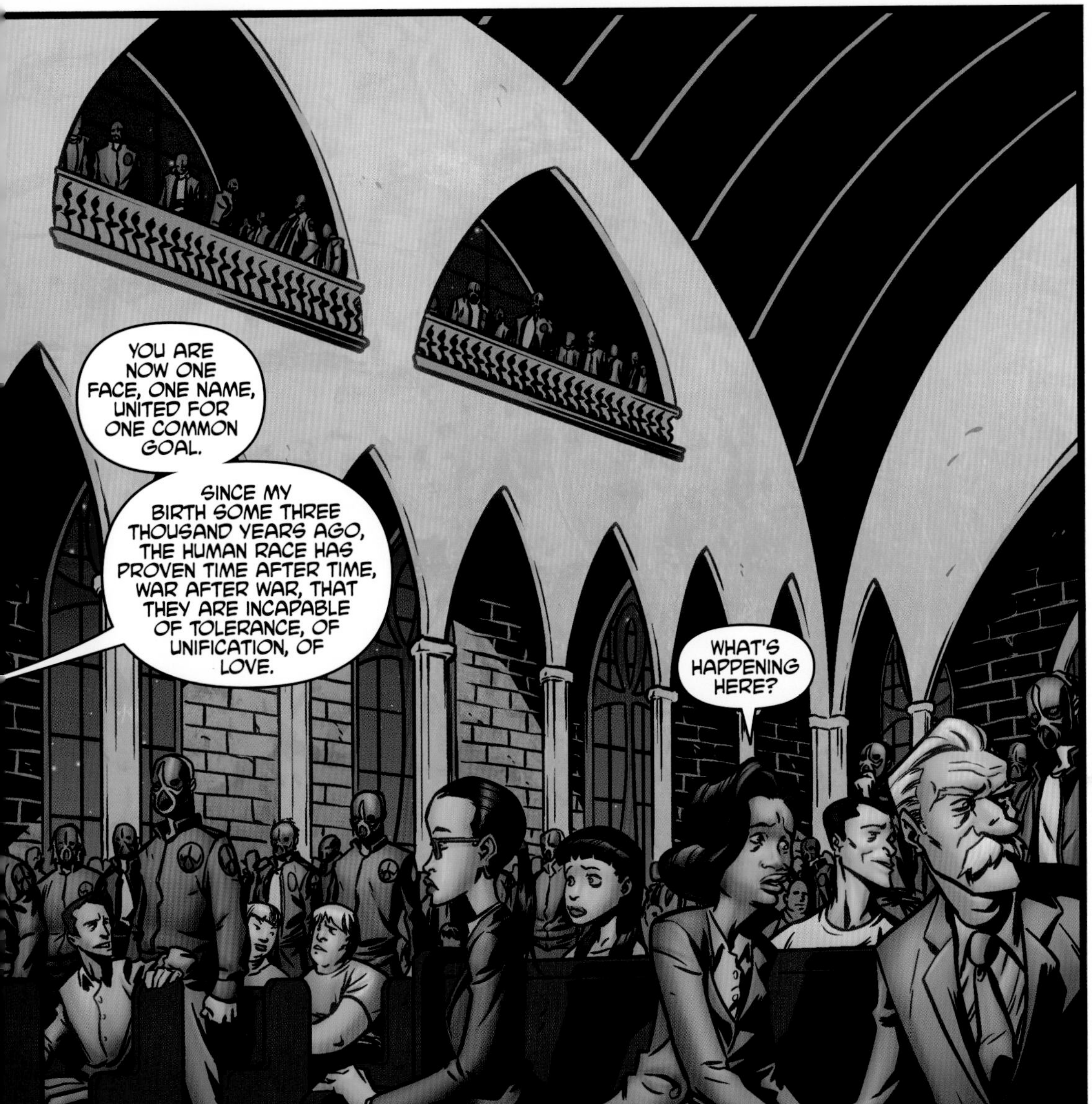
YOU ARE NOW ONE FACE, ONE NAME, UNITED FOR ONE COMMON GOAL.
SINCE MY BIRTH SOME THREE THOUSAND YEARS AGO, THE HUMAN RACE HAS PROVEN TIME AFTER TIME, WAR AFTER WAR, THAT THEY ARE INCAPABLE OF TOLERANCE, OF UNIFICATION, OF LOVE.
WHAT'S HAPPENING HERE?

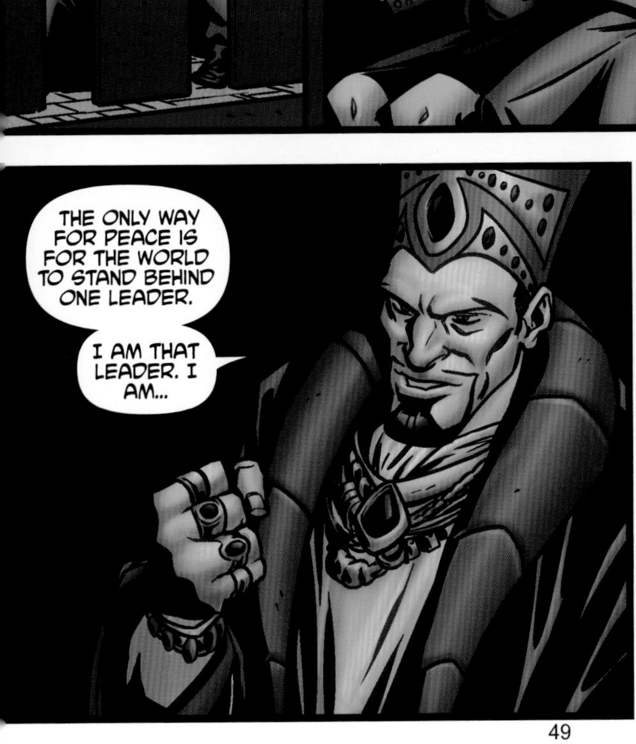
THE ONLY WAY FOR PEACE IS FOR THE WORLD TO STAND BEHIND ONE LEADER.
I AM THAT LEADER. I AM...

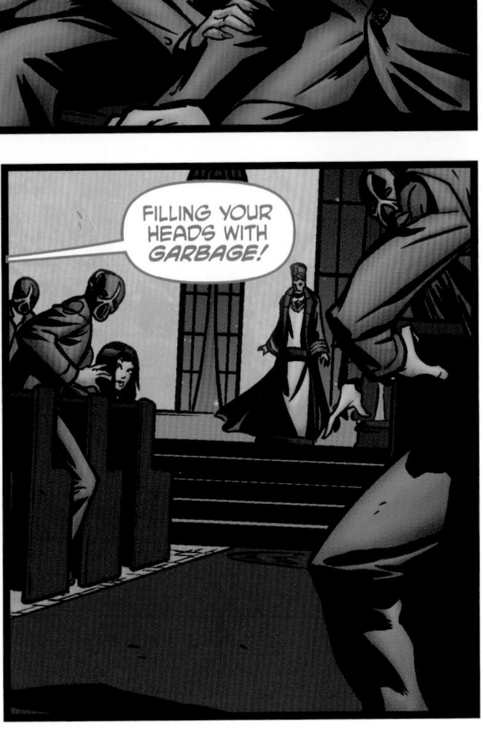
FILLING YOUR HEADS WITH *GARBAGE!*

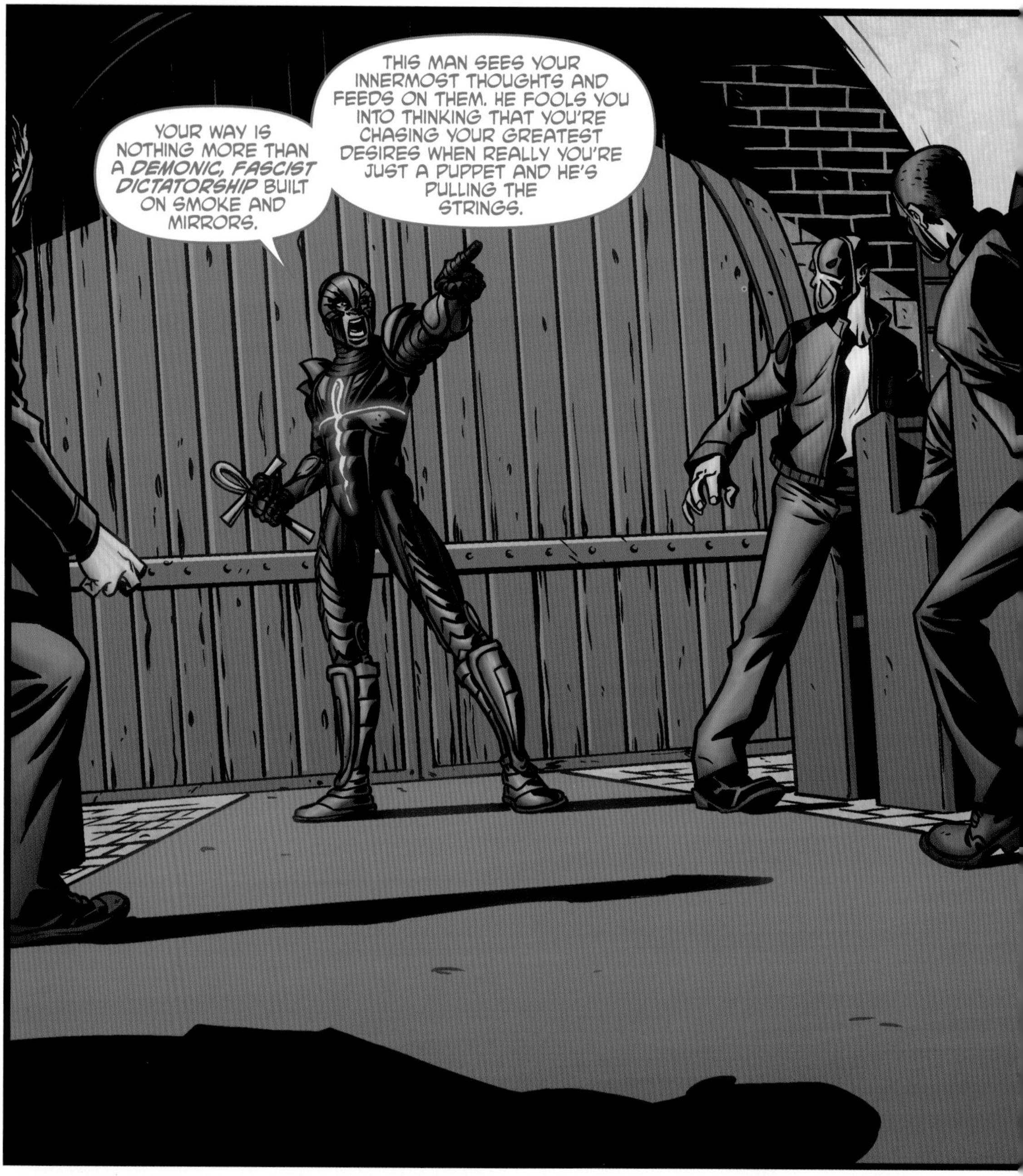
YOUR WAY IS NOTHING MORE THAN A DEMONIC, FASCIST DICTATORSHIP BUILT ON SMOKE AND MIRRORS.
THIS MAN SEES YOUR INNERMOST THOUGHTS AND FEEDS ON THEM. HE FOOLS YOU INTO THINKING THAT YOU'RE CHASING YOUR GREATEST DESIRES WHEN REALLY YOU'RE JUST A PUPPET AND HE'S PULLING THE STRINGS.

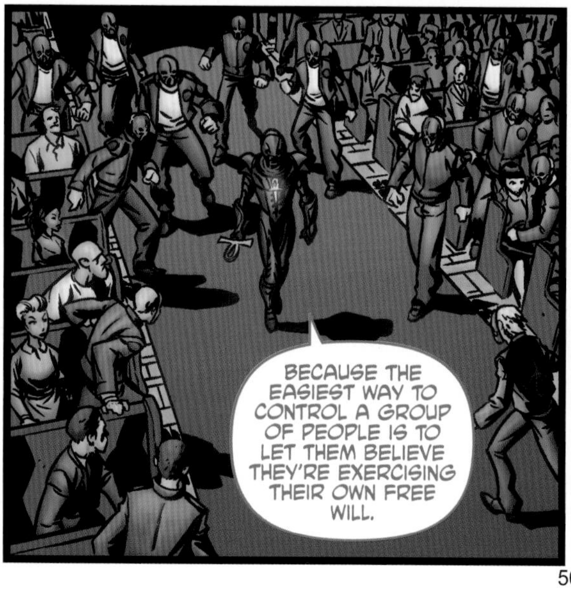
BECAUSE THE EASIEST WAY TO CONTROL A GROUP OF PEOPLE IS TO LET THEM BELIEVE THEY'RE EXERCISING THEIR OWN FREE WILL.

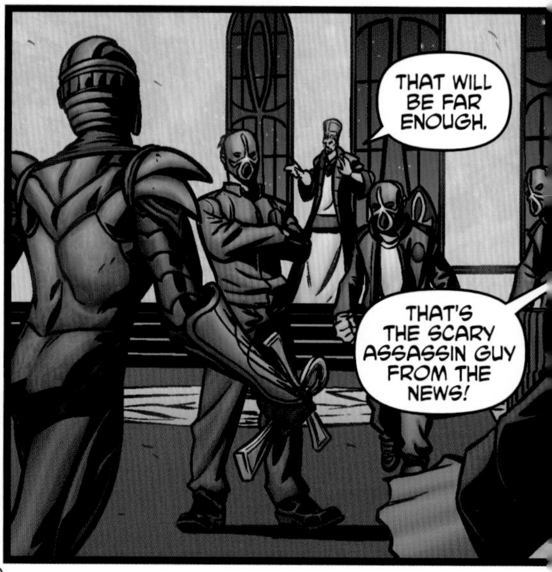
THAT WILL BE FAR ENOUGH.
THAT'S THE SCARY ASSASSIN GUY FROM THE NEWS!

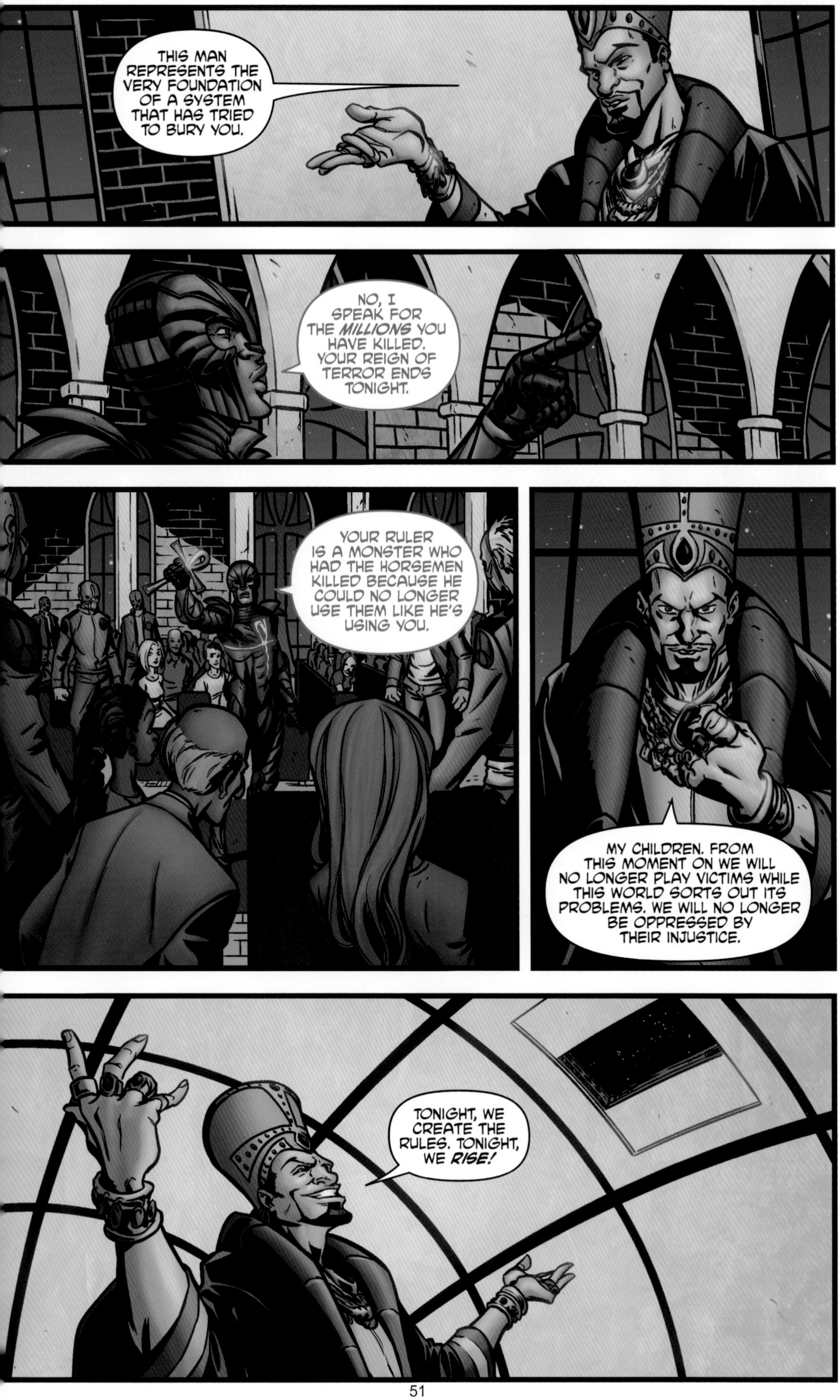
THIS MAN REPRESENTS THE VERY FOUNDATION OF A SYSTEM THAT HAS TRIED TO BURY YOU.
NO, I SPEAK FOR THE *MILLIONS* YOU HAVE KILLED. YOUR REIGN OF TERROR ENDS TONIGHT.
YOUR RULER IS A MONSTER WHO HAD THE HORSEMEN KILLED BECAUSE HE COULD NO LONGER USE THEM LIKE HE'S USING YOU.
MY CHILDREN. FROM THIS MOMENT ON WE WILL NO LONGER PLAY VICTIMS WHILE THIS WORLD SORTS OUT ITS PROBLEMS. WE WILL NO LONGER BE OPPRESSED BY THEIR INJUSTICE.
TONIGHT, WE CREATE THE RULES. TONIGHT, WE *RISE!*

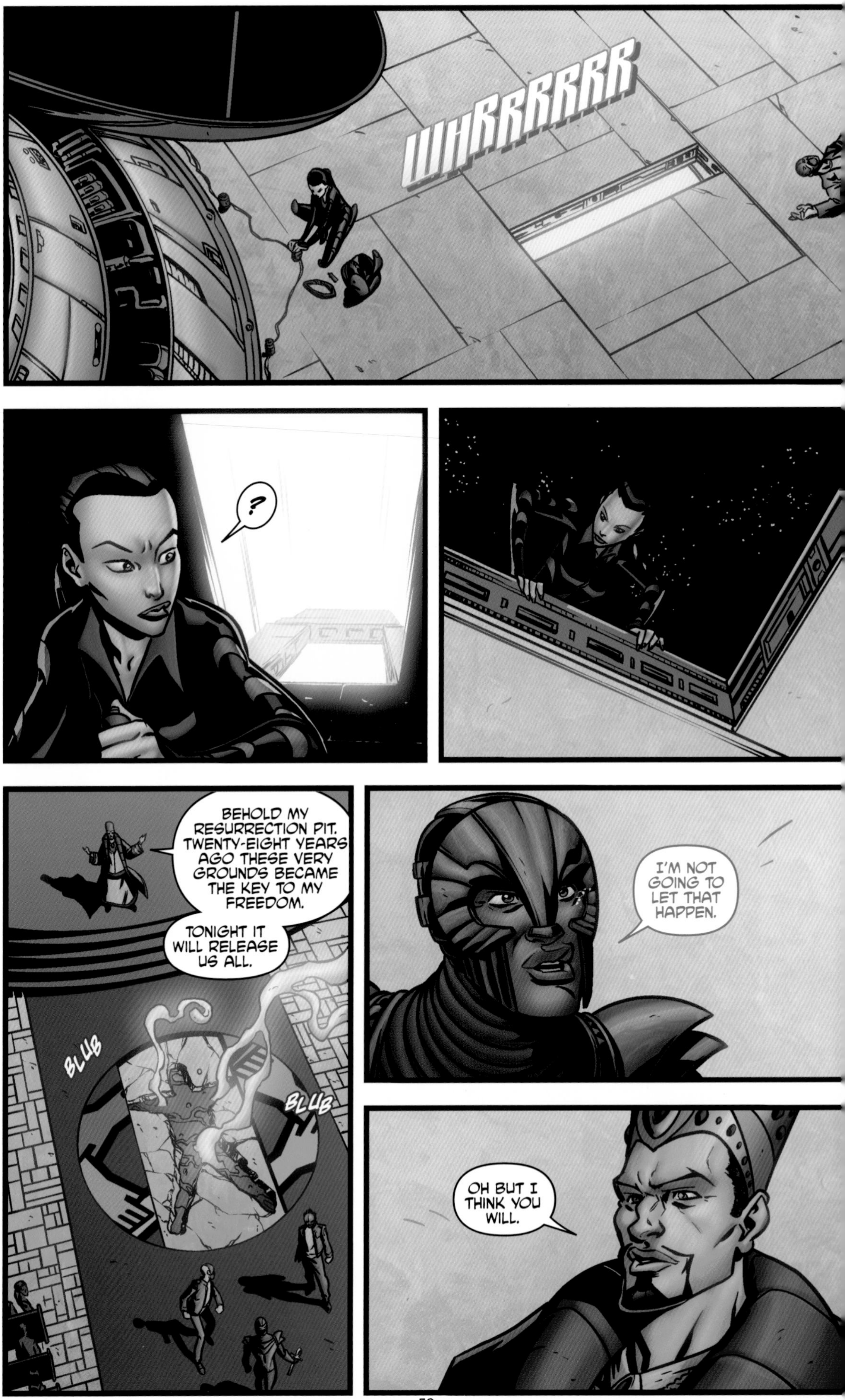
WHRRRRRR
?
BEHOLD MY RESURRECTION PIT. TWENTY-EIGHT YEARS AGO THESE VERY GROUNDS BECAME THE KEY TO MY FREEDOM.
TONIGHT IT WILL RELEASE US ALL.
BLUB
BLUB
I'M NOT GOING TO LET THAT HAPPEN.
OH BUT I THINK YOU WILL.

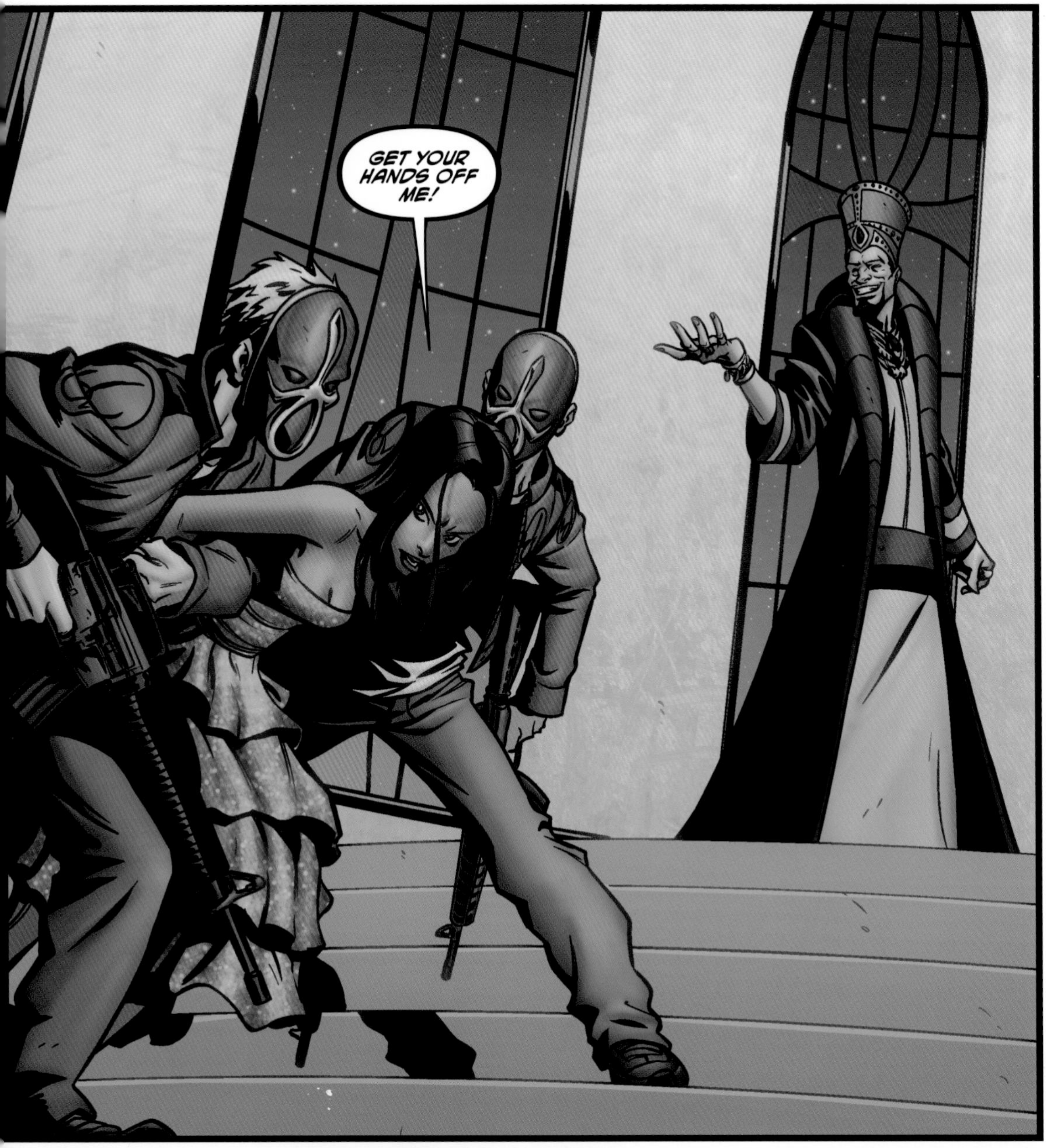
GET YOUR HANDS OFF ME!

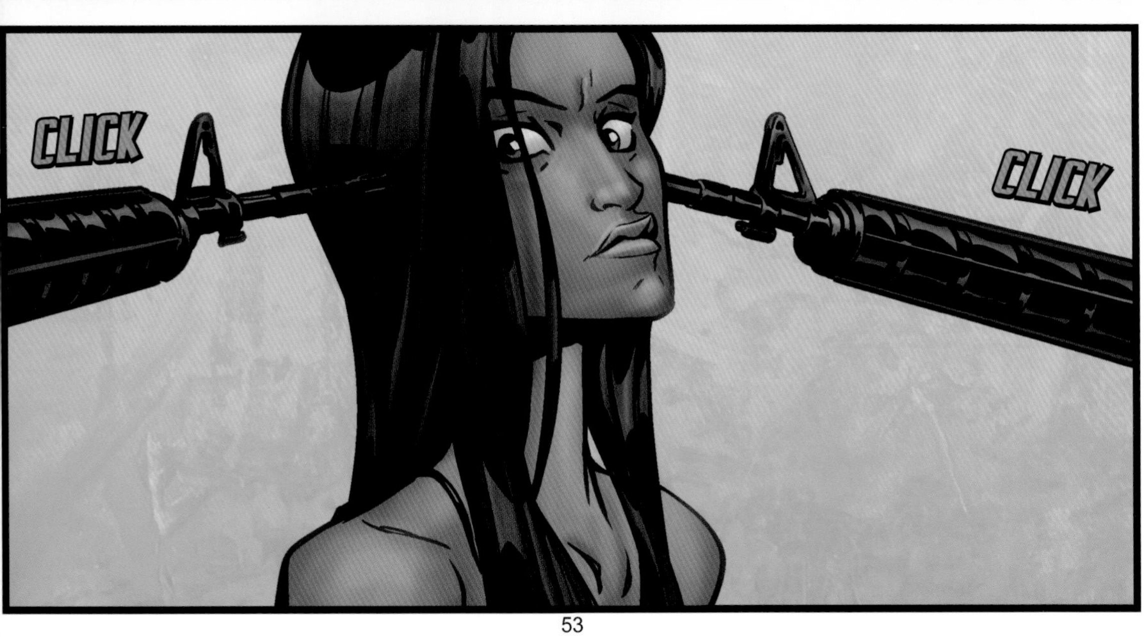
CLICK
CLICK

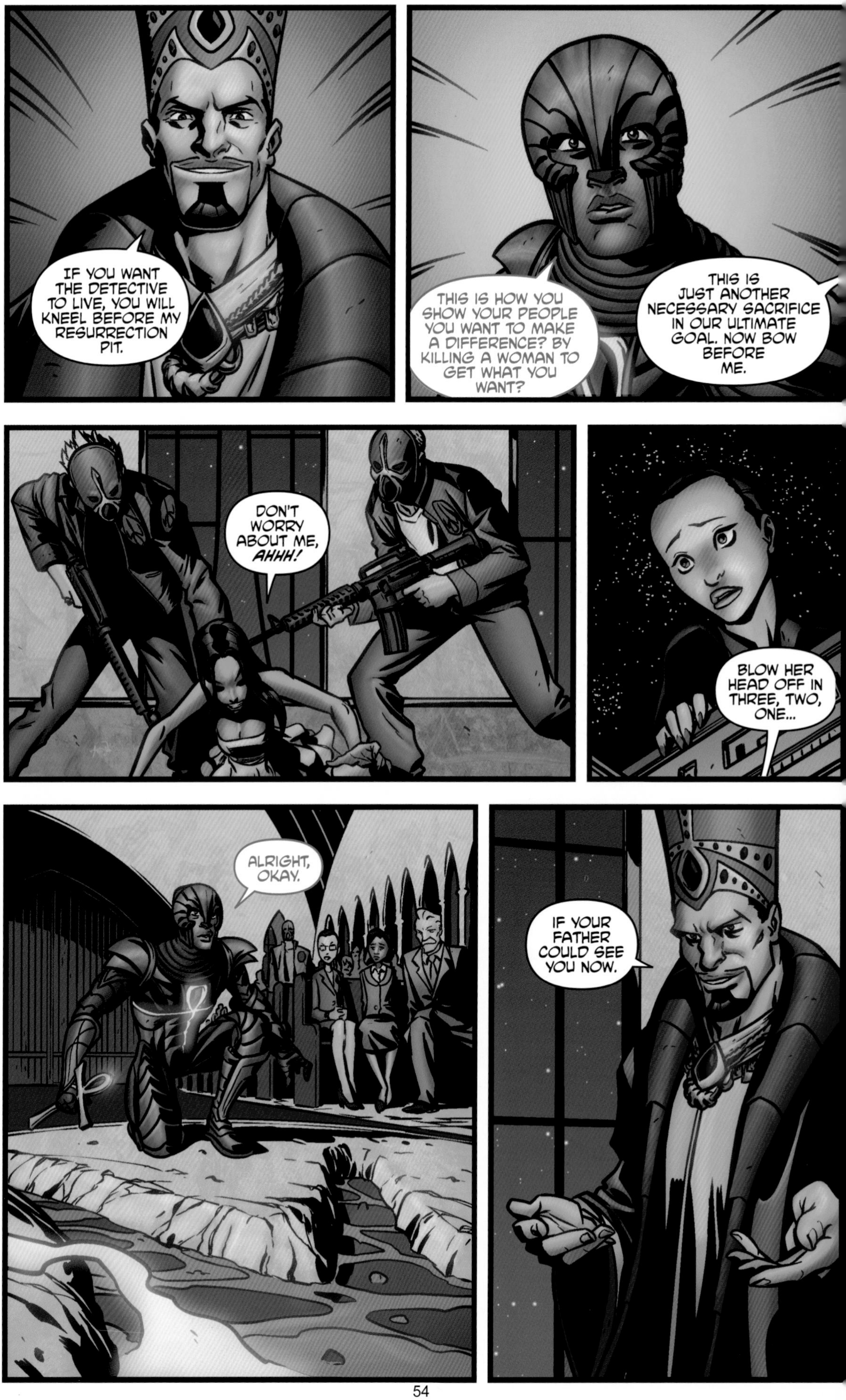
IF YOU WANT THE DETECTIVE TO LIVE, YOU WILL KNEEL BEFORE MY RESURRECTION PIT.
THIS IS HOW YOU SHOW YOUR PEOPLE YOU WANT TO MAKE A DIFFERENCE? BY KILLING A WOMAN TO GET WHAT YOU WANT?
THIS IS JUST ANOTHER NECESSARY SACRIFICE IN OUR ULTIMATE GOAL. NOW BOW BEFORE ME.
DON'T WORRY ABOUT ME, *AHHH!*
BLOW HER HEAD OFF IN THREE, TWO, ONE...
ALRIGHT, OKAY.
IF YOUR FATHER COULD SEE YOU NOW.

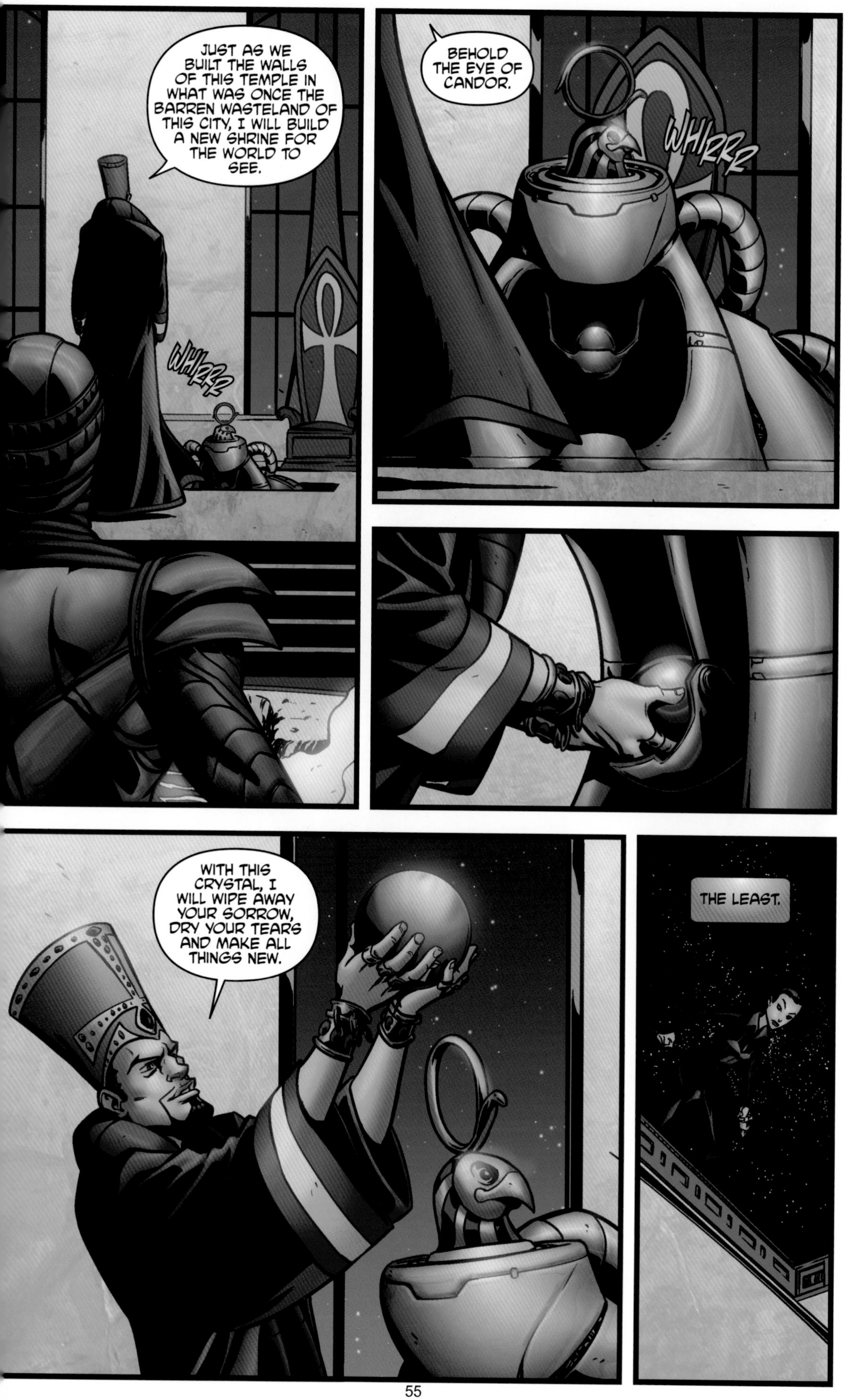

JUST AS WE BUILT THE WALLS OF THIS TEMPLE IN WHAT WAS ONCE THE BARREN WASTELAND OF THIS CITY, I WILL BUILD A NEW SHRINE FOR THE WORLD TO SEE.
WHIRRR
BEHOLD THE EYE OF CANDOR.
WHIRRR
WITH THIS CRYSTAL, I WILL WIPE AWAY YOUR SORROW, DRY YOUR TEARS AND MAKE ALL THINGS NEW.
THE LEAST.

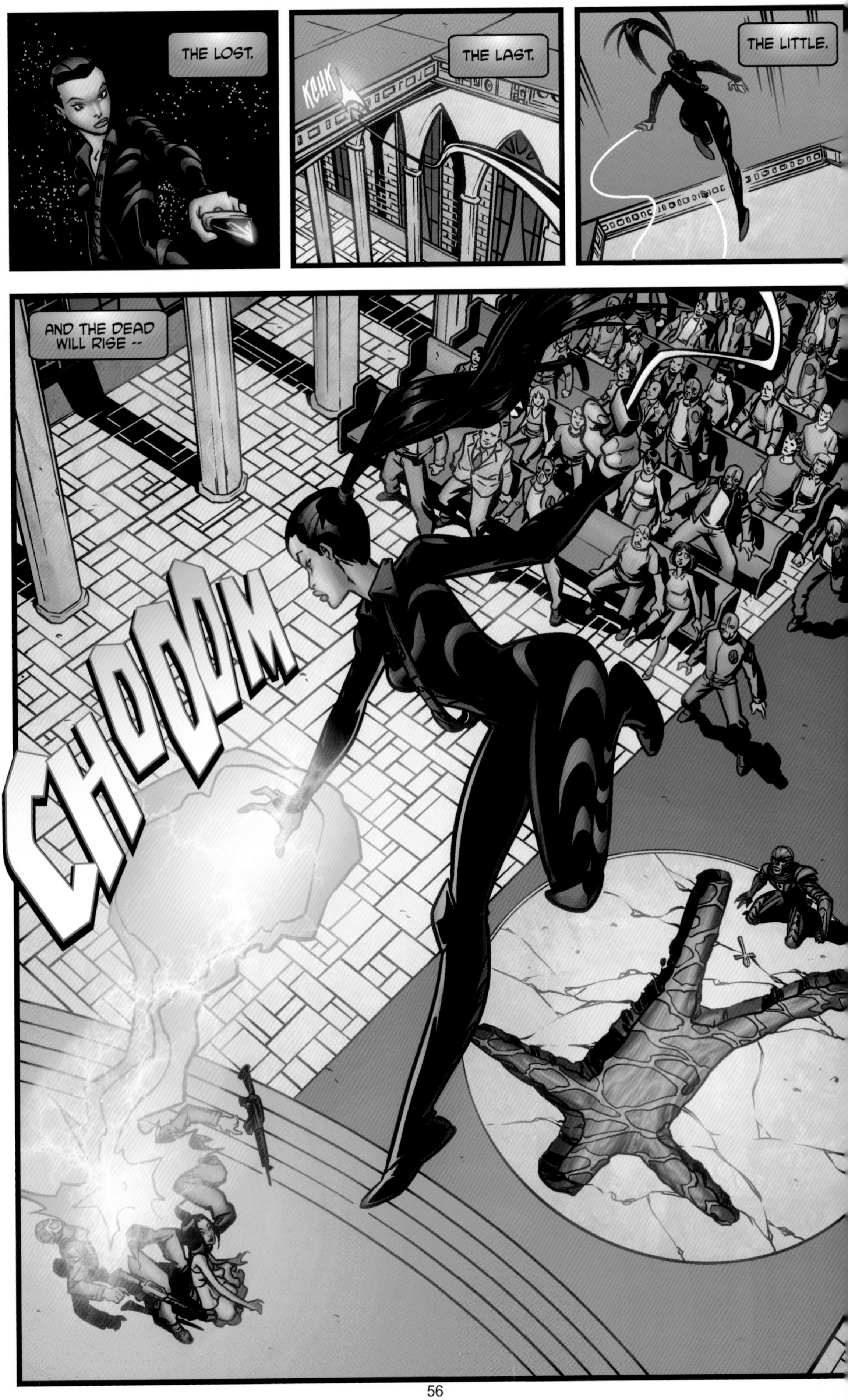
THE LOST.
KCHK
THE LAST.
THE LITTLE.
AND THE DEAD WILL RISE --
CHOOOM

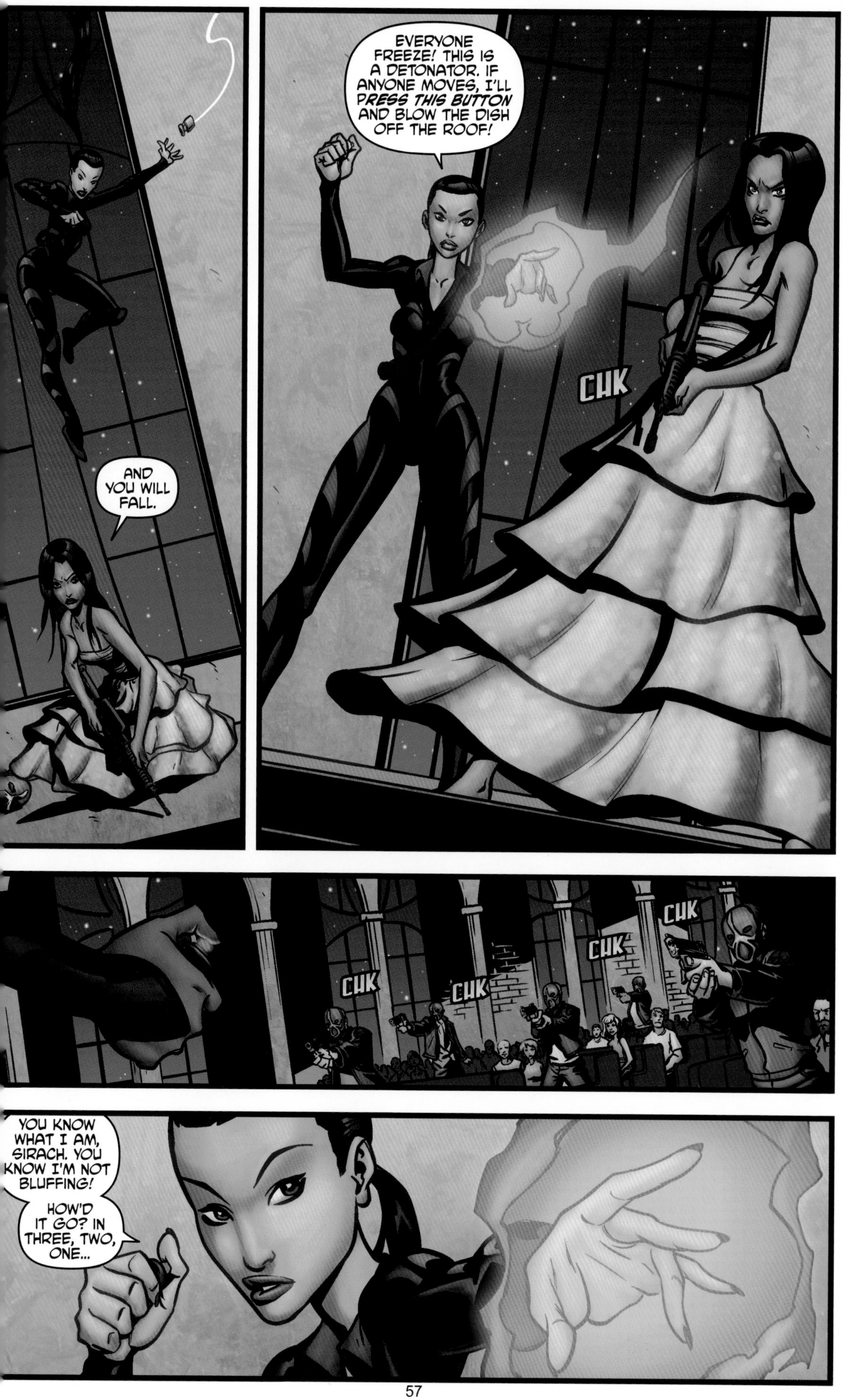
AND YOU WILL FALL.
EVERYONE FREEZE! THIS IS A DETONATOR. IF ANYONE MOVES, I'LL PRESS THIS BUTTON AND BLOW THE DISH OFF THE ROOF!
CHK
CHK
CHK
CHK
CHK
YOU KNOW WHAT I AM, SIRACH. YOU KNOW I'M NOT BLUFFING!
HOW'D IT GO? IN THREE, TWO, ONE...

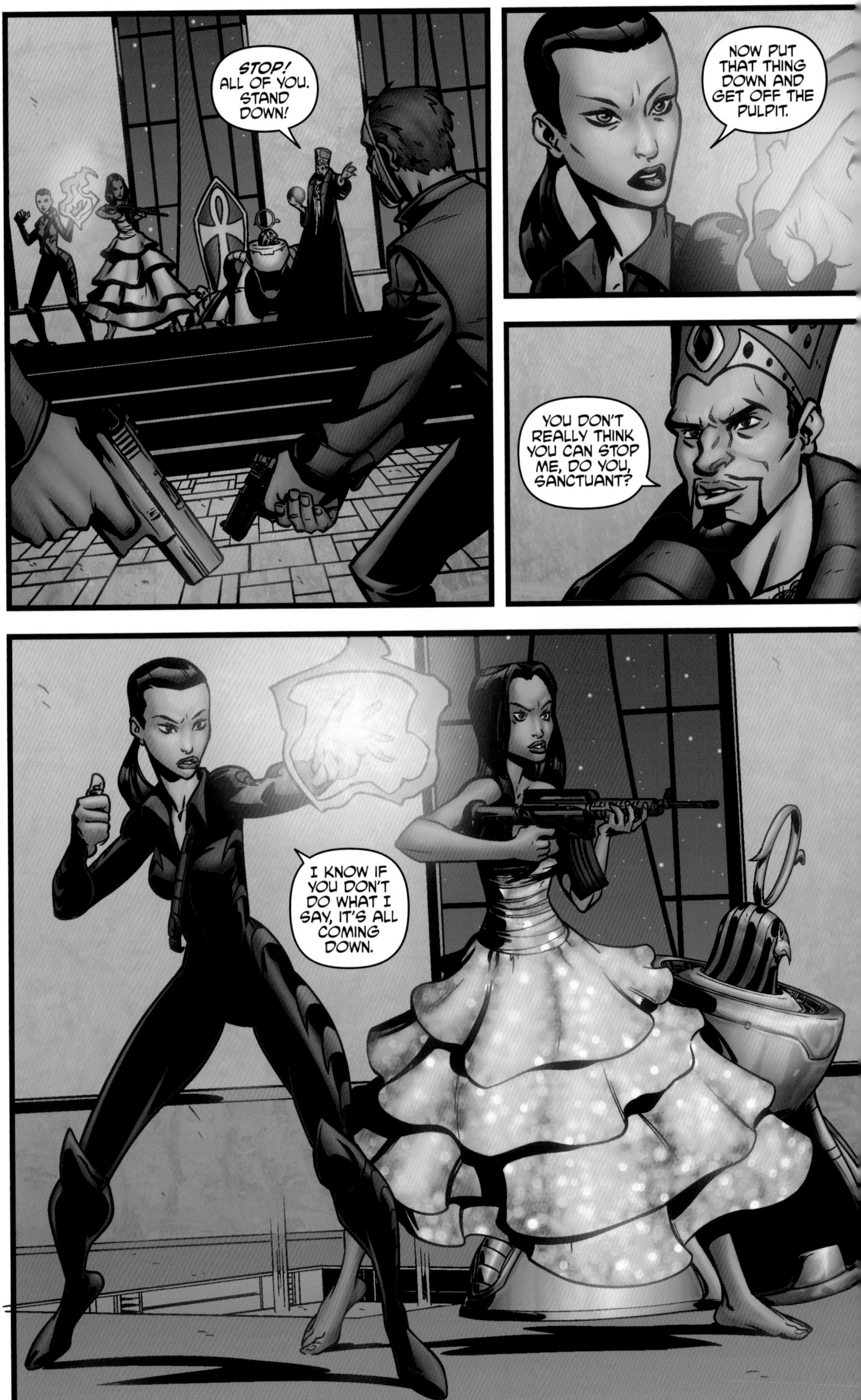
STOP! ALL OF YOU. STAND DOWN!
NOW PUT THAT THING DOWN AND GET OFF THE PULPIT.
YOU DON'T REALLY THINK YOU CAN STOP ME, DO YOU, SANCTUANT?
I KNOW IF YOU DON'T DO WHAT I SAY, IT'S ALL COMING DOWN.

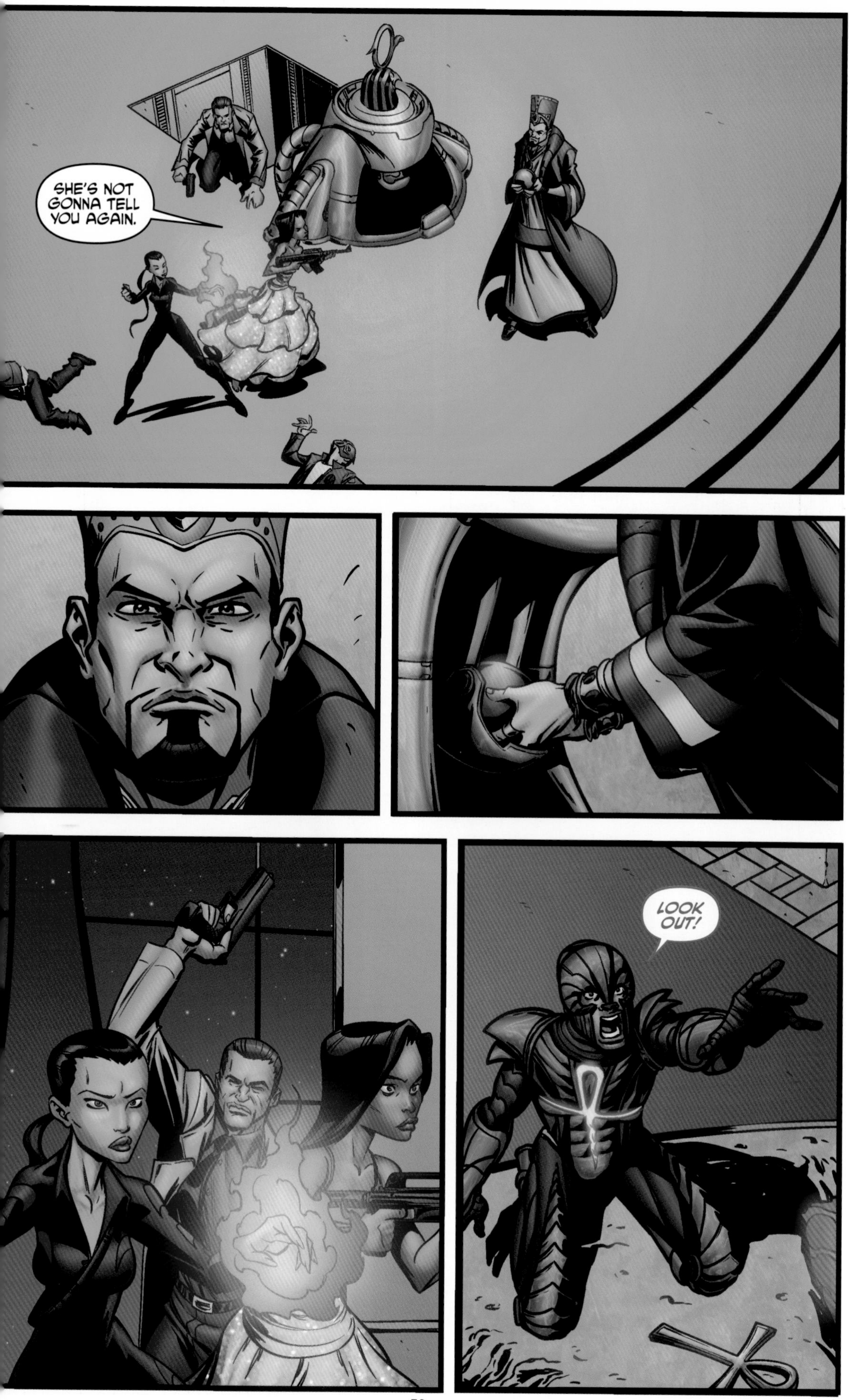
SHE'S NOT GONNA TELL YOU AGAIN.
LOOK OUT!

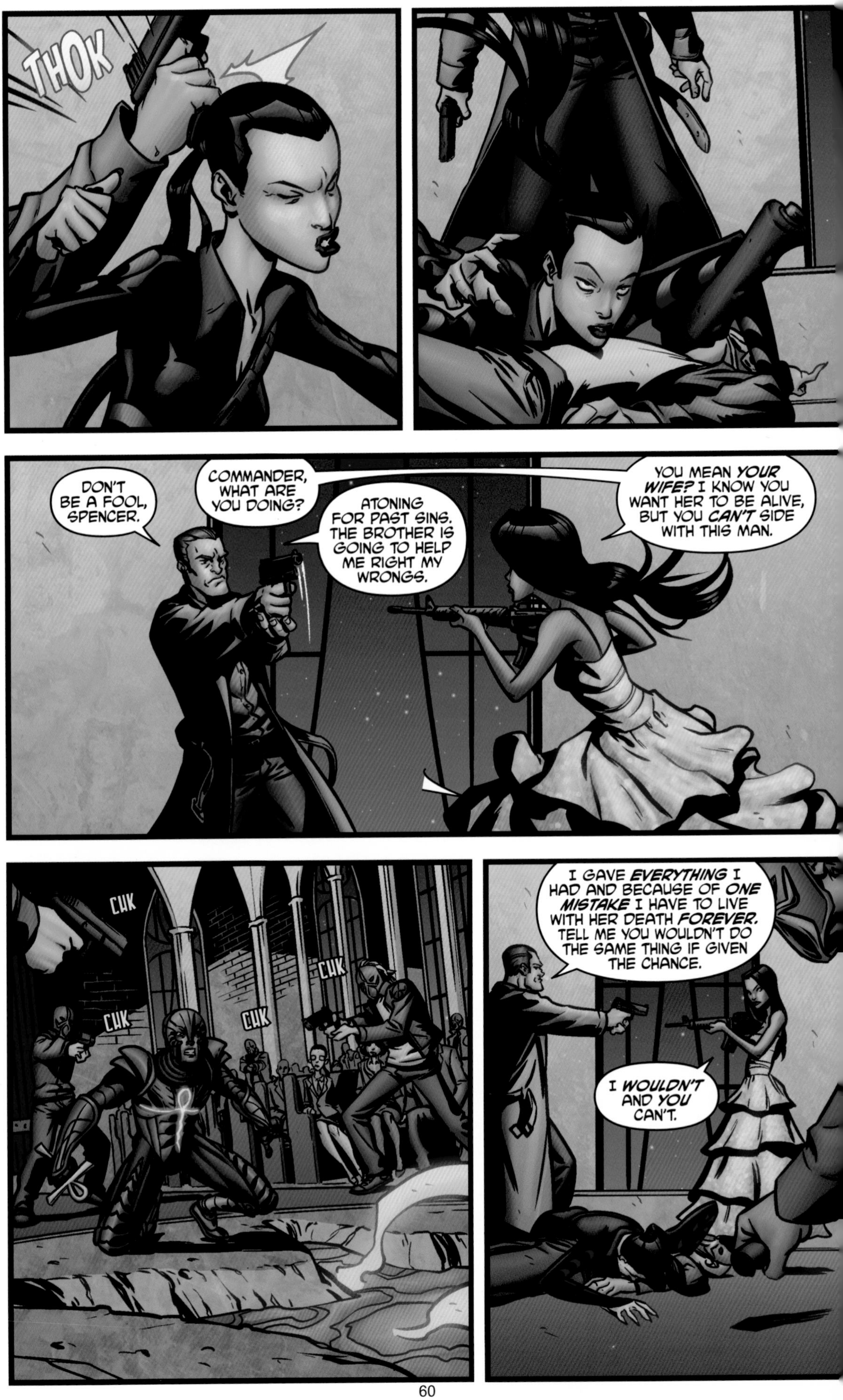
THOK
DON'T BE A FOOL, SPENCER.
COMMANDER, WHAT ARE YOU DOING?
ATONING FOR PAST SINS. THE BROTHER IS GOING TO HELP ME RIGHT MY WRONGS.
YOU MEAN *YOUR WIFE?* I KNOW YOU WANT HER TO BE ALIVE, BUT YOU *CAN'T* SIDE WITH THIS MAN.
CHK
CHK
CHK
CHK
I GAVE *EVERYTHING* I HAD AND BECAUSE OF *ONE MISTAKE* I HAVE TO LIVE WITH HER DEATH *FOREVER.* TELL ME YOU WOULDN'T DO THE SAME THING IF GIVEN THE CHANCE.
I *WOULDN'T* AND *YOU* CAN'T.

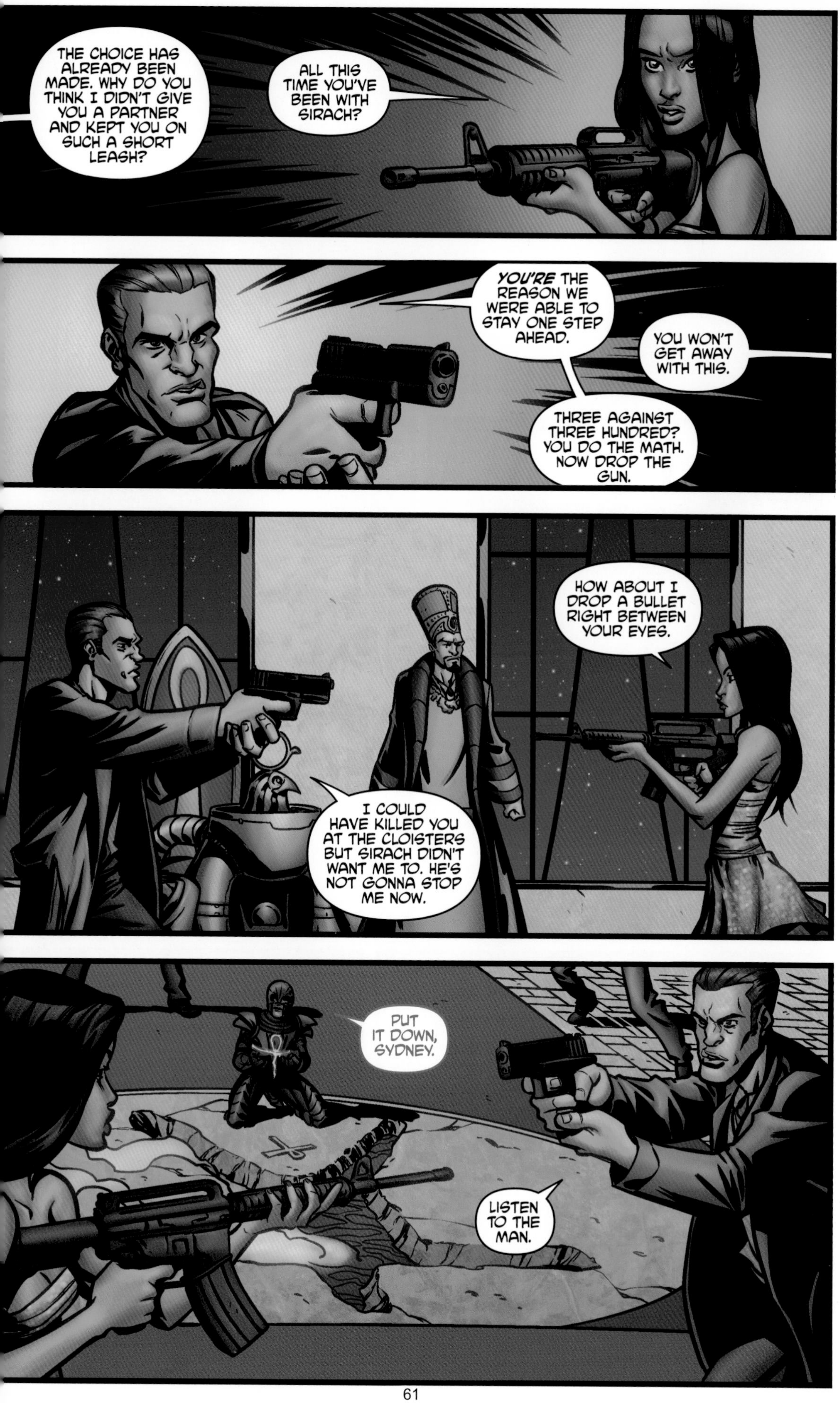
THE CHOICE HAS ALREADY BEEN MADE. WHY DO YOU THINK I DIDN'T GIVE YOU A PARTNER AND KEPT YOU ON SUCH A SHORT LEASH?
ALL THIS TIME YOU'VE BEEN WITH SIRACH?
YOU'RE THE REASON WE WERE ABLE TO STAY ONE STEP AHEAD.
YOU WON'T GET AWAY WITH THIS.
THREE AGAINST THREE HUNDRED? YOU DO THE MATH. NOW DROP THE GUN.
HOW ABOUT I DROP A BULLET RIGHT BETWEEN YOUR EYES.
I COULD HAVE KILLED YOU AT THE CLOISTERS BUT SIRACH DIDN'T WANT ME TO. HE'S NOT GONNA STOP ME NOW.
PUT IT DOWN, SYDNEY.
LISTEN TO THE MAN.

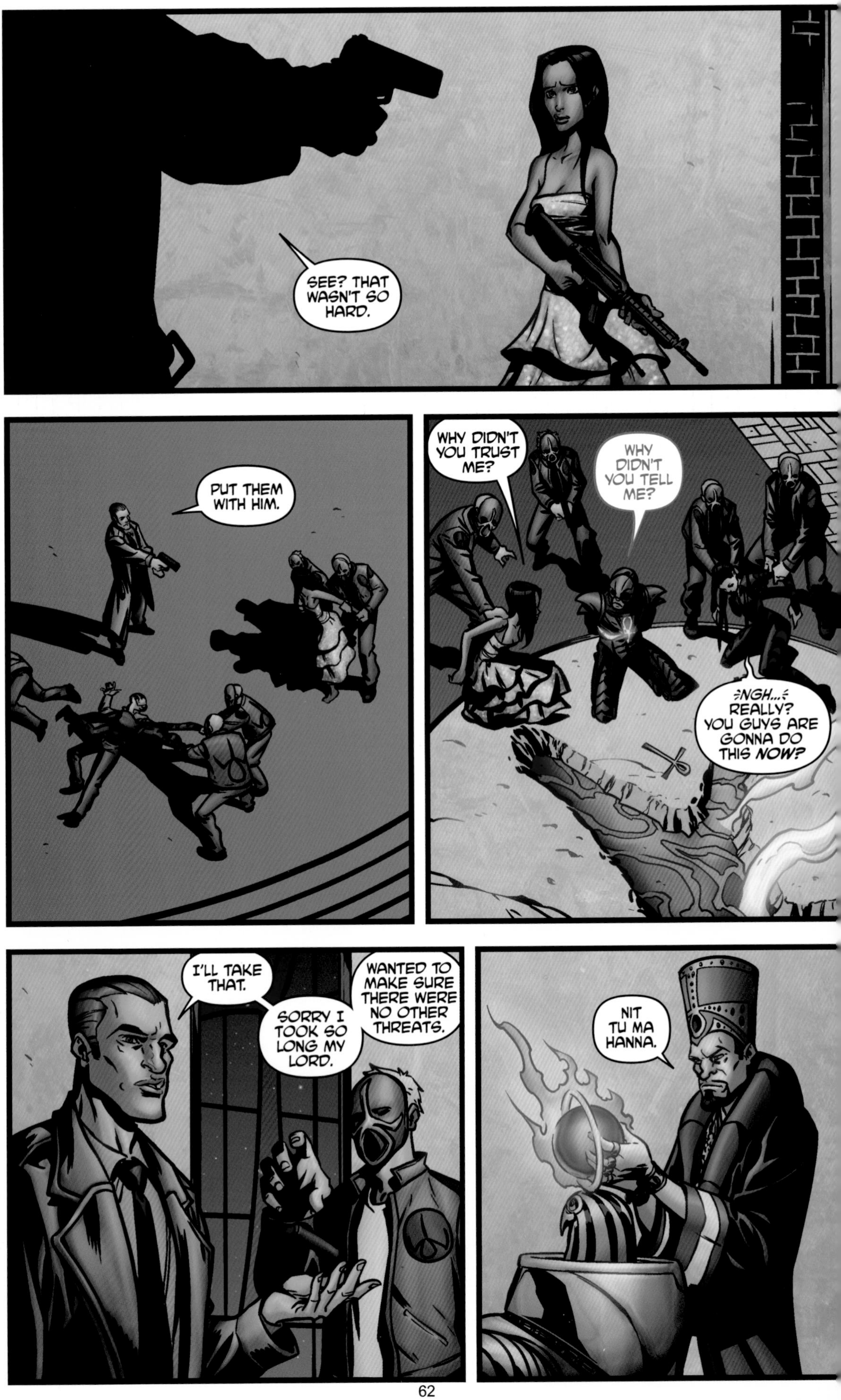
SEE? THAT WASN'T SO HARD.
PUT THEM WITH HIM.
WHY DIDN'T YOU TRUST ME?
WHY DIDN'T YOU TELL ME?
NGH... REALLY? YOU GUYS ARE GONNA DO THIS NOW?
I'LL TAKE THAT.
SORRY I TOOK SO LONG MY LORD.
WANTED TO MAKE SURE THERE WERE NO OTHER THREATS.
NIT TU MA HANNA.

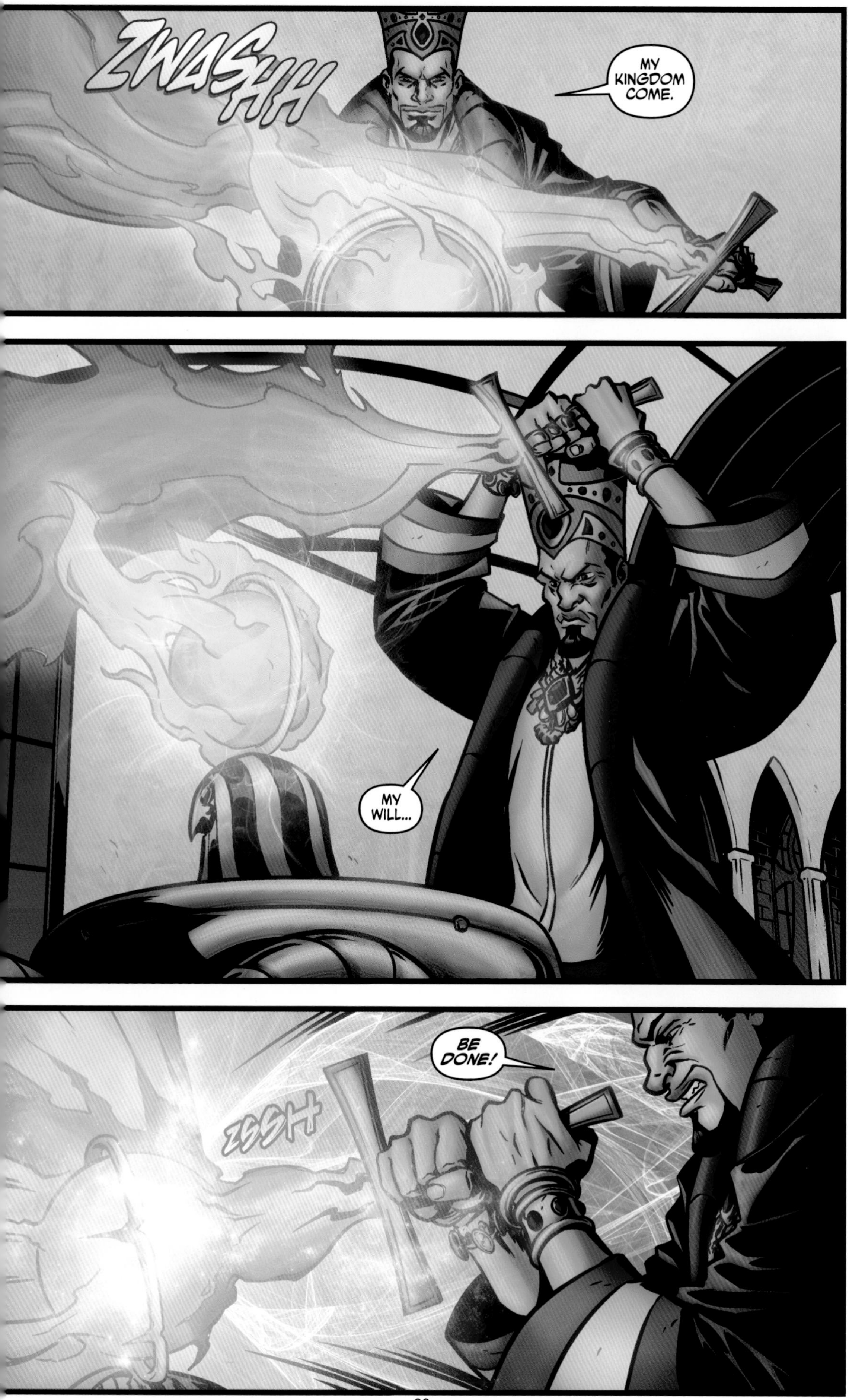
ZWASHH
MY KINGDOM COME.
MY WILL...
BE DONE!
ZSSH

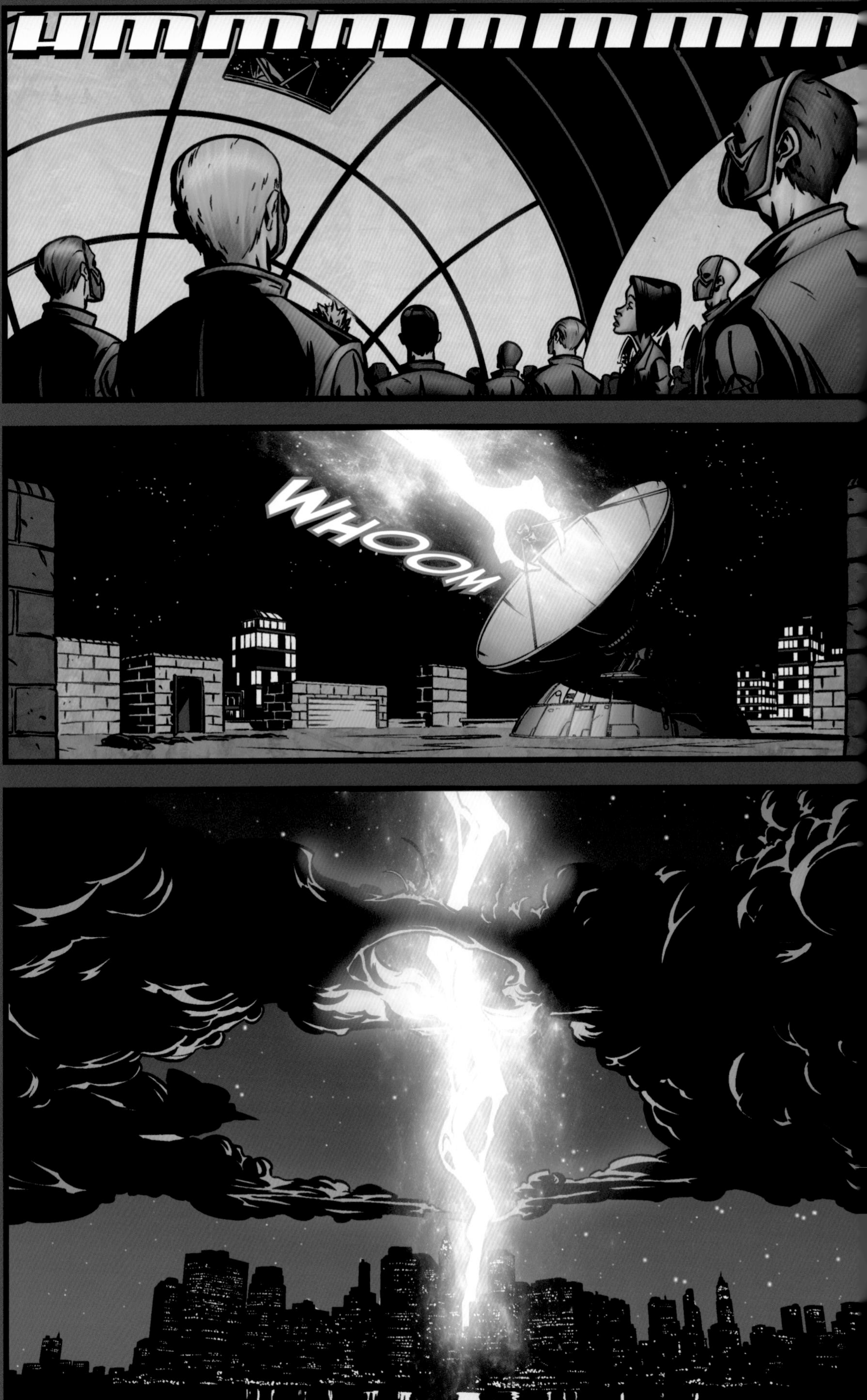
HMMMMMMMMM
WHOOM

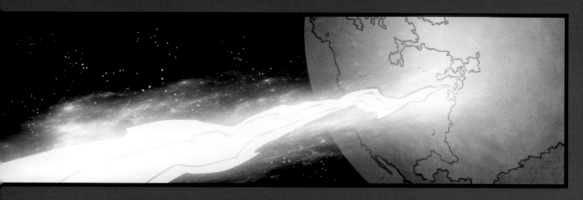

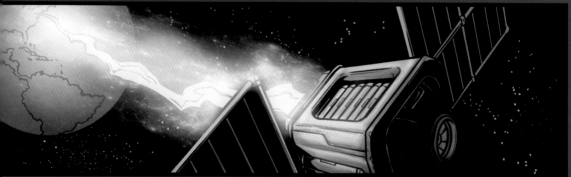

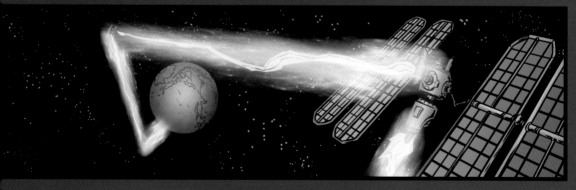

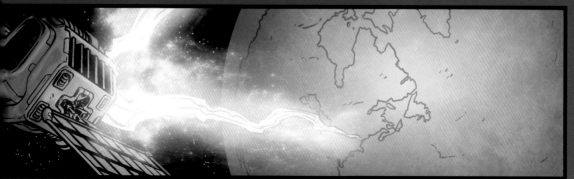

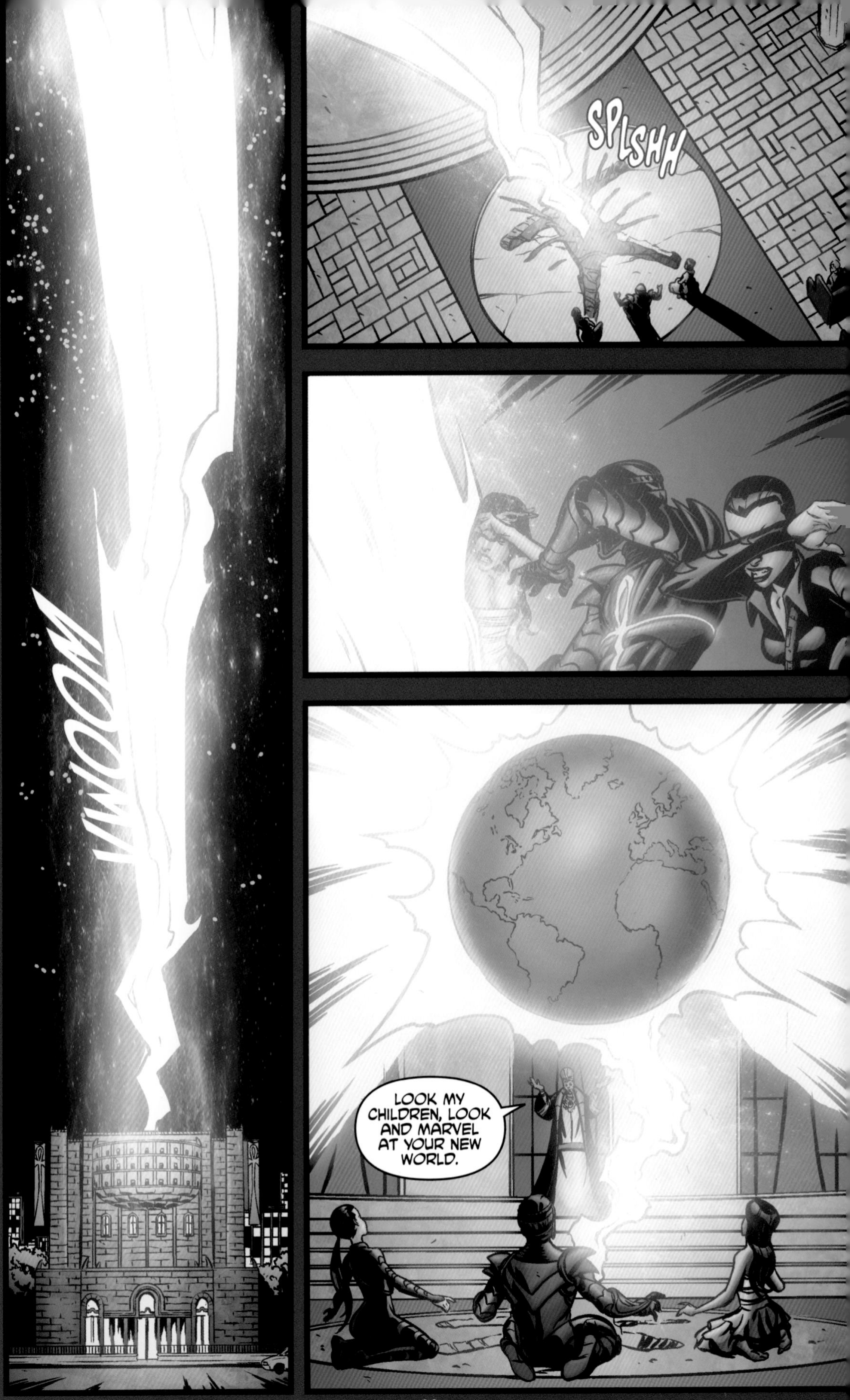
VWOOM
SPLSHH
LOOK MY CHILDREN, LOOK AND MARVEL AT YOUR NEW WORLD.

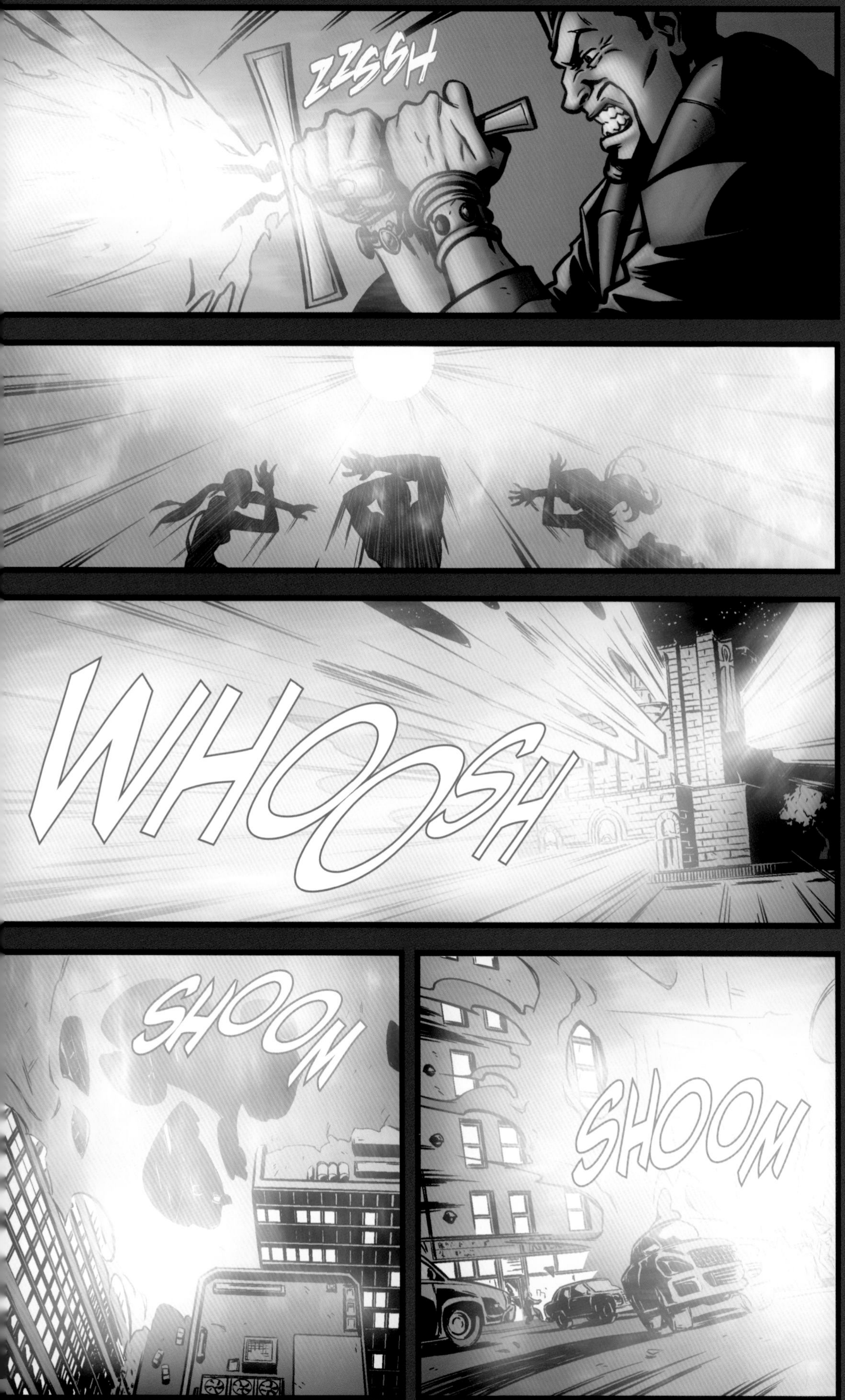
ZZSSH
WHOOSH
SHOOM
SHOOM

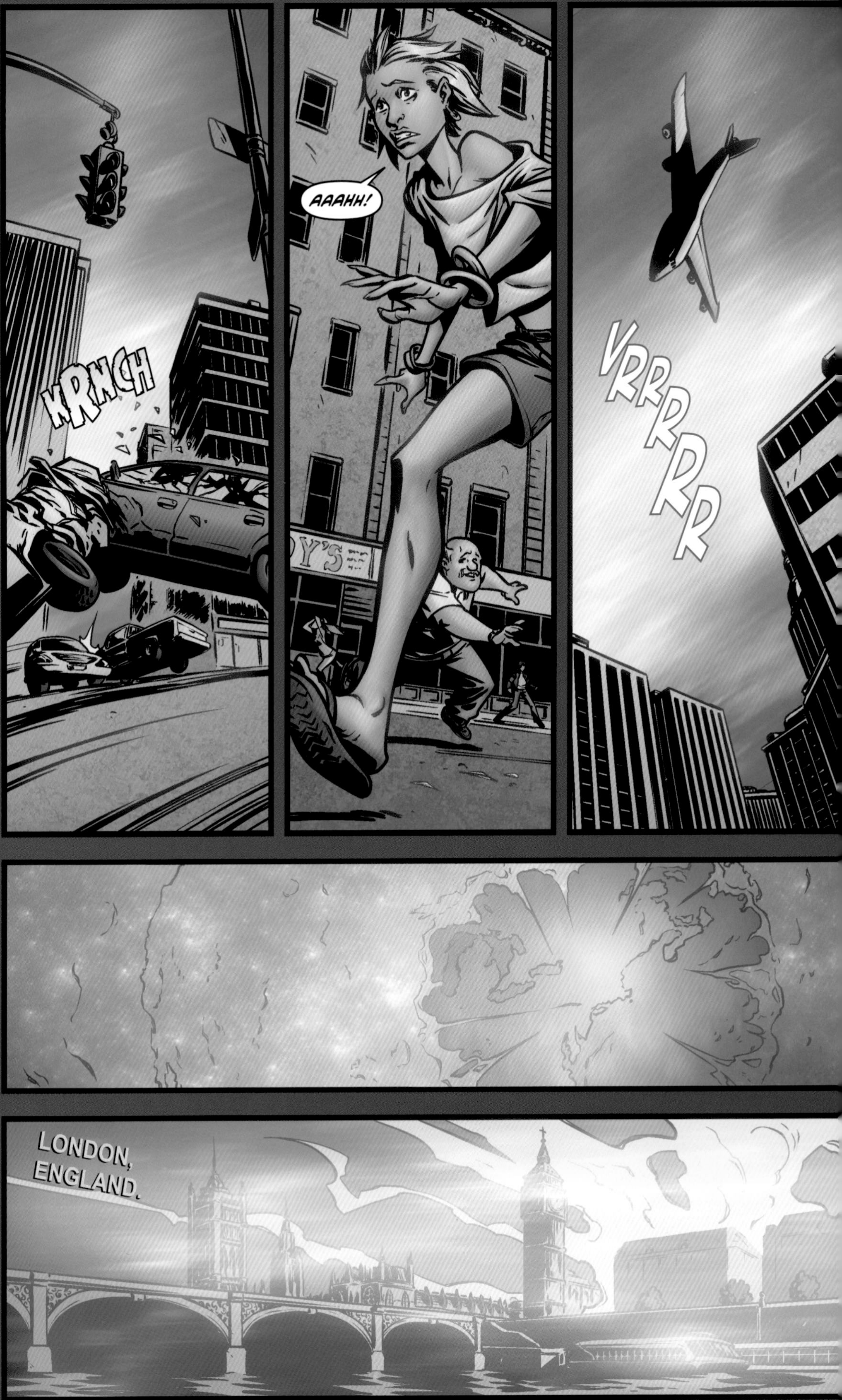
KRNCH
AAAHH!
VRRRRR
LONDON, ENGLAND.

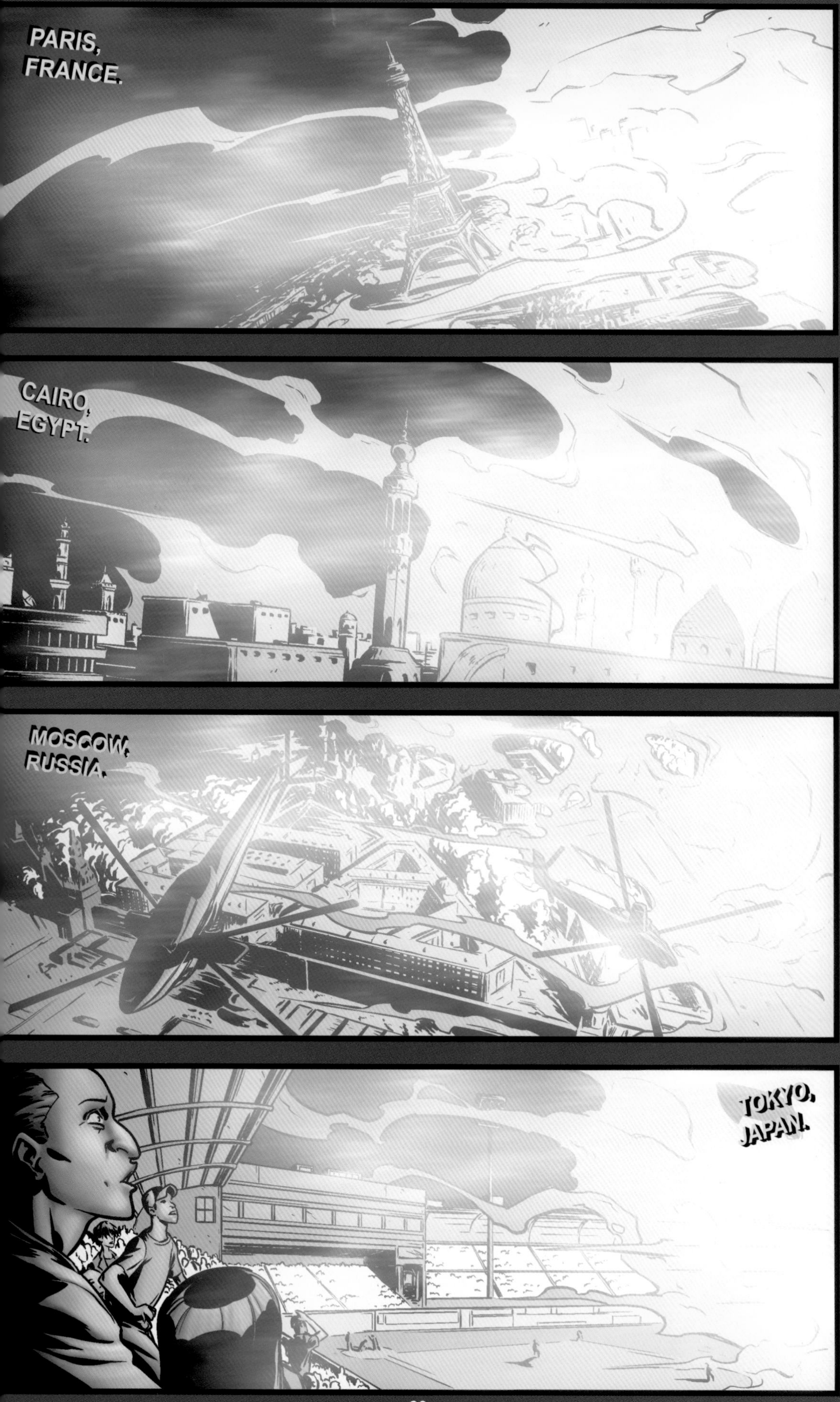
PARIS, FRANCE.
CAIRO, EGYPT.
MOSCOW, RUSSIA.
TOKYO, JAPAN.

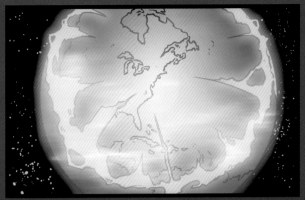

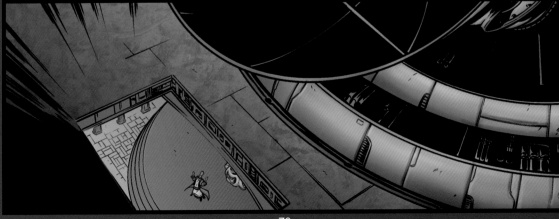

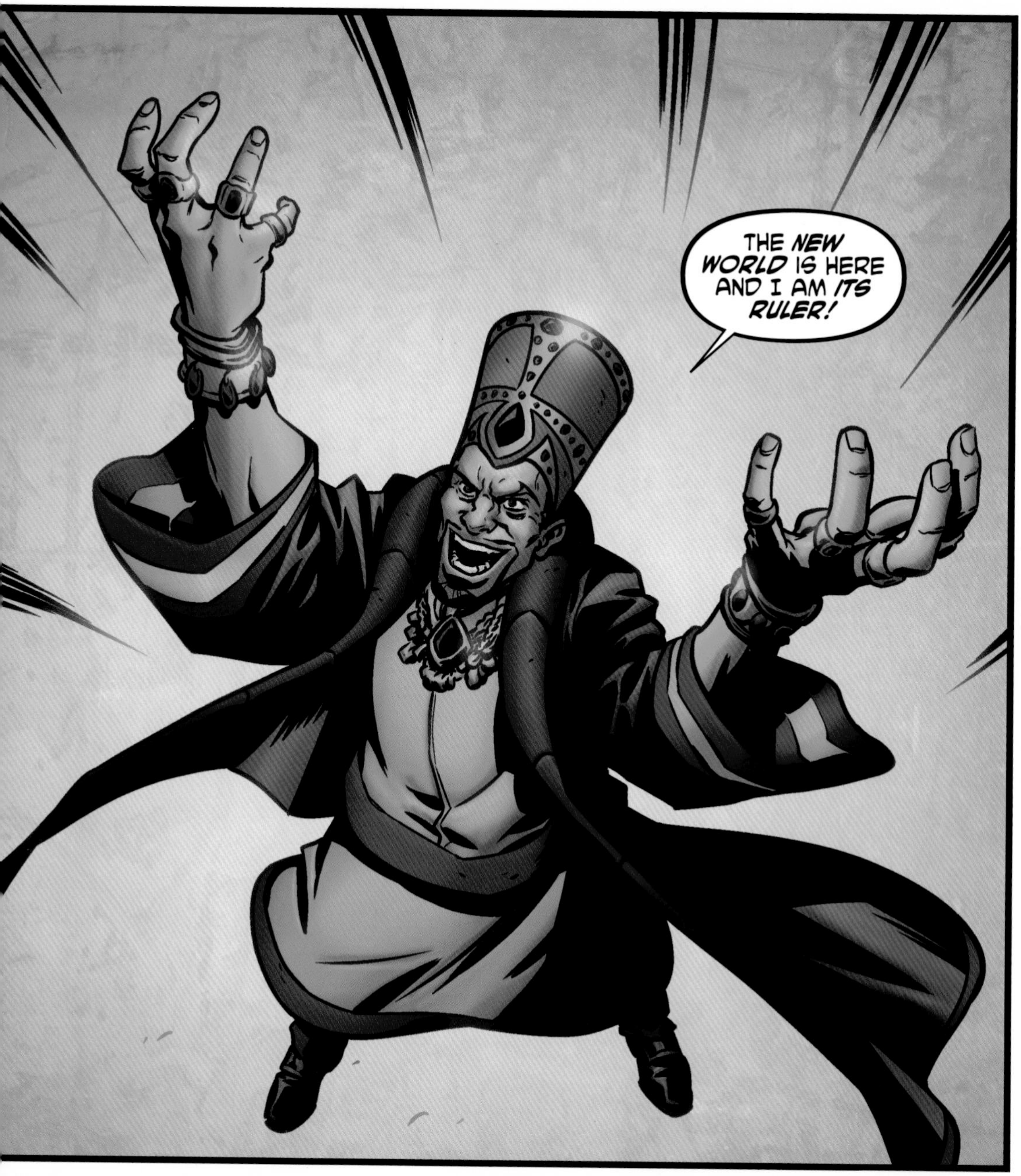
THE *NEW WORLD* IS HERE AND I AM *ITS RULER!*

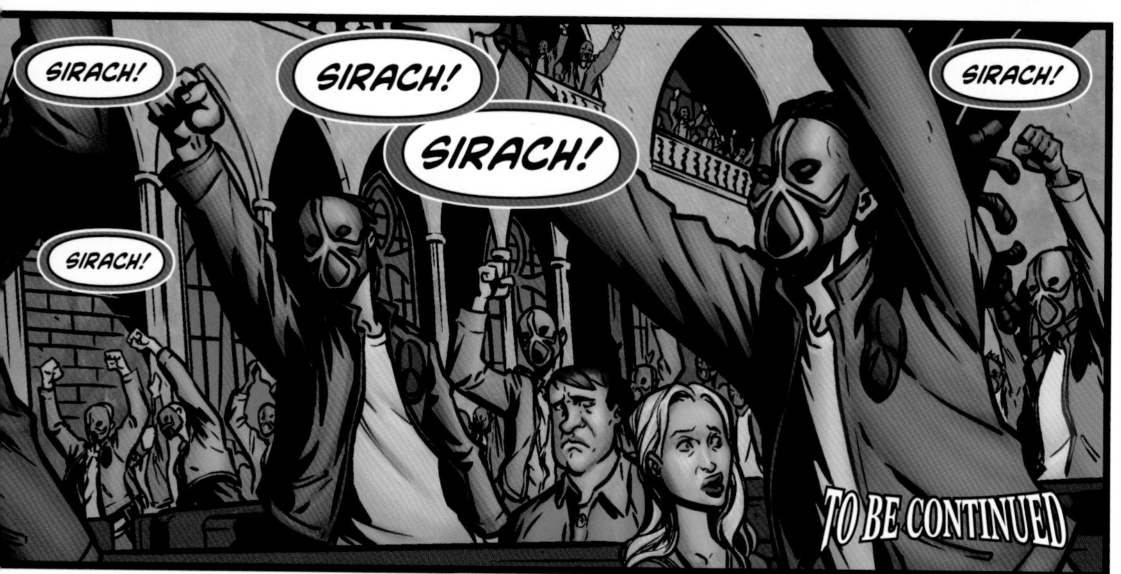
SIRACH!
SIRACH!
SIRACH!
SIRACH!
SIRACH!
TO BE CONTINUED

CHAPTER ⑭

For all the evils they had conquered before, they were not prepared for their most deadly adversary. Oh, if the ravens could have warned us of this darkness! Oh, If the sun could have pierced the despair! But humanity suffered, the world groaned, and even the Mantamaji were unsure they could prevail.

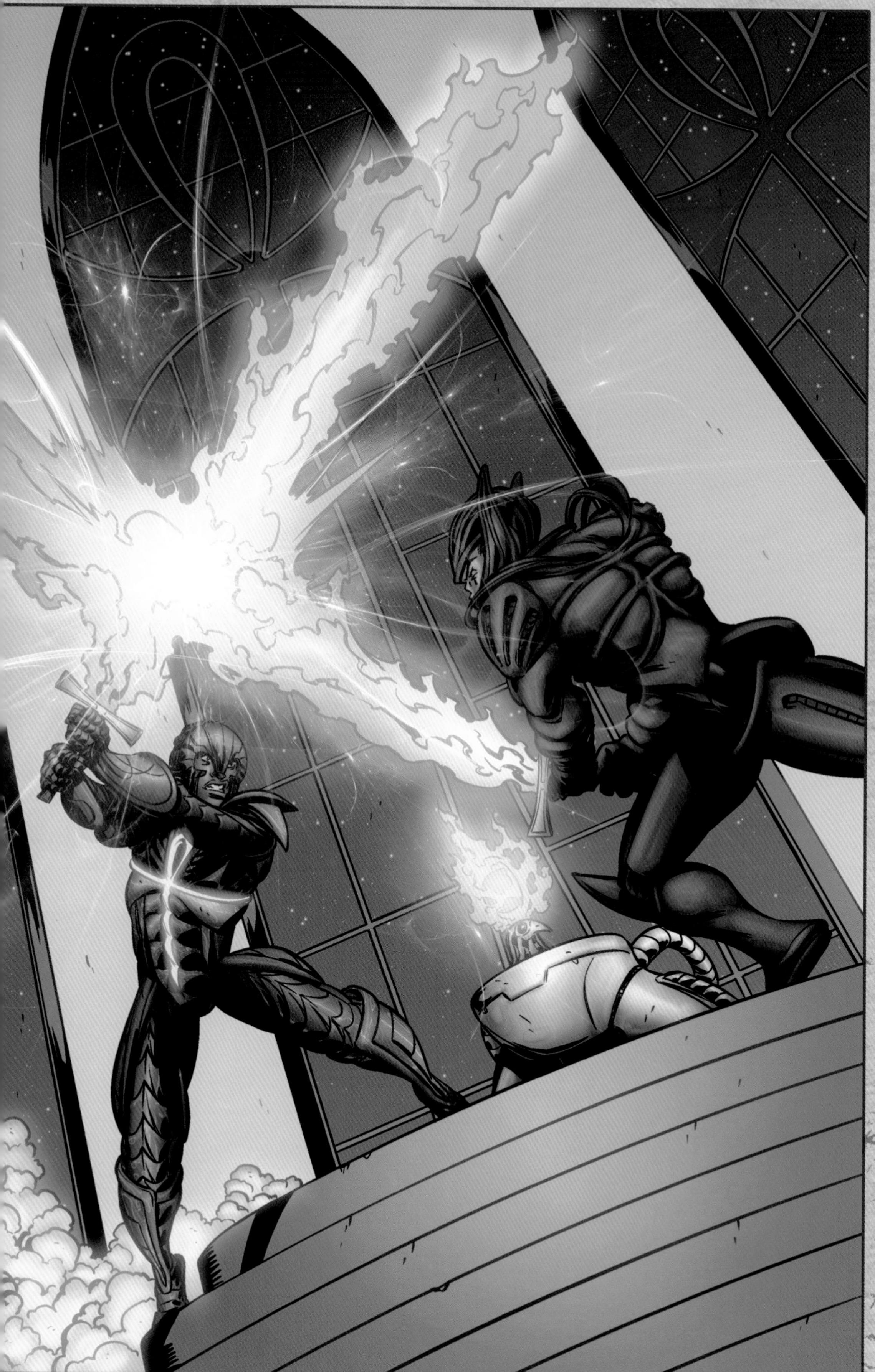

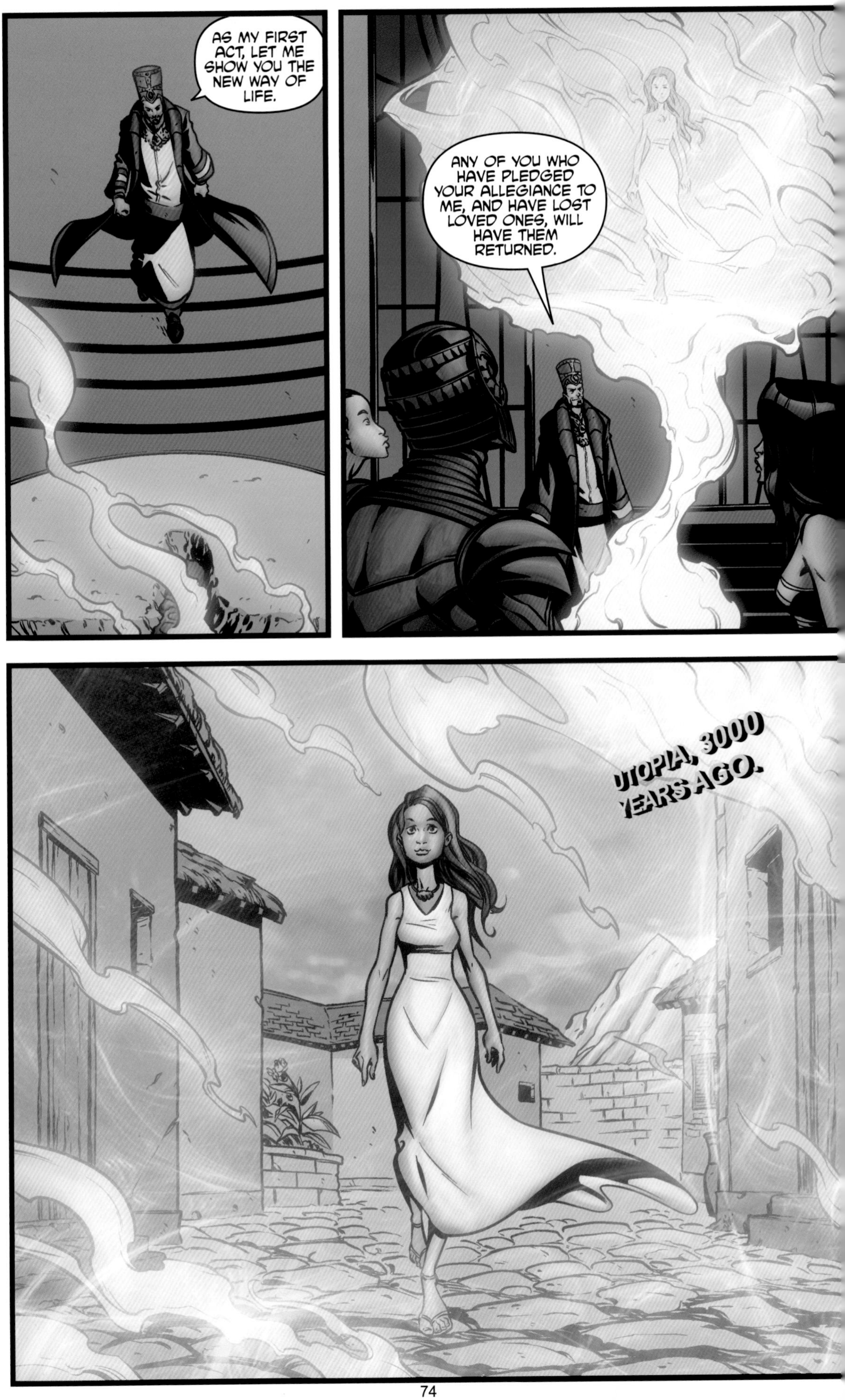
AS MY FIRST ACT, LET ME SHOW YOU THE NEW WAY OF LIFE.
ANY OF YOU WHO HAVE PLEDGED YOUR ALLEGIANCE TO ME, AND HAVE LOST LOVED ONES, WILL HAVE THEM RETURNED.
UTOPIA, 3000 YEARS AGO.

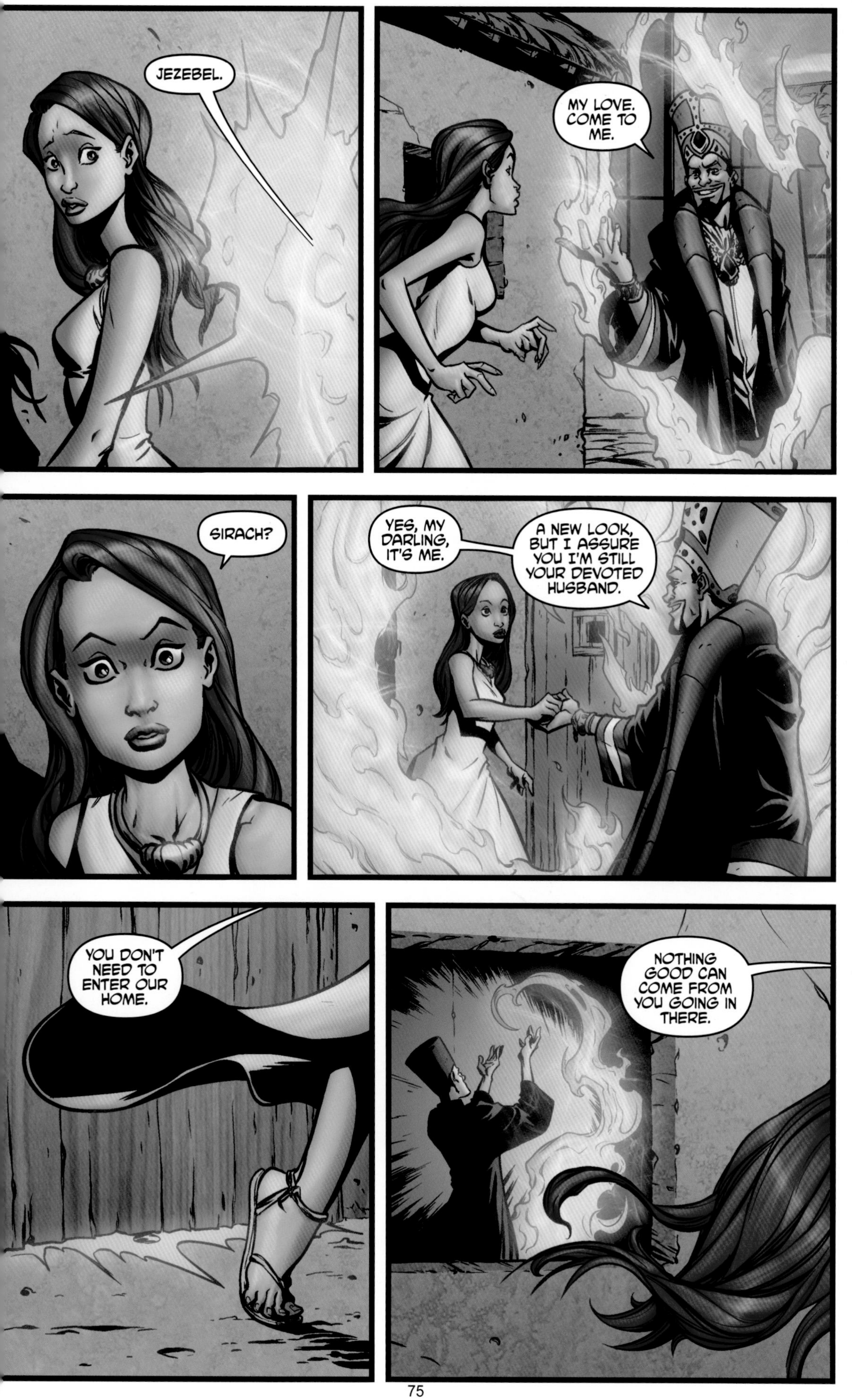
JEZEBEL.
MY LOVE. COME TO ME.
SIRACH?
YES, MY DARLING, IT'S ME.
A NEW LOOK, BUT I ASSURE YOU I'M STILL YOUR DEVOTED HUSBAND.
YOU DON'T NEED TO ENTER OUR HOME.
NOTHING GOOD CAN COME FROM YOU GOING IN THERE.

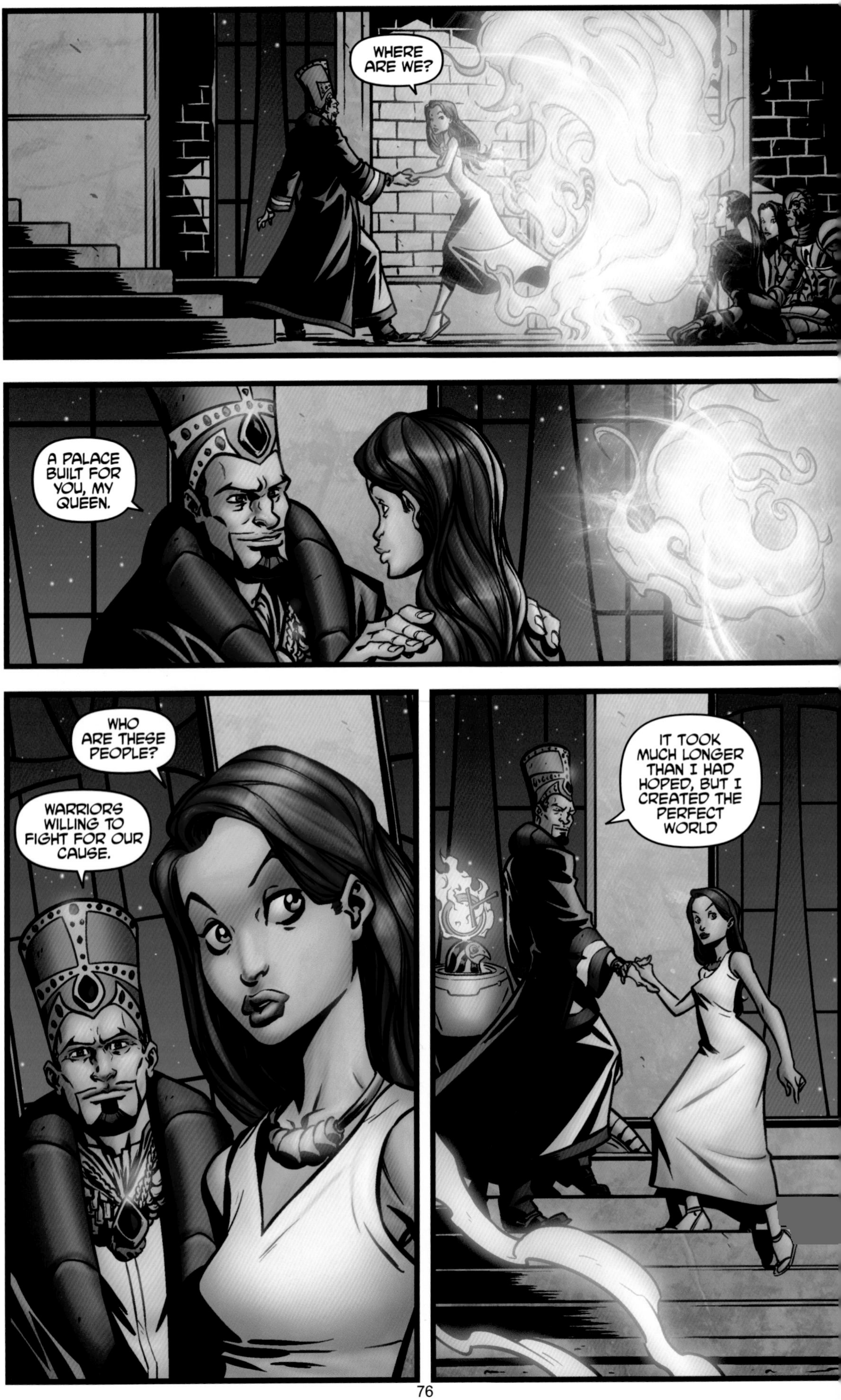
WHERE ARE WE?
A PALACE BUILT FOR YOU, MY QUEEN.
WHO ARE THESE PEOPLE?
WARRIORS WILLING TO FIGHT FOR OUR CAUSE.
IT TOOK MUCH LONGER THAN I HAD HOPED, BUT I CREATED THE PERFECT WORLD

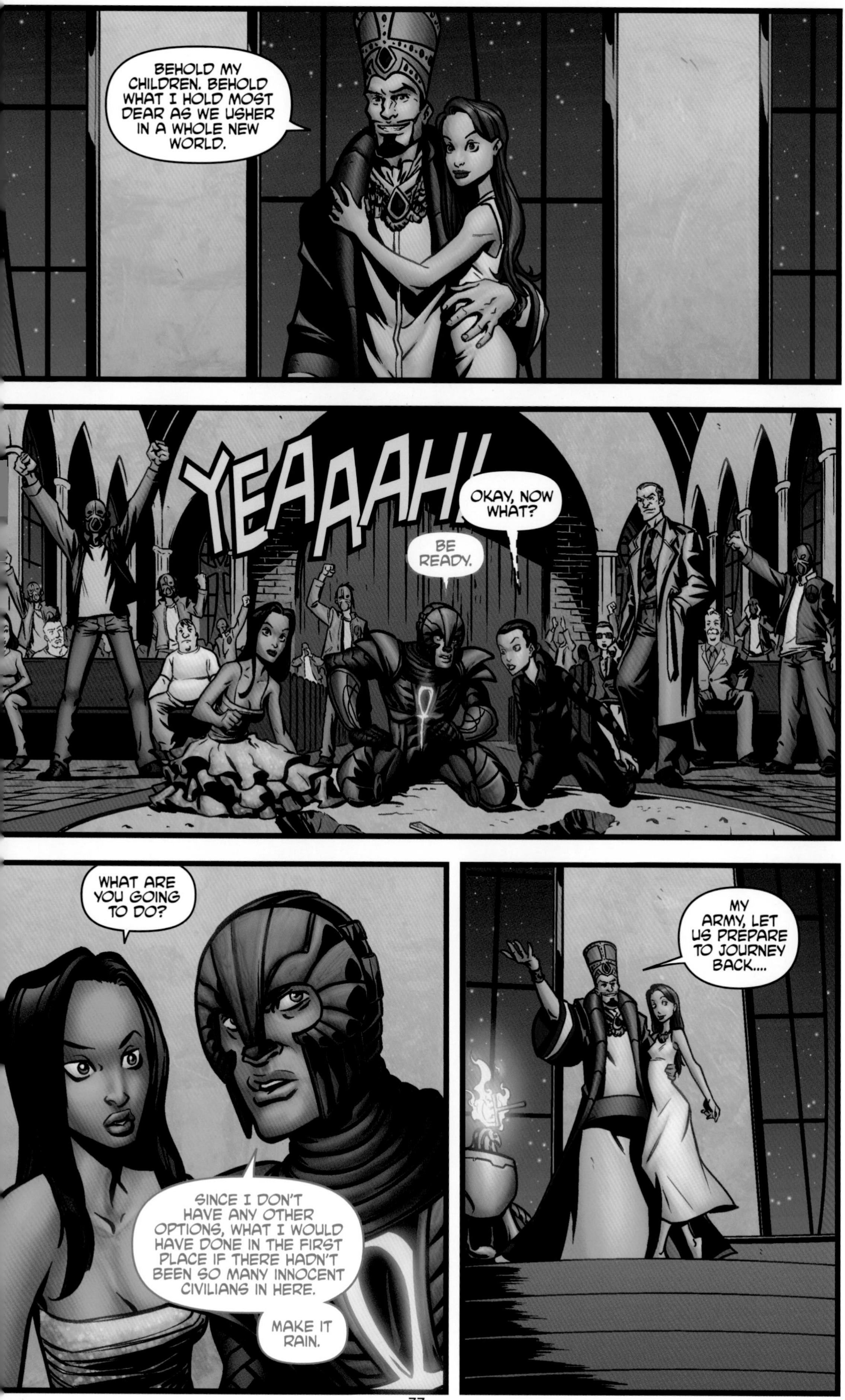

BEHOLD MY CHILDREN. BEHOLD WHAT I HOLD MOST DEAR AS WE USHER IN A WHOLE NEW WORLD.
YEAAAH!
OKAY, NOW WHAT?
BE READY.
WHAT ARE YOU GOING TO DO?
SINCE I DON'T HAVE ANY OTHER OPTIONS, WHAT I WOULD HAVE DONE IN THE FIRST PLACE IF THERE HADN'T BEEN SO MANY INNOCENT CIVILIANS IN HERE.
MAKE IT RAIN.
MY ARMY, LET US PREPARE TO JOURNEY BACK....

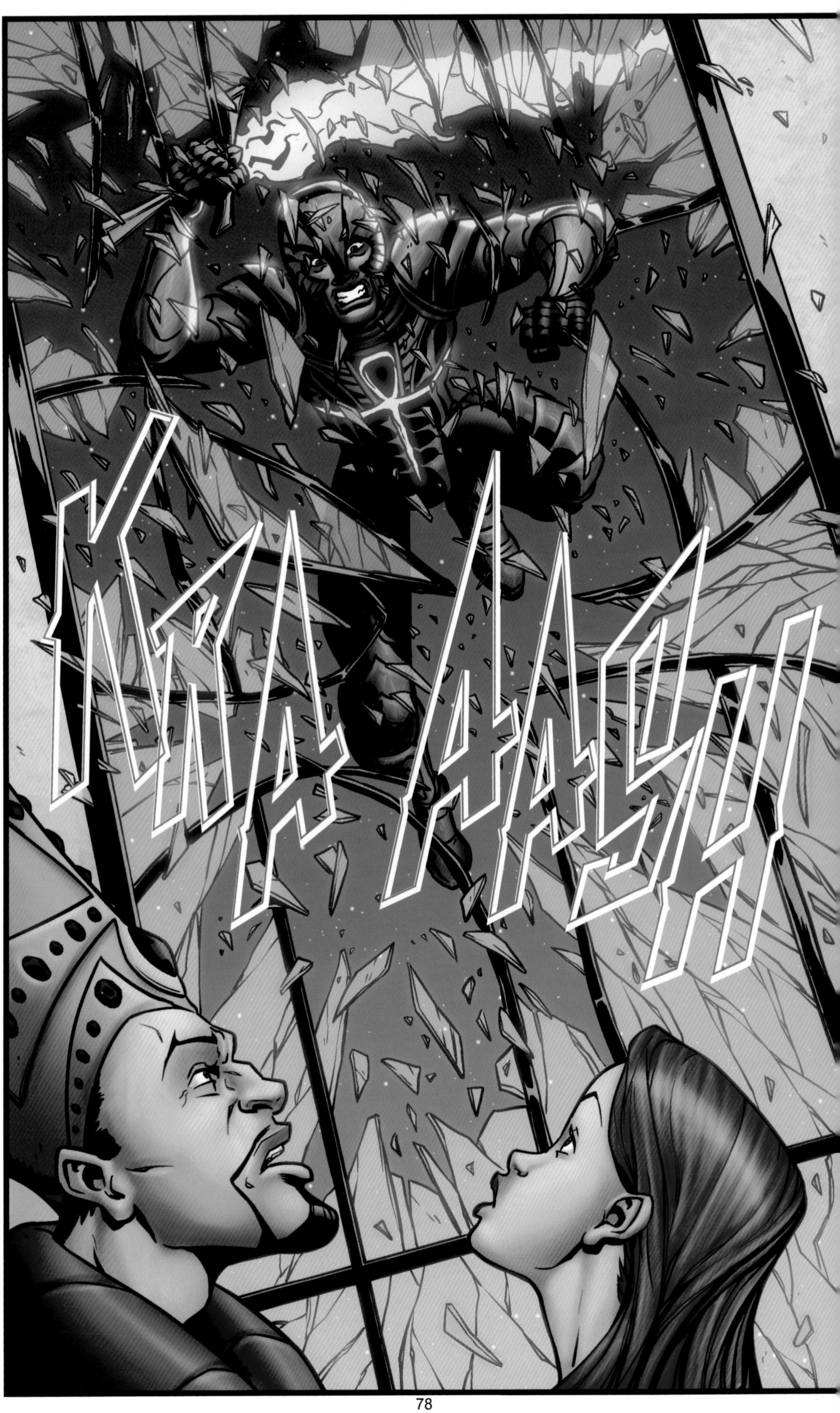
KRA-AASH!

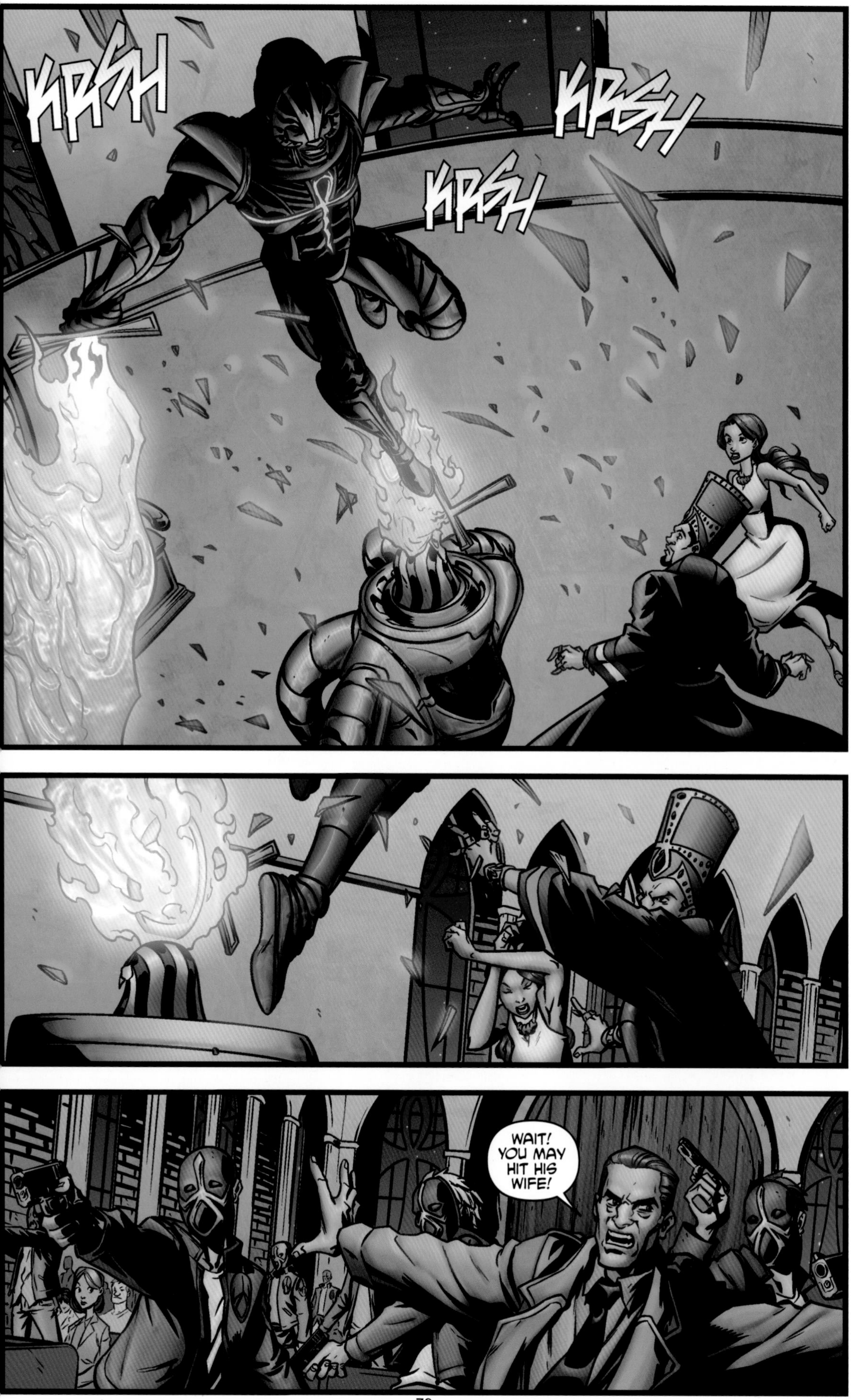
KRSH
KRSH
KRSH
WAIT! YOU MAY HIT HIS WIFE!

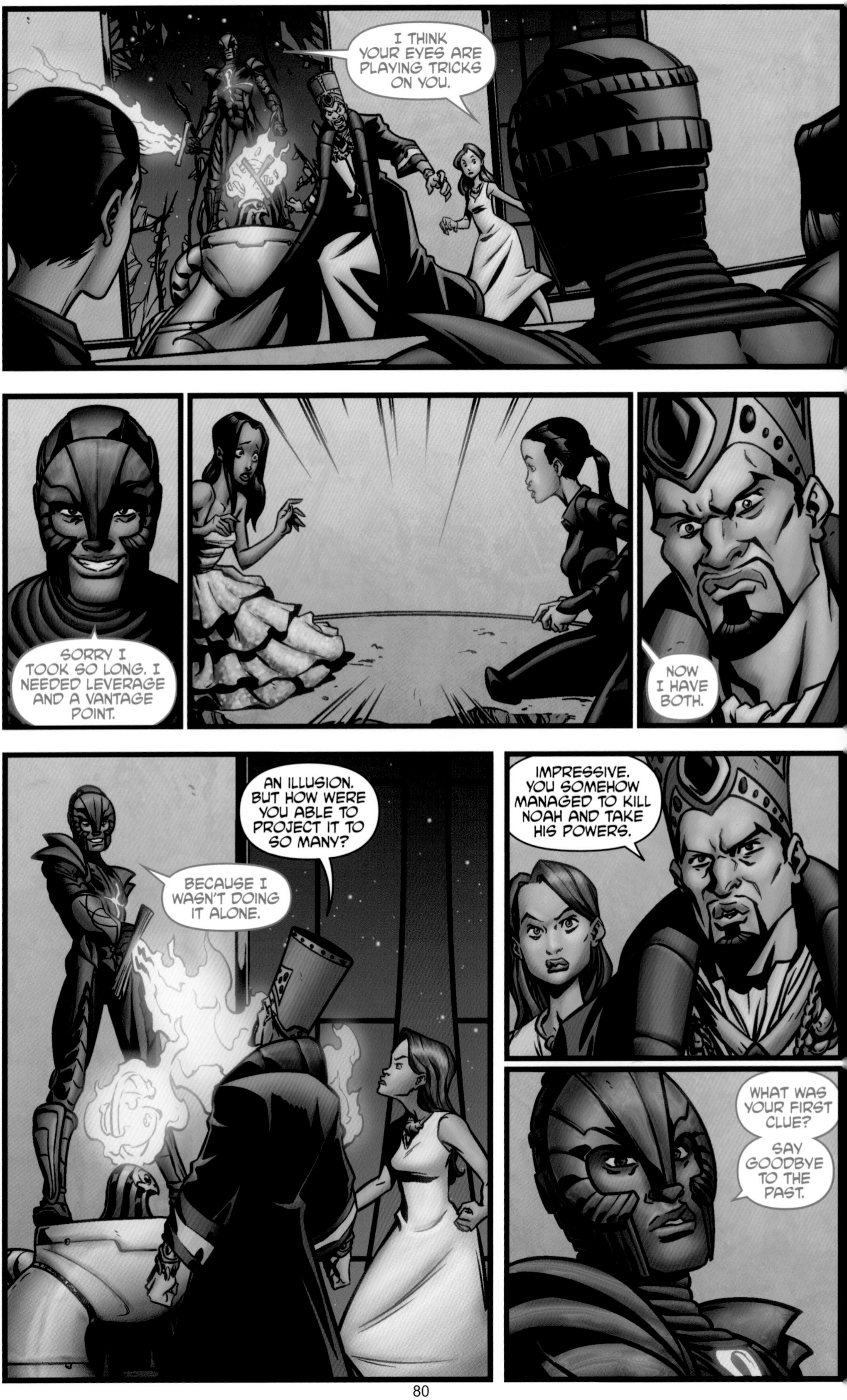
I THINK YOUR EYES ARE PLAYING TRICKS ON YOU.
SORRY I TOOK SO LONG. I NEEDED LEVERAGE AND A VANTAGE POINT.
NOW I HAVE BOTH.
AN ILLUSION. BUT HOW WERE YOU ABLE TO PROJECT IT TO SO MANY?
BECAUSE I WASN'T DOING IT ALONE.
IMPRESSIVE. YOU SOMEHOW MANAGED TO KILL NOAH AND TAKE HIS POWERS.
WHAT WAS YOUR FIRST CLUE?
SAY GOODBYE TO THE PAST.

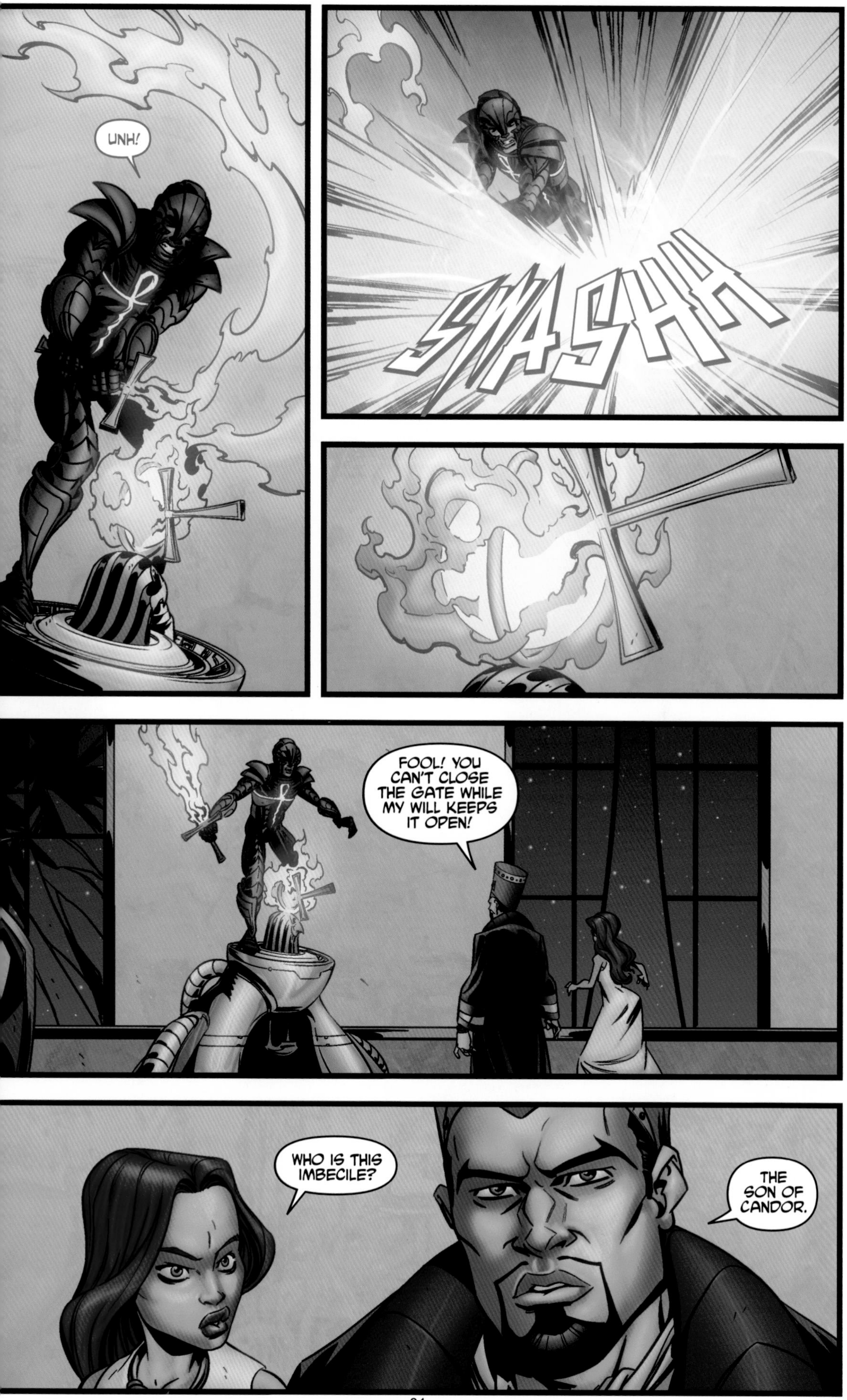

UNH!
SWASHH
FOOL! YOU CAN'T CLOSE THE GATE WHILE MY WILL KEEPS IT OPEN!
WHO IS THIS IMBECILE?
THE SON OF CANDOR.

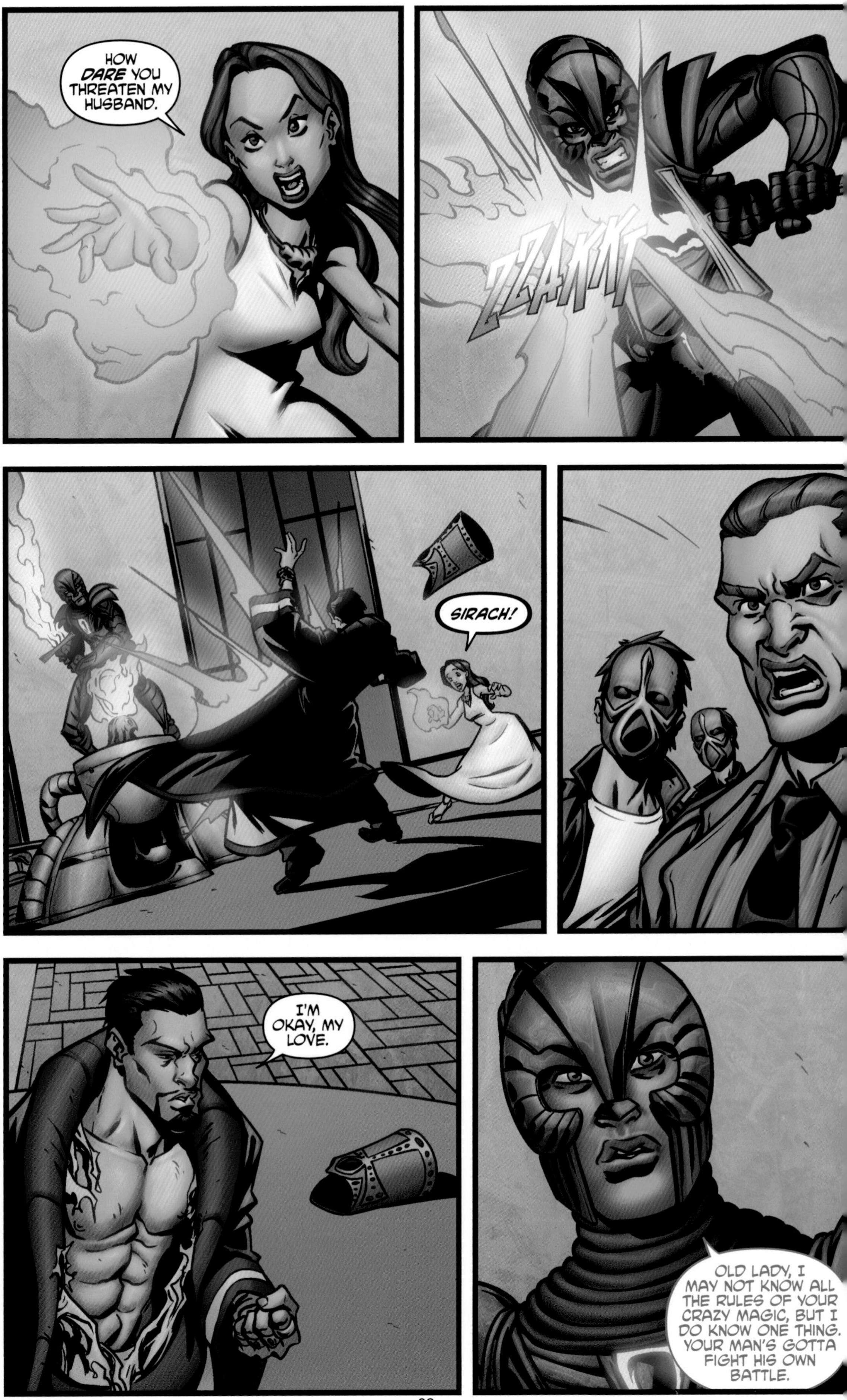
HOW DARE YOU THREATEN MY HUSBAND.
ZZAKKT
SIRACH!
I'M OKAY, MY LOVE.
OLD LADY, I MAY NOT KNOW ALL THE RULES OF YOUR CRAZY MAGIC, BUT I DO KNOW ONE THING. YOUR MAN'S GOTTA FIGHT HIS OWN BATTLE.

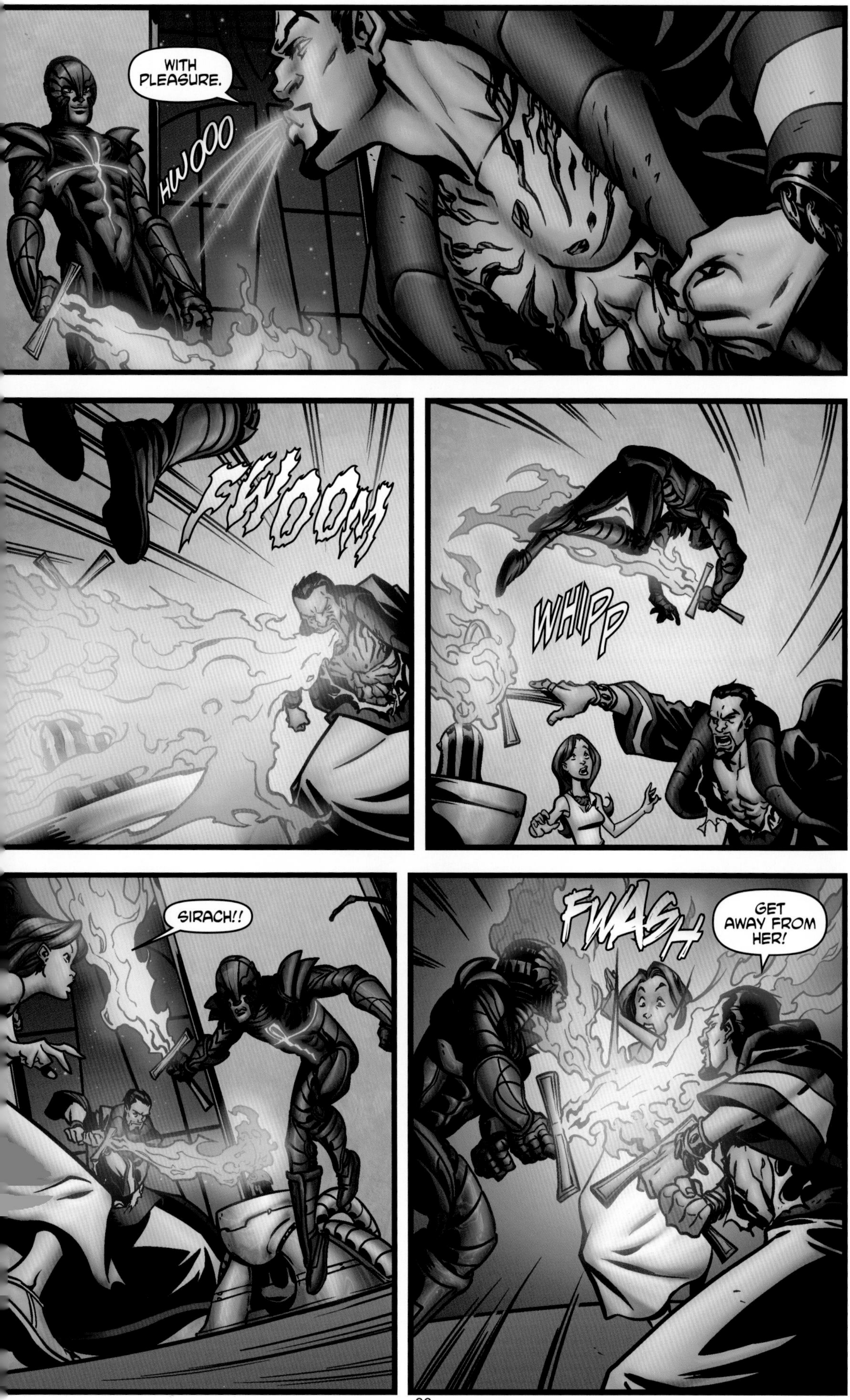
WITH PLEASURE.
HWOOO
FWOOM
WHIPP
SIRACH!!
FWASH
GET AWAY FROM HER!

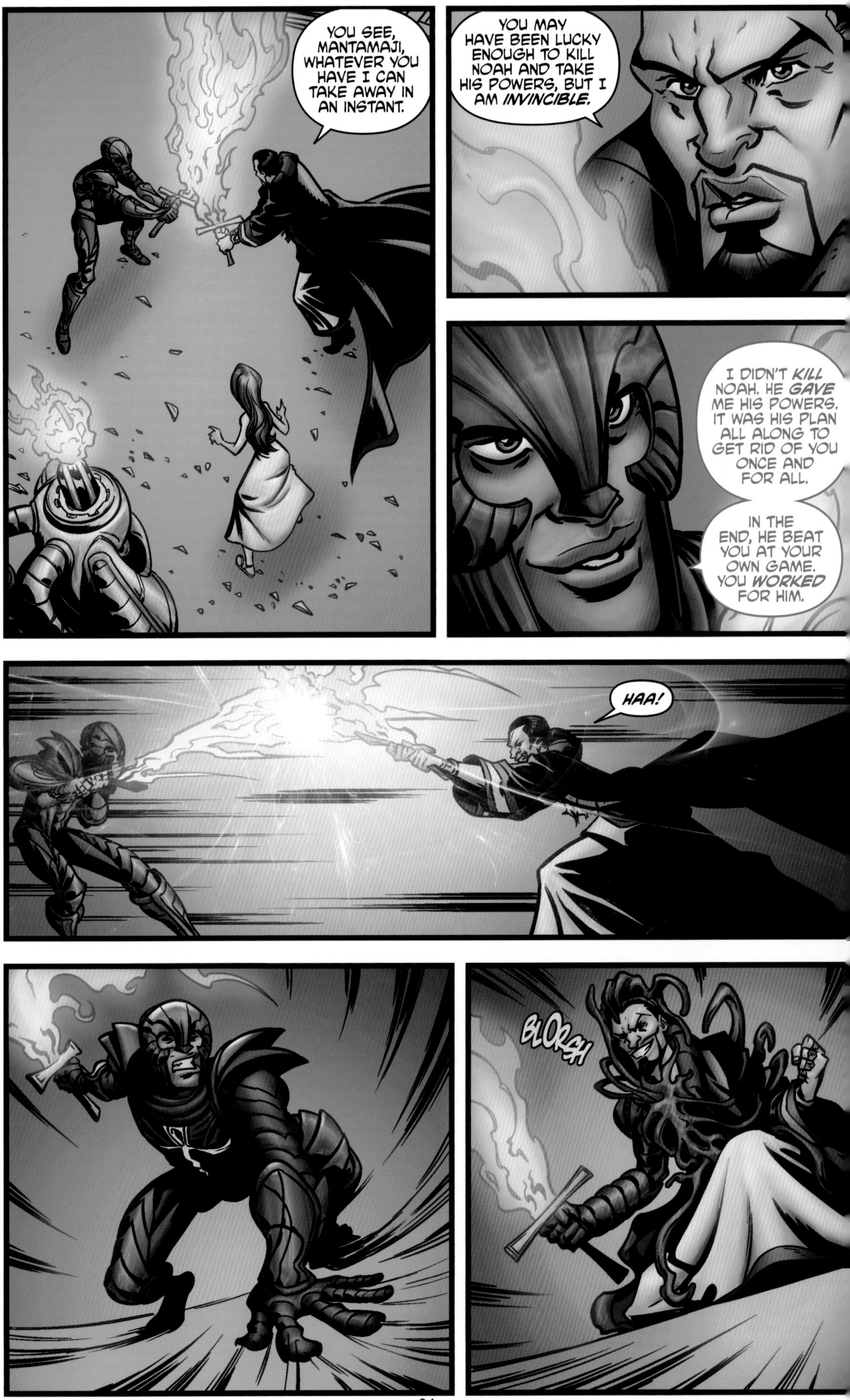
YOU SEE, MANTAMAJI, WHATEVER YOU HAVE I CAN TAKE AWAY IN AN INSTANT.
YOU MAY HAVE BEEN LUCKY ENOUGH TO KILL NOAH AND TAKE HIS POWERS, BUT I AM *INVINCIBLE.*
I DIDN'T *KILL* NOAH. HE *GAVE* ME HIS POWERS. IT WAS HIS PLAN ALL ALONG TO GET RID OF YOU ONCE AND FOR ALL.
IN THE END, HE BEAT YOU AT YOUR OWN GAME. YOU *WORKED* FOR HIM.
HAA!
BLORSH

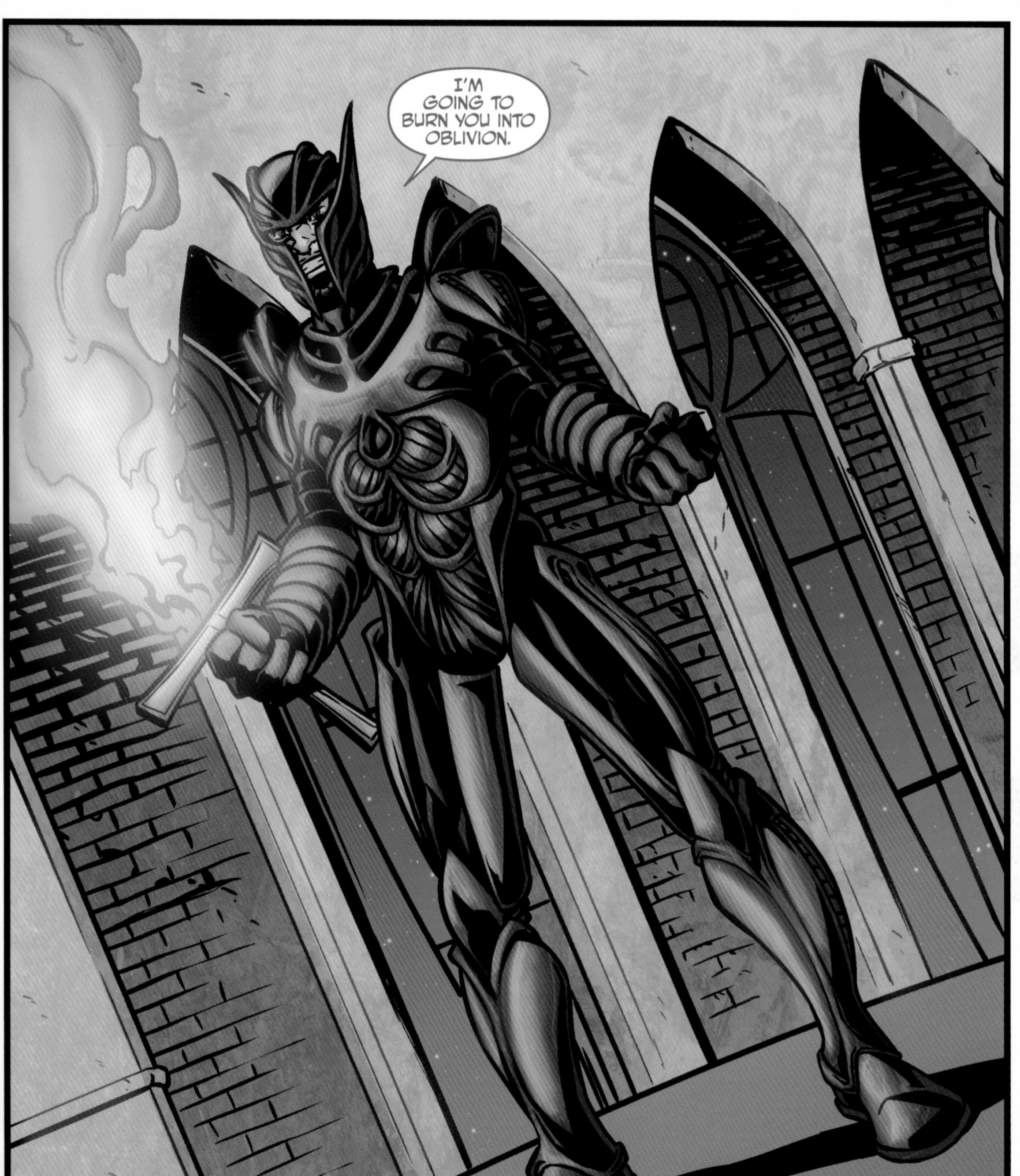
I'M GOING TO BURN YOU INTO OBLIVION.

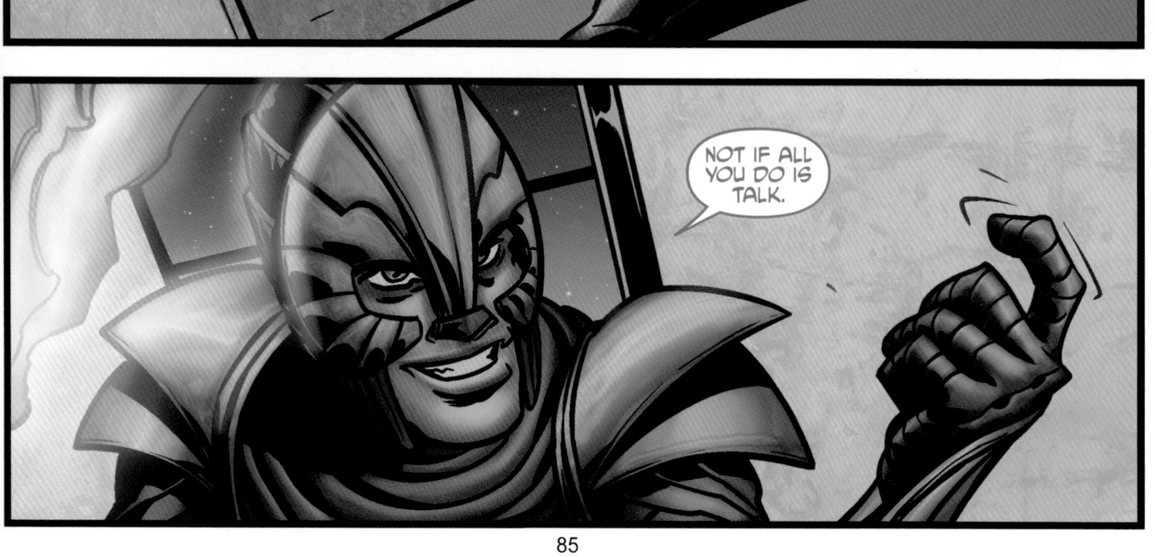
NOT IF ALL YOU DO IS TALK.

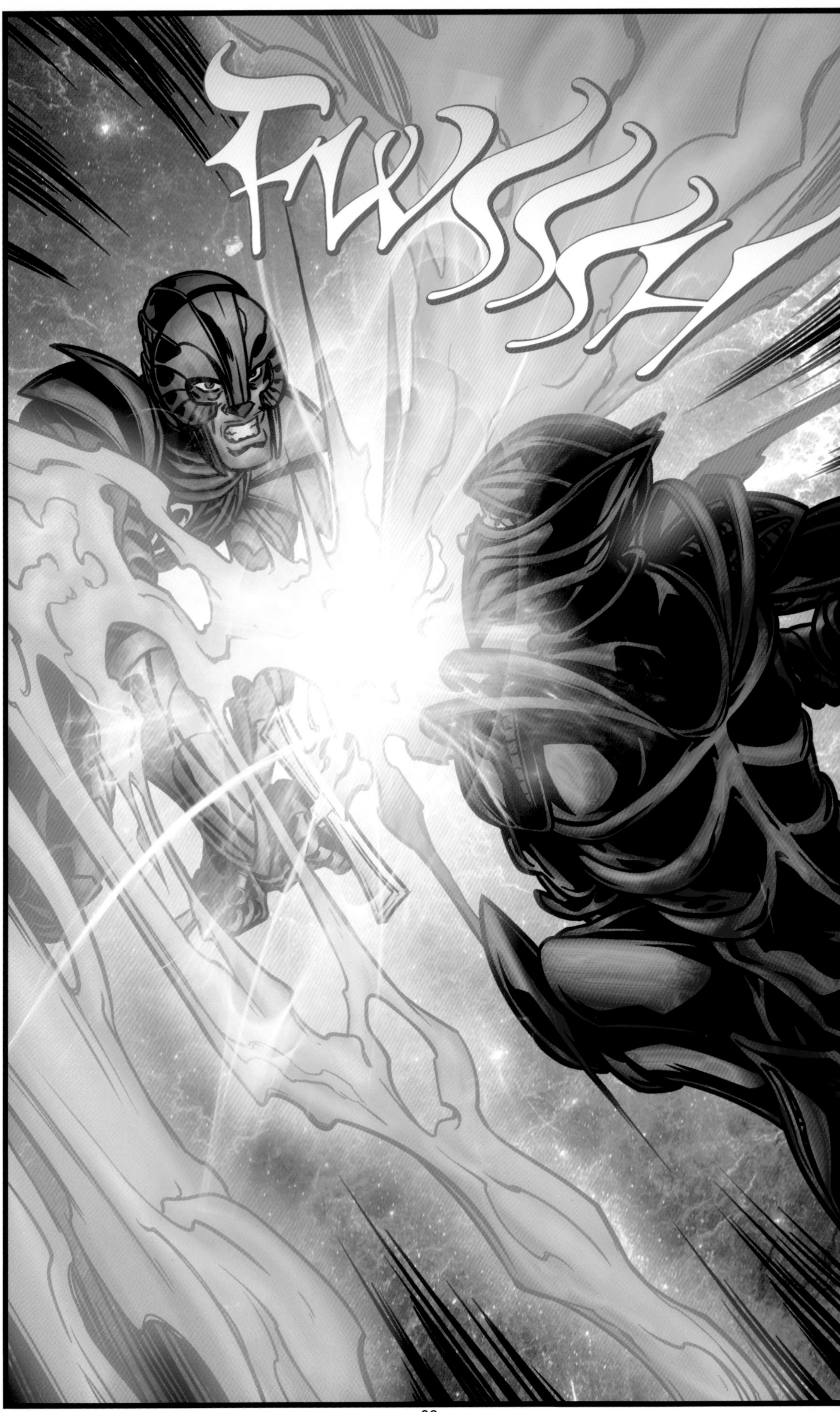
FWSSH

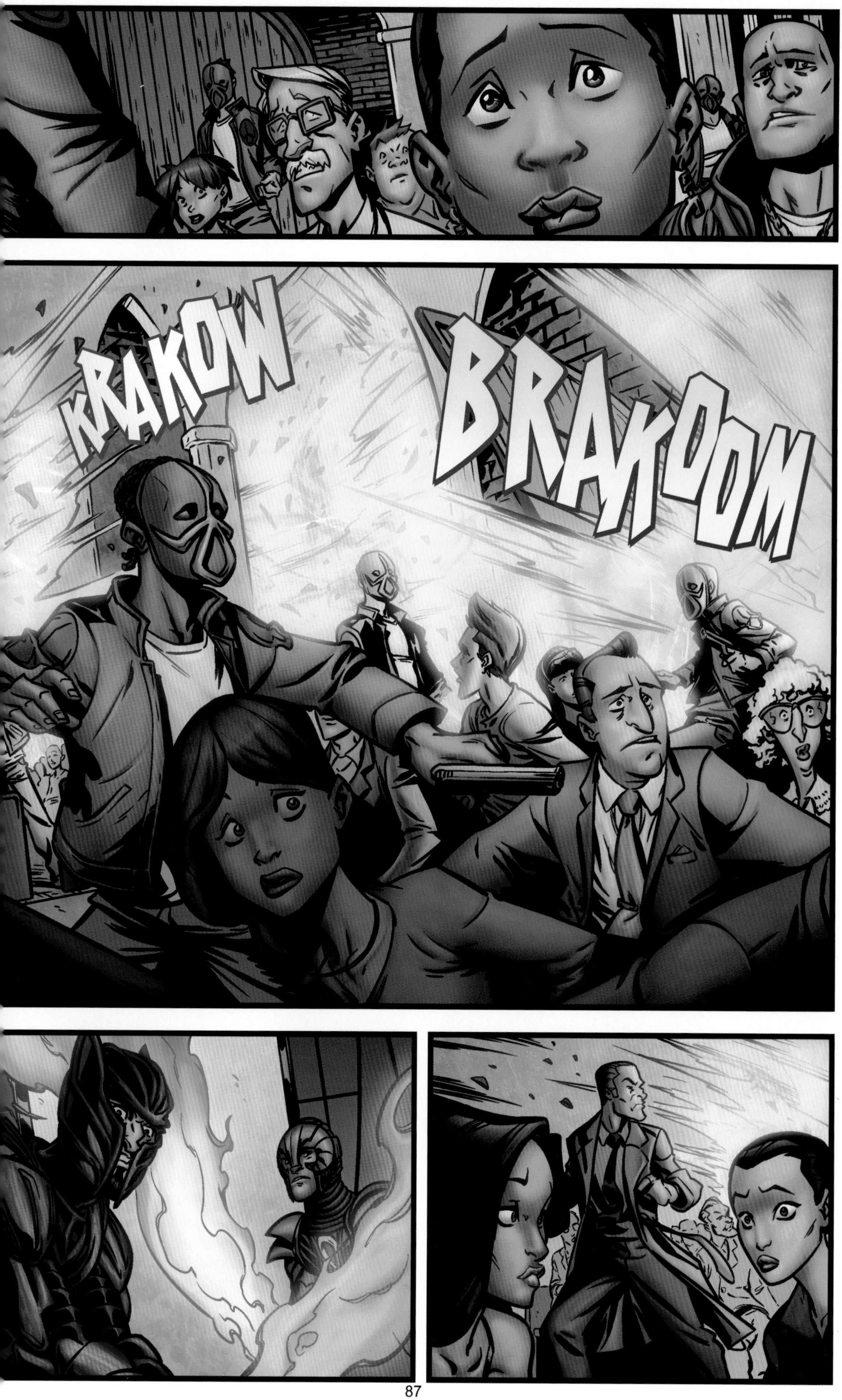
KRAKOW
BRAKOOM

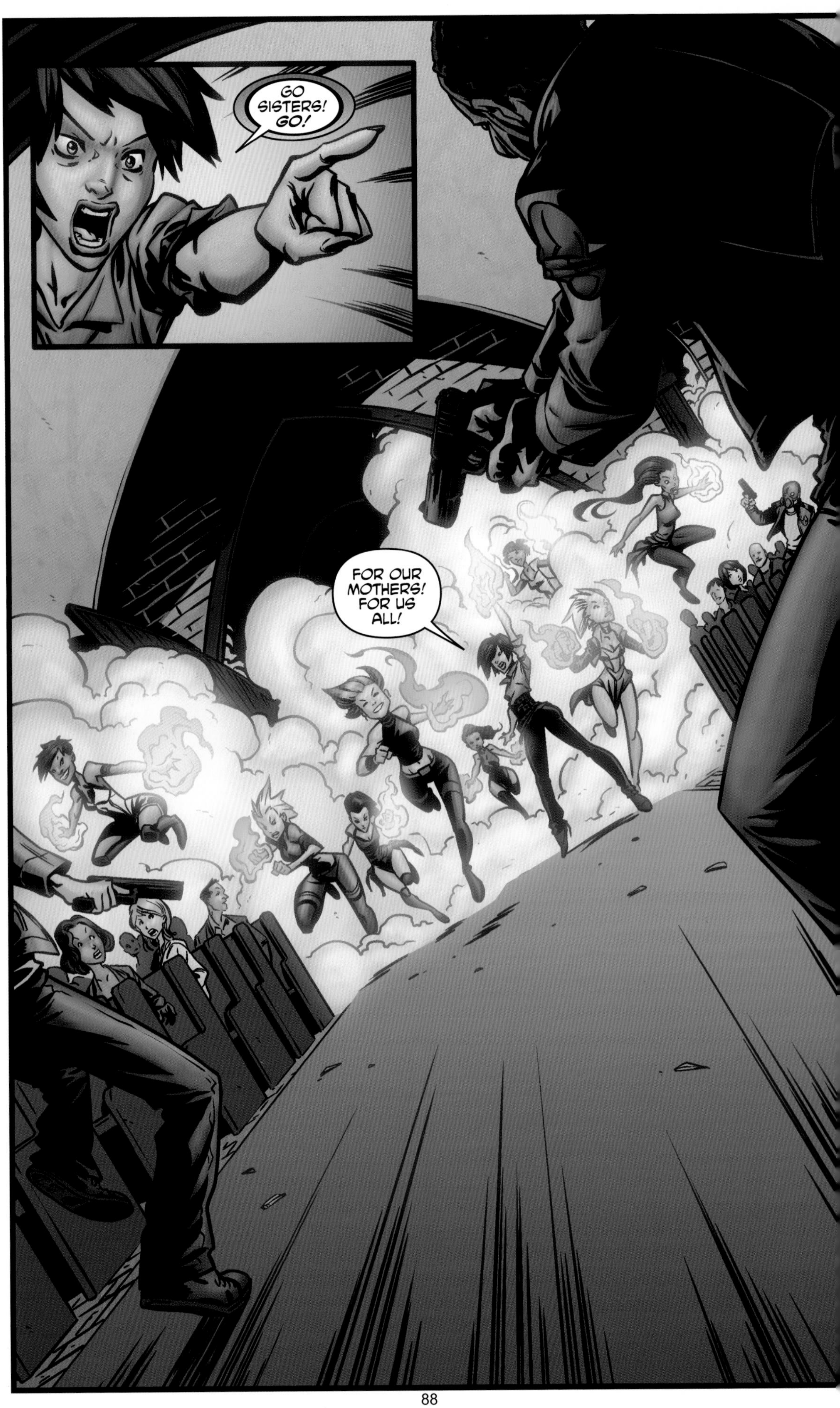
GO SISTERS! GO!
FOR OUR MOTHERS! FOR US ALL!

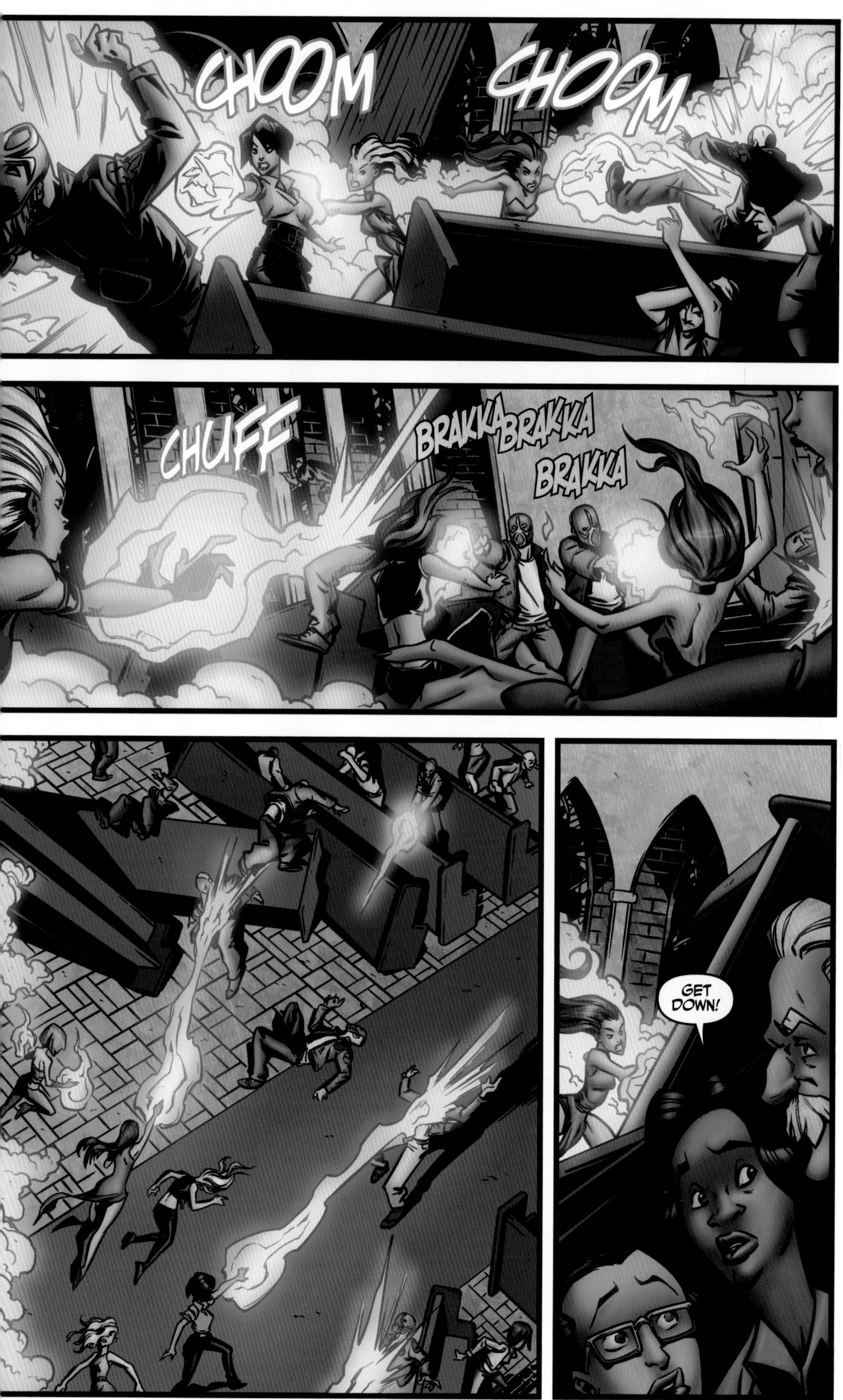
CHOOM
CHOOM
CHUFF
BRAKKA BRAKKA
BRAKKA
GET DOWN!

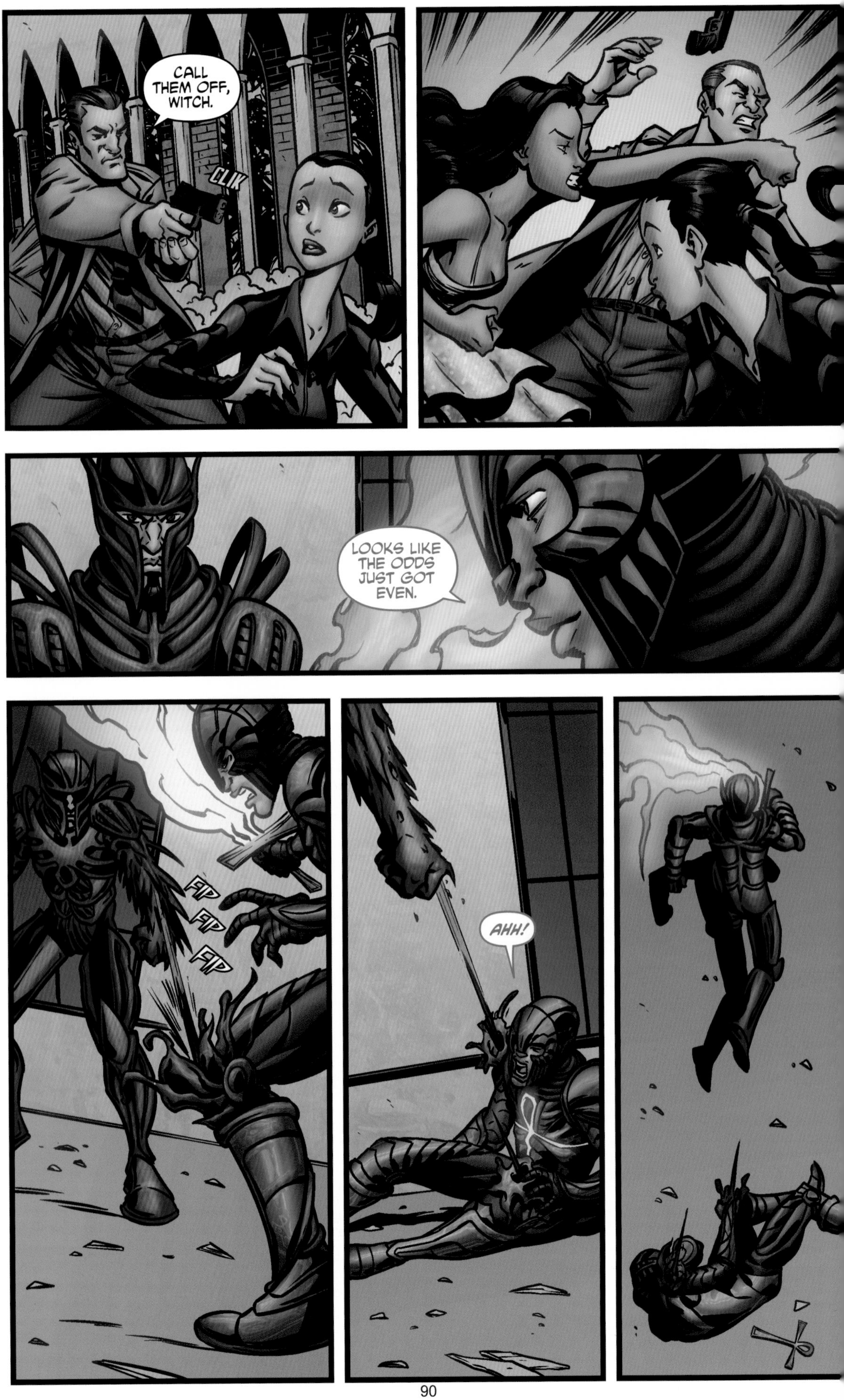
CALL THEM OFF, WITCH.
CLIK
LOOKS LIKE THE ODDS JUST GOT EVEN.
RIP
RIP
RIP
AHH!

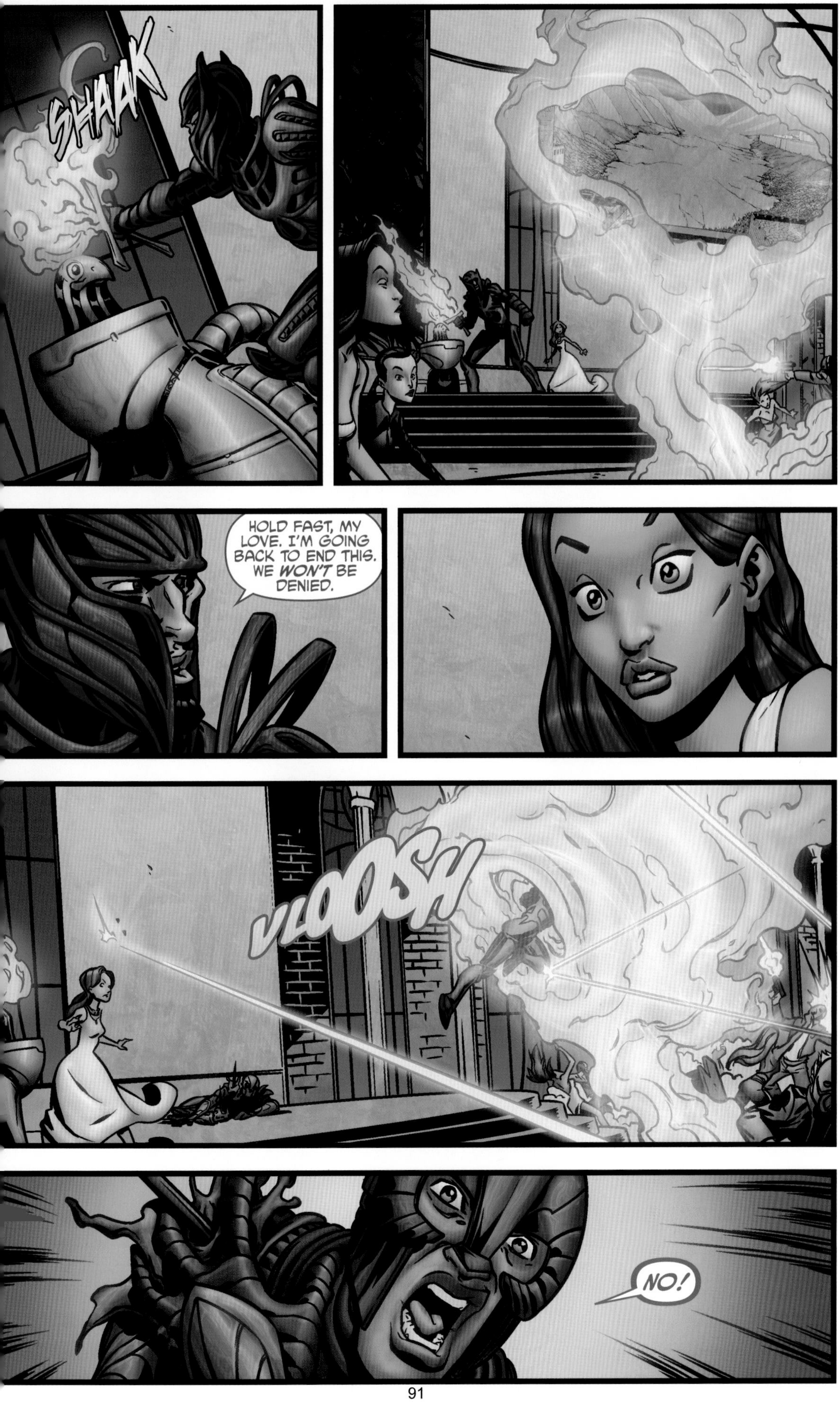
SHAAK
HOLD FAST, MY LOVE. I'M GOING BACK TO END THIS. WE WON'T BE DENIED.
VLOOSH
NO!

UTOPIA, AFRICA
3000 YEARS AGO

TONIGHT WE STAND AT THE GATES TO OUR HOME.

TONIGHT WE DEFEND THE INNOCENT AGAINST ONE OF OUR OWN.

TONIGHT WE FIGHT FOR THE FUTURE FOR ALL MANKIND. FOR THIS IS WHAT WE WERE MADE TO DO!

YEAH!

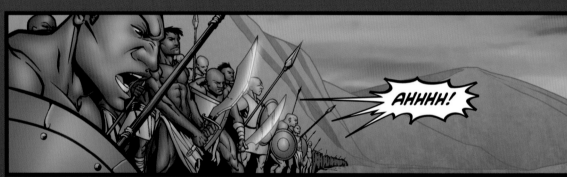

AHHHH!

DAAA!!

AAH!

YARR!!

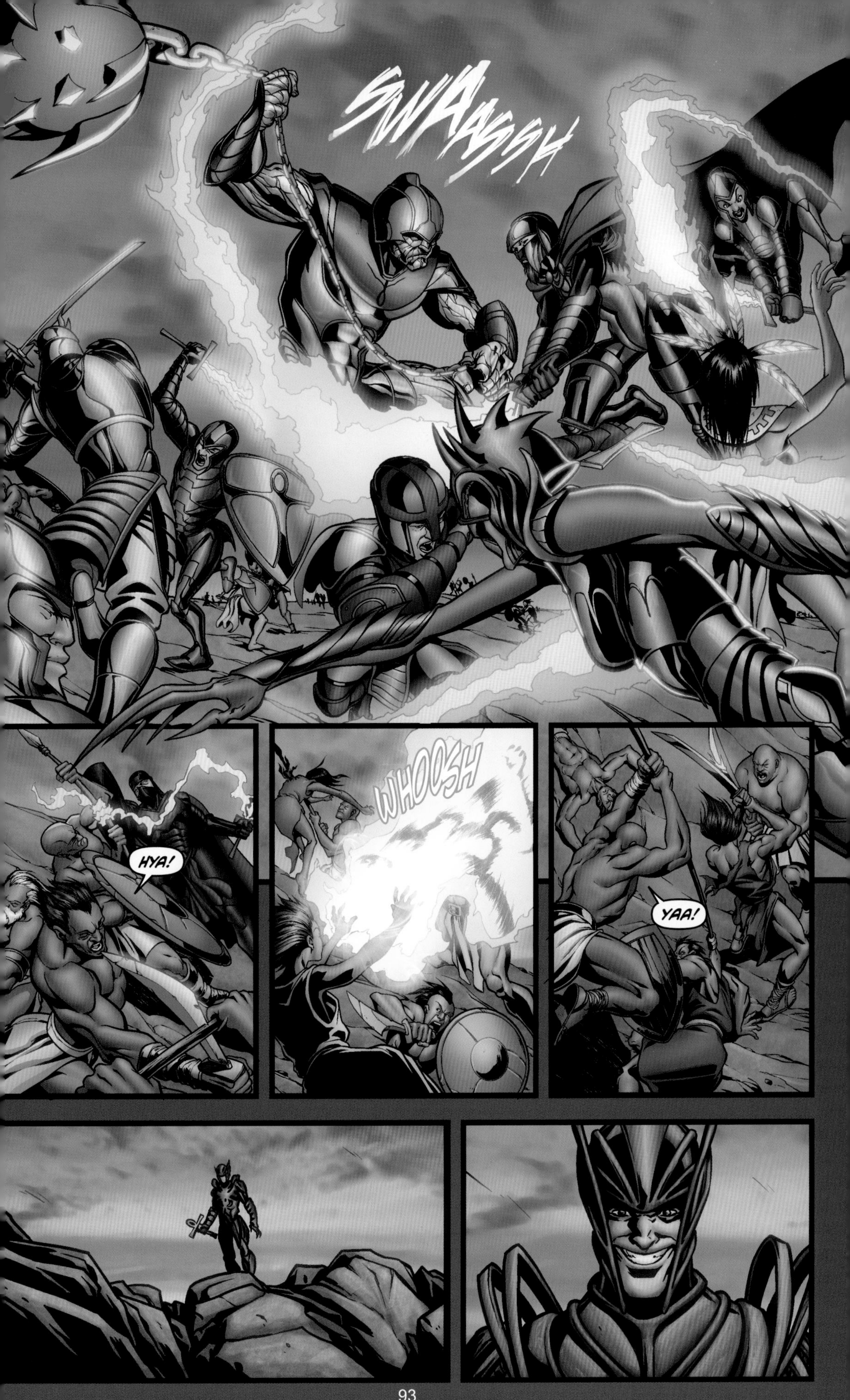
SWAASSH
HYA!
WHOOSH
YAA!

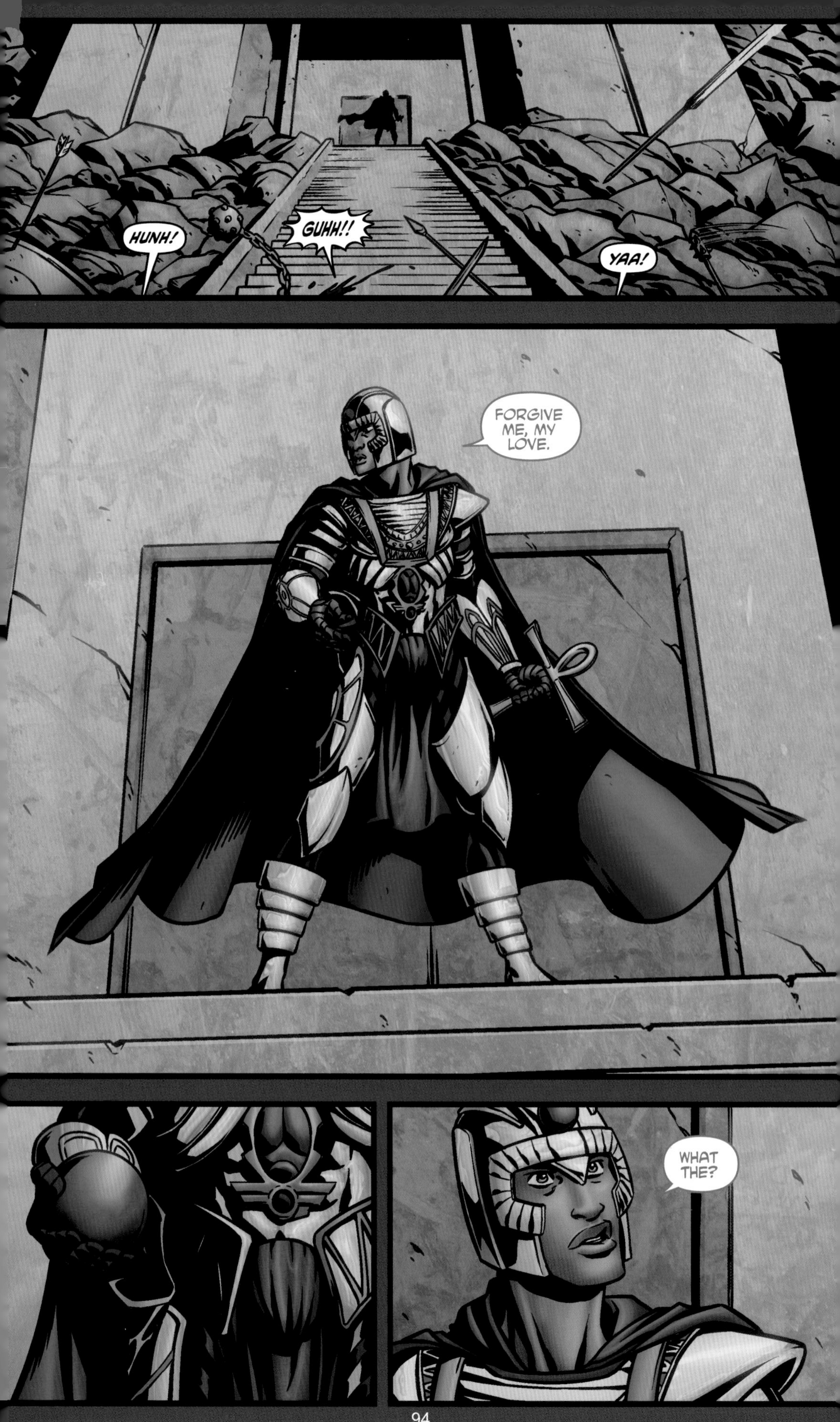
HUNH!
GUHH!!
YAA!
FORGIVE ME, MY LOVE.
WHAT THE?

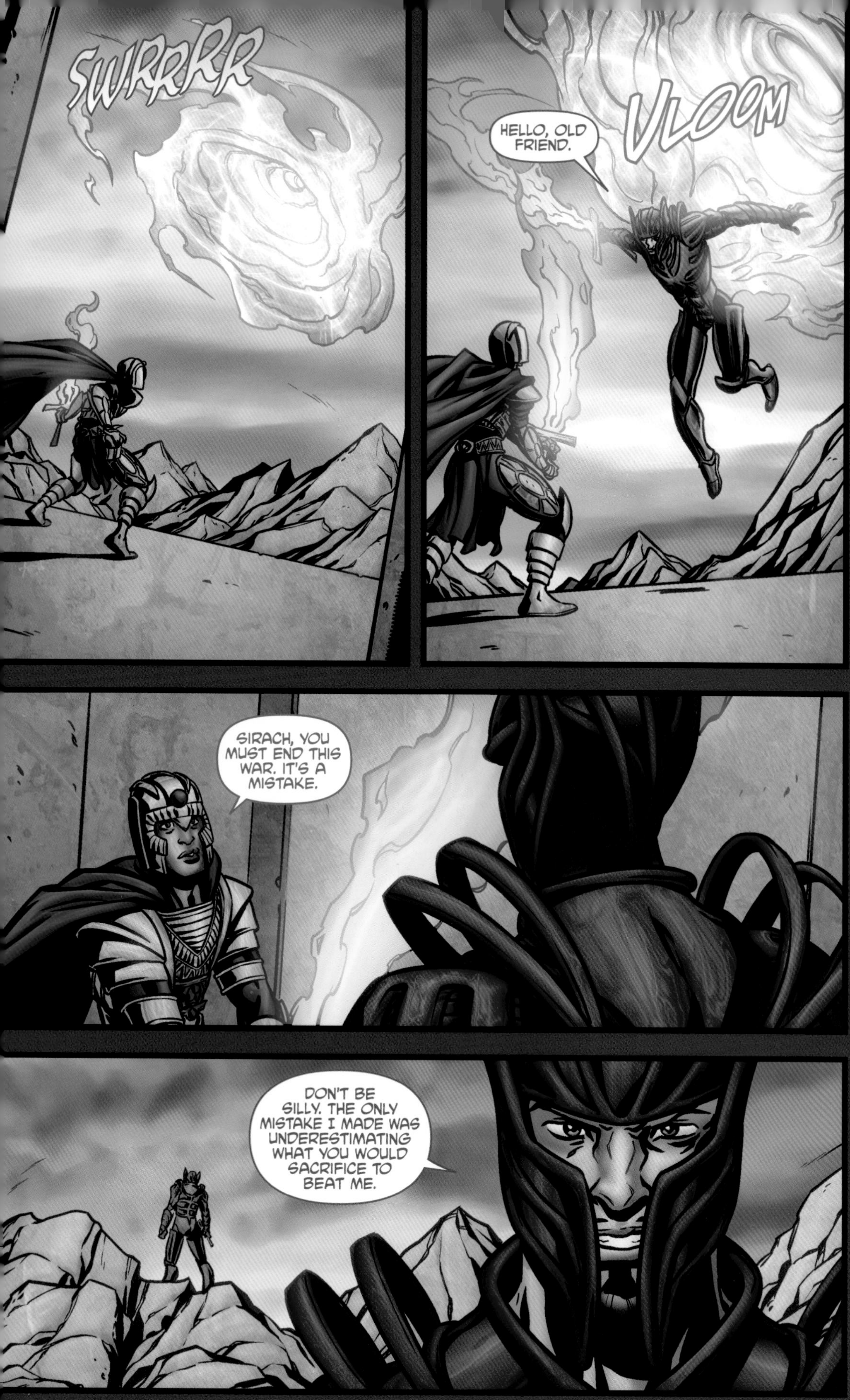
SWRRRR
HELLO, OLD FRIEND.
VLOOM
SIRACH, YOU MUST END THIS WAR. IT'S A MISTAKE.
DON'T BE SILLY. THE ONLY MISTAKE I MADE WAS UNDERESTIMATING WHAT YOU WOULD SACRIFICE TO BEAT ME.

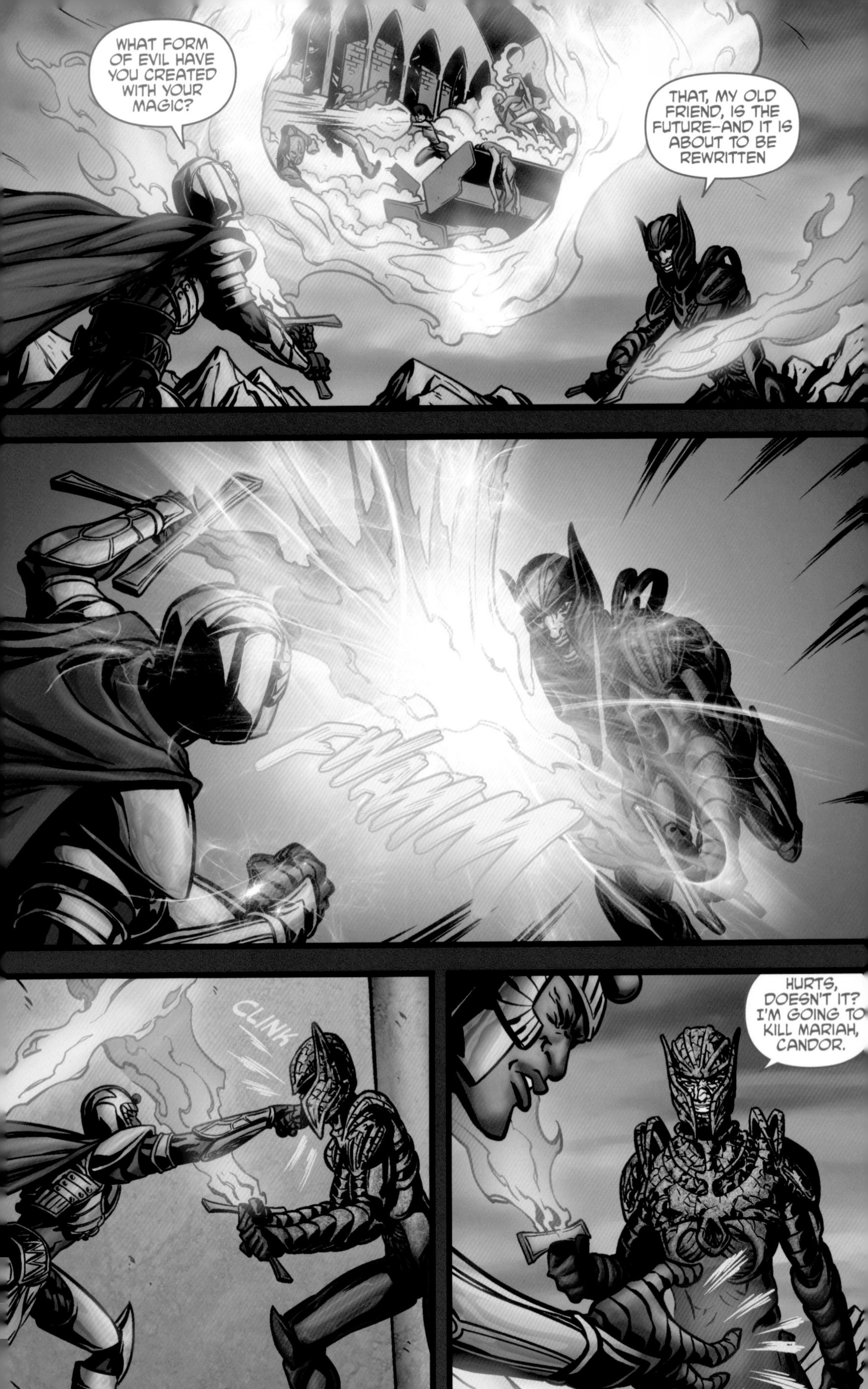
WHAT FORM OF EVIL HAVE YOU CREATED WITH YOUR MAGIC?
THAT, MY OLD FRIEND, IS THE FUTURE--AND IT IS ABOUT TO BE REWRITTEN
CLINK
HURTS, DOESN'T IT? I'M GOING TO KILL MARIAH, CANDOR.

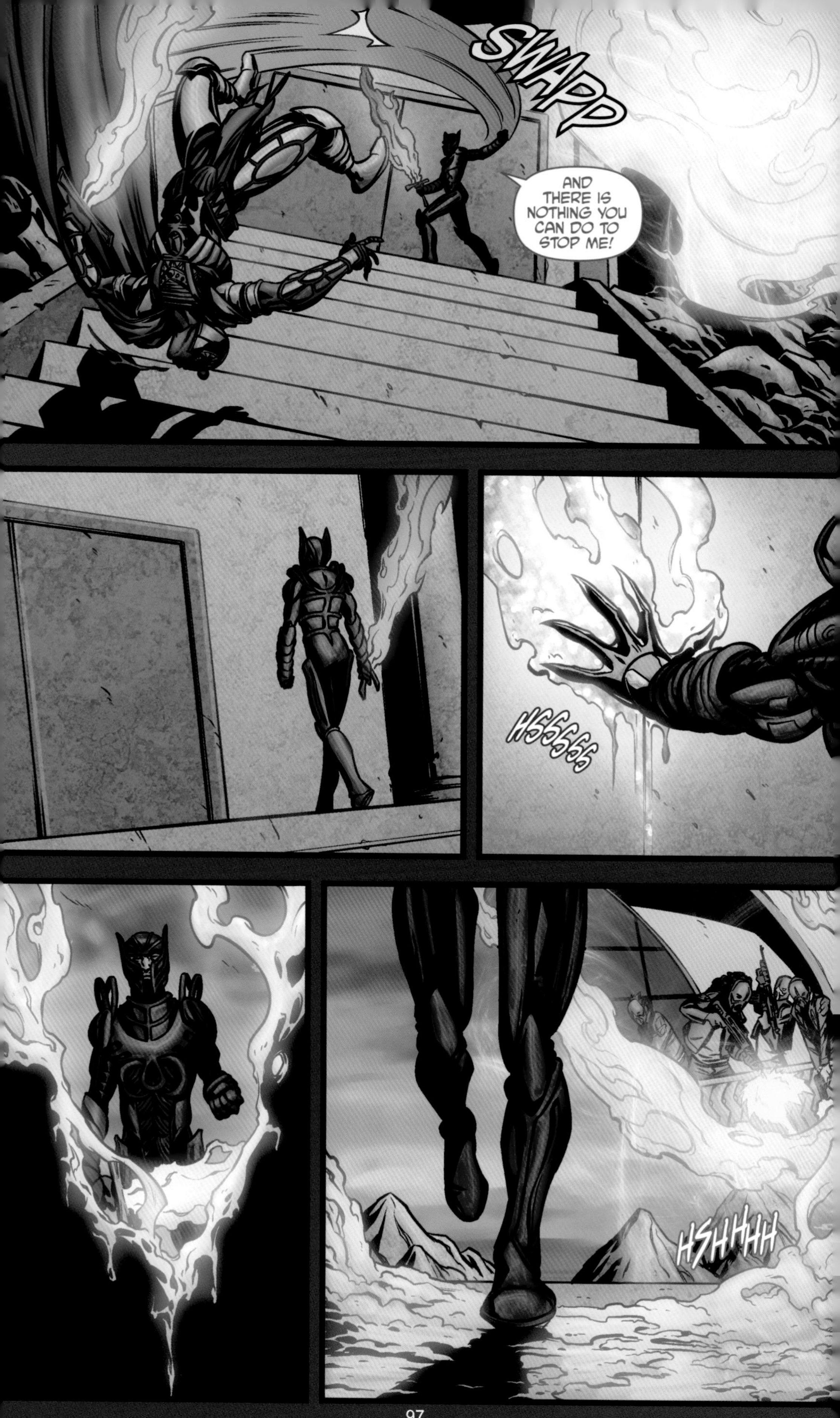
SWAPP
AND THERE IS NOTHING YOU CAN DO TO STOP ME!
HSSSSS
HSHHHH

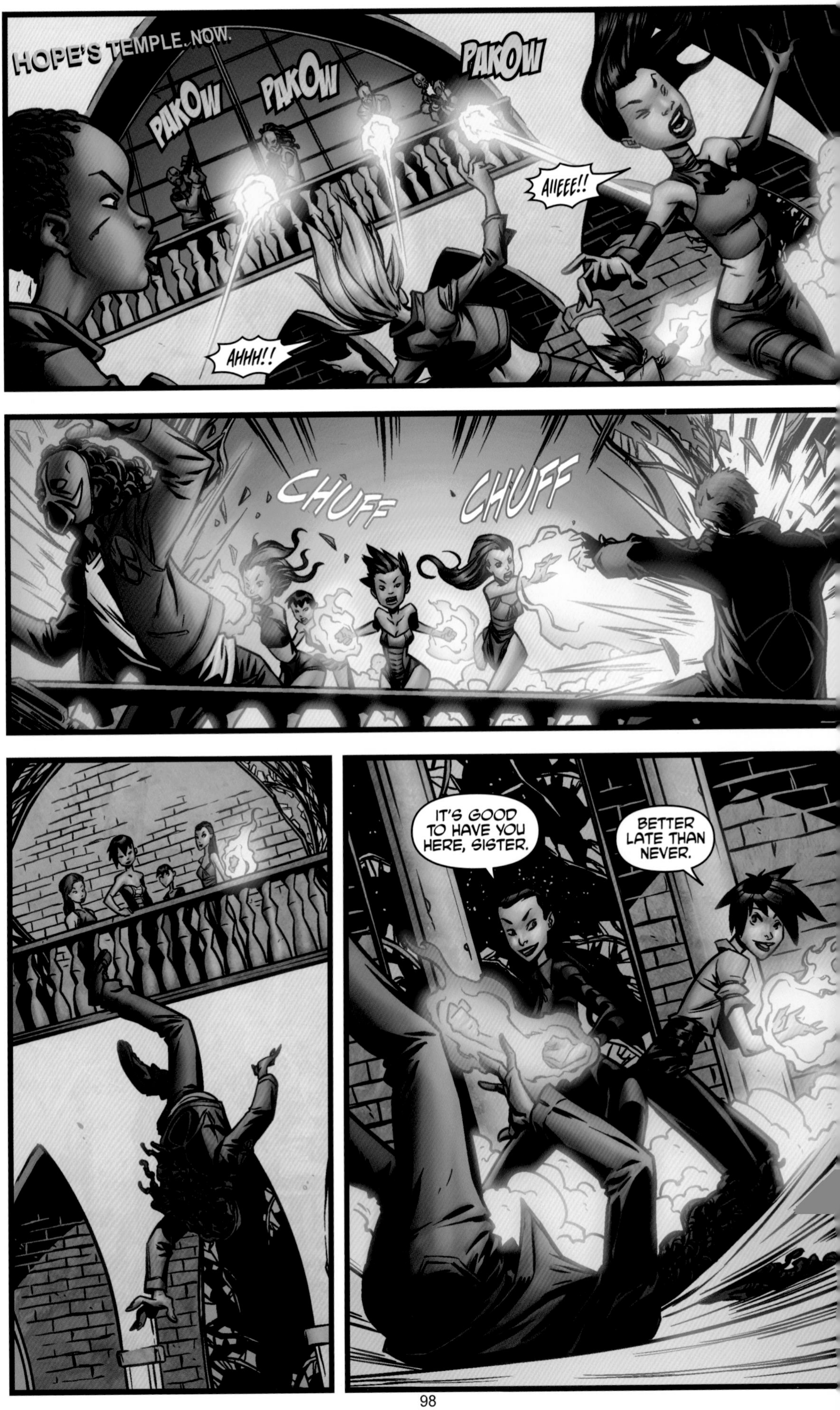
HOPE'S TEMPLE. NOW.
PAKOW
PAKOW
PAKOW
AIIEEE!!
AHHH!!
CHUFF
CHUFF
IT'S GOOD TO HAVE YOU HERE, SISTER.
BETTER LATE THAN NEVER.

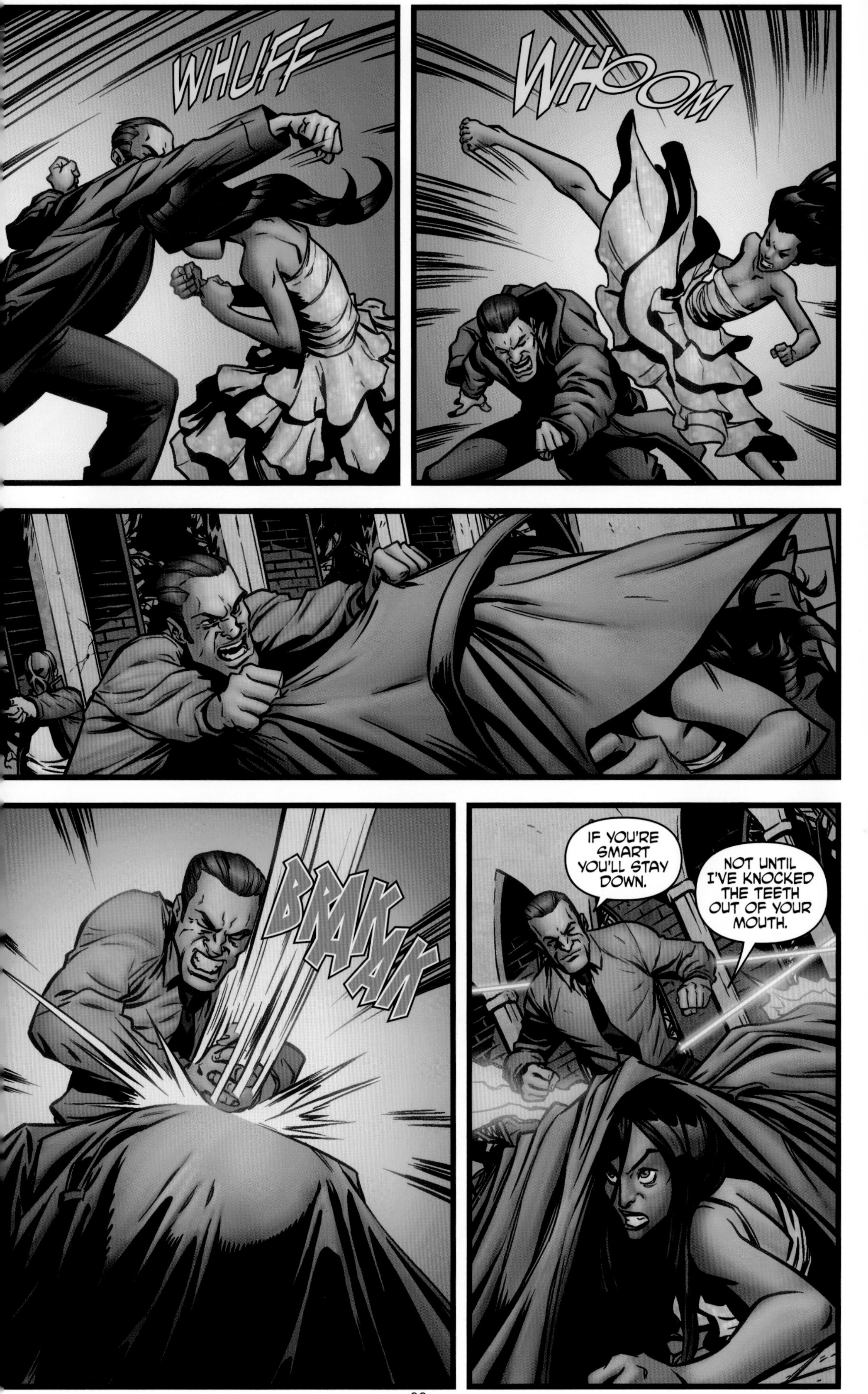
WHUFF
WHOOM
BRAKK
IF YOU'RE SMART YOU'LL STAY DOWN.
NOT UNTIL I'VE KNOCKED THE TEETH OUT OF YOUR MOUTH.

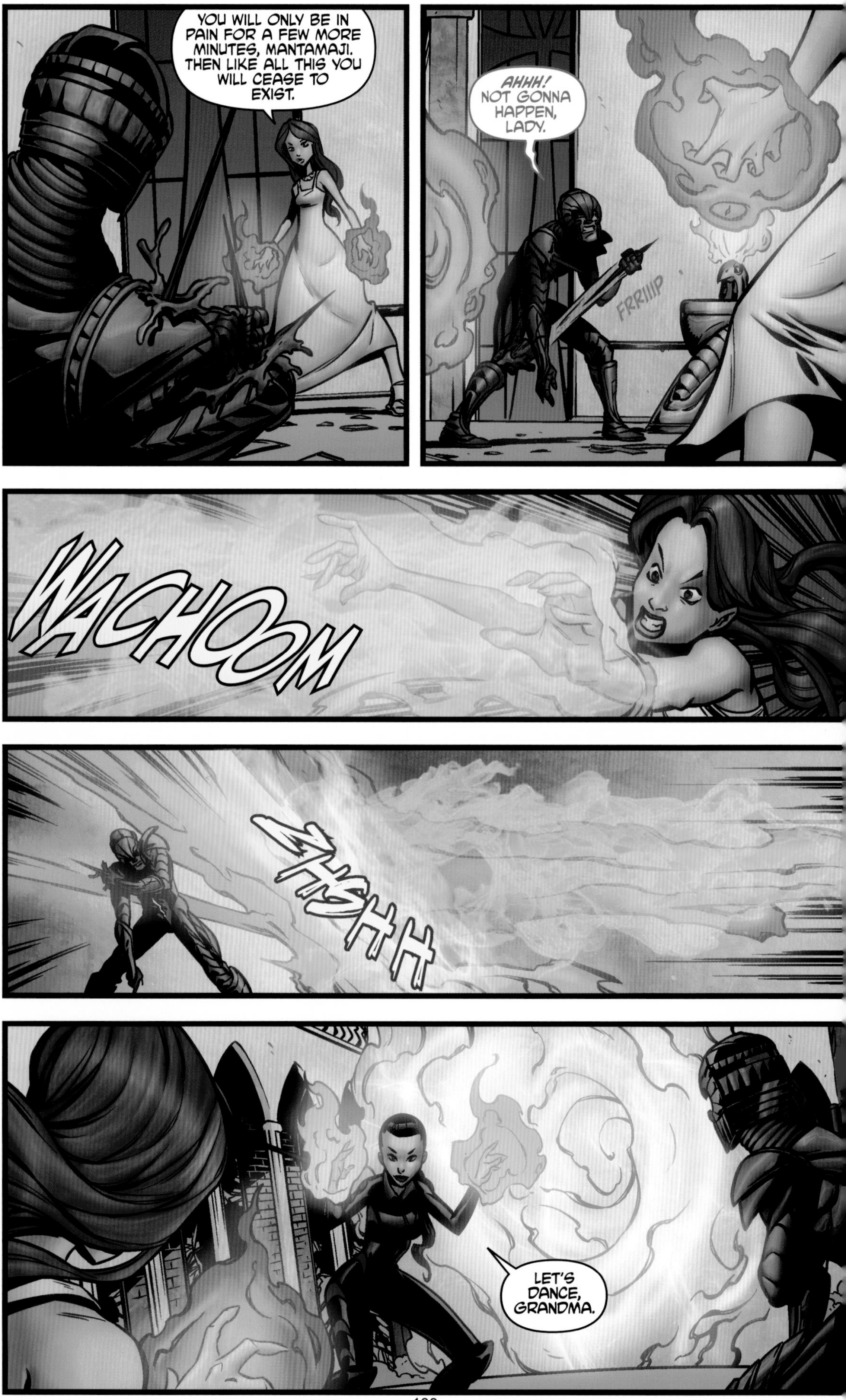
YOU WILL ONLY BE IN PAIN FOR A FEW MORE MINUTES, MANTAMAJI. THEN LIKE ALL THIS YOU WILL CEASE TO EXIST.
AHHH! NOT GONNA HAPPEN, LADY.
FRRIIIP
WACHOOM
ZHSHHH
LET'S DANCE, GRANDMA.

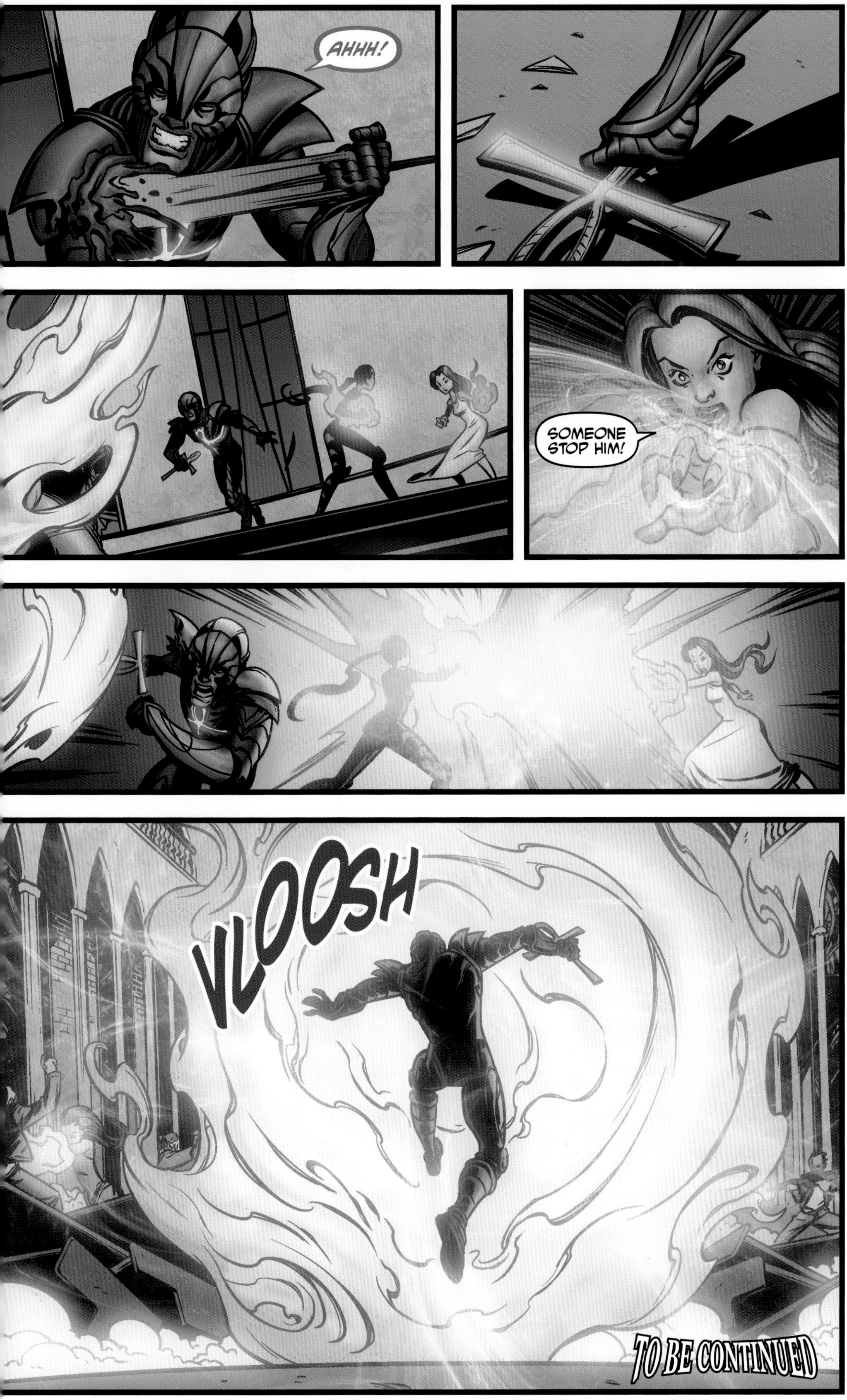
AHHH!
SOMEONE STOP HIM!
VLOOSH
TO BE CONTINUED

CHAPTER ⑮

The Mantamaji and Sanctuants believed—and rightly—that family is the source of strength. For what good is sacrifice if the warmth in the hearth-stove goes out? But their enemies believed that family was also a weakness, for what is love if not vulnerability? In this—alas, a thousand times alas—their enemies believed rightly, too.

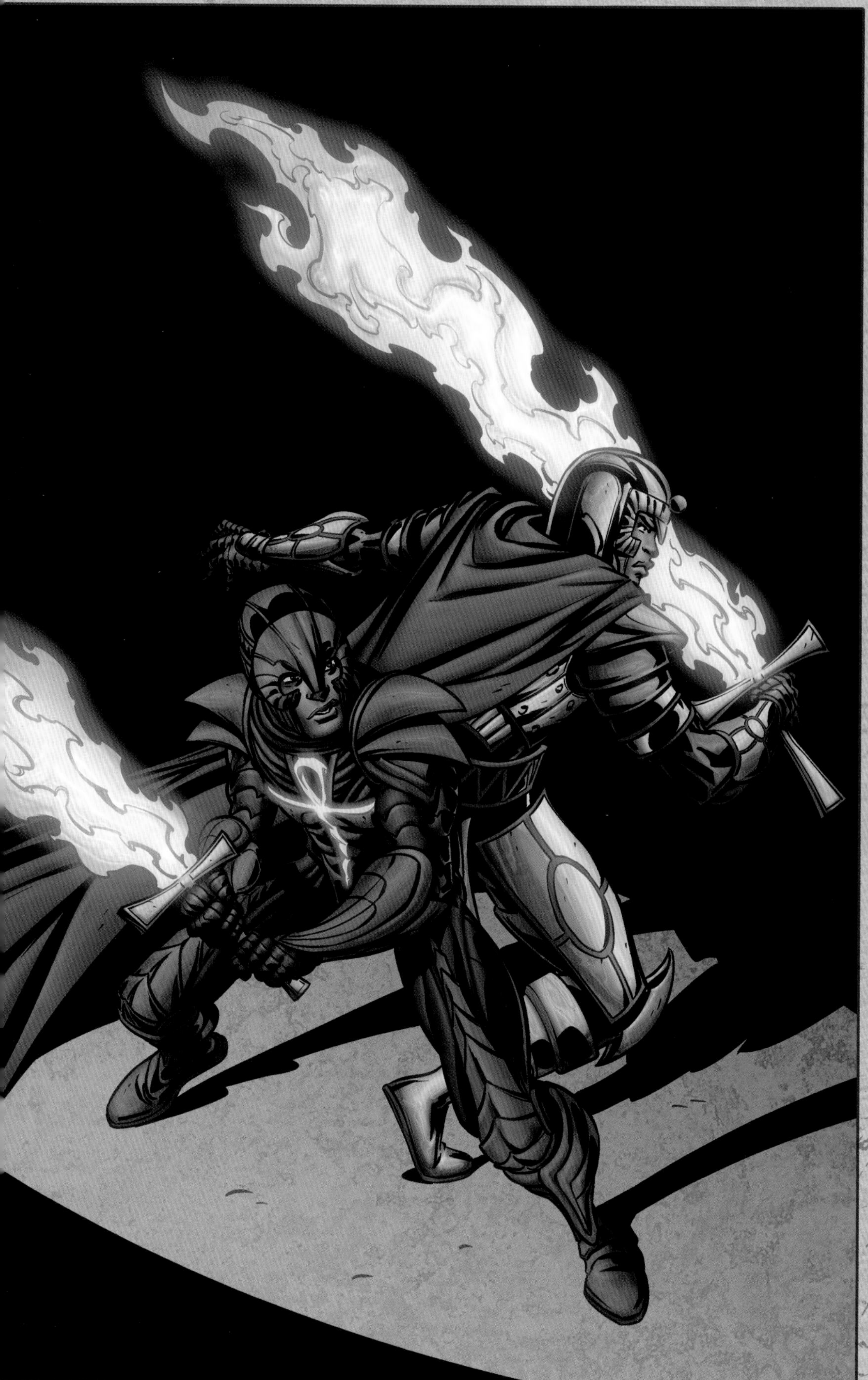

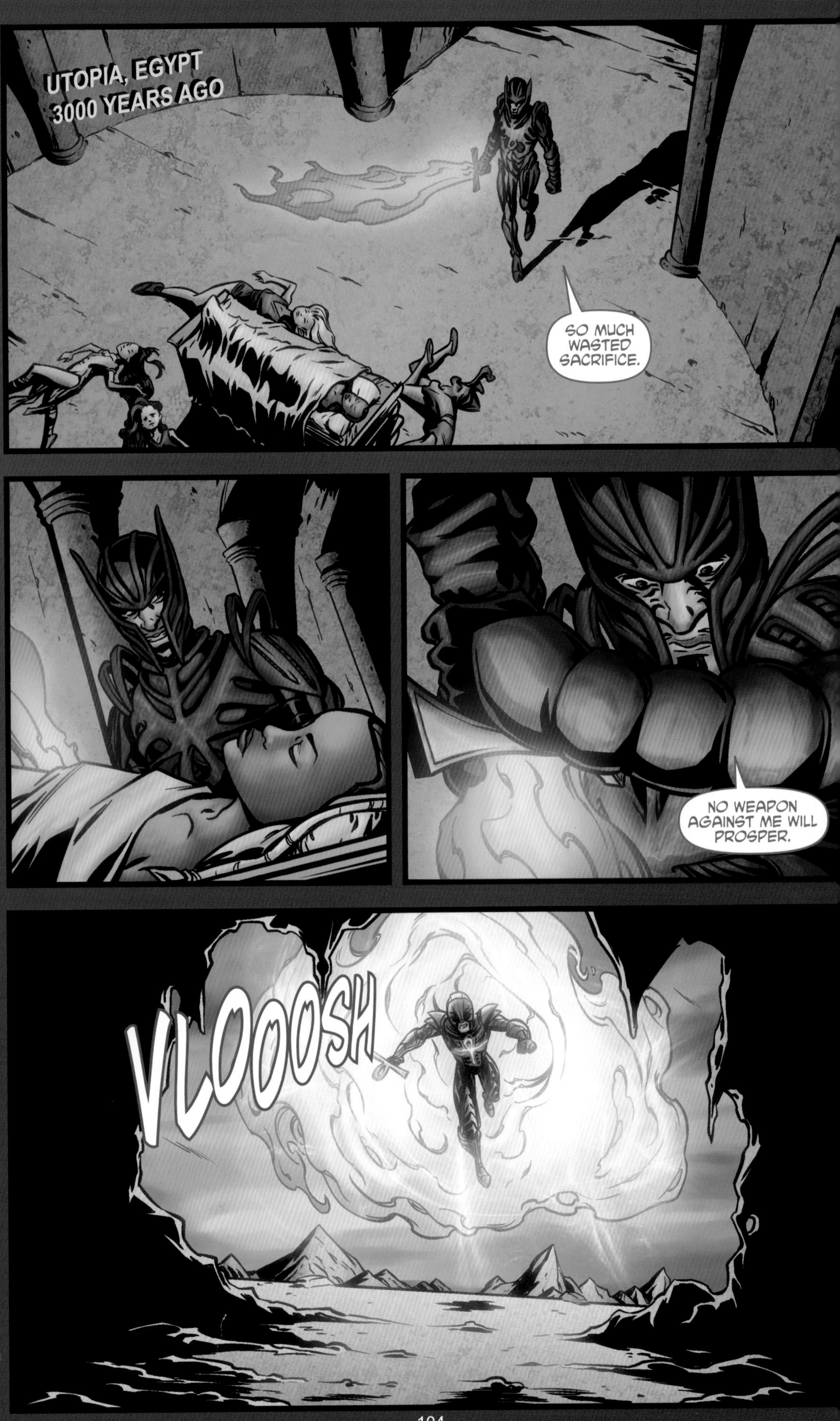
UTOPIA, EGYPT
3000 YEARS AGO
SO MUCH WASTED SACRIFICE.
NO WEAPON AGAINST ME WILL PROSPER.
VLOOOSH

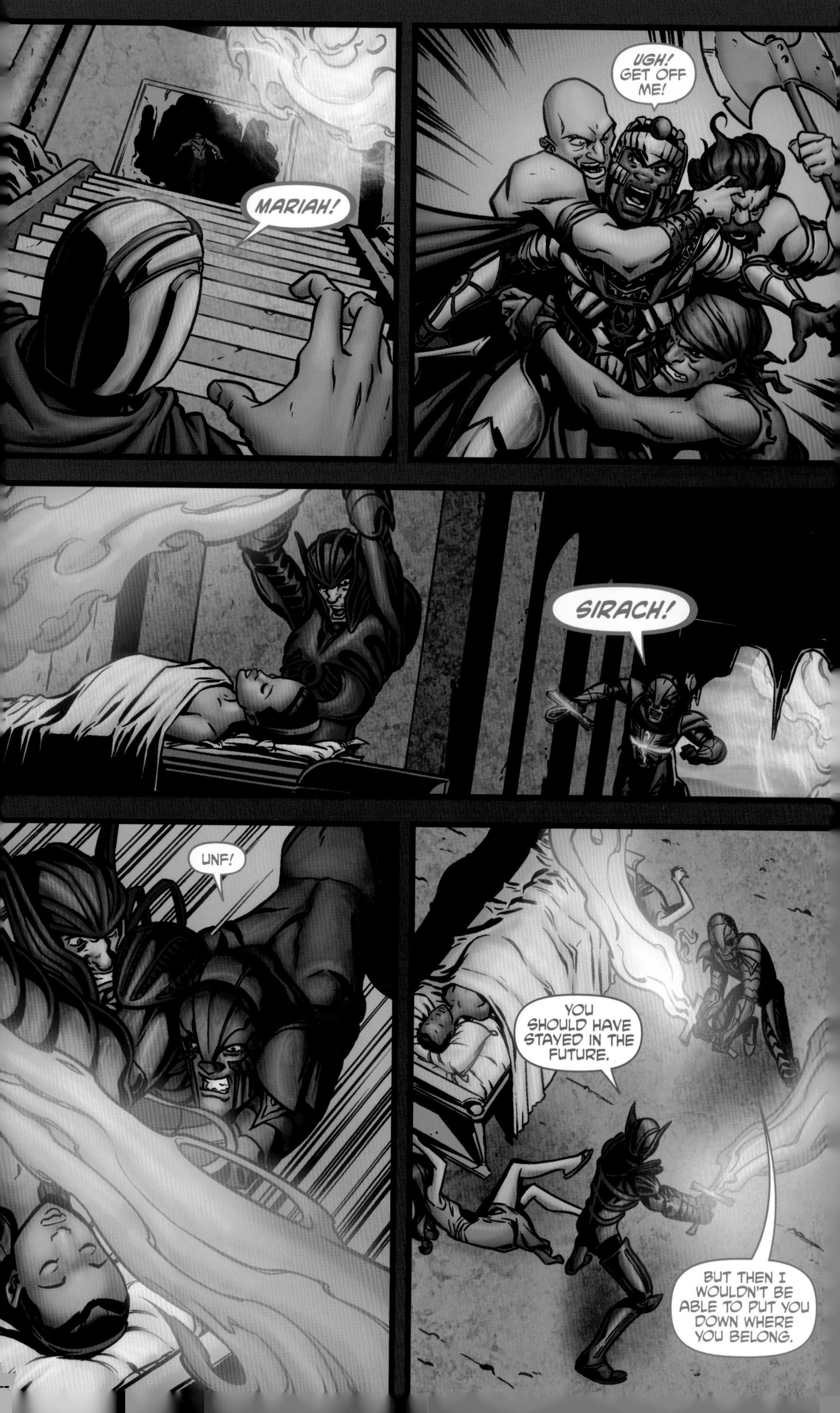
MARIAH!
UGH! GET OFF ME!
SIRACH!
UNF!
YOU SHOULD HAVE STAYED IN THE FUTURE.
BUT THEN I WOULDN'T BE ABLE TO PUT YOU DOWN WHERE YOU BELONG.

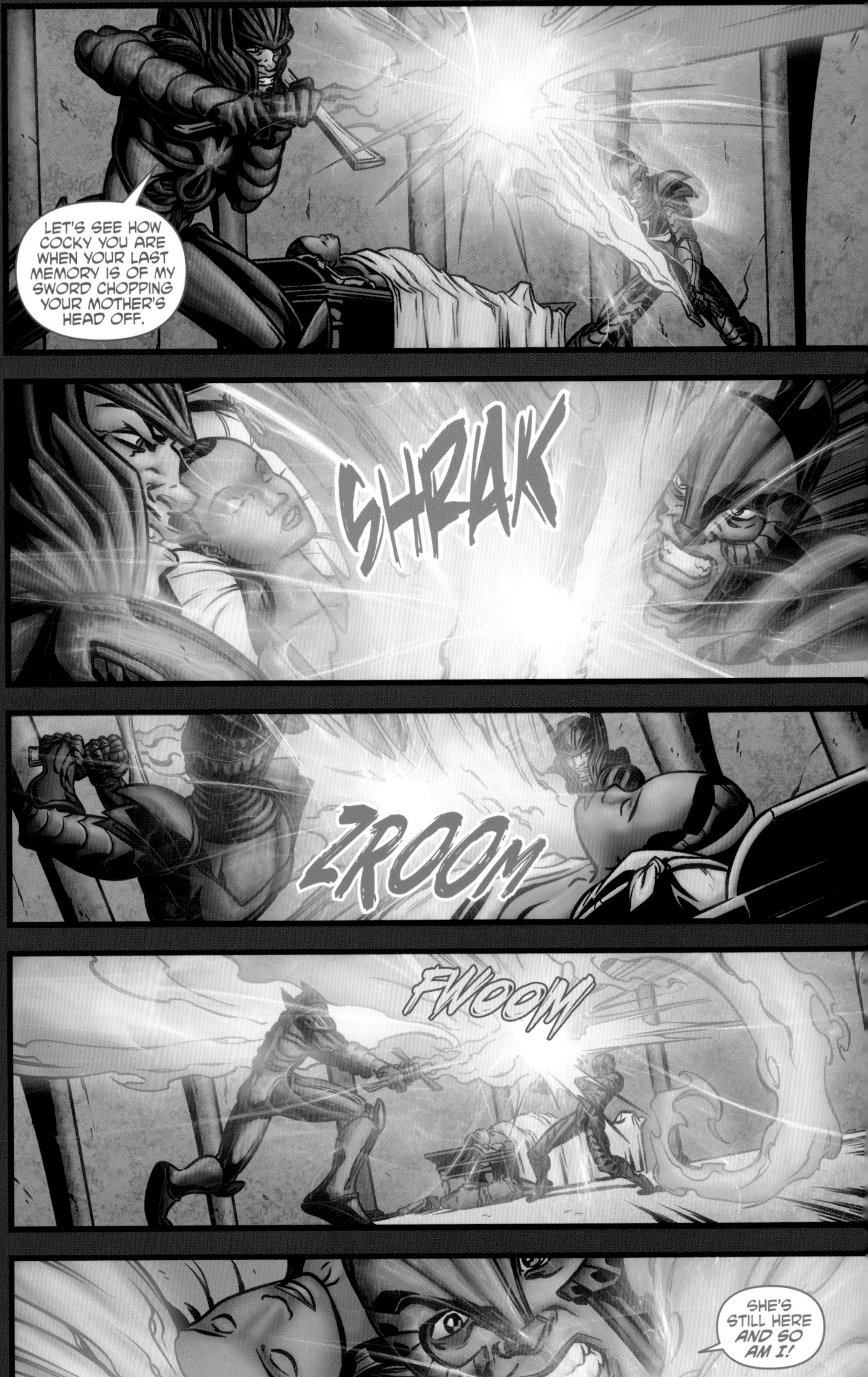
LET'S SEE HOW COCKY YOU ARE WHEN YOUR LAST MEMORY IS OF MY SWORD CHOPPING YOUR MOTHER'S HEAD OFF.
SHRAK
ZROOM
FWOOM
SHE'S STILL HERE AND SO AM I!

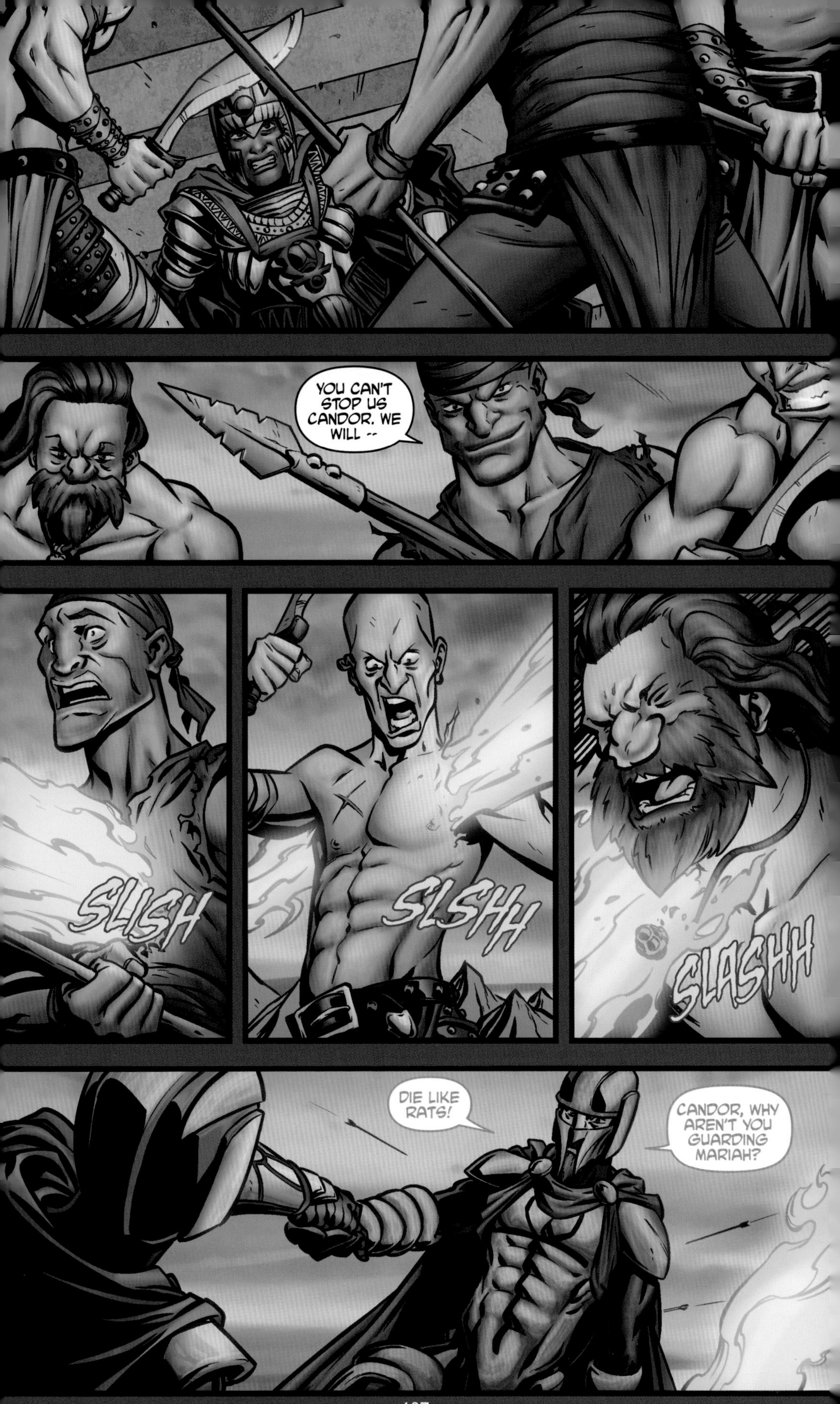
YOU CAN'T STOP US CANDOR. WE WILL --
SLISH
SLSHH
SLASHH
DIE LIKE RATS!
CANDOR, WHY AREN'T YOU GUARDING MARIAH?

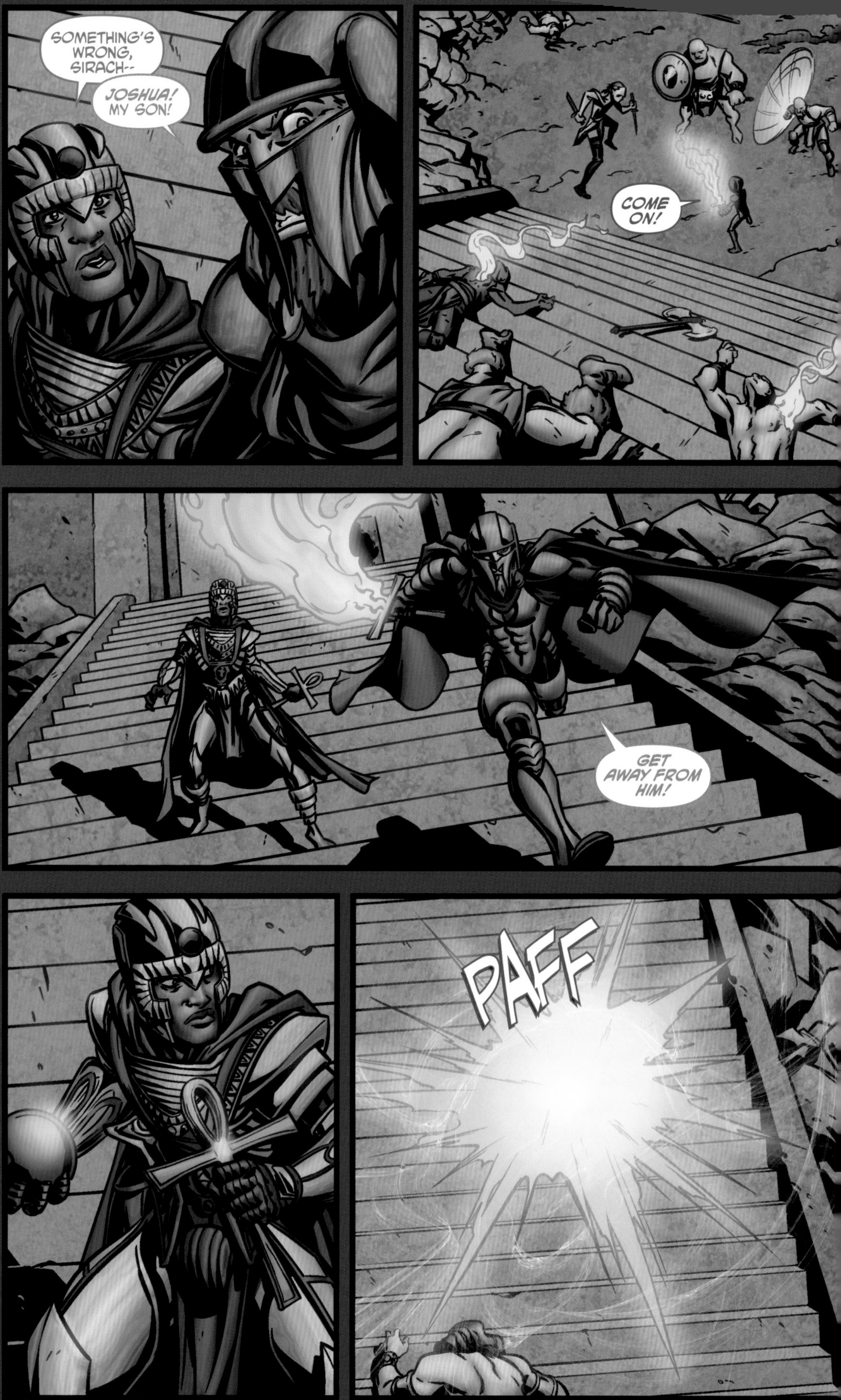
SOMETHING'S WRONG, SIRACH--
JOSHUA! MY SON!
COME ON!
GET AWAY FROM HIM!
PAFF

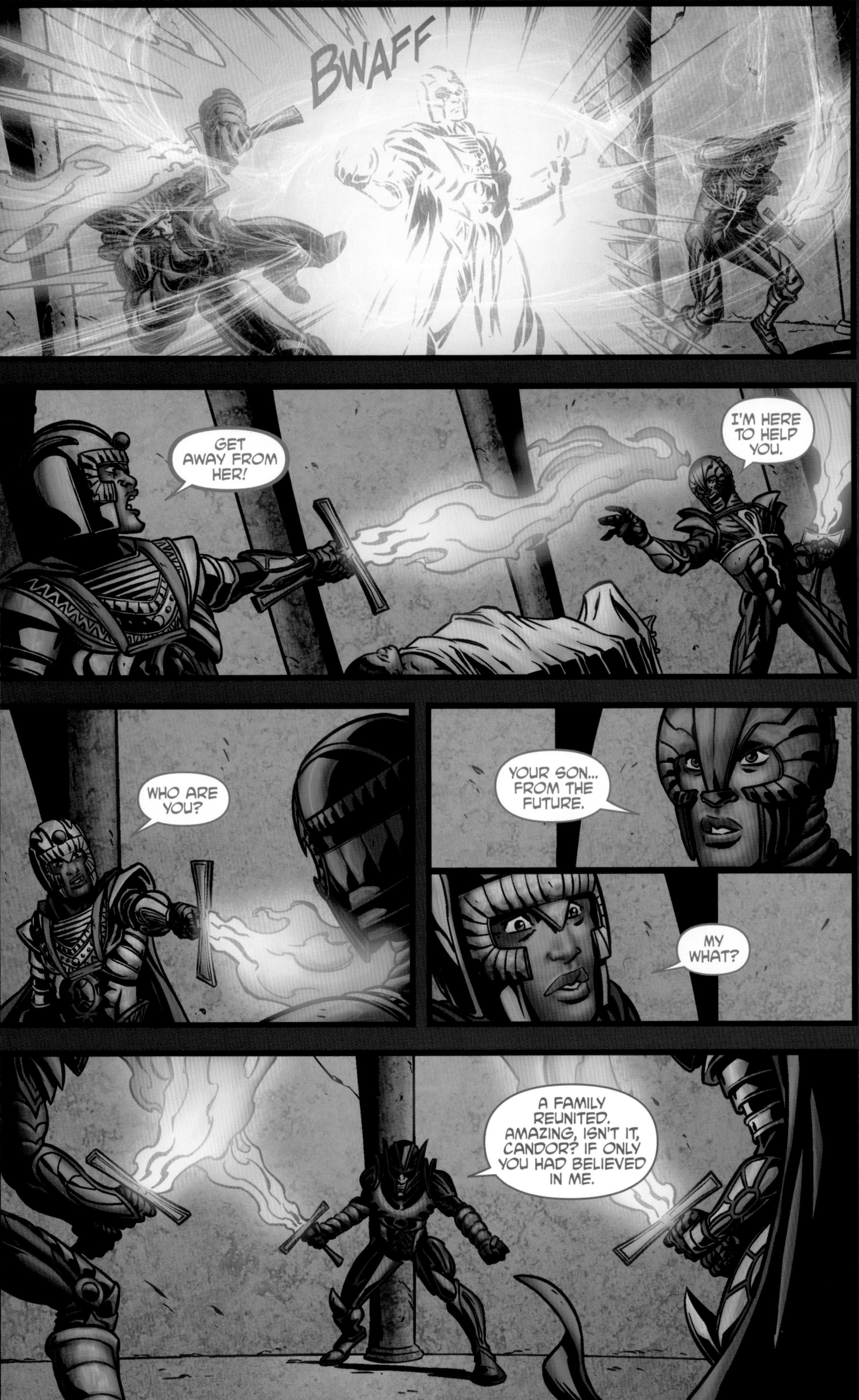
BWAFF
GET AWAY FROM HER!
I'M HERE TO HELP YOU.
WHO ARE YOU?
YOUR SON... FROM THE FUTURE.
MY WHAT?
A FAMILY REUNITED. AMAZING, ISN'T IT, CANDOR? IF ONLY YOU HAD BELIEVED IN ME.

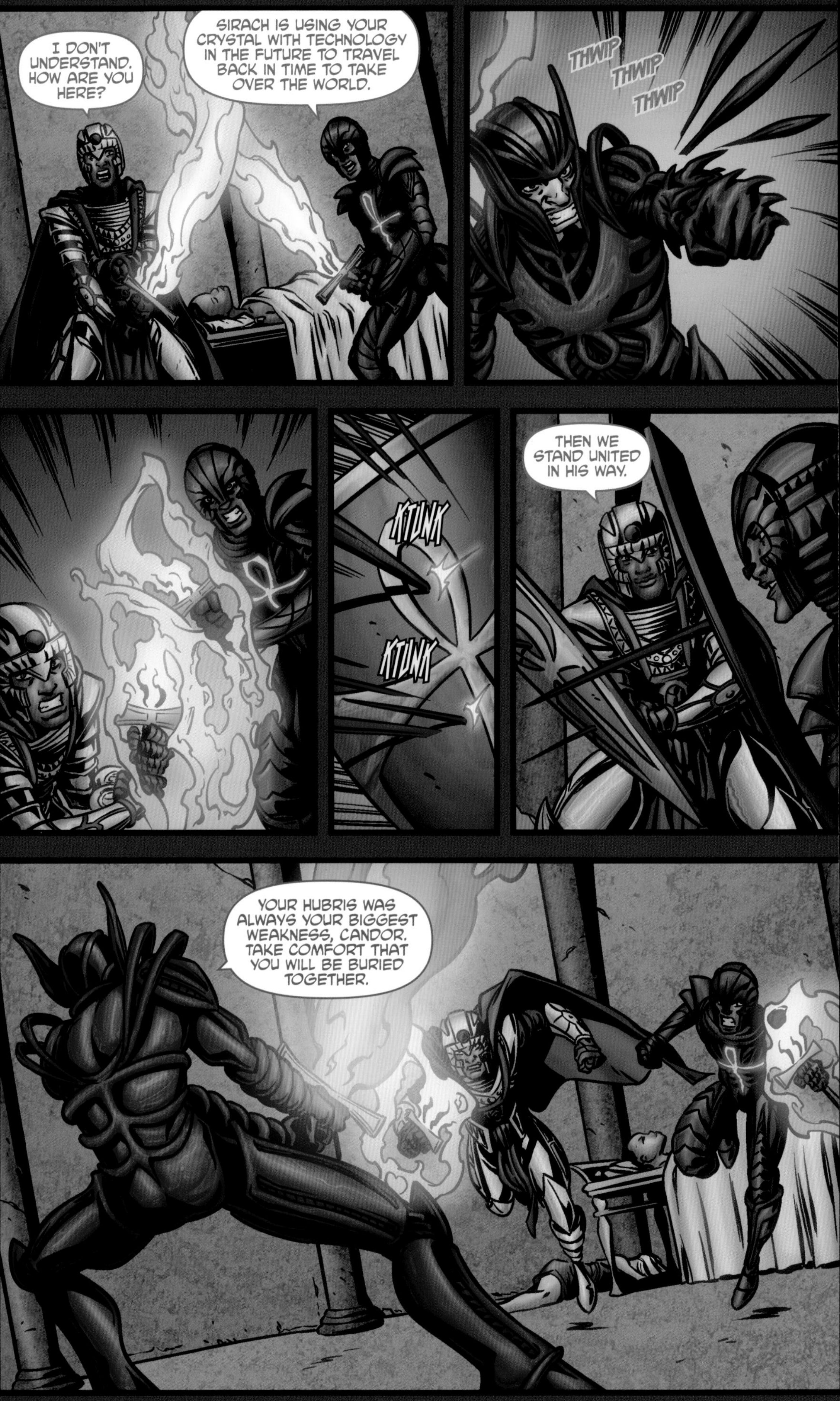
I DON'T UNDERSTAND. HOW ARE YOU HERE?
SIRACH IS USING YOUR CRYSTAL WITH TECHNOLOGY IN THE FUTURE TO TRAVEL BACK IN TIME TO TAKE OVER THE WORLD.
THWIP
THWIP
THWIP
KTUNK
KTUNK
THEN WE STAND UNITED IN HIS WAY.
YOUR HUBRIS WAS ALWAYS YOUR BIGGEST WEAKNESS, CANDOR. TAKE COMFORT THAT YOU WILL BE BURIED TOGETHER.

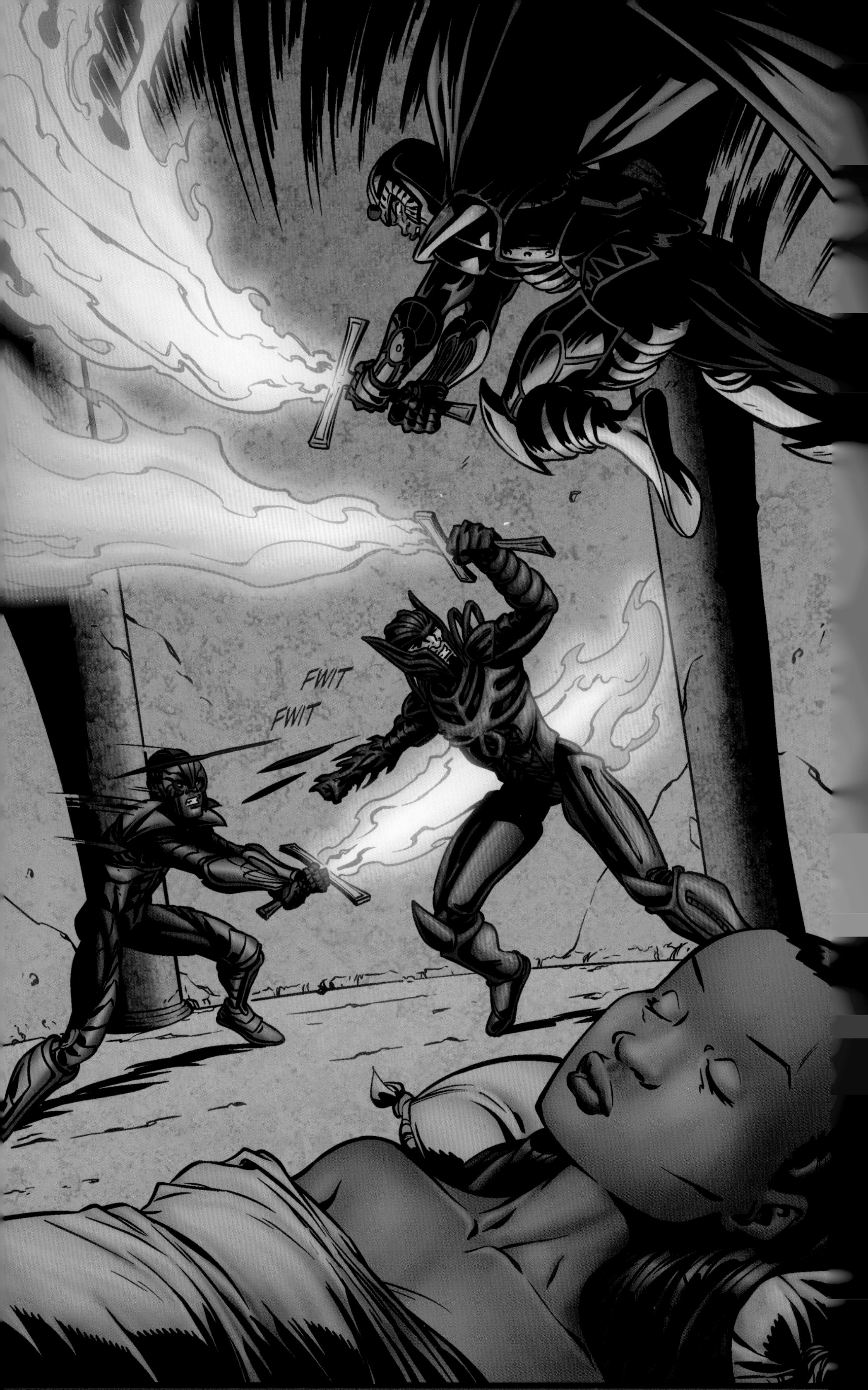
FWIT
FWIT

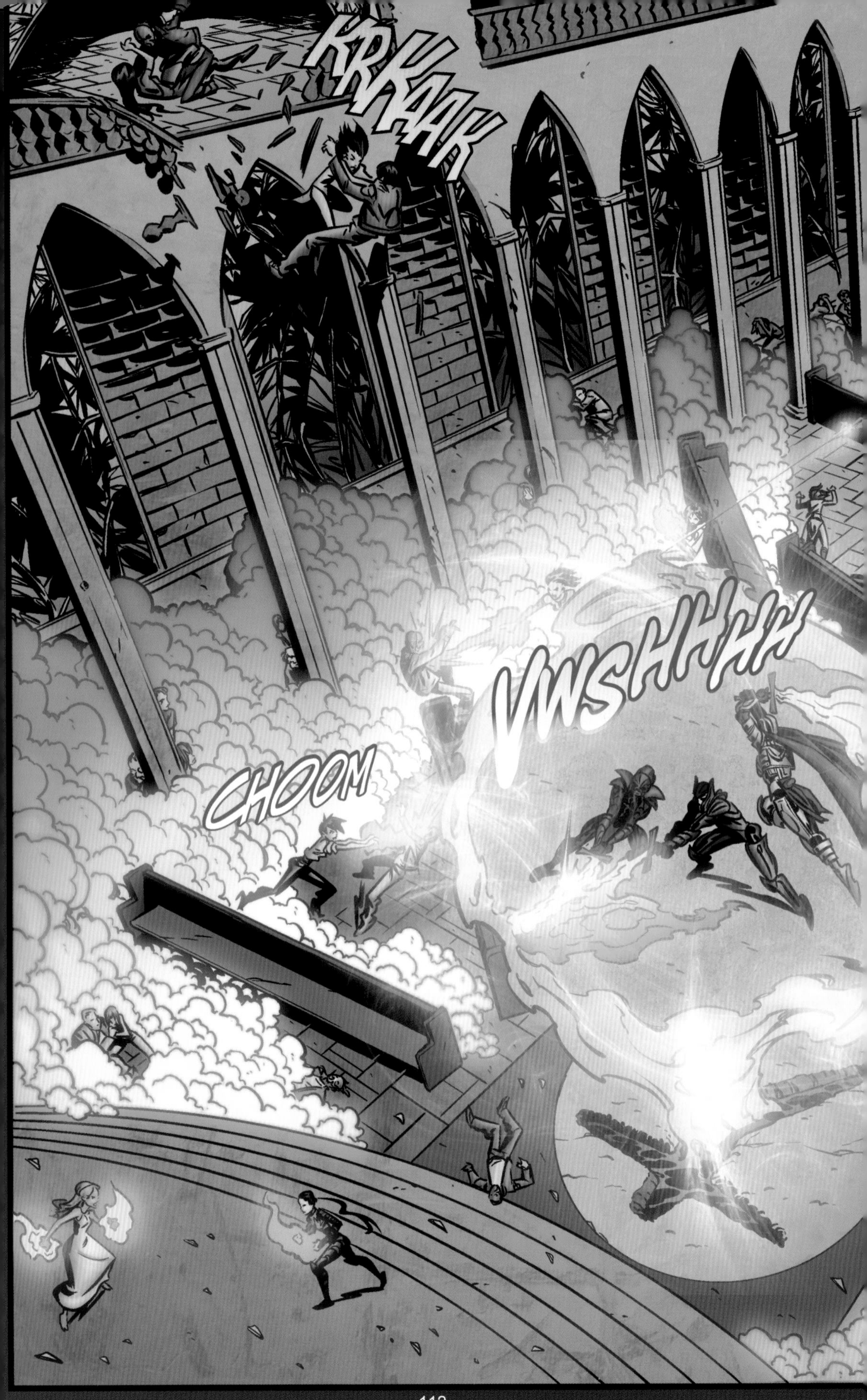
KRKAAK
VWSHHHH
CHOOM

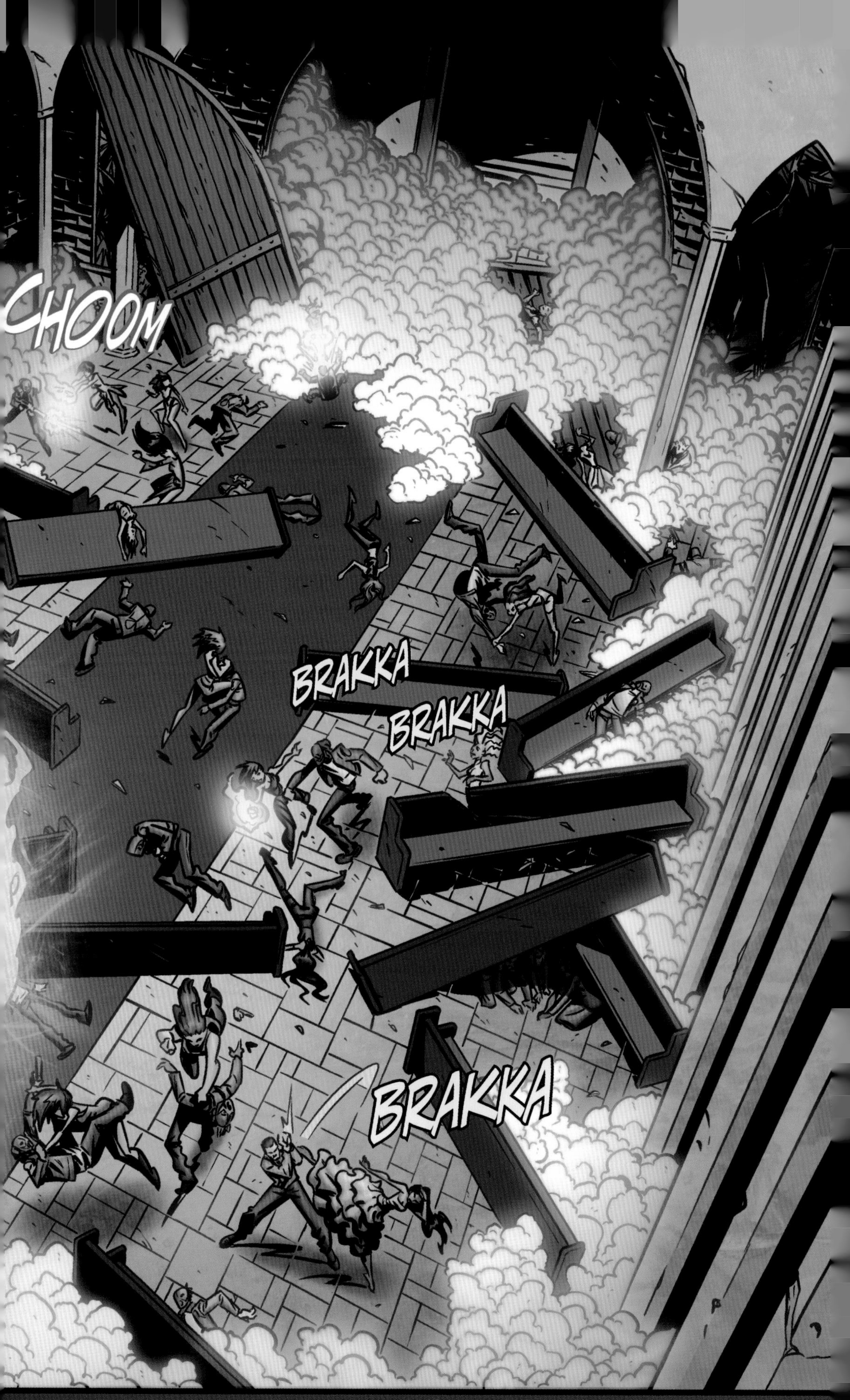
CHOOM
BRAKKA
BRAKKA
BRAKKA

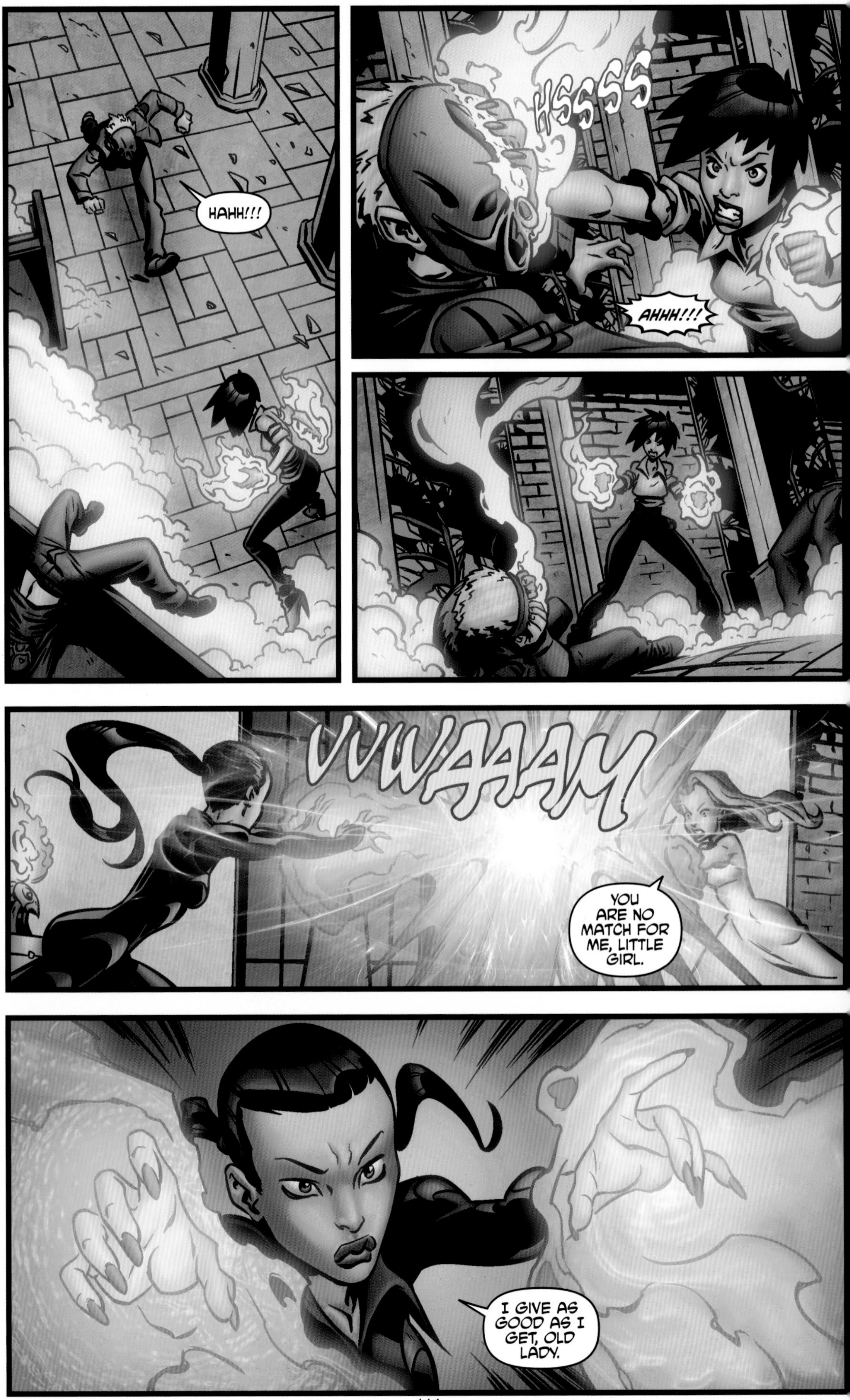
HAHH!!!
HSSSS
AHHH!!!
VVWAAAM
YOU ARE NO MATCH FOR ME, LITTLE GIRL.
I GIVE AS GOOD AS I GET, OLD LADY.

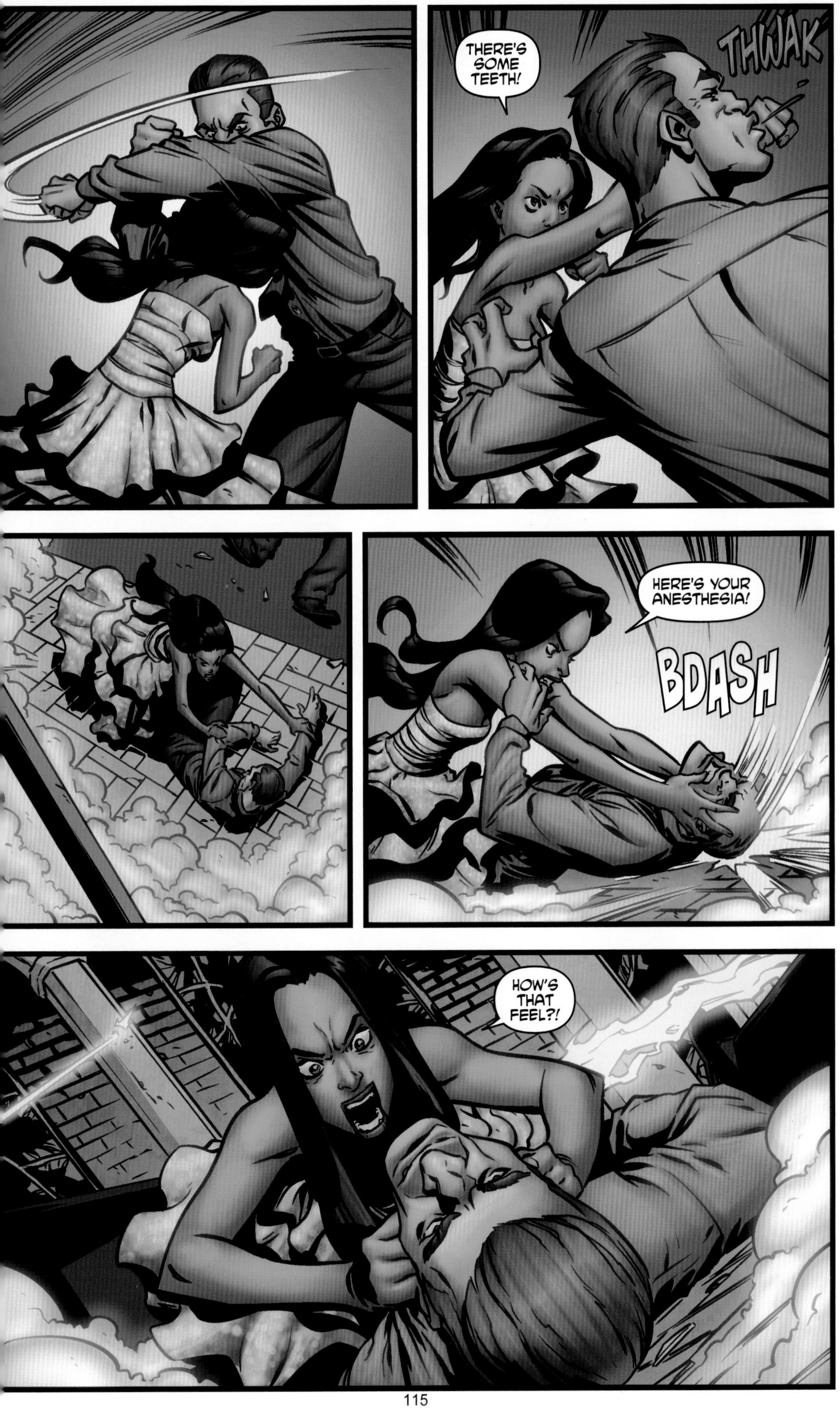
THERE'S SOME TEETH!
THWAK
HERE'S YOUR ANESTHESIA!
BDASH
HOW'S THAT FEEL?!

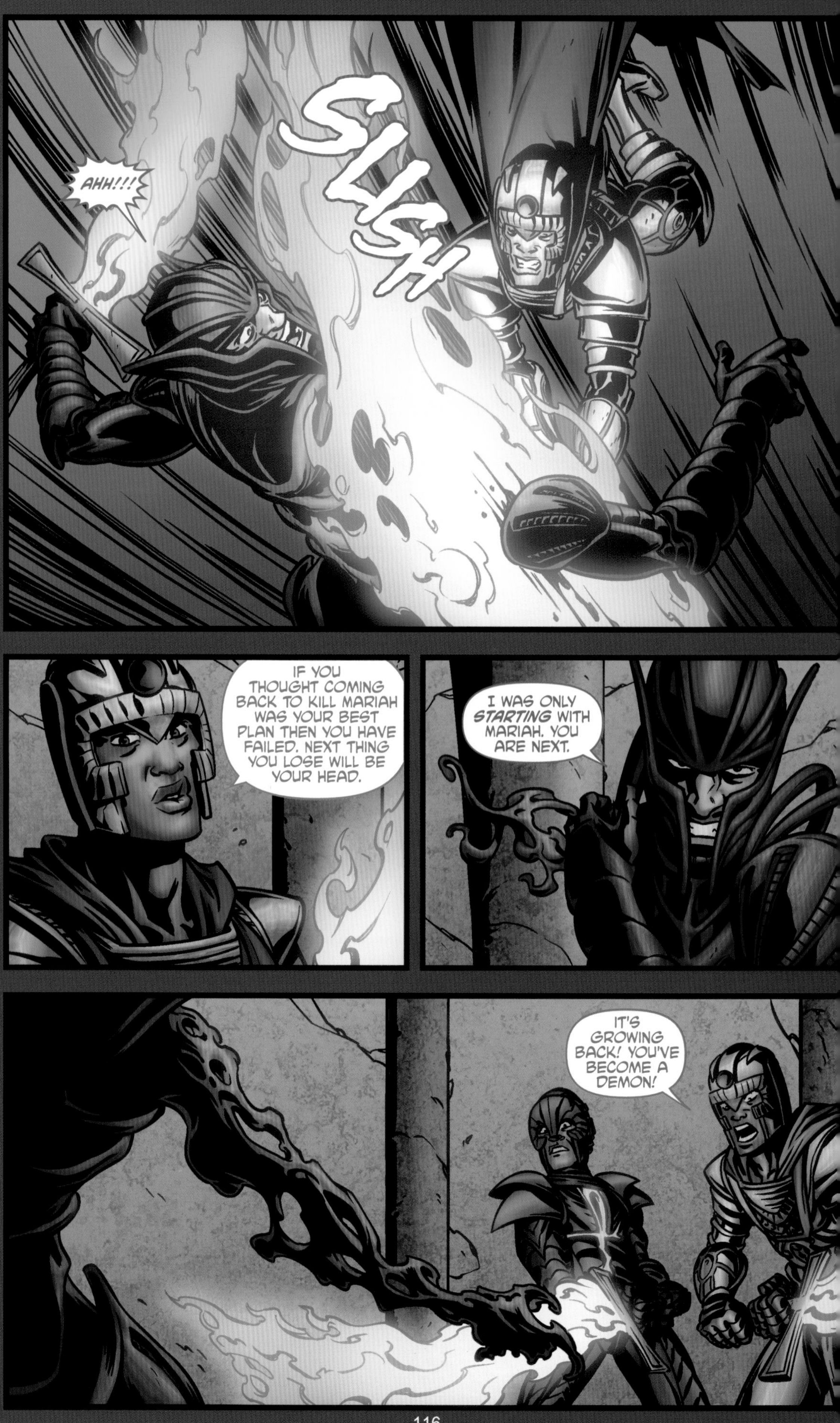

AHH!!!
SLISH
IF YOU THOUGHT COMING BACK TO KILL MARIAH WAS YOUR BEST PLAN THEN YOU HAVE FAILED. NEXT THING YOU LOSE WILL BE YOUR HEAD.
I WAS ONLY *STARTING* WITH MARIAH. YOU ARE NEXT.
IT'S GROWING BACK! YOU'VE BECOME A DEMON!

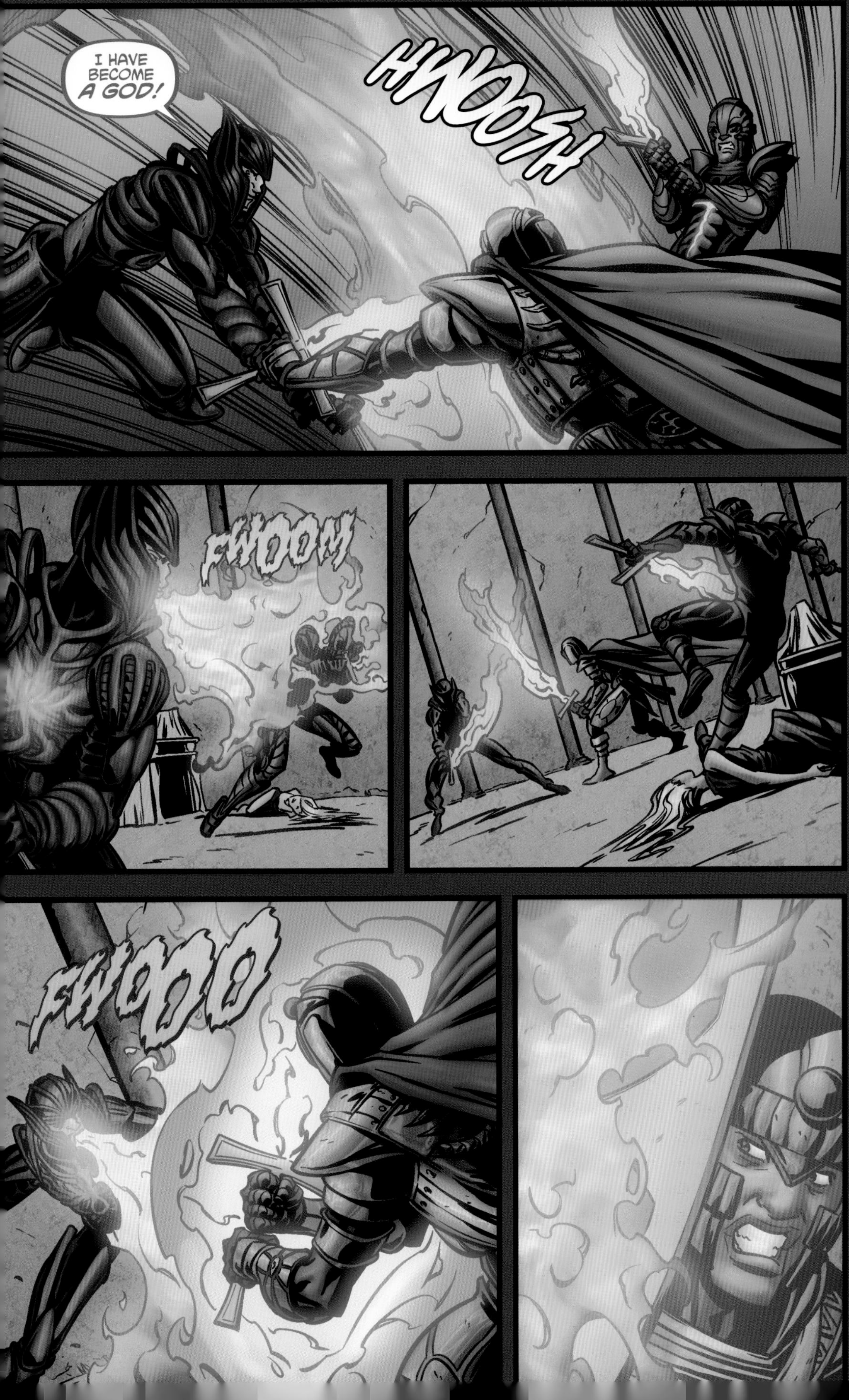

I HAVE BECOME A GOD!
HWOOSH
FWOOM
FWOOO

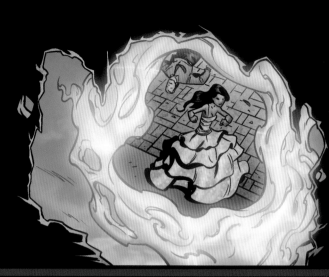

SYDNEY, USE THE DETONATOR TO BLOW THE SATELLITE.

SYDNEY, USE THE DETONATOR TO BLOW THE SATELLITE.

BUT YOU'LL BE TRAPPED IN THE PAST.

I DON'T MATTER. EVERYONE ELSE DOES.

NO, THERE MUST BE ANOTHER WAY.

WE DON'T HAVE TIME. *BLOW IT.*

ELIJAH, *PLEASE--*

THIS IS MY CHOICE. I'LL FIND MY WAY BACK TO YOU. I PROMISE.

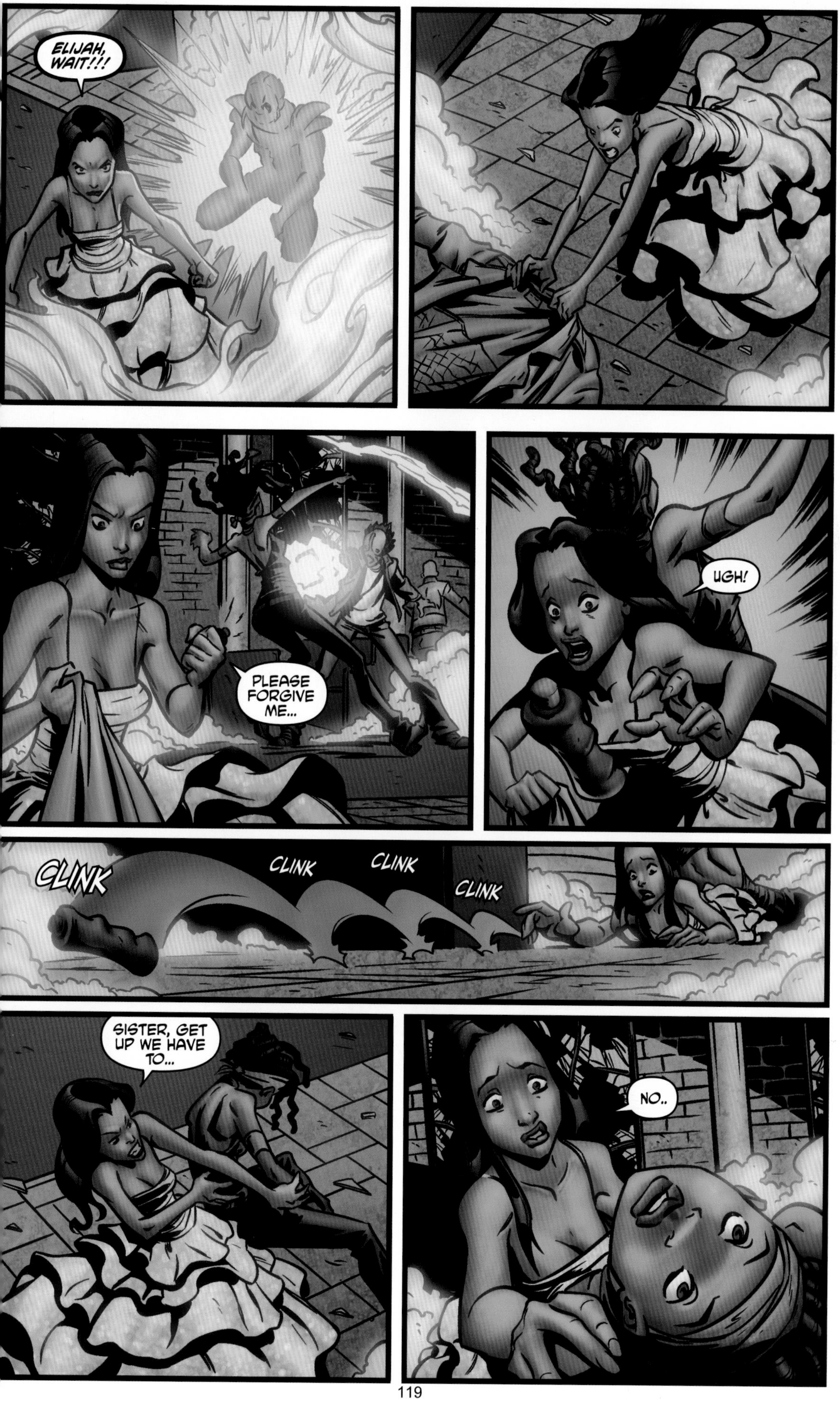
ELIJAH, WAIT!!!
PLEASE FORGIVE ME...
UGH!
CLINK
CLINK
CLINK
CLINK
SISTER, GET UP WE HAVE TO...
NO..

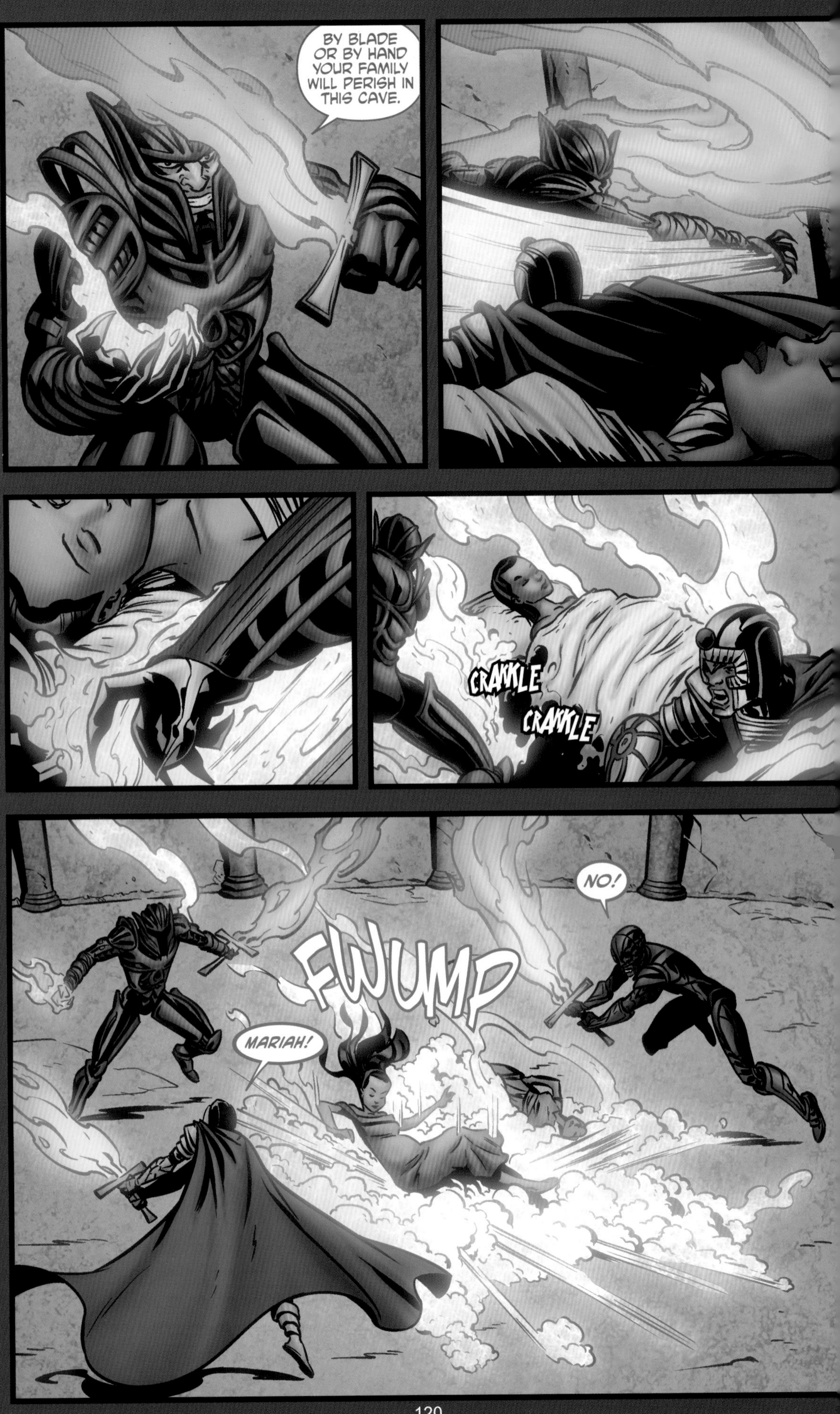
BY BLADE OR BY HAND YOUR FAMILY WILL PERISH IN THIS CAVE.
CRAKKLE
CRAKKLE
NO!
FWUMP
MARIAH!

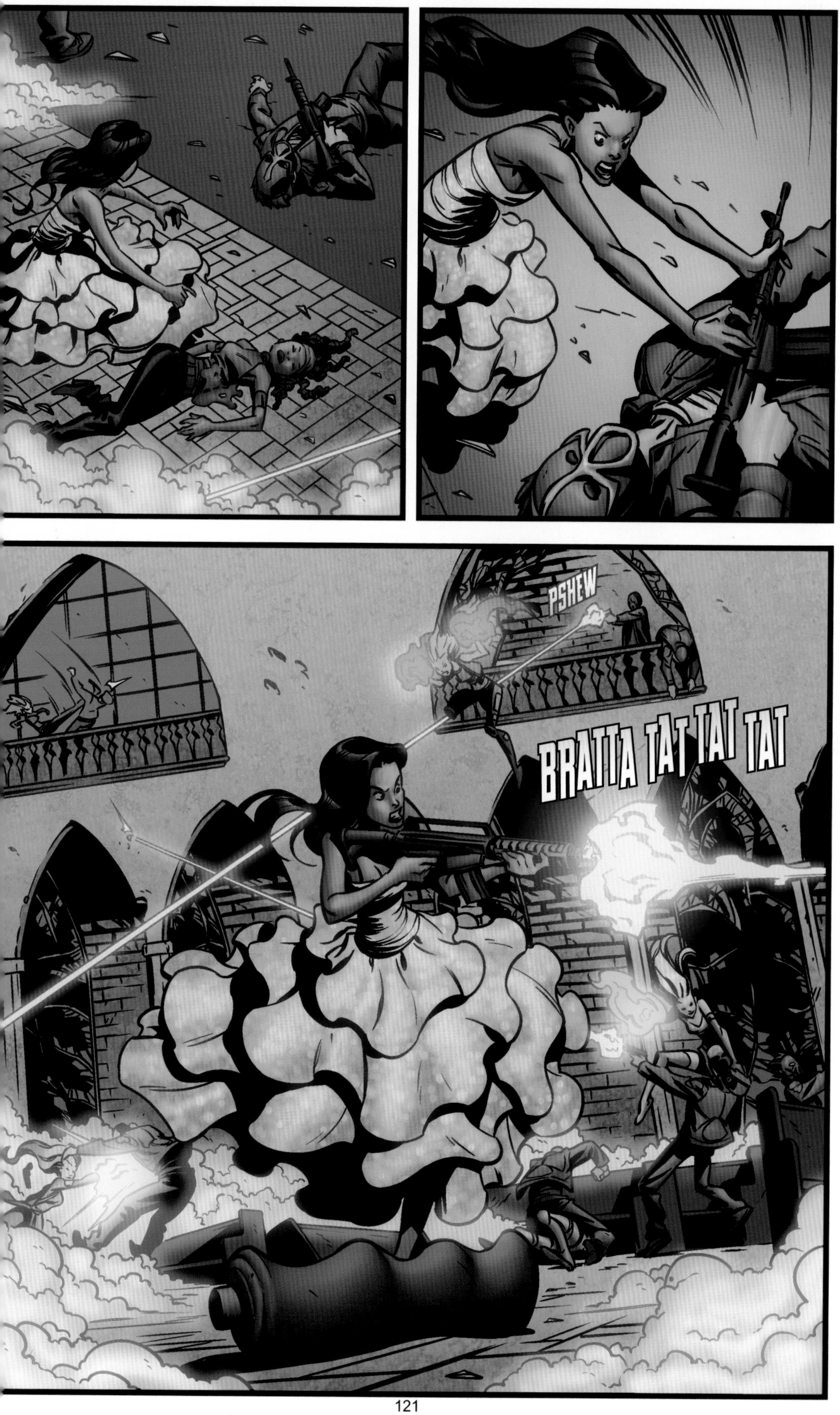
PSHEW
BRATTA TAT TAT TAT

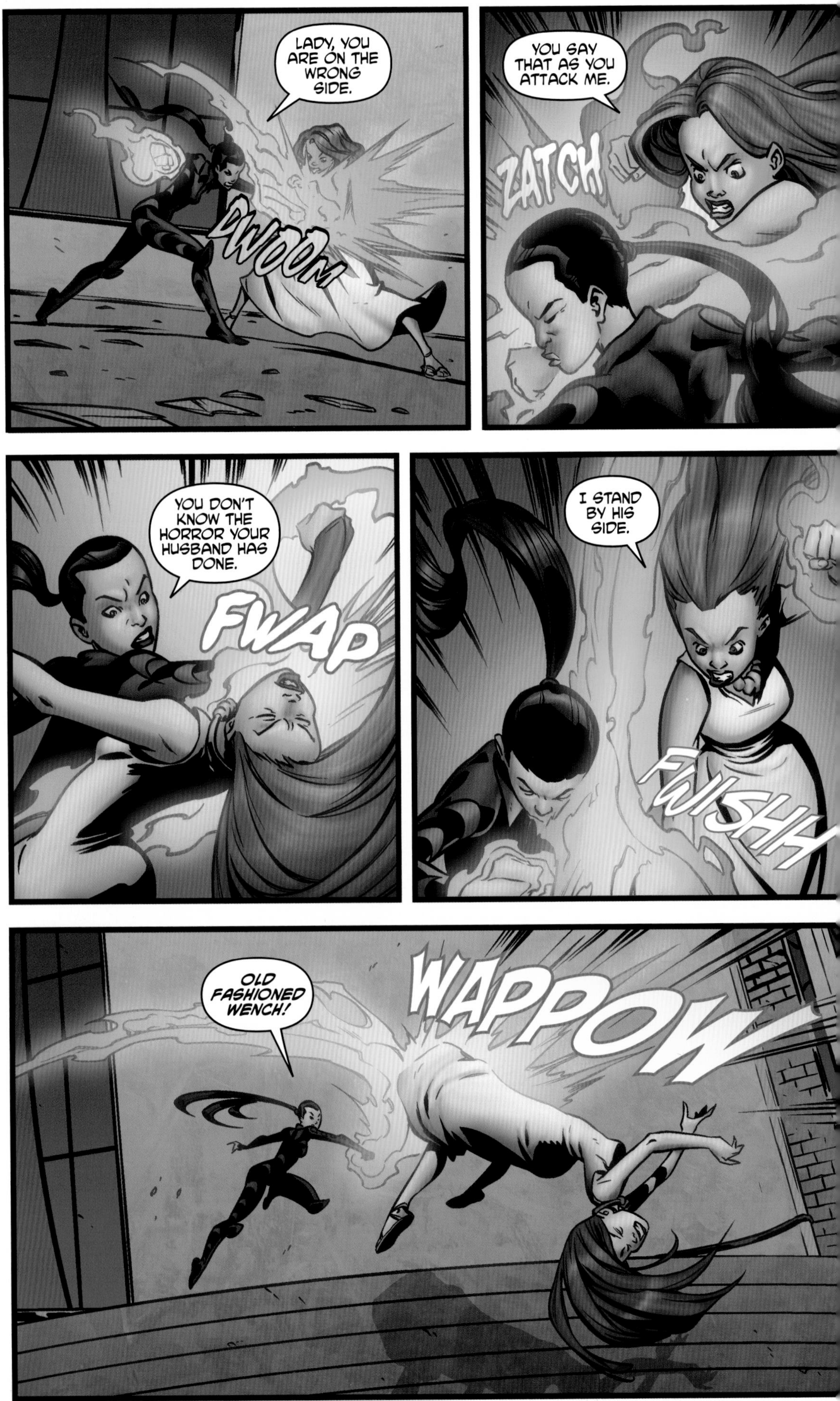
LADY, YOU ARE ON THE WRONG SIDE.
DWOOM
YOU SAY THAT AS YOU ATTACK ME.
ZATCH
YOU DON'T KNOW THE HORROR YOUR HUSBAND HAS DONE.
FWAP
I STAND BY HIS SIDE.
FWISHH
OLD FASHIONED WENCH!
WAPPOW

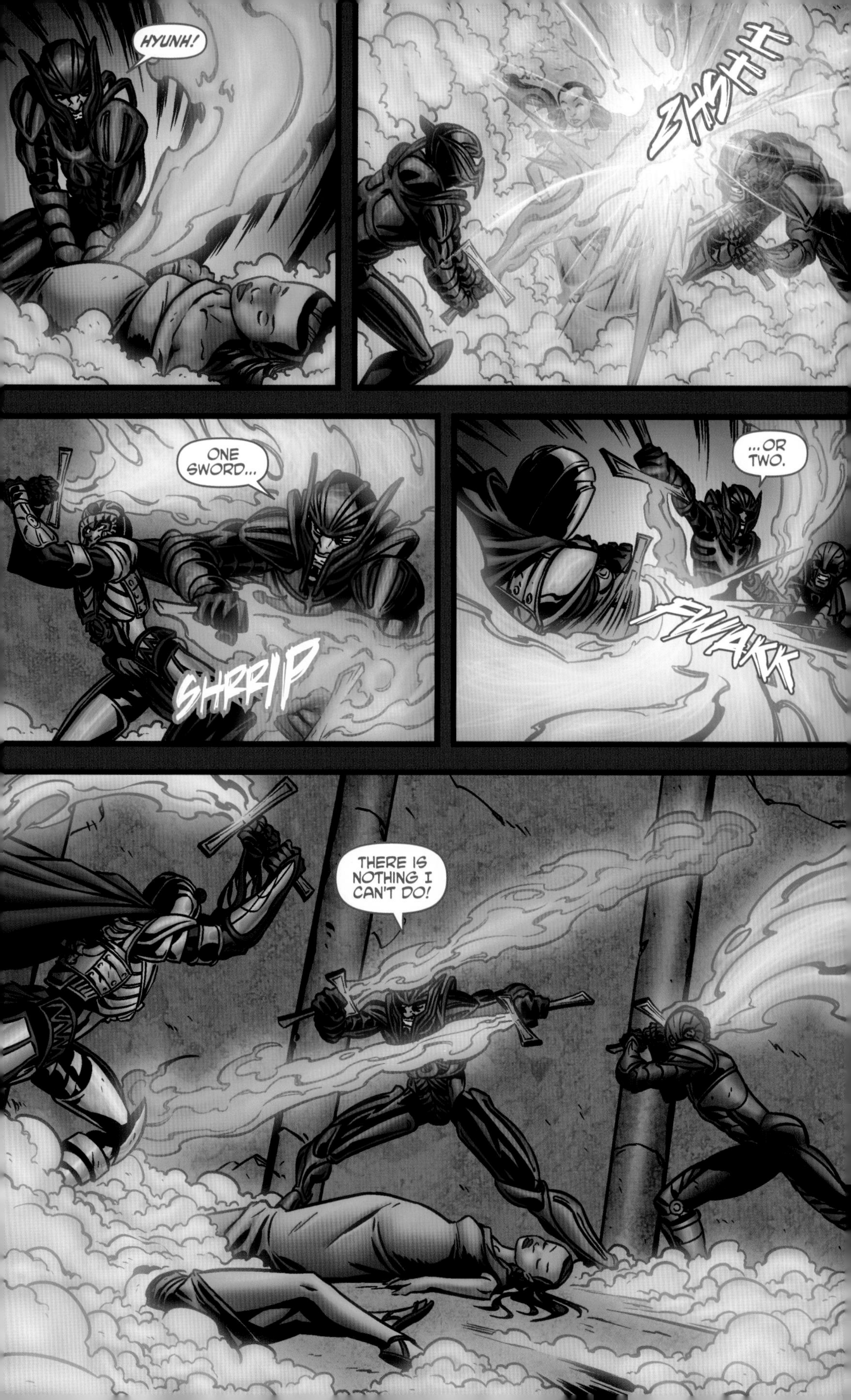
HYUNH!
ZHSHH
ONE SWORD...
SHRRIP
...OR TWO.
FWAKK
THERE IS NOTHING I CAN'T DO!

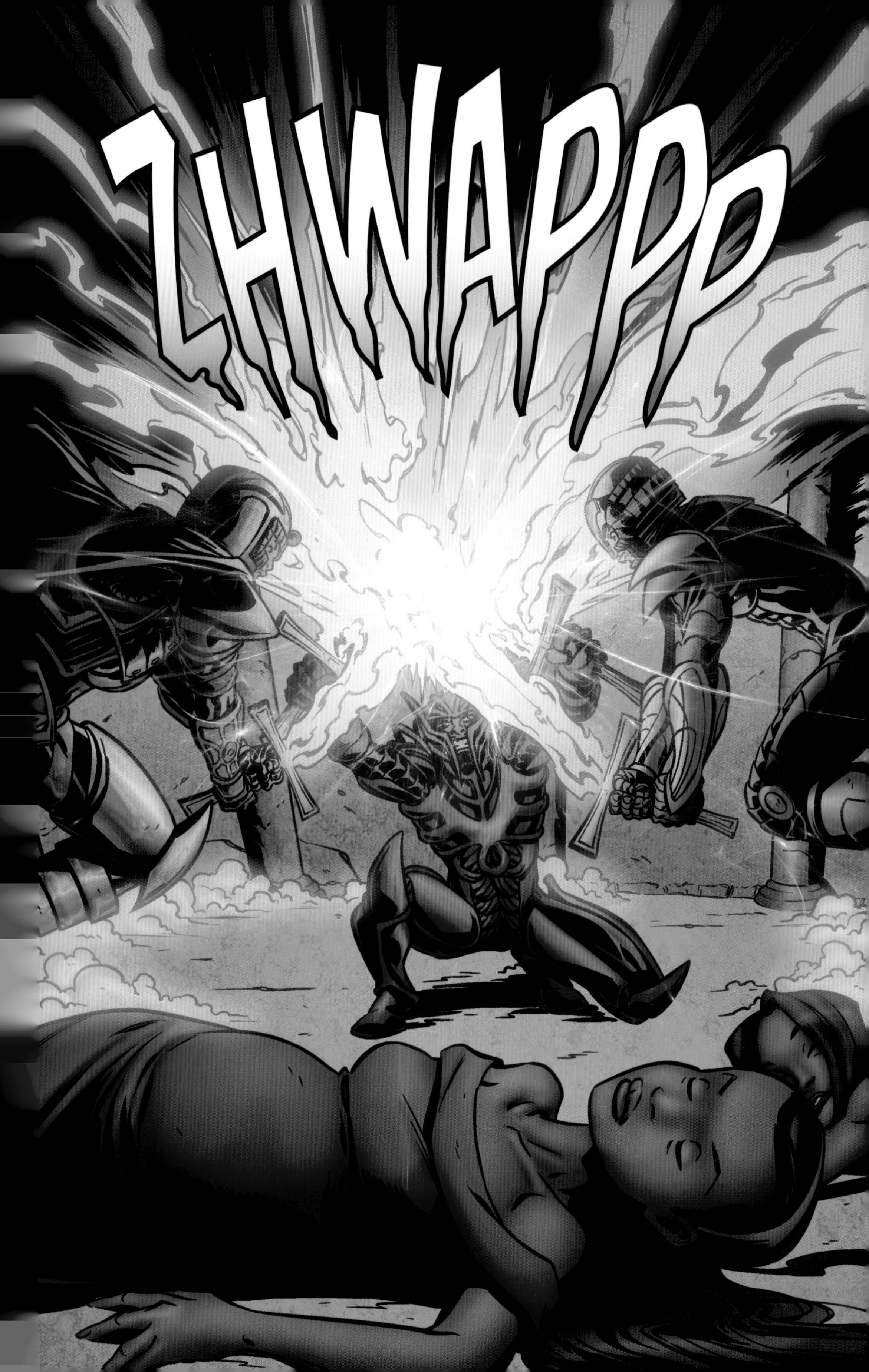
ZHWAPPP

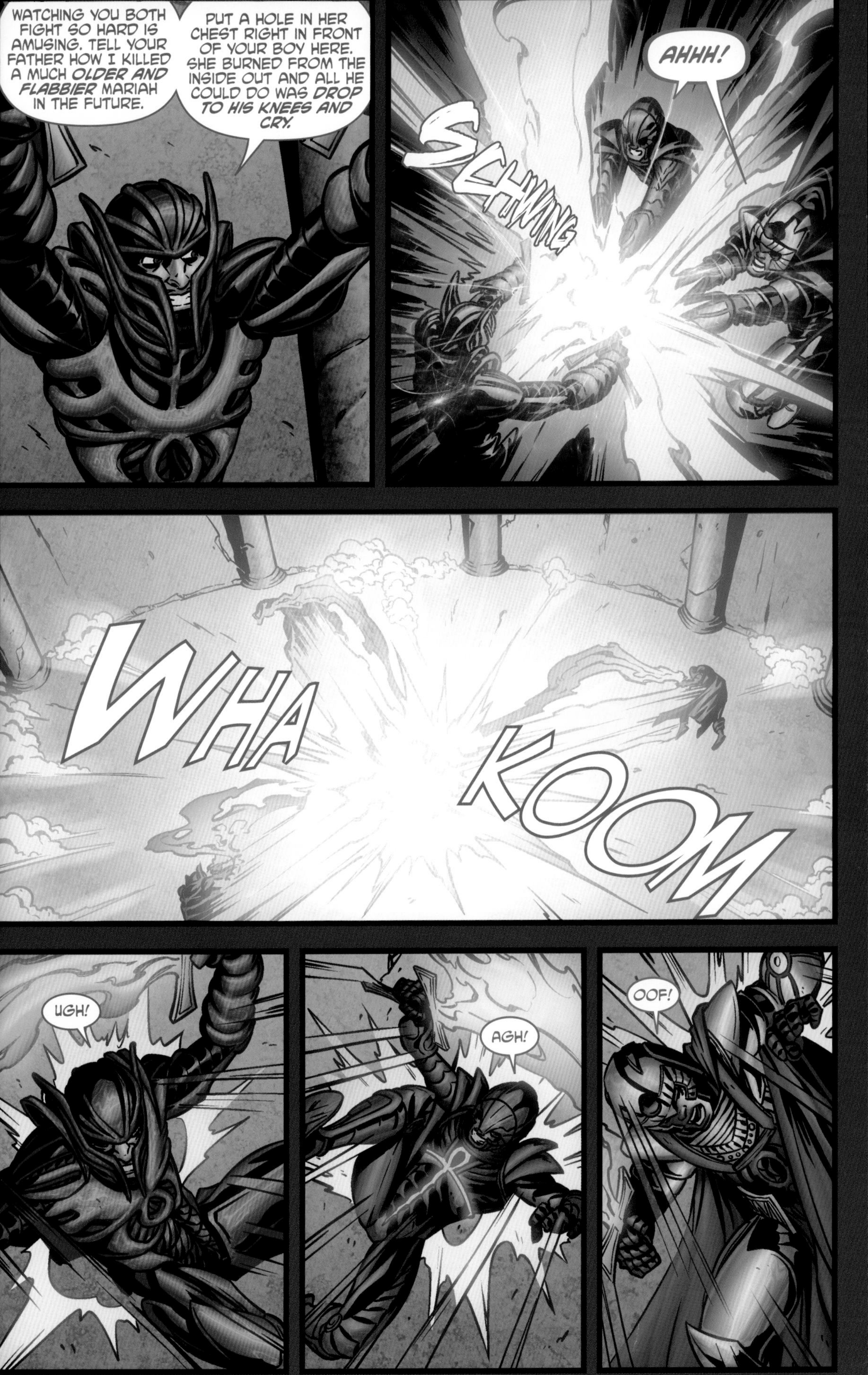
WATCHING YOU BOTH FIGHT SO HARD IS AMUSING. TELL YOUR FATHER HOW I KILLED A MUCH OLDER AND FLABBIER MARIAH IN THE FUTURE.
PUT A HOLE IN HER CHEST RIGHT IN FRONT OF YOUR BOY HERE. SHE BURNED FROM THE INSIDE OUT AND ALL HE COULD DO WAS DROP TO HIS KNEES AND CRY.
AHHH!
SCHWING
WHA
KOOM
UGH!
AGH!
OOF!

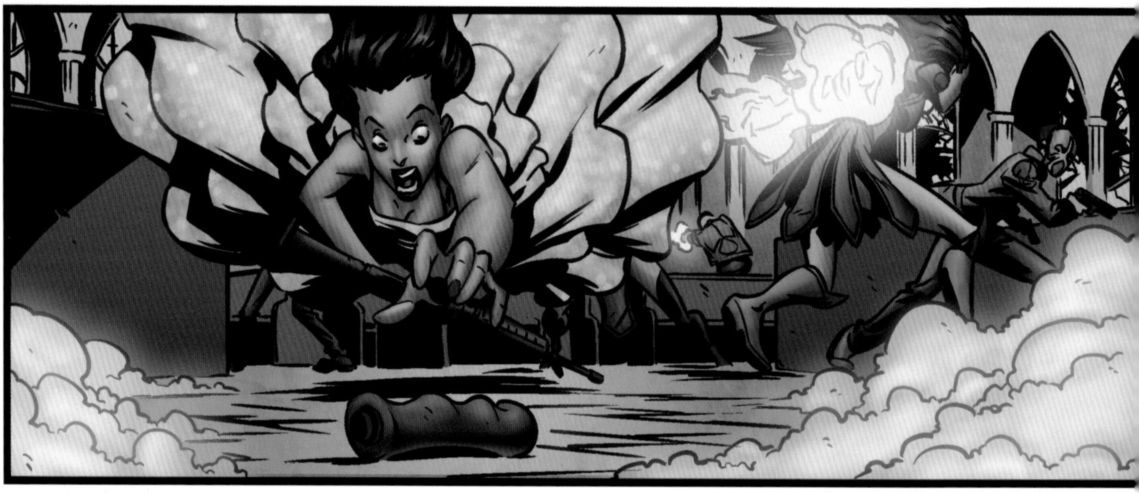

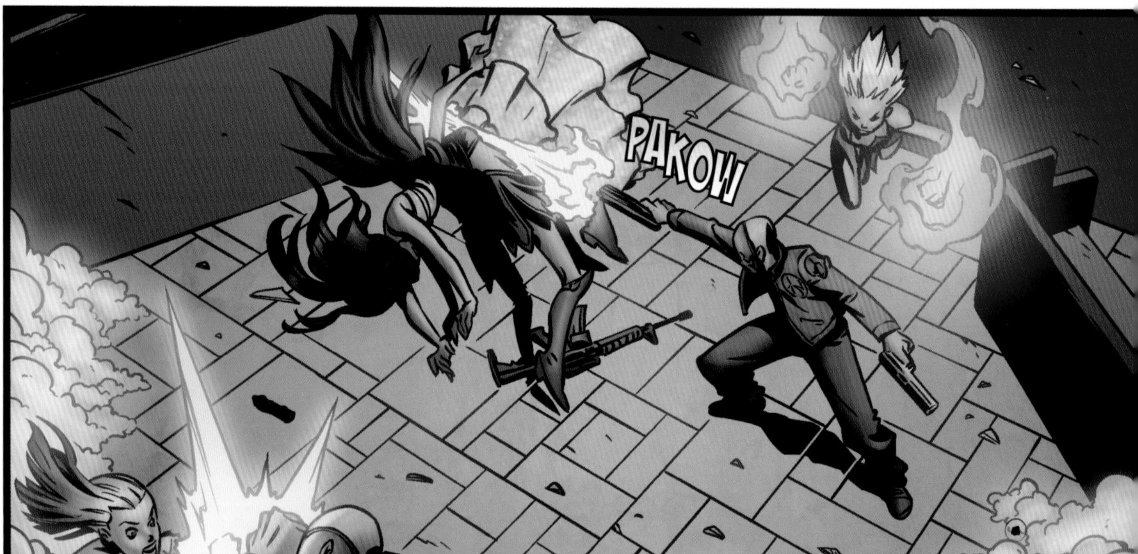
PAKOW

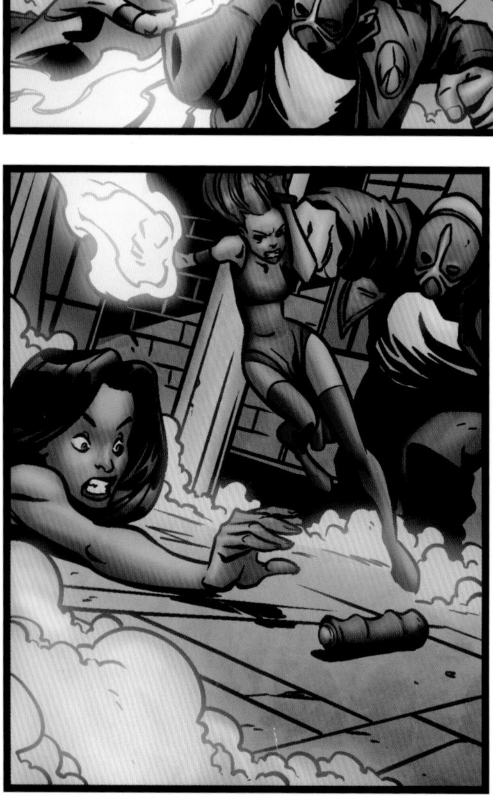

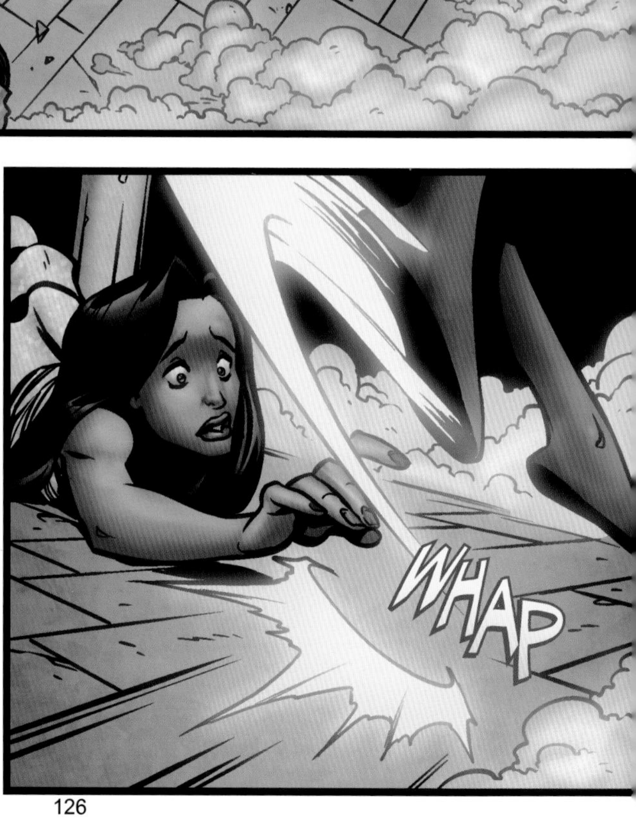
WHAP

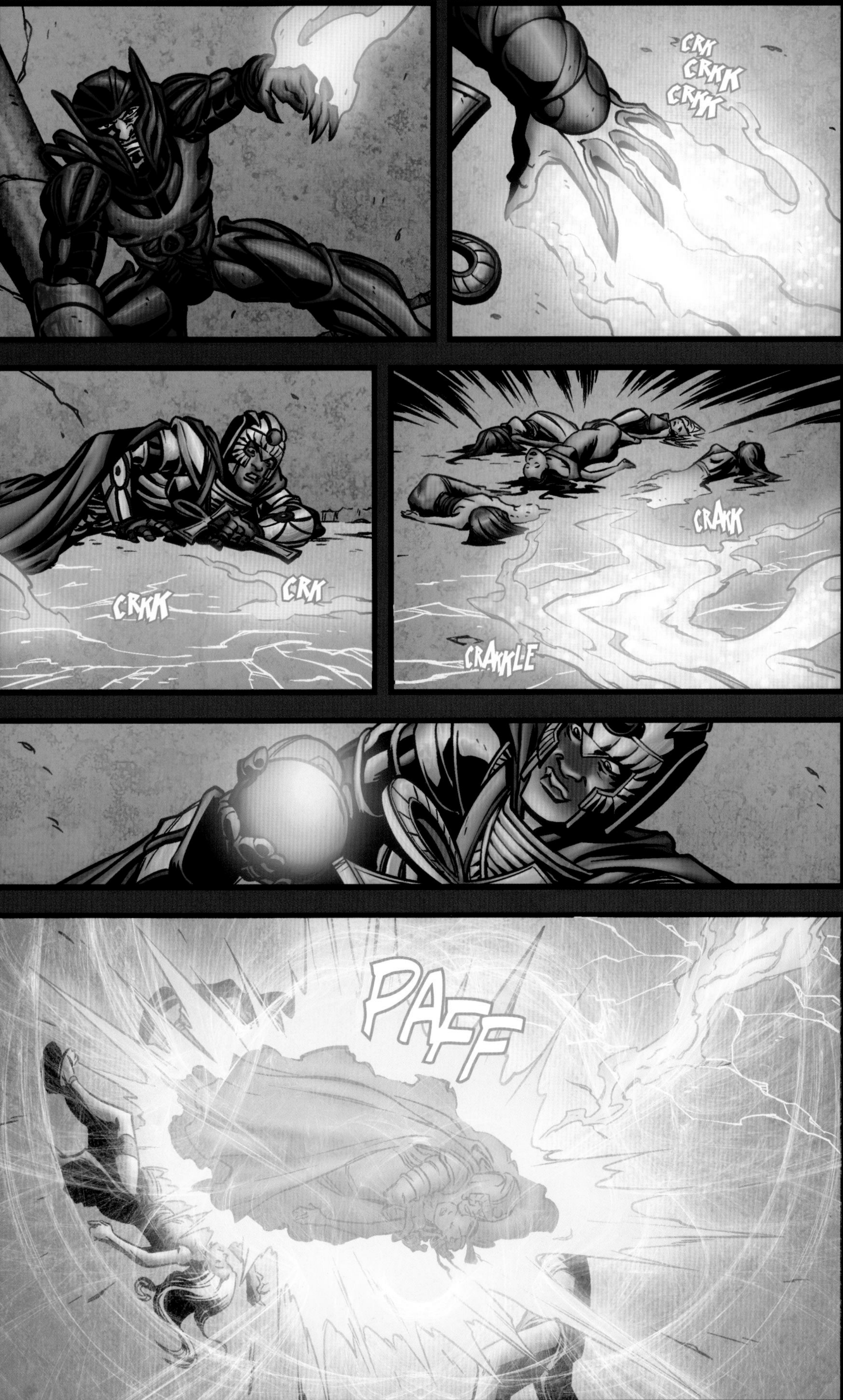
CRK
CRKK
CRKK
CRKK
CRK
CRAKK
CRAKKLE
PAFF

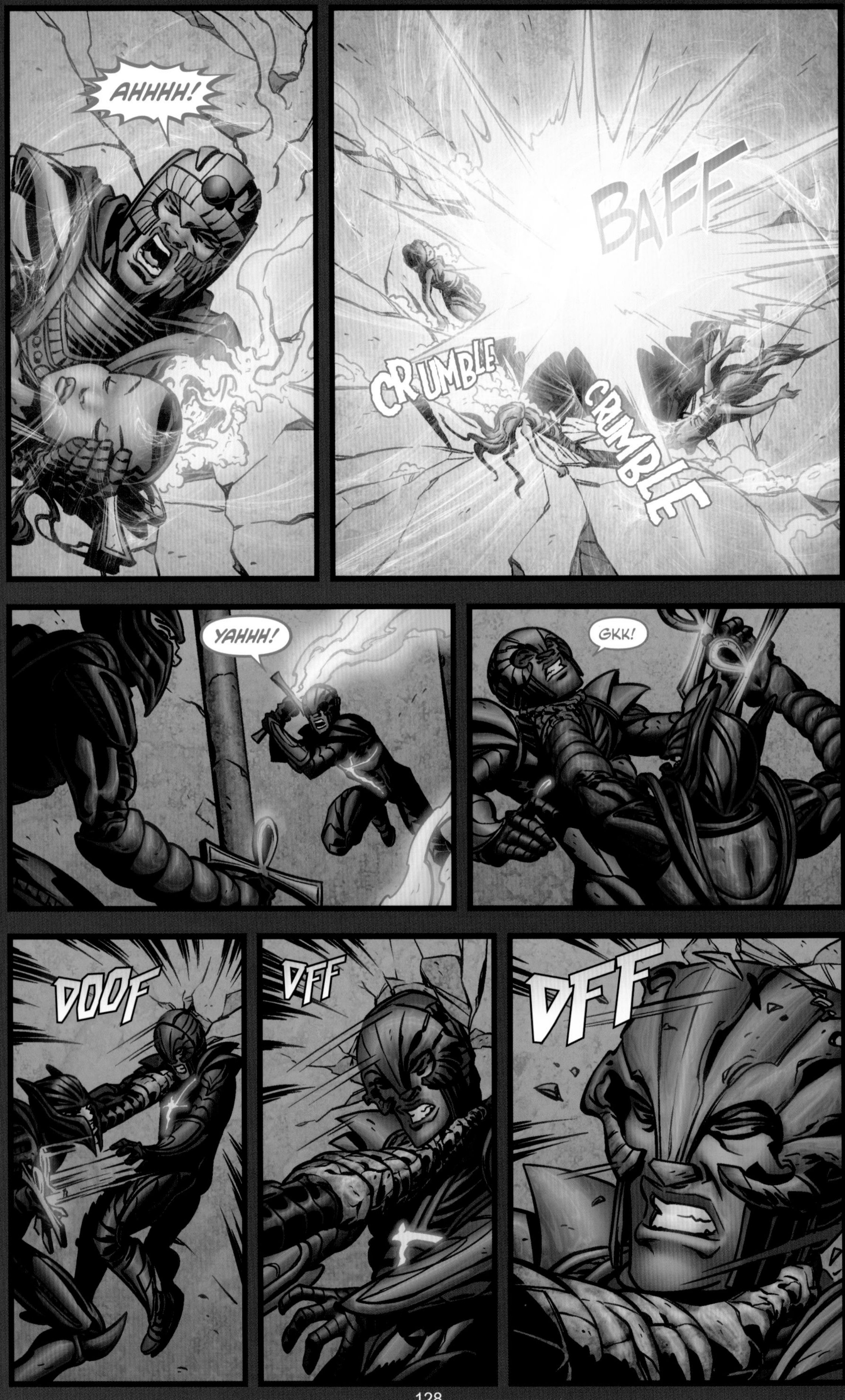
AHHHH!
BAFF
CRUMBLE
CRUMBLE
YAHHH!
GKK!
DOOF
DFF
DFF

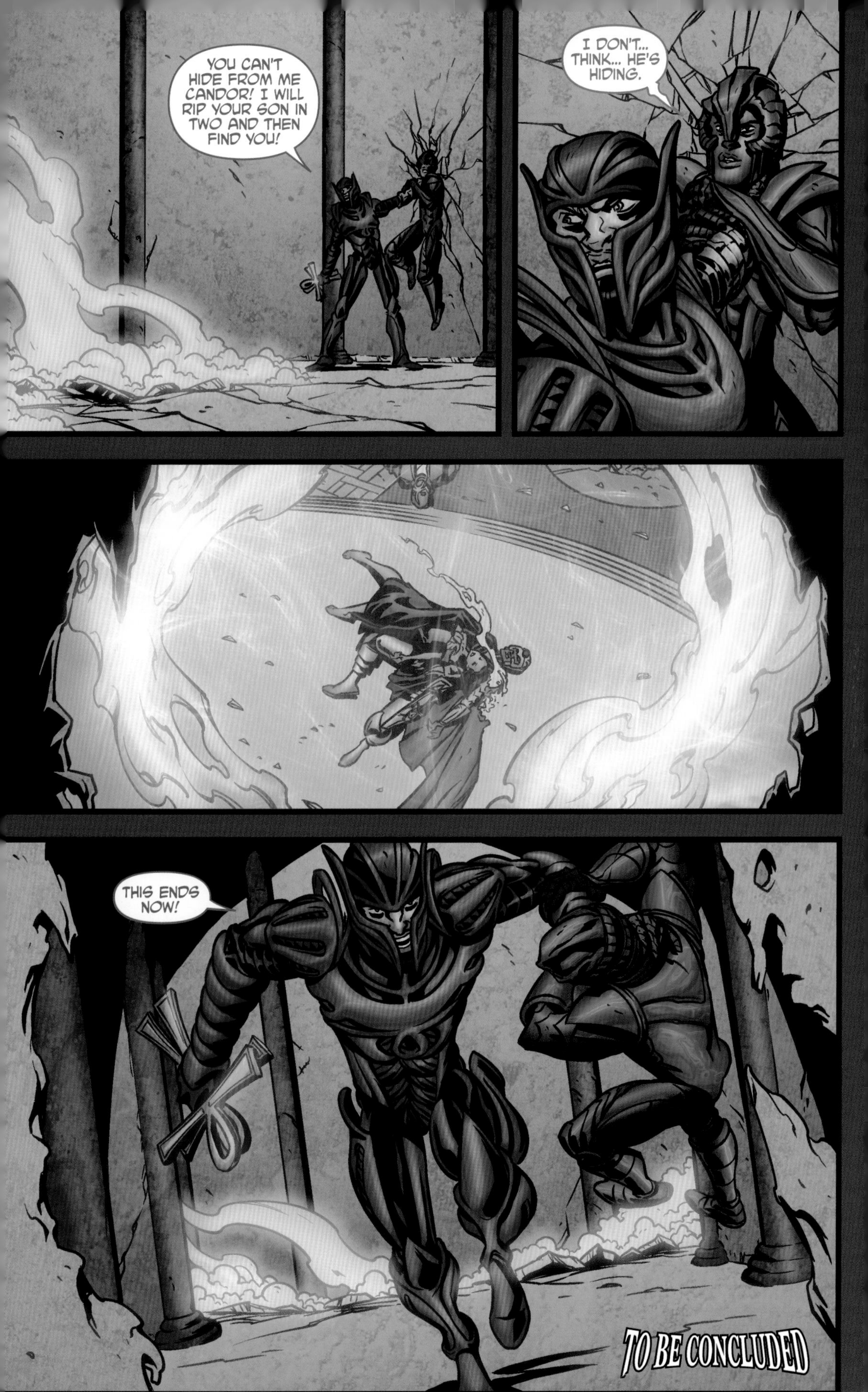
YOU CAN'T HIDE FROM ME CANDOR! I WILL RIP YOUR SON IN TWO AND THEN FIND YOU!
I DON'T... THINK... HE'S HIDING.
THIS ENDS NOW!
TO BE CONCLUDED

CHAPTER 16

The Mantamaji knew there would be no day beyond this one, and this day was bleak and terrible. They fought, therefore, not only with brute force, but with mind and soul and spirit, giving everything they had inside them. For on the last day of your life, why hide two coins beneath your pillow? What good is tomorrow's bread?

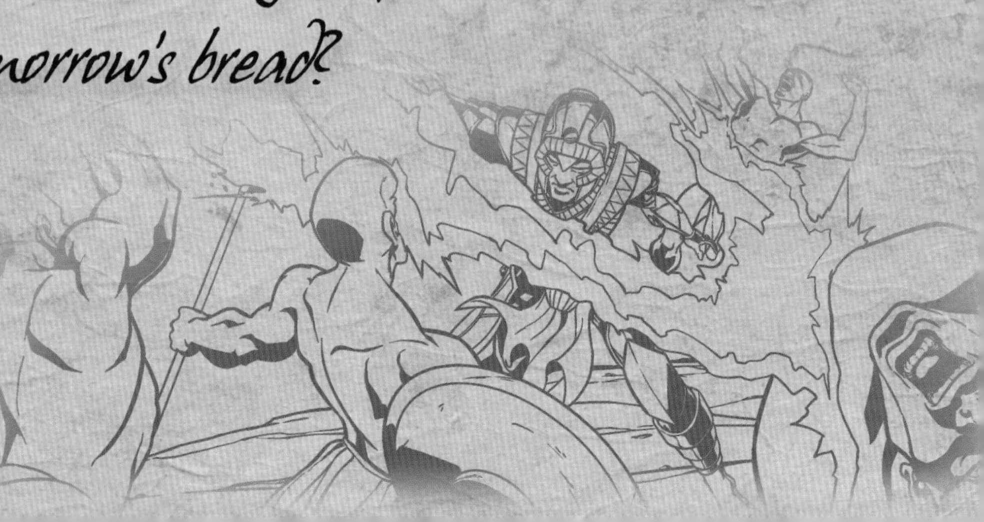

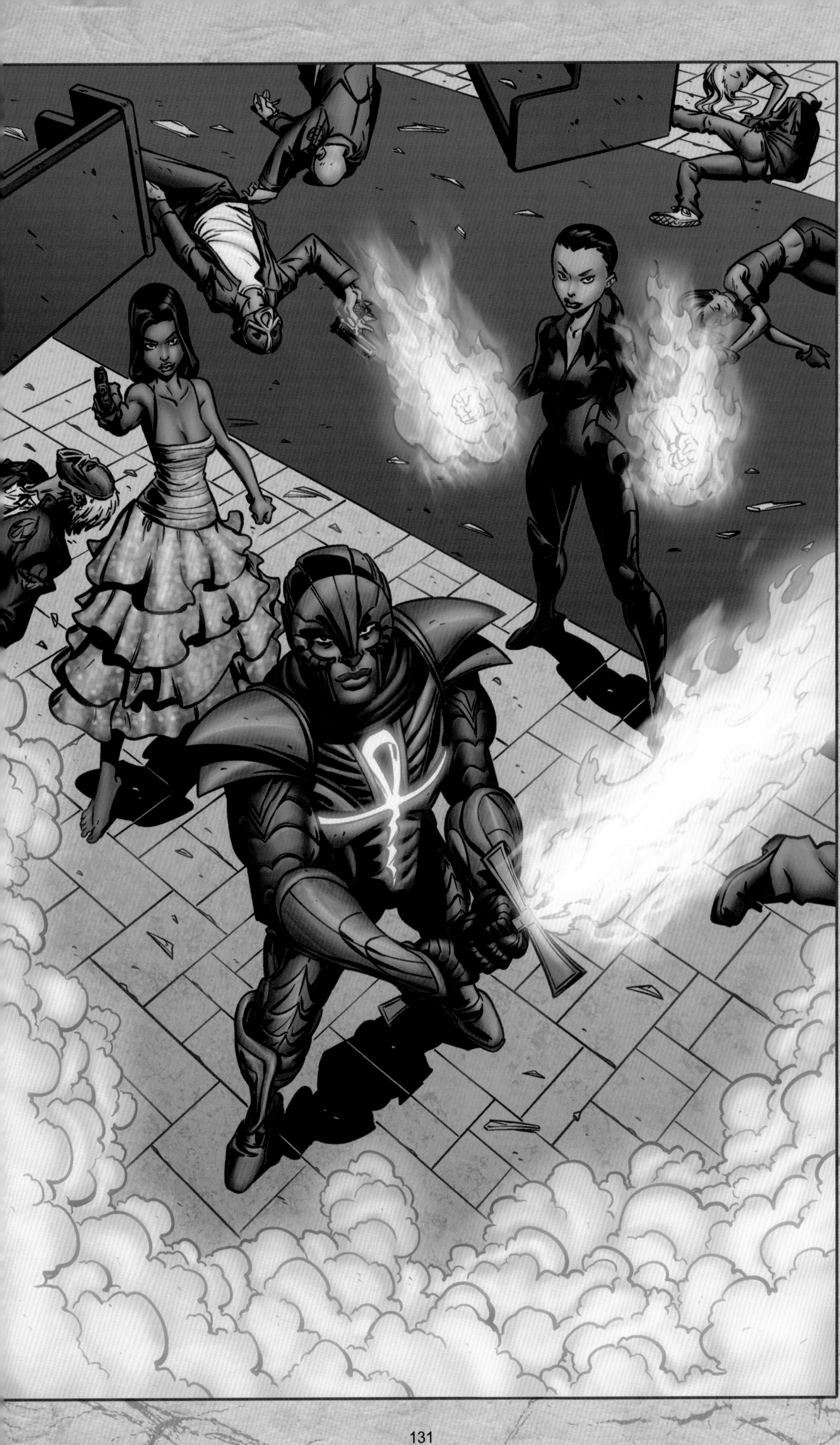

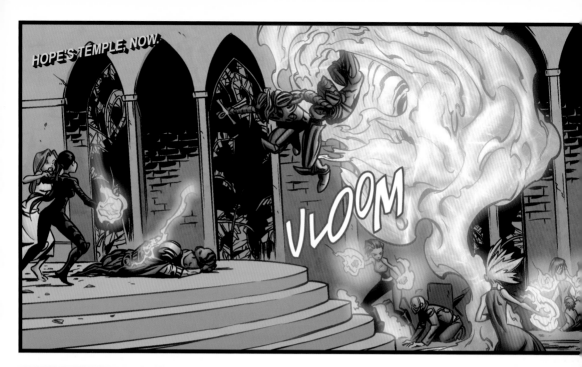

VLOOM

ENOUGH OF THE GAMES. THE PAST, THE FUTURE. I CONTROL IT ALL.

LET HIM GO OR I'LL PAINT THE WALLS WITH YOUR WIFE'S BRAINS.

IF YOU KILL HER, SILLY GIRL, I WILL SIMPLY GO BACK TO AN EARLIER TIME AND BRING HER HERE AGAIN.

KNIGHTS, ON YOUR FEET! SURROUND THEM.

DON'T LISTEN TO HIM.

CLK

MY KNIGHTS, I WILL GIVE YOU GLORY OVER ALL THESE MEN, *KINGDOMS* YOU CAN RULE.

CANDOR, THIS IS WHAT IT LOOKS LIKE TO WATCH SOMEONE YOU LOVE DIE.

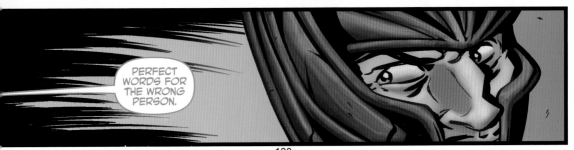

PERFECT WORDS FOR THE WRONG PERSON.

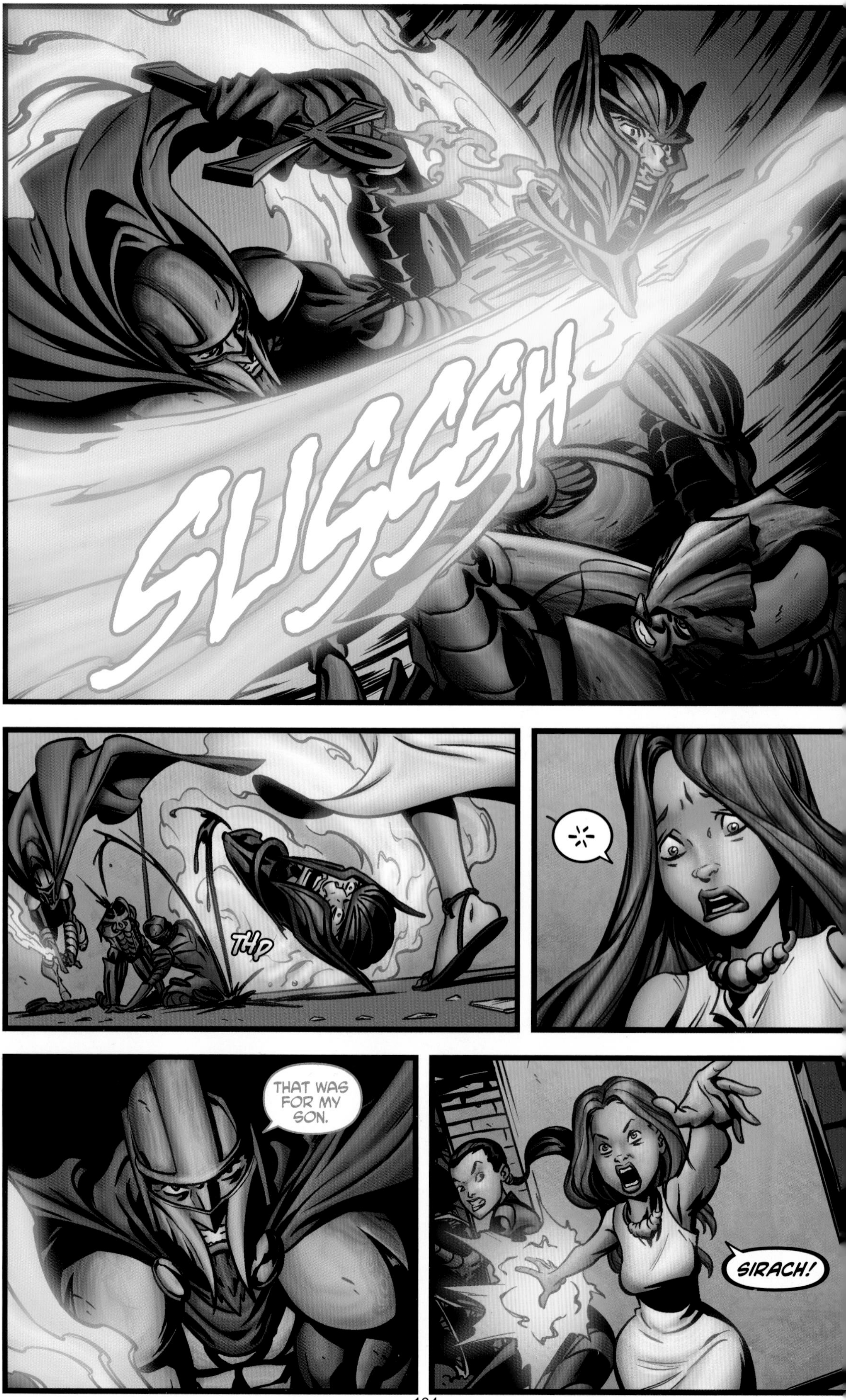
SUSSSH
THD
THAT WAS FOR MY SON.
SIRACH!

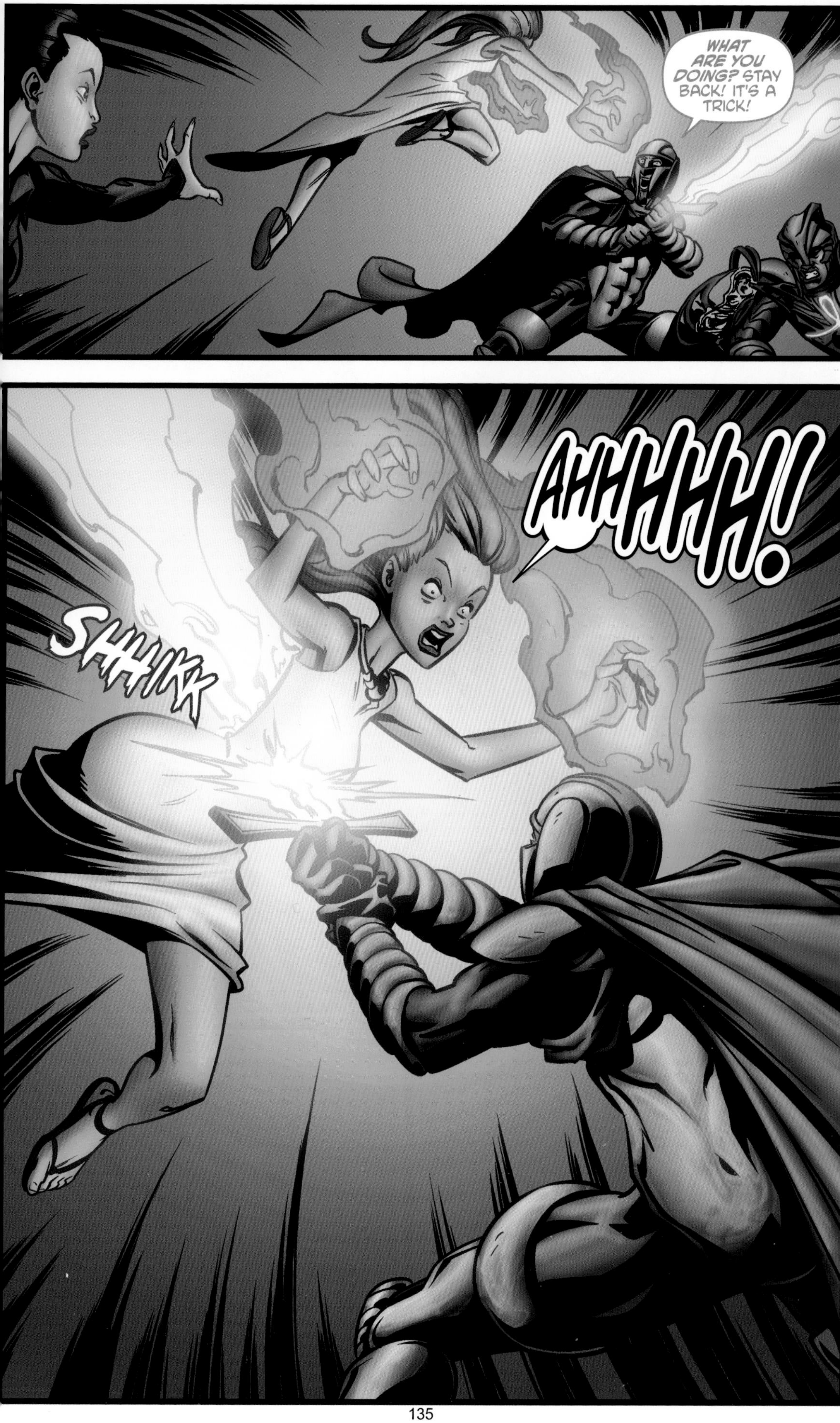
WHAT ARE YOU DOING? STAY BACK! IT'S A TRICK!
SHHIKK
AHHHHH!

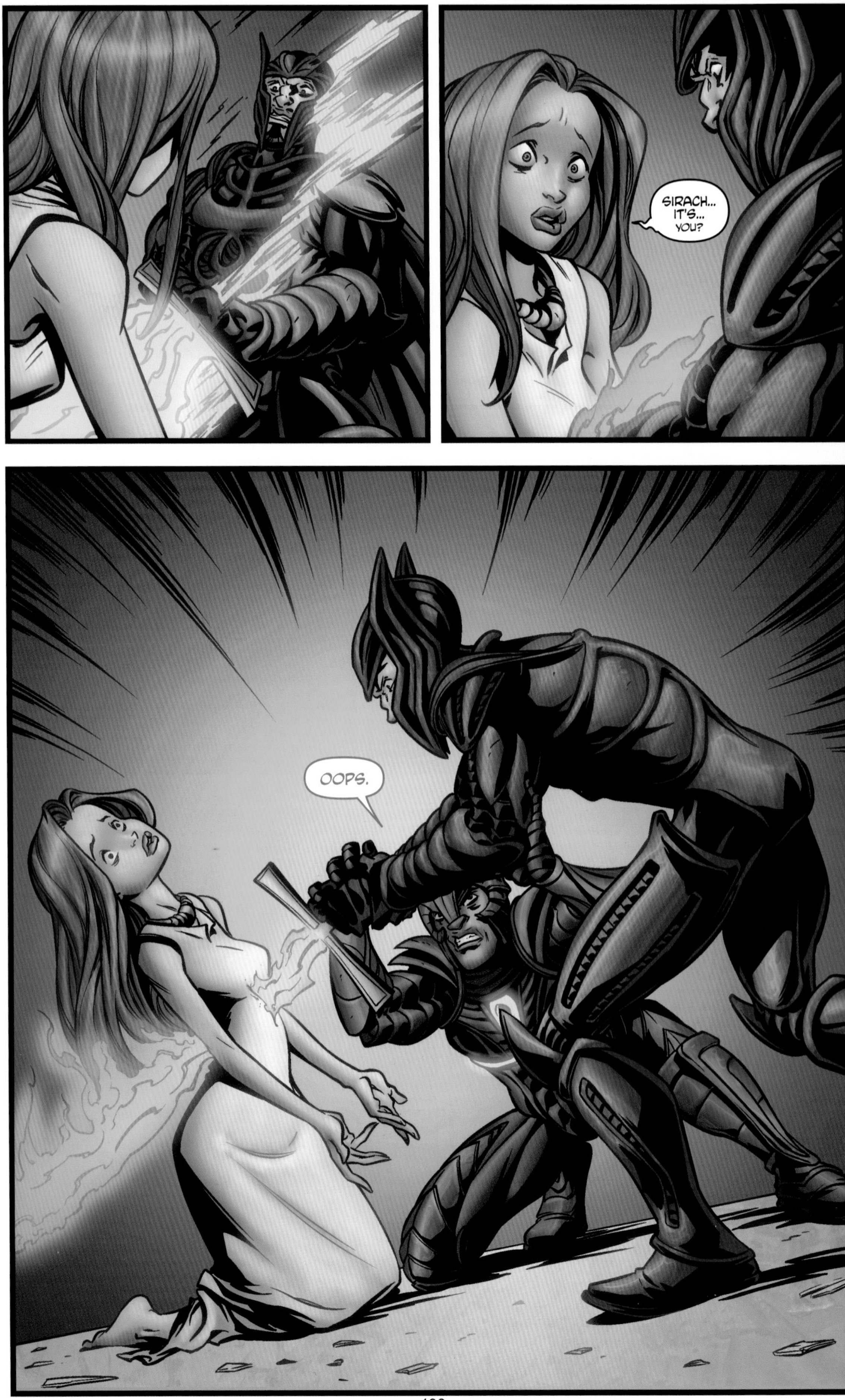
SIRACH... IT'S... YOU?
OOPS.

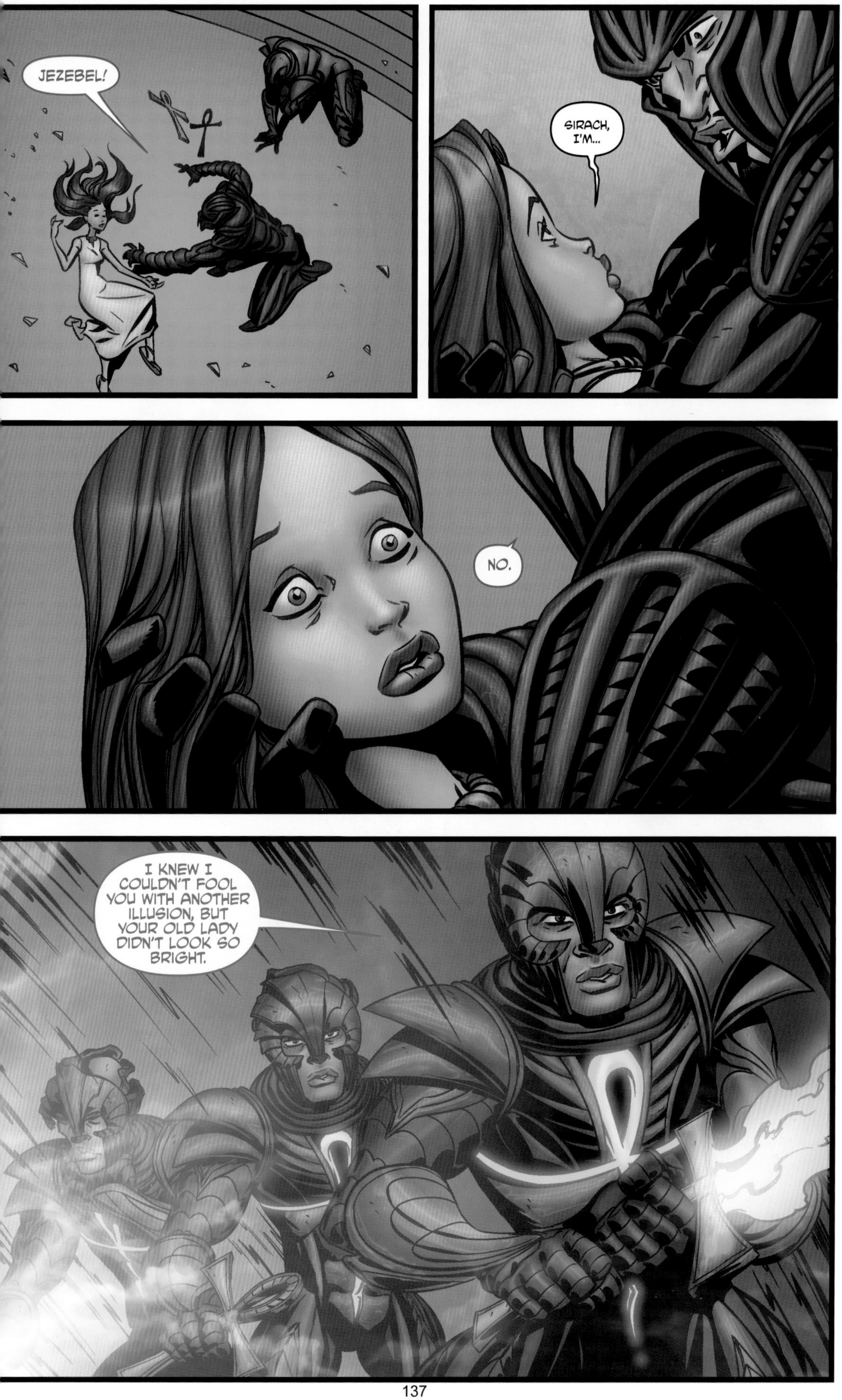
JEZEBEL!
SIRACH, I'M...
NO.
I KNEW I COULDN'T FOOL YOU WITH ANOTHER ILLUSION, BUT YOUR OLD LADY DIDN'T LOOK SO BRIGHT.

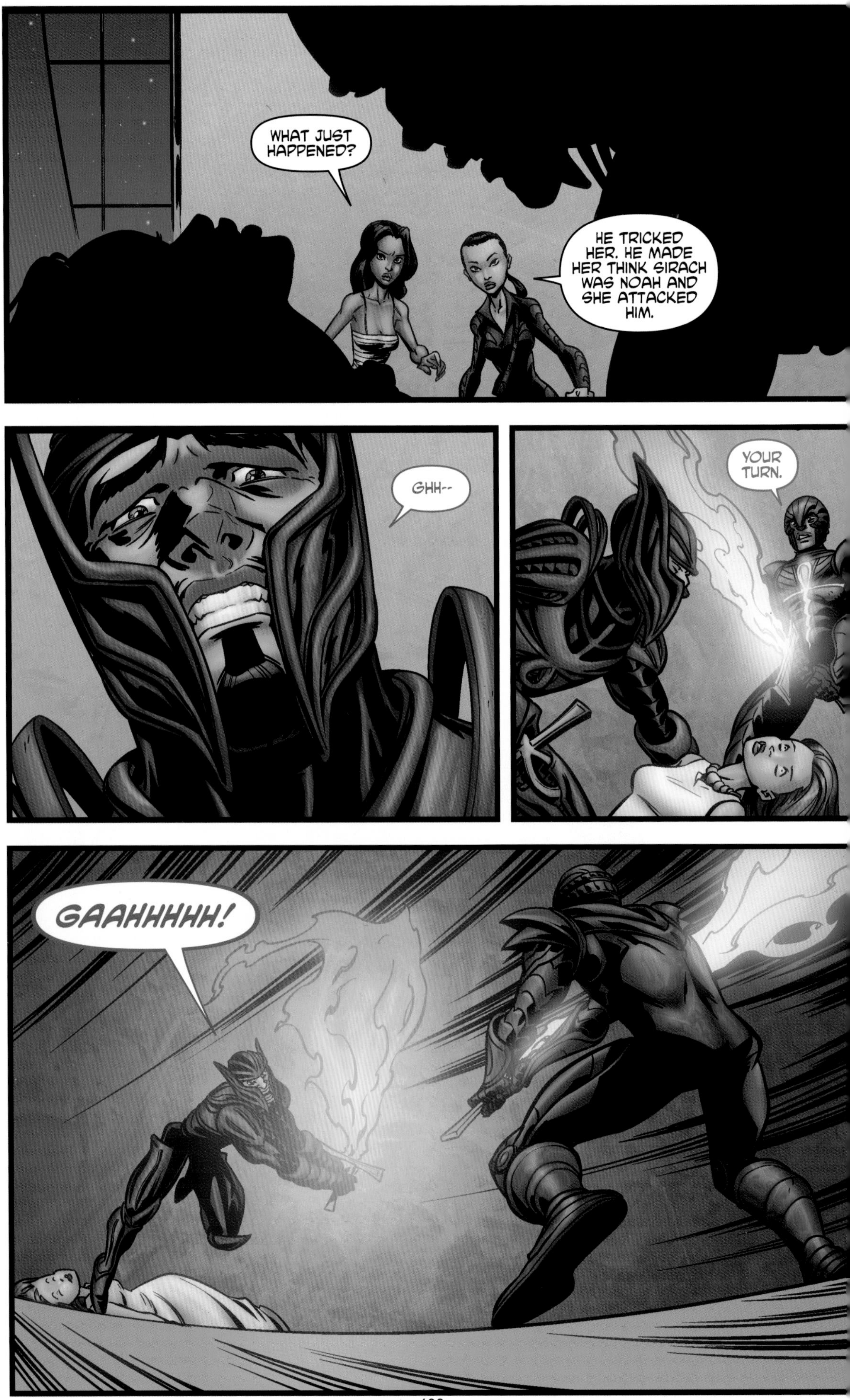
WHAT JUST HAPPENED?
HE TRICKED HER. HE MADE HER THINK SIRACH WAS NOAH AND SHE ATTACKED HIM.
GHH--
YOUR TURN.
GAAHHHHH!

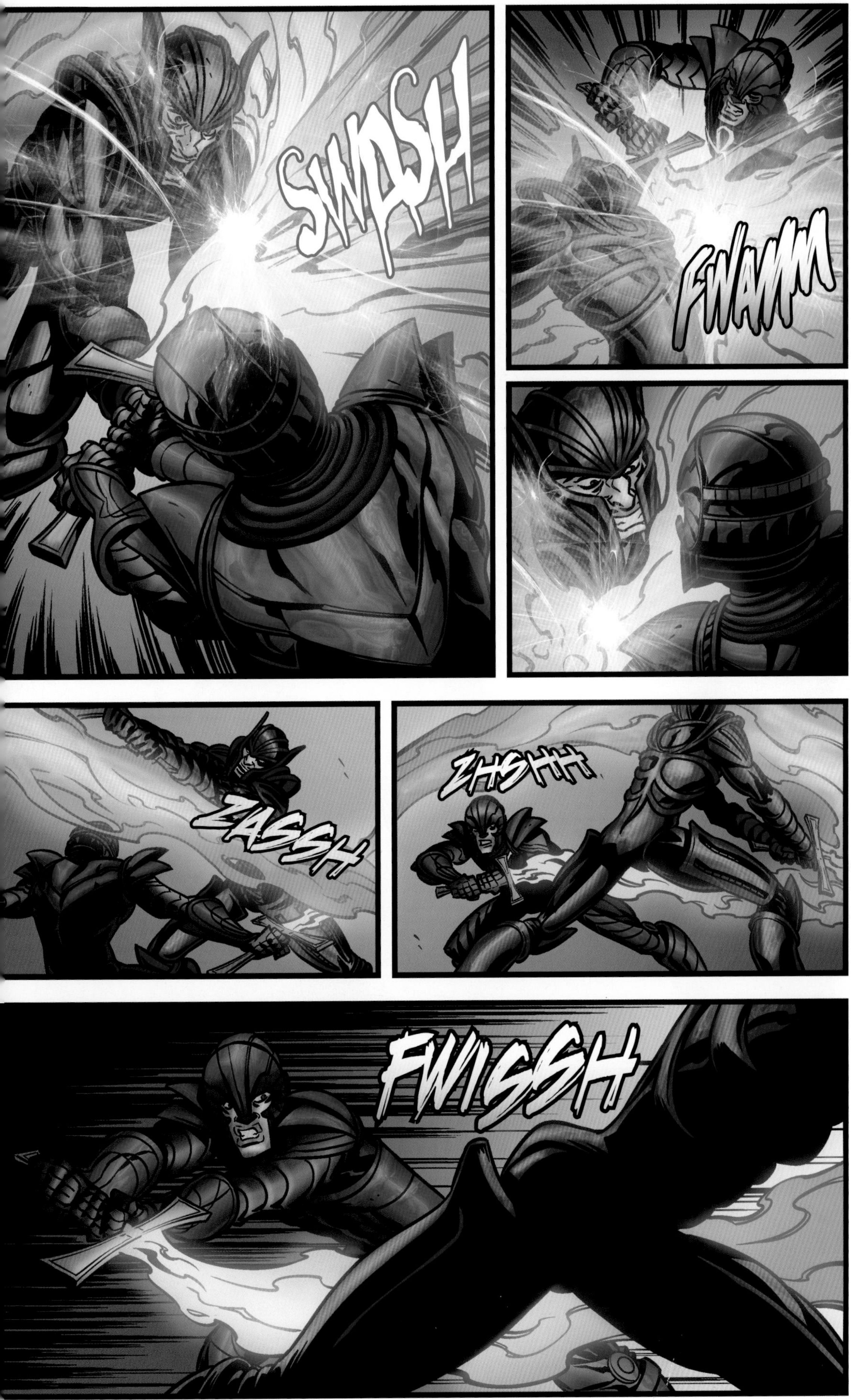
SWOSH
FWAMM
ZASSH
ZHSHH
FWISSH

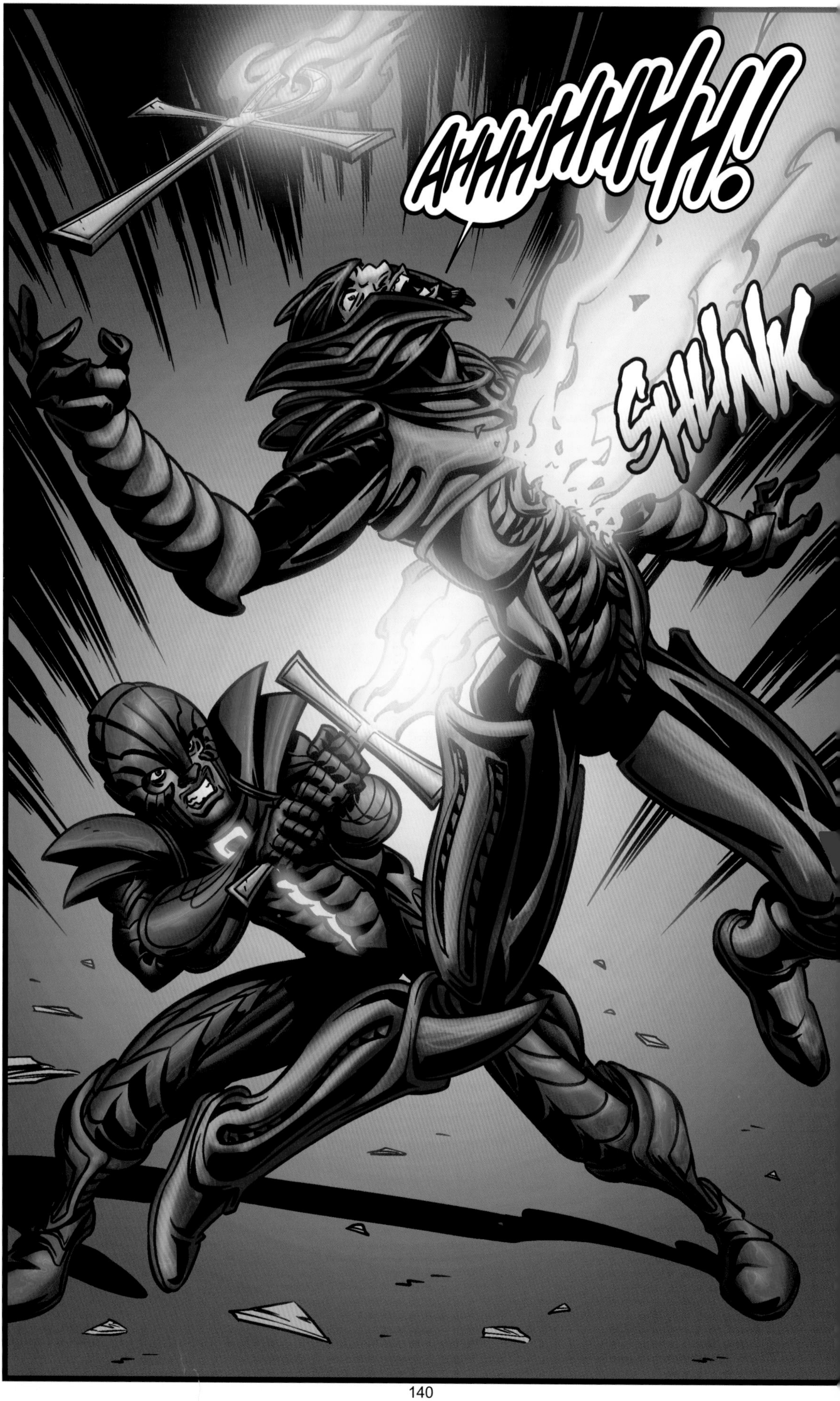
AHHHHHHHH!
SHUNK

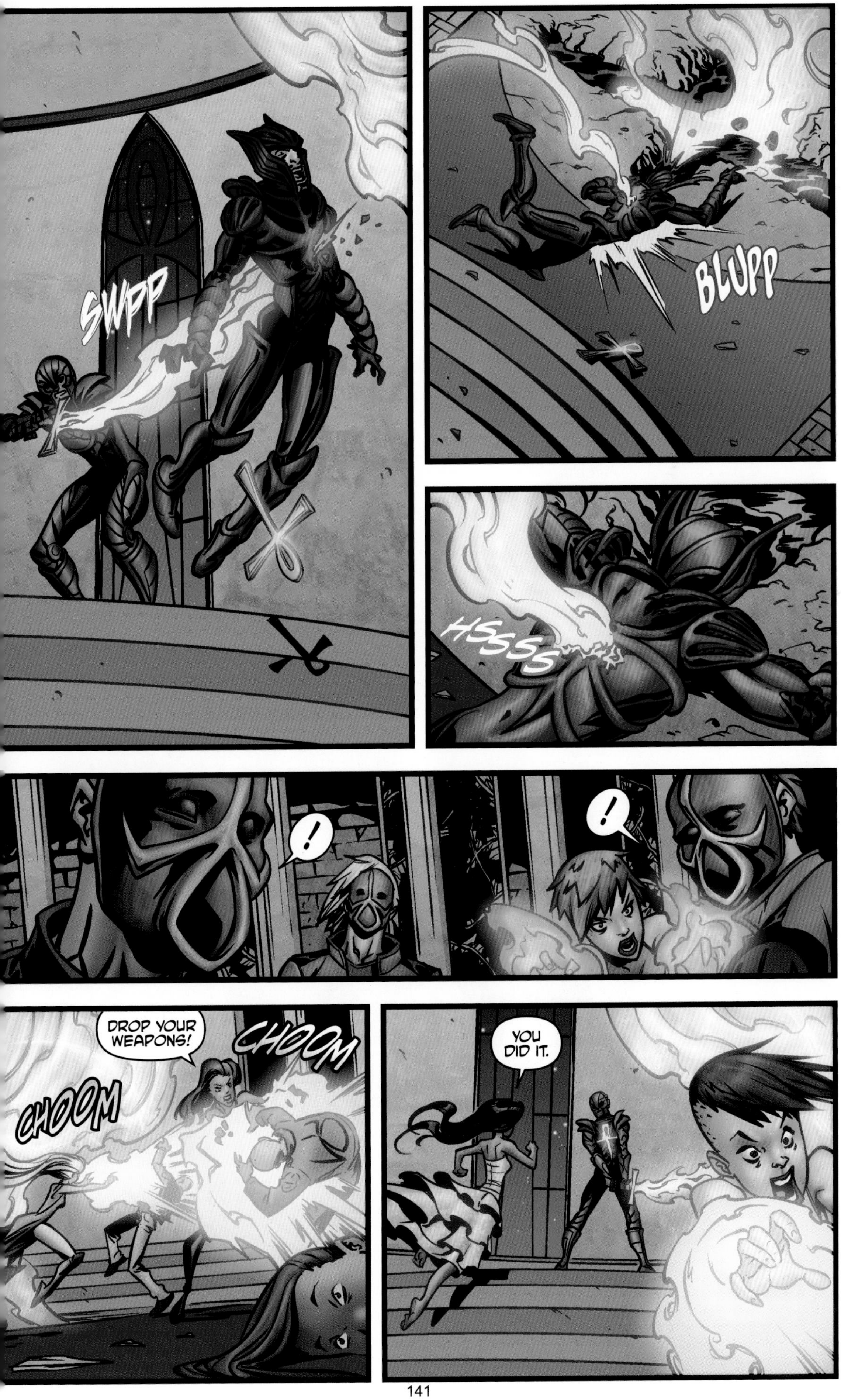

SWPP
BLUPP
HSSSS
!
!
DROP YOUR WEAPONS!
CHOOM
CHOOM
YOU DID IT.

YOU DEFEATED HIM.

HE'S NOT DEAD, JUST DOWN.

NICELY DONE. YOU USED HIS RAGE AGAINST HIM.

HE'S BEEN DOING THAT TO ME FOR A WEEK. ANY IDEA ON HOW TO MAKE THIS MORE PERMANENT?

IF SIRACH HAS BEEN LIVING BETWEEN TWO TIME PERIODS, IT MAY BE POSSIBLE TO TRAP HIM IN TIME ITSELF.

HOW?

THE GEM ALLOWS US TO TRAVEL THROUGH TIME AND SPACE, BUT IT HAS NEVER BEEN STRETCHED SO FAR BEFORE.

RIGHT NOW, SIRACH'S POWER—HIS WILL, HIS MAGIC TECHNOLOGY—ARE KEEPING IT OPEN. IF YOU USE YOUR MANTAMAJI POWER TO SLAM IT SHUT, THE CONNECTION COULD SNAP BACK LIKE A BOWSTRING, AND TRAP HIM INSIDE.

BUT HOW DO I SNAP BACK TIME?

TIME *WANTS* TO BE RESTORED TO NORMAL.

JUST LISTEN TO THE CRYSTAL, FIND ITS STRESS POINTS, AND PULL WHERE SIRACH IS PUSHING THE HARDEST.

YOU CAN DO THIS. IT'S MY CRYSTAL, AND YOU'RE MY SON.

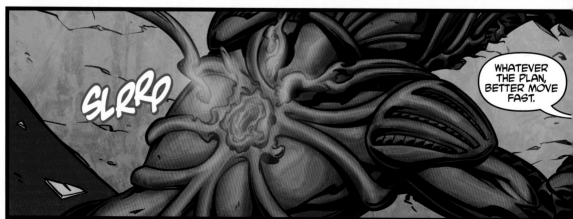

SLRRP

WHATEVER THE PLAN, BETTER MOVE FAST.

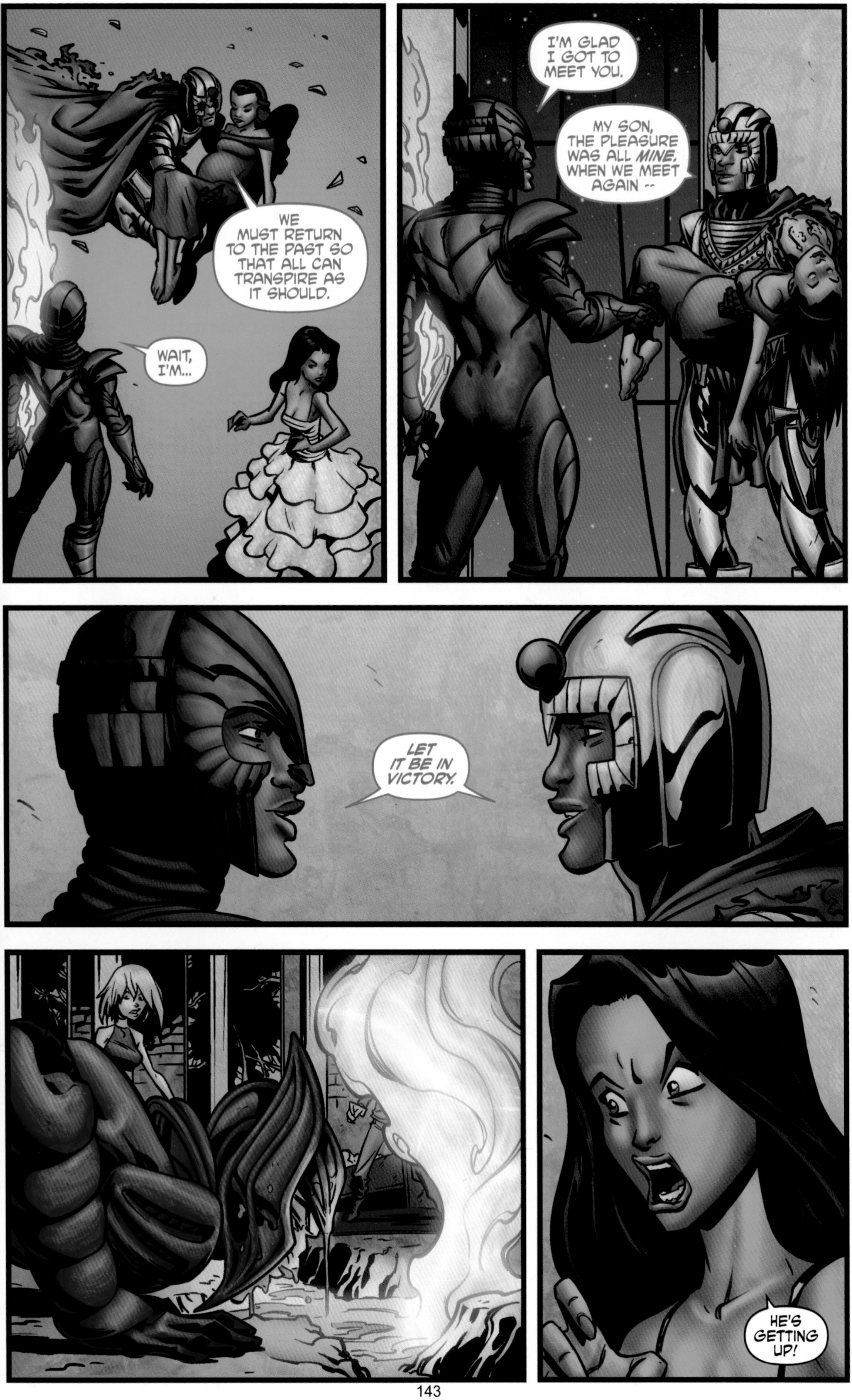
WE MUST RETURN TO THE PAST SO THAT ALL CAN TRANSPIRE AS IT SHOULD.
WAIT, I'M...
I'M GLAD I GOT TO MEET YOU.
MY SON, THE PLEASURE WAS ALL *MINE.* WHEN WE MEET AGAIN --
LET IT BE IN VICTORY.
HE'S GETTING UP!

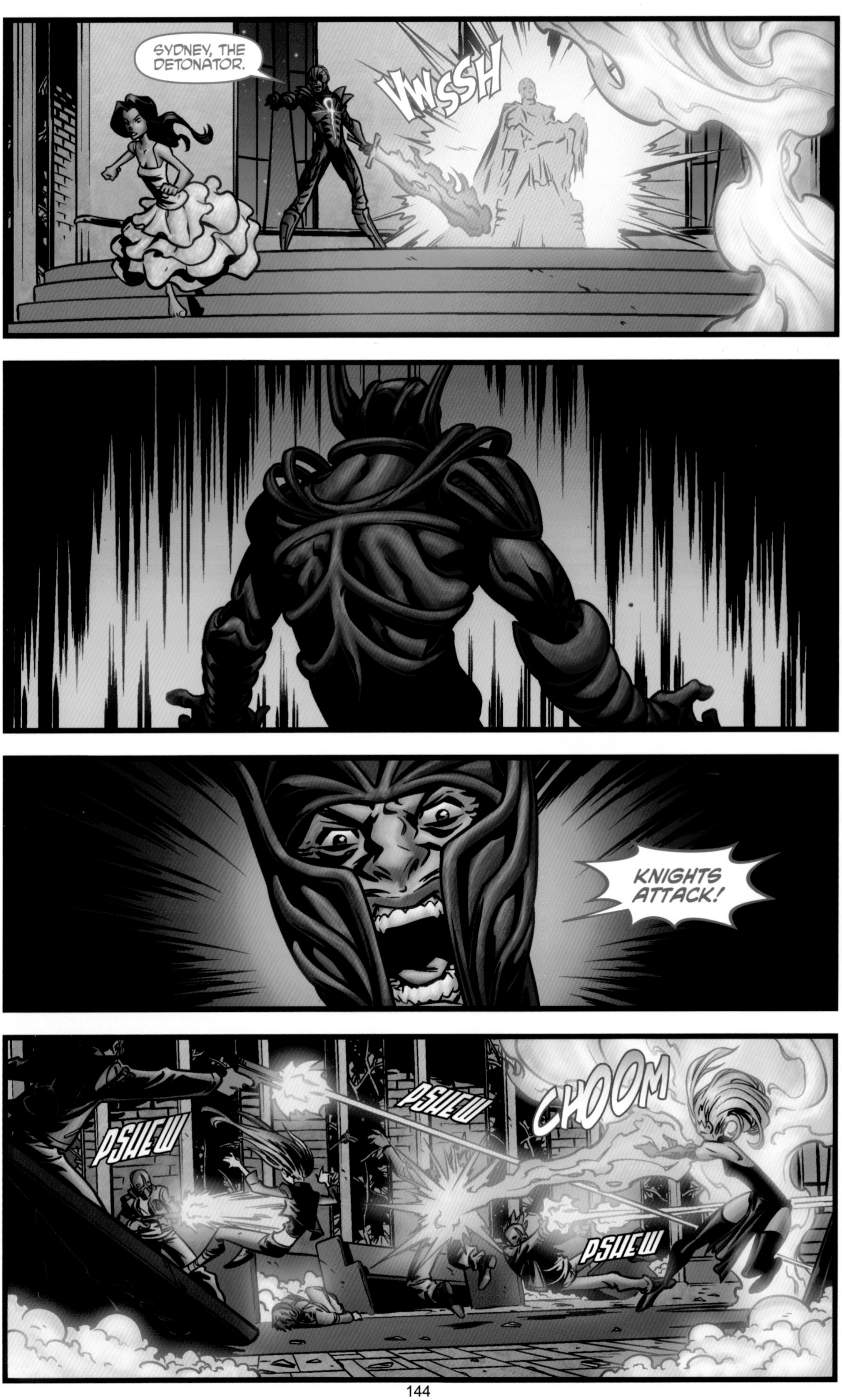
SYDNEY, THE DETONATOR.
VWSSH
KNIGHTS ATTACK!
PSHEW
PSHEW
CHOOM
PSHEW

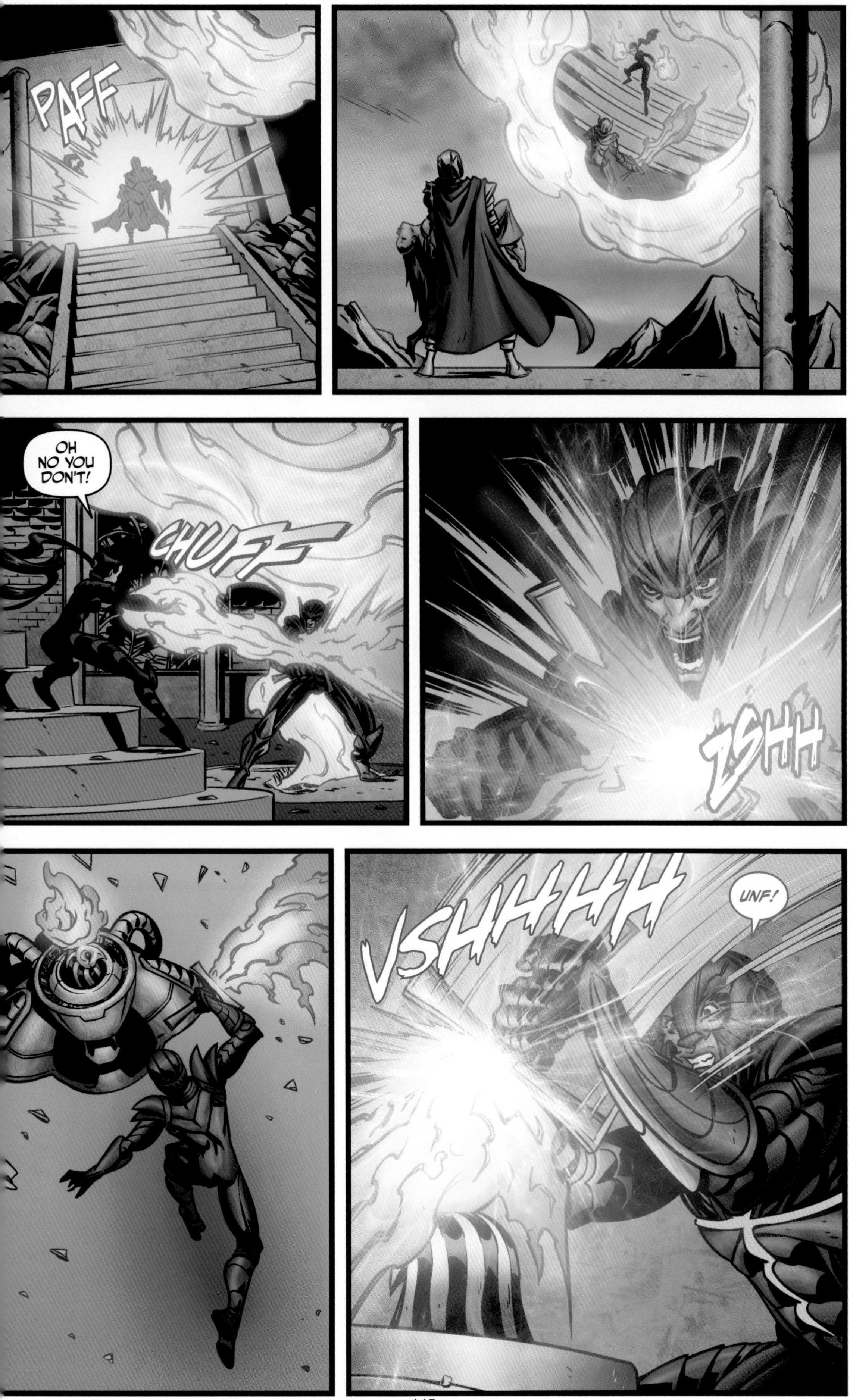
PAFF
OH NO YOU DON'T!
CHUFF
ZSHH
VSHHHH
UNF!

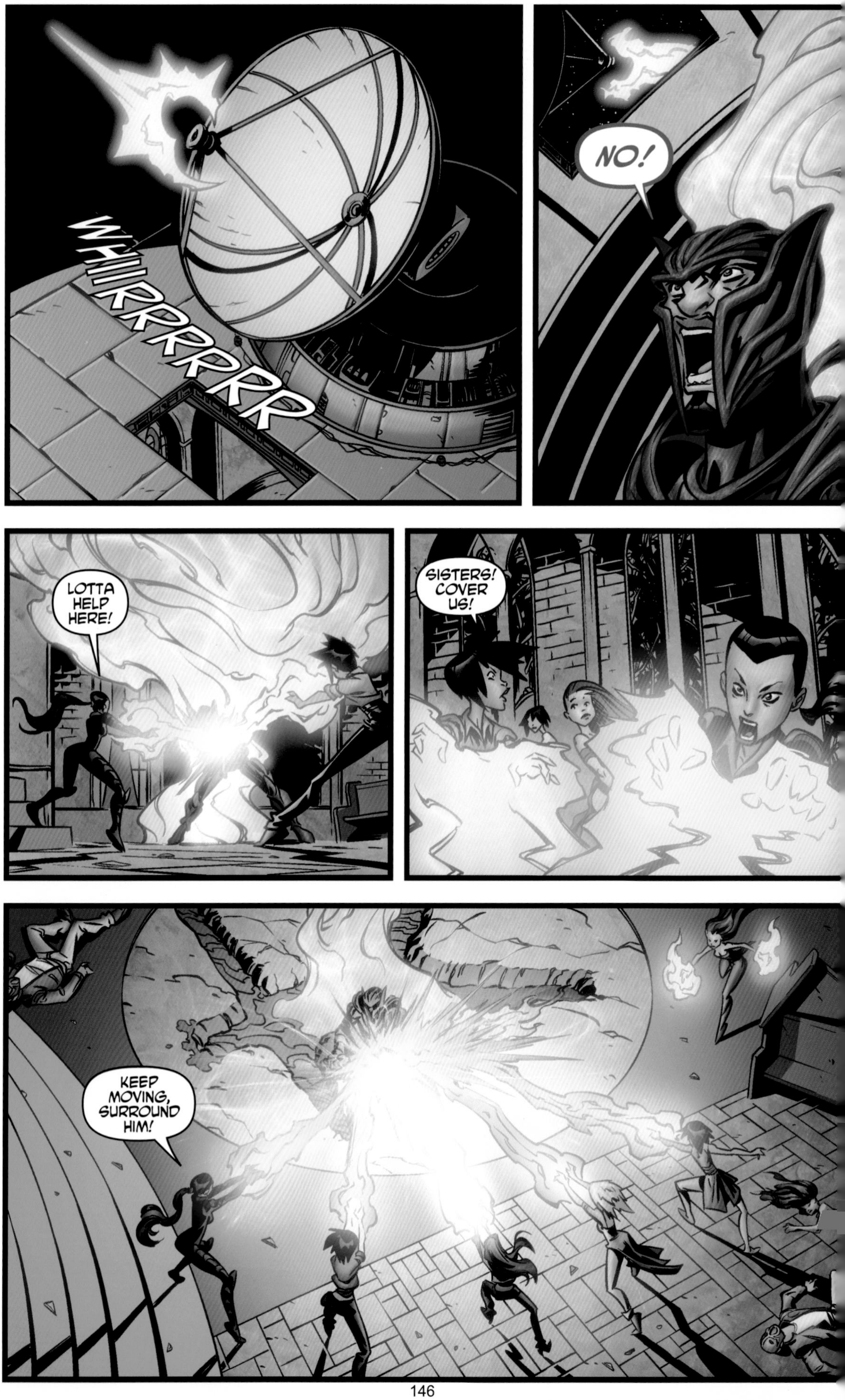
WHIRRRRRR
NO!
LOTTA HELP HERE!
SISTERS! COVER US!
KEEP MOVING, SURROUND HIM!

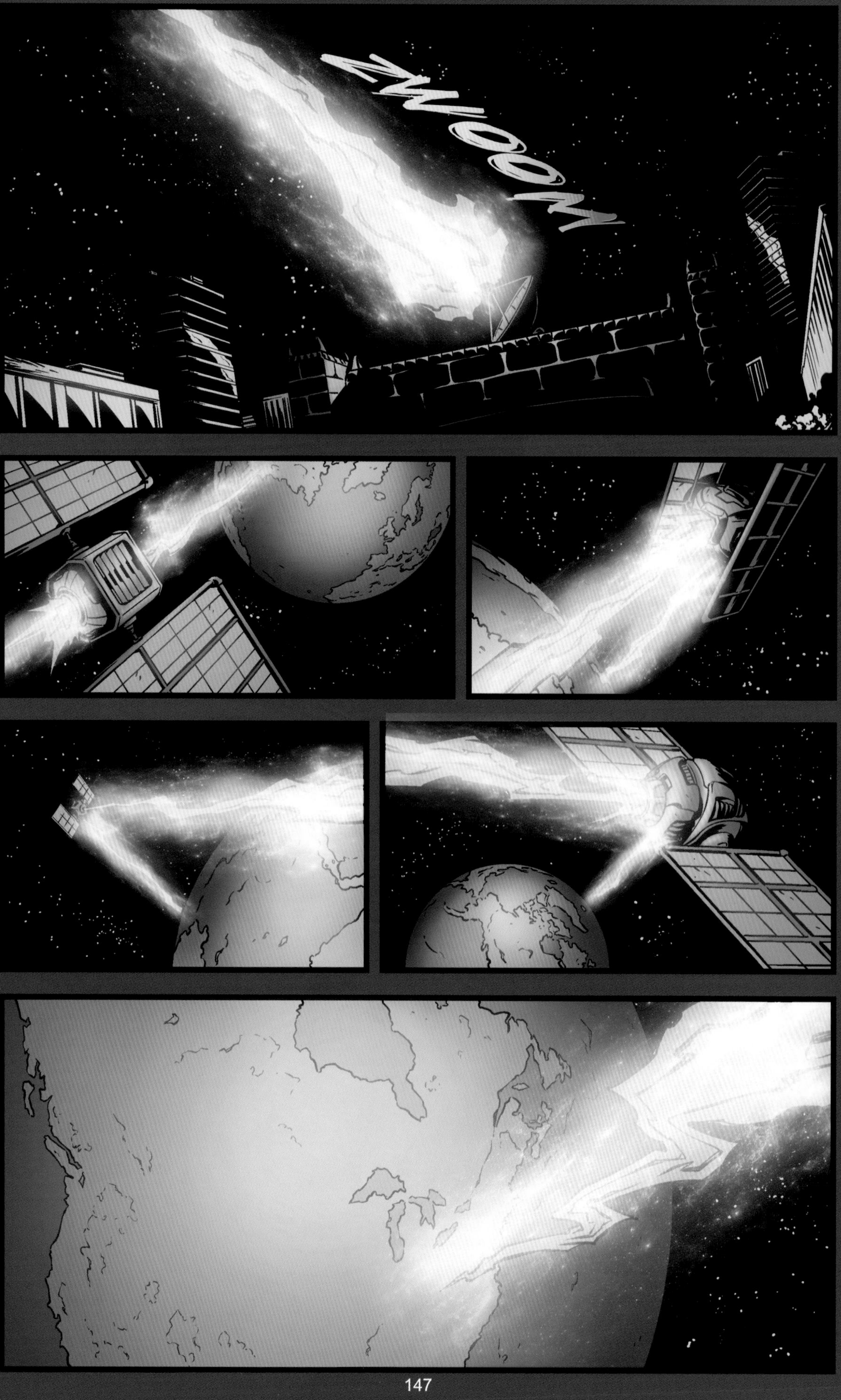
ZWOOM

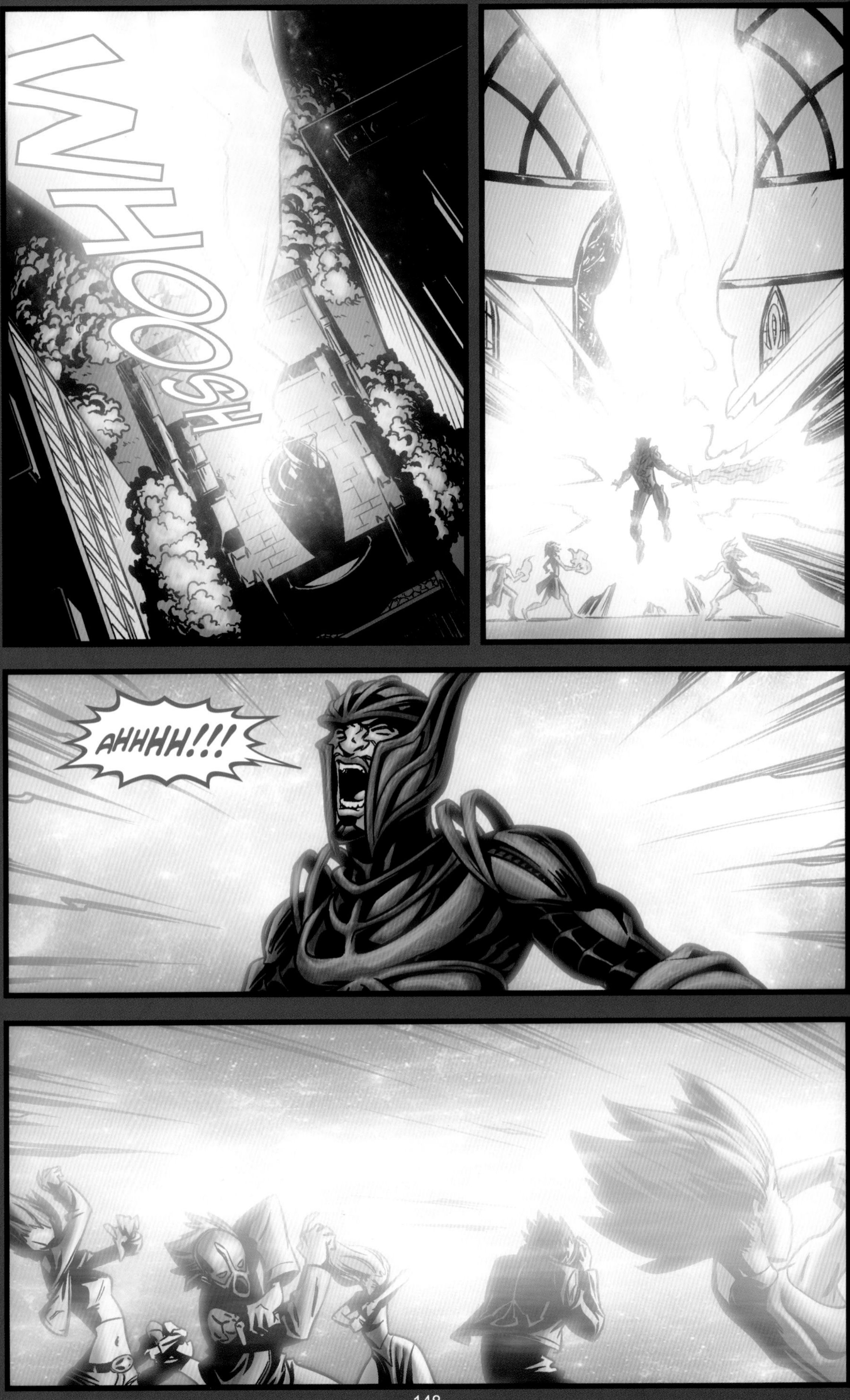
WHOOSH
AHHHH!!!

SHOOM
FWSSH
SHOOM

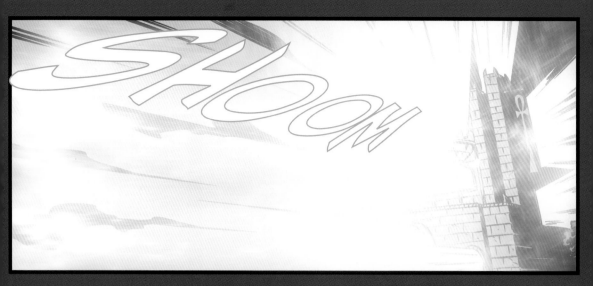

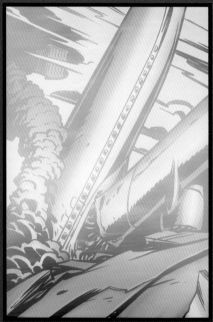

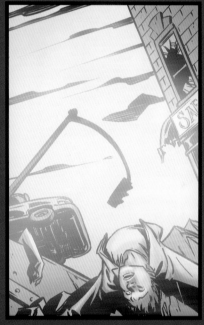

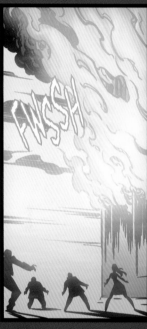

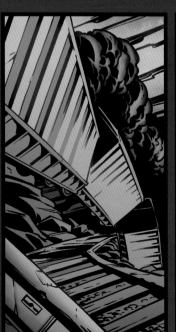

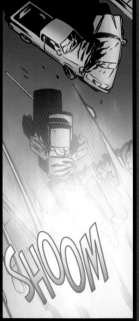

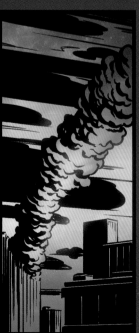

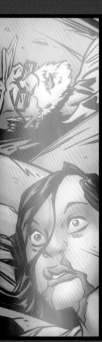

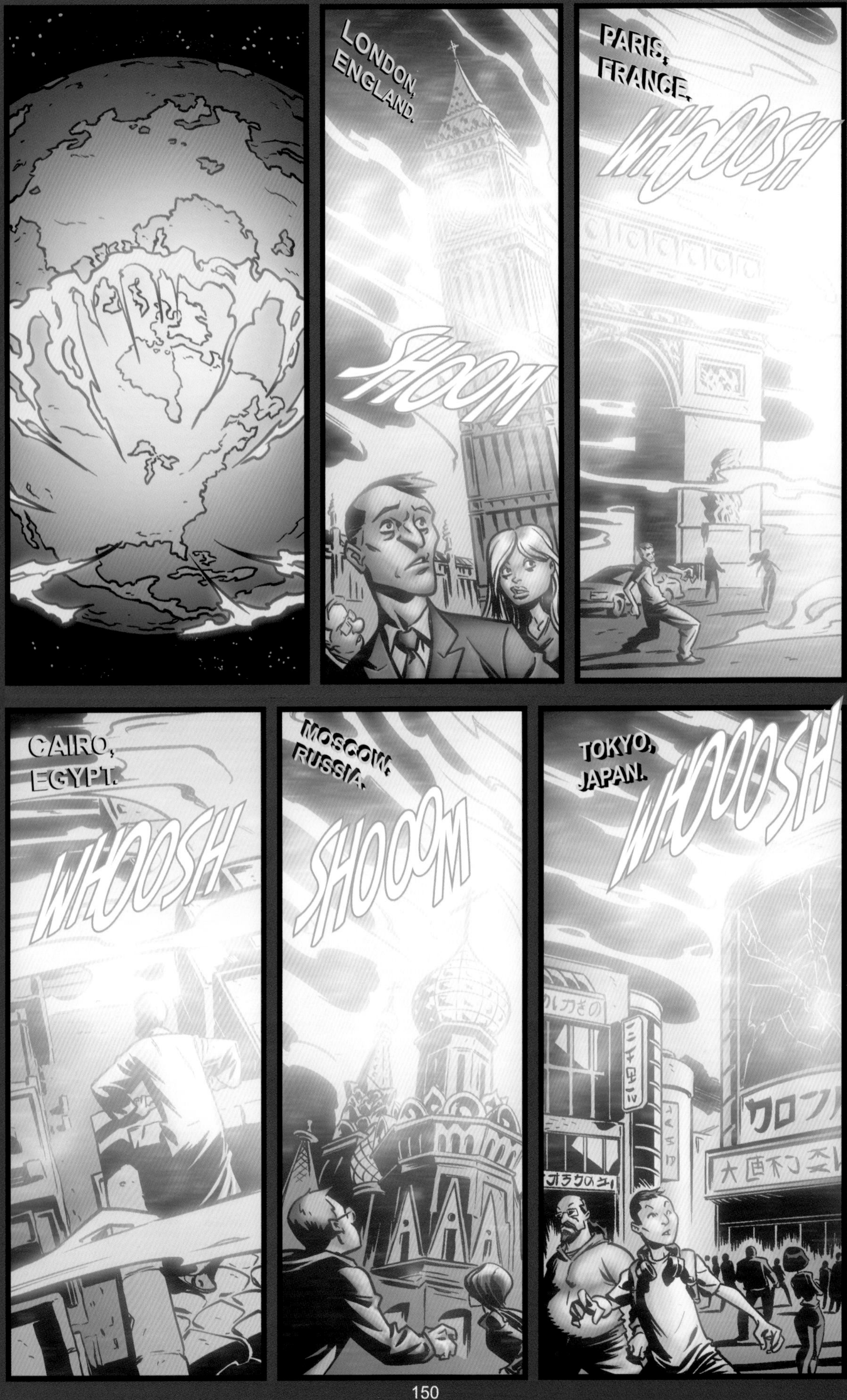

LONDON, ENGLAND.
SHOOM
PARIS, FRANCE.
WHOOOSH
CAIRO, EGYPT.
WHOOSH
MOSCOW, RUSSIA.
SHOOOM
TOKYO, JAPAN.
WHOOOSH

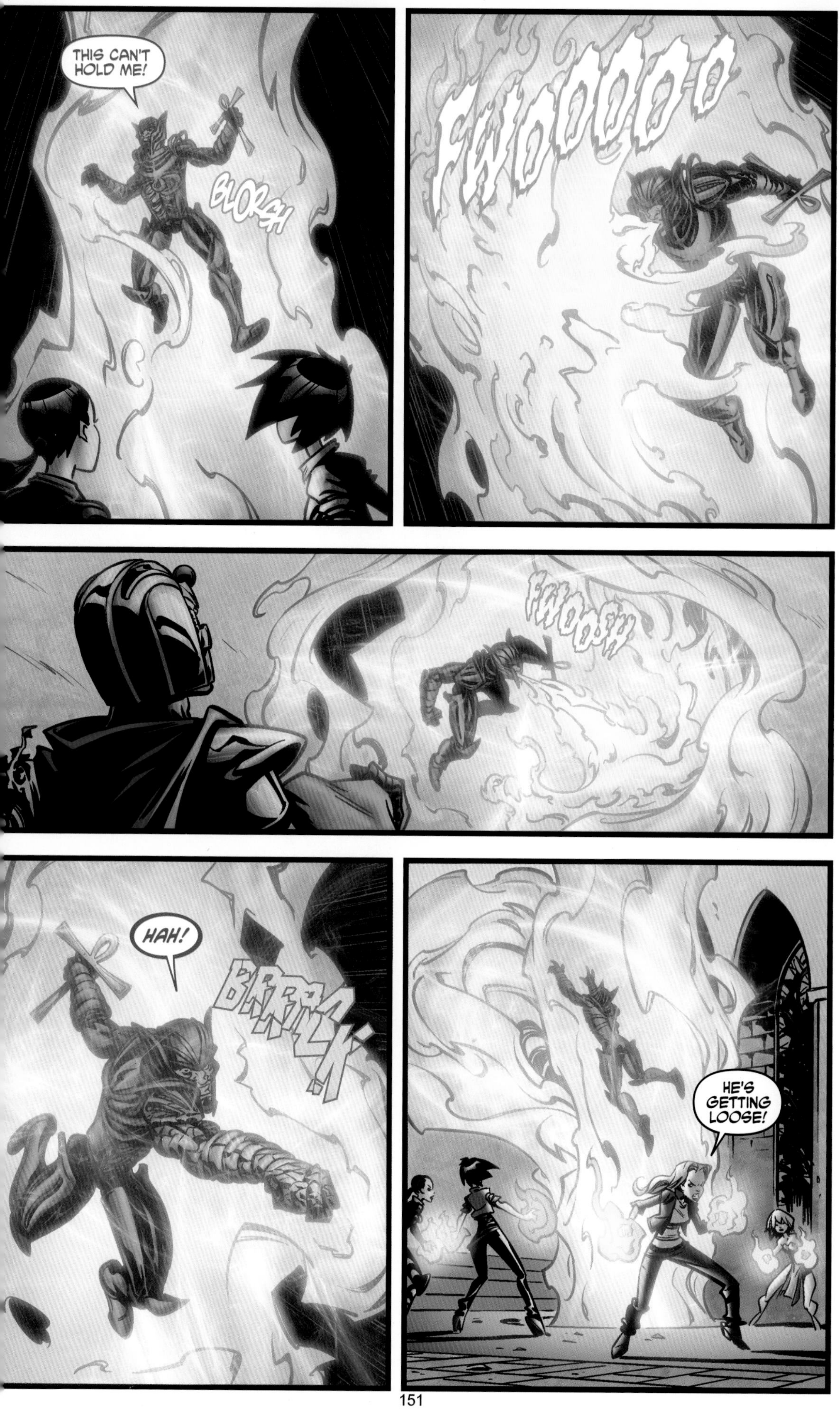
THIS CAN'T HOLD ME!
BLORSH
FWOOOOO
FWOOSH
HAH!
BRRRAK
HE'S GETTING LOOSE!

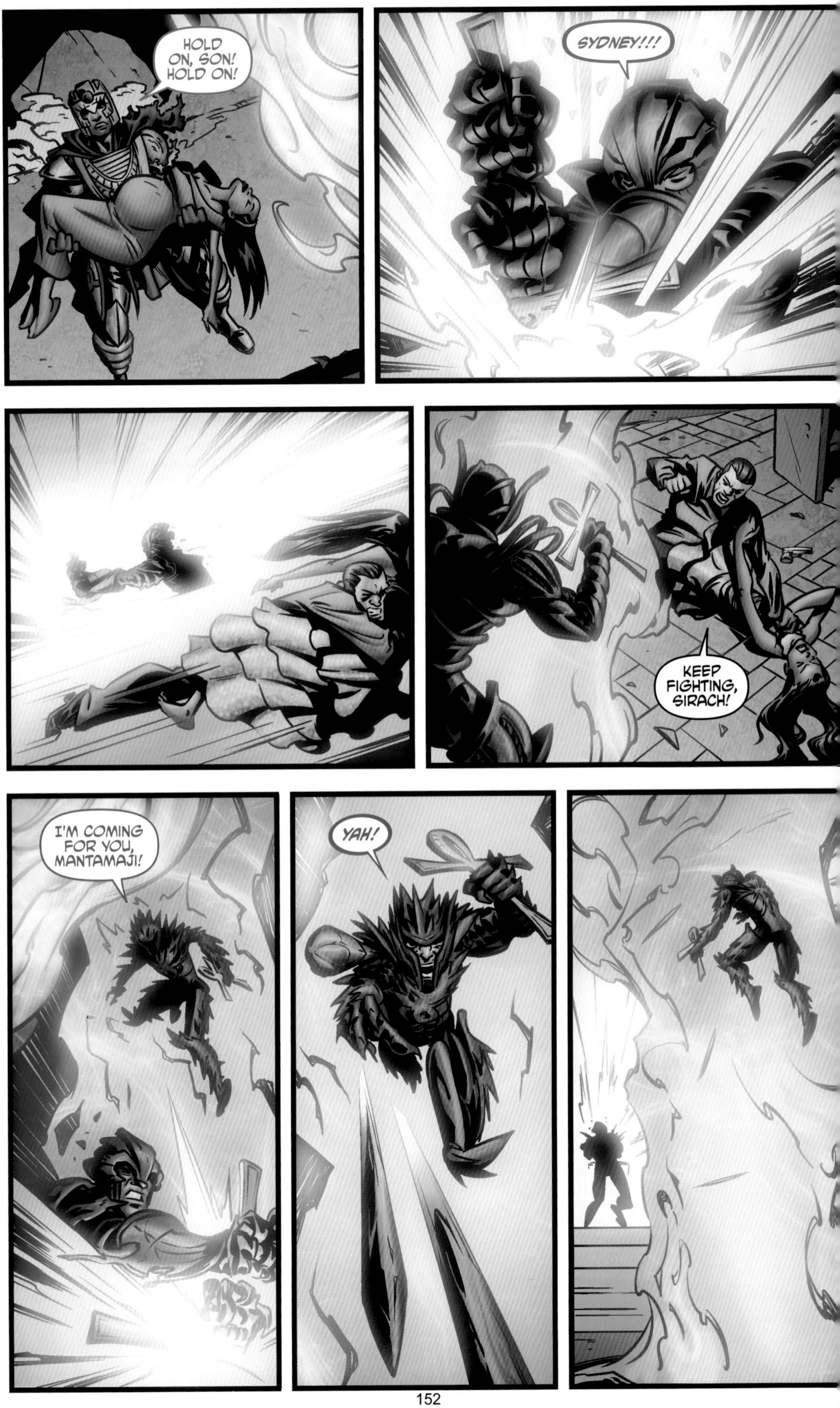
HOLD ON, SON! HOLD ON!
SYDNEY!!!
KEEP FIGHTING, SIRACH!
I'M COMING FOR YOU, MANTAMAJI!
YAH!

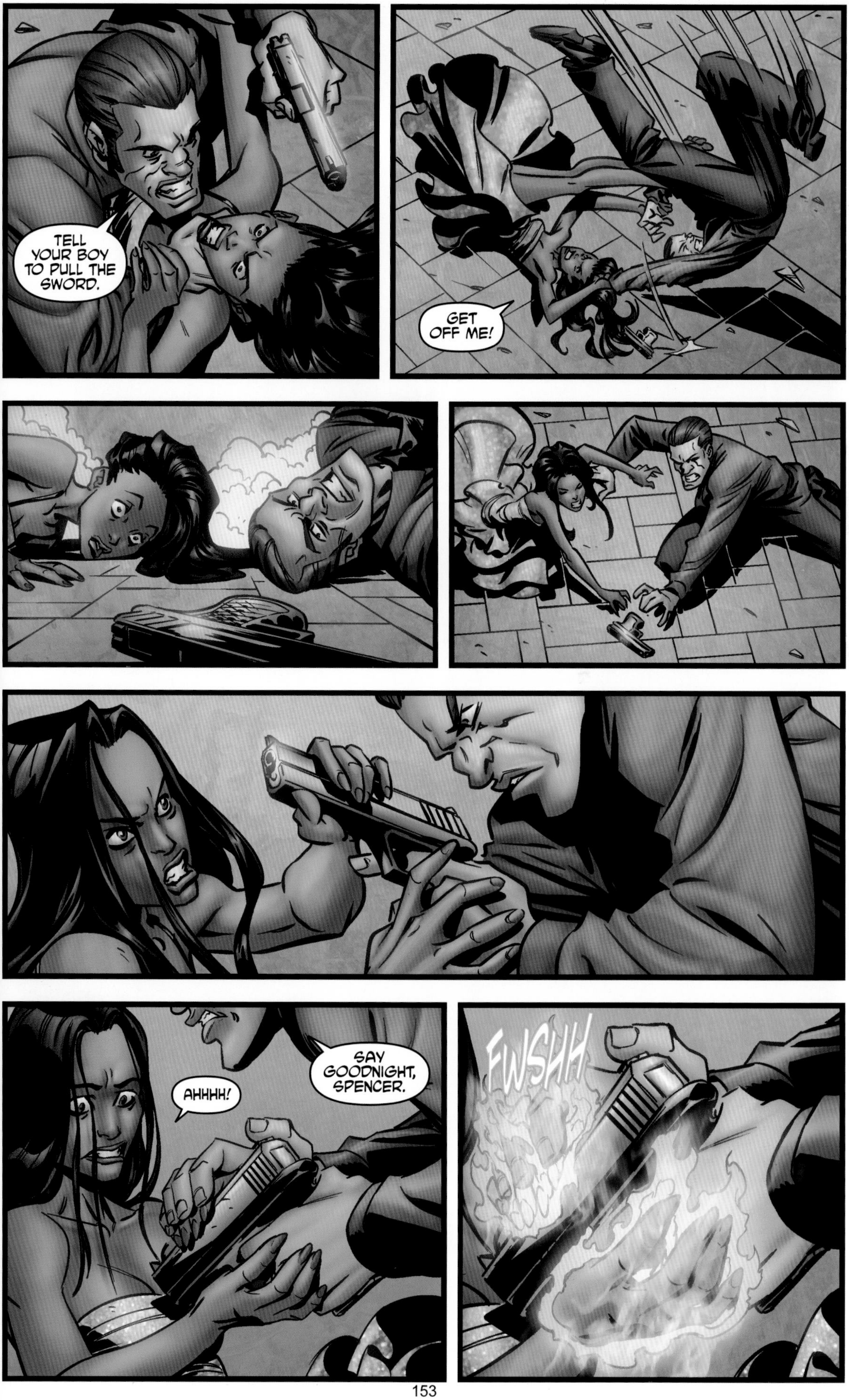
TELL YOUR BOY TO PULL THE SWORD.
GET OFF ME!
AHHHH!
SAY GOODNIGHT, SPENCER.
FWSHH

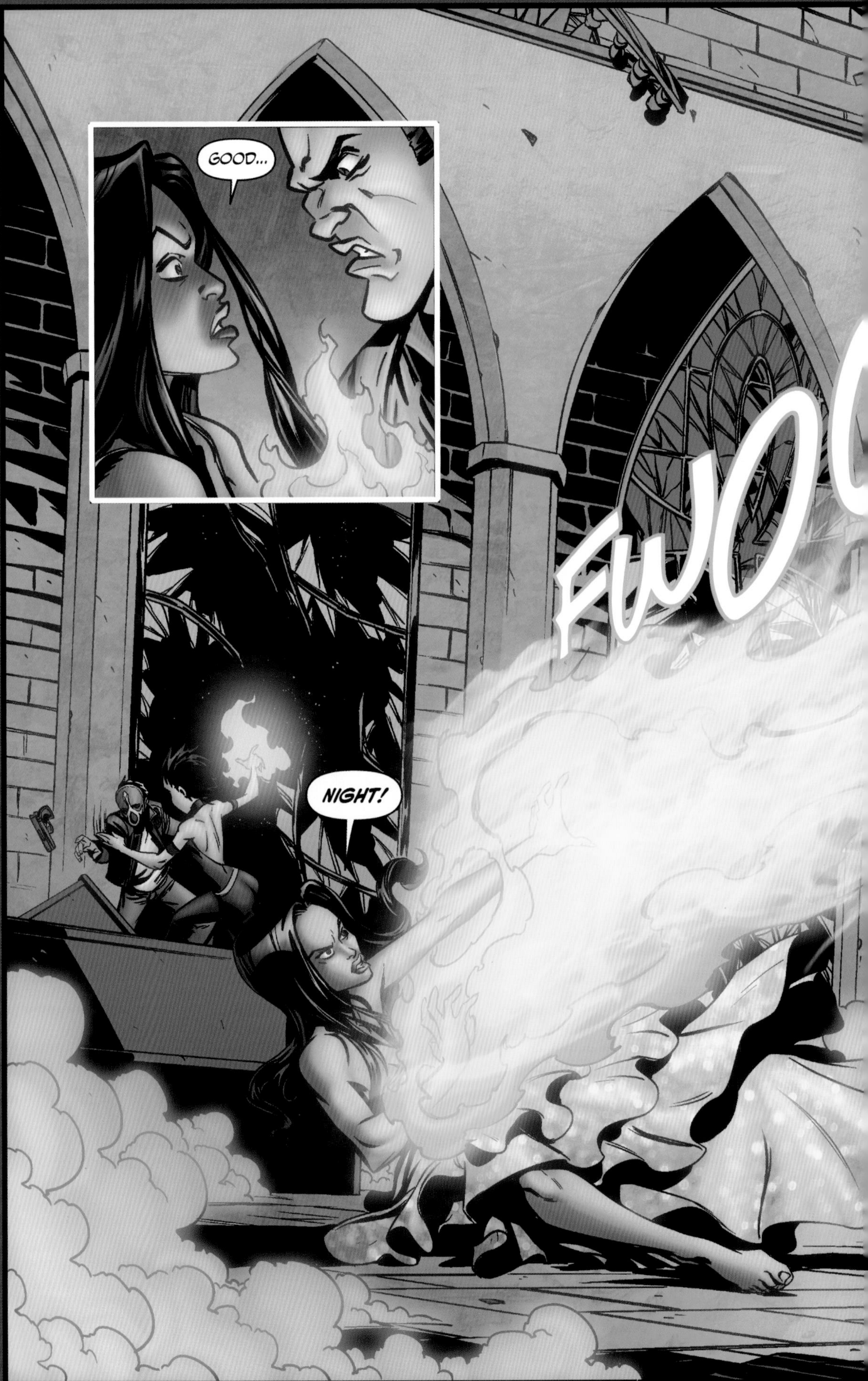
GOOD...
NIGHT!
FWOO

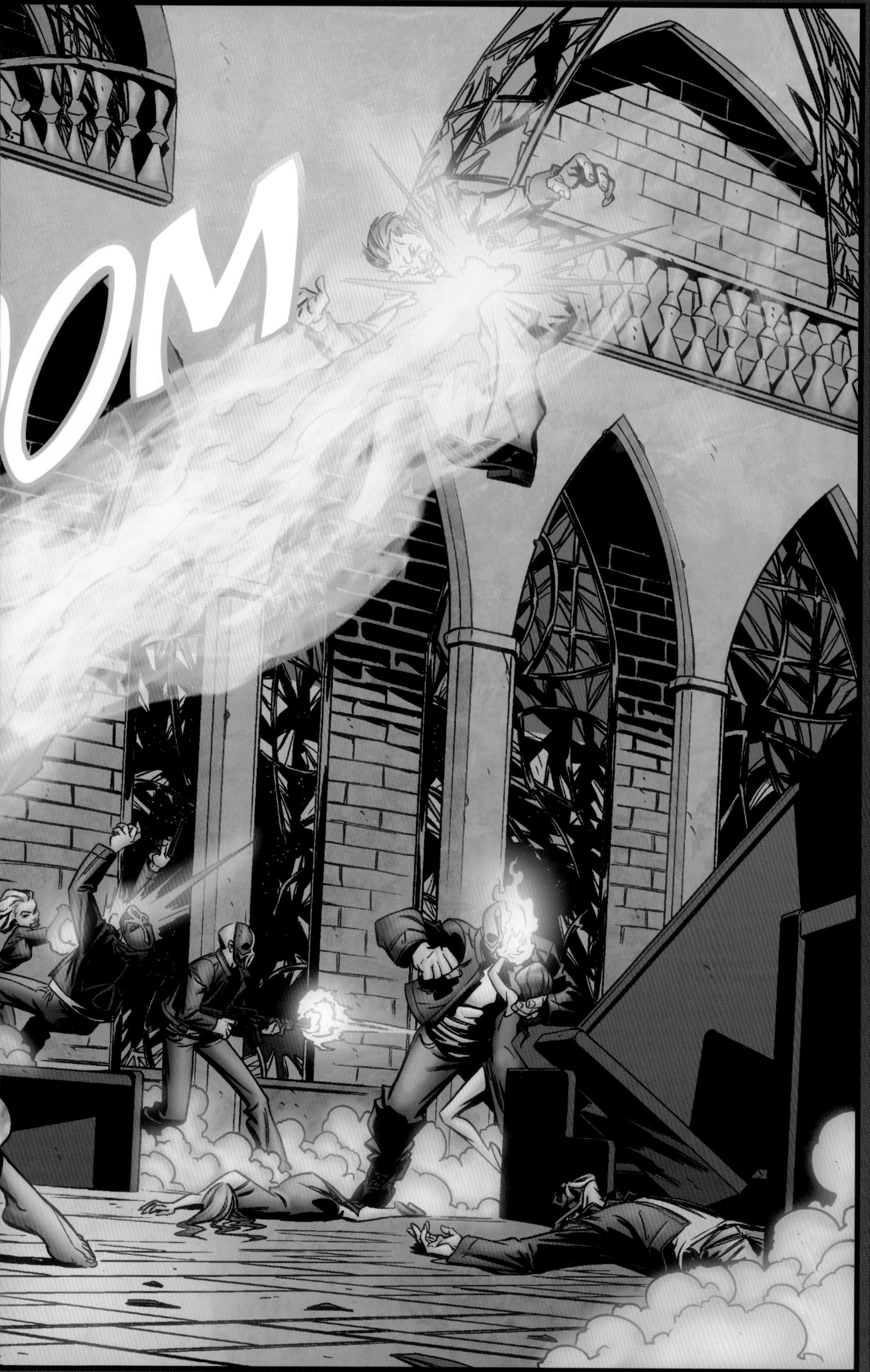

OOM

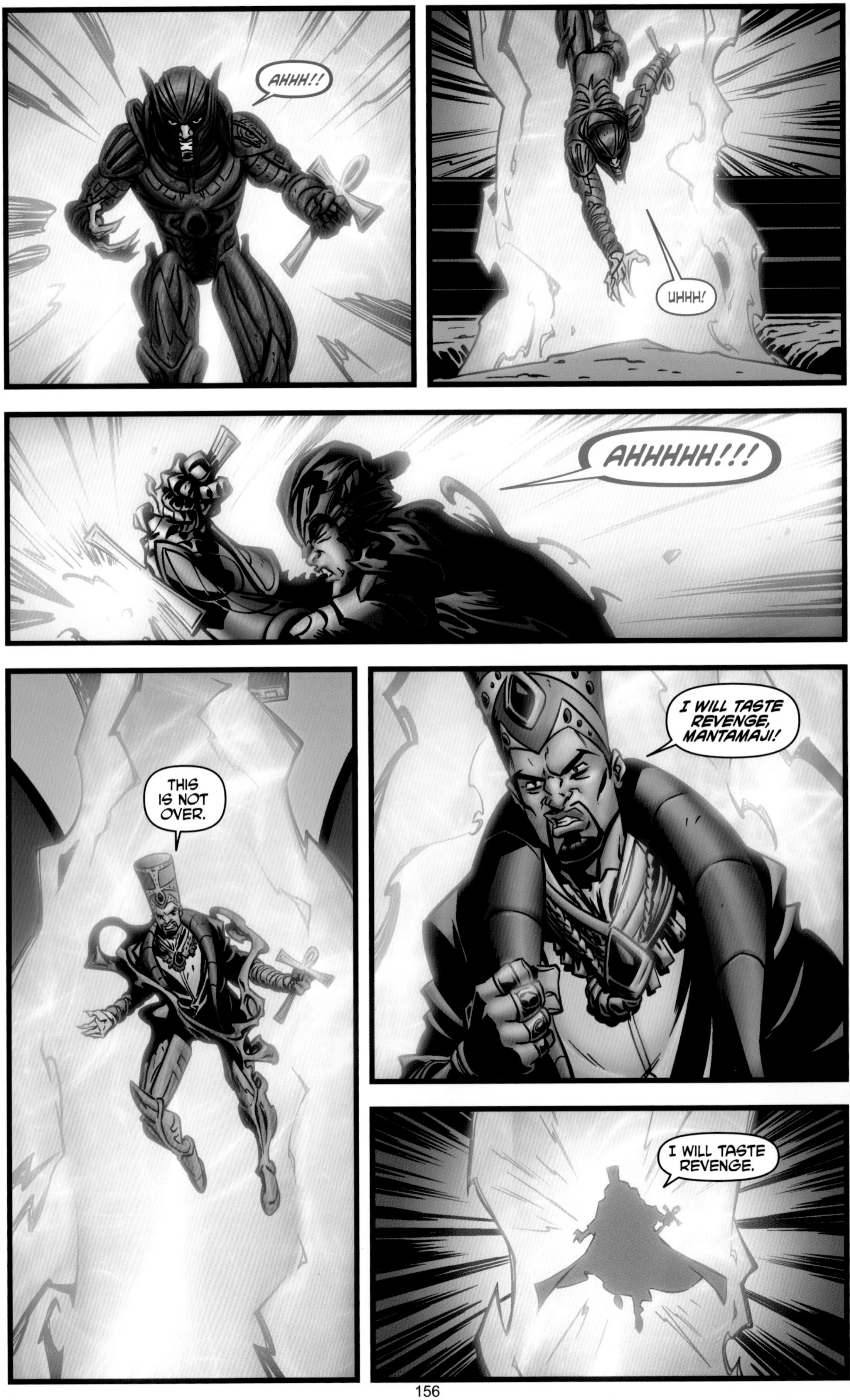
AHHH!!
UHHH!
AHHHHH!!!
THIS IS NOT OVER.
I WILL TASTE REVENGE, MANTAMAJI!
I WILL TASTE REVENGE.

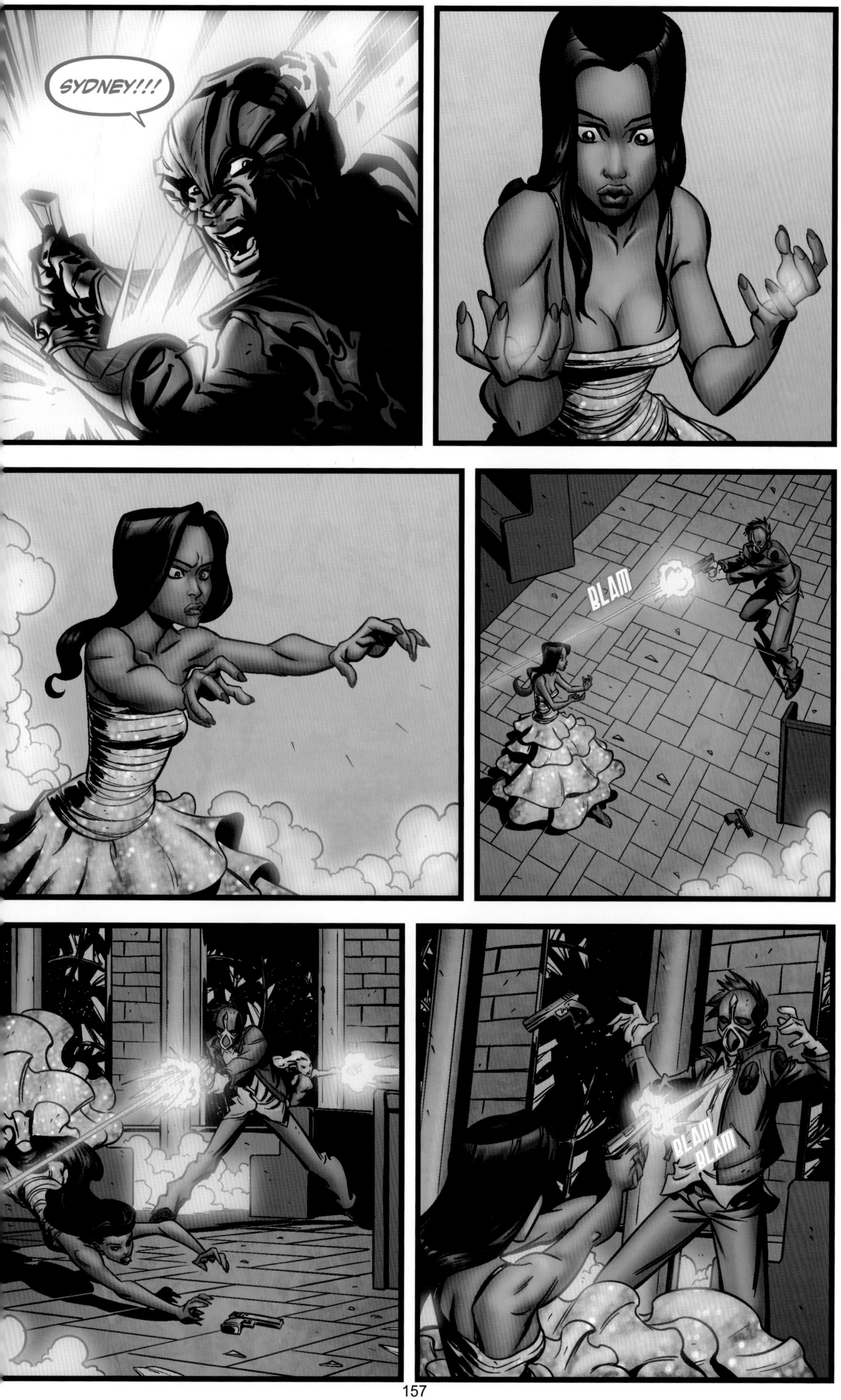
SYDNEY!!!
BLAM
BLAM
BLAM

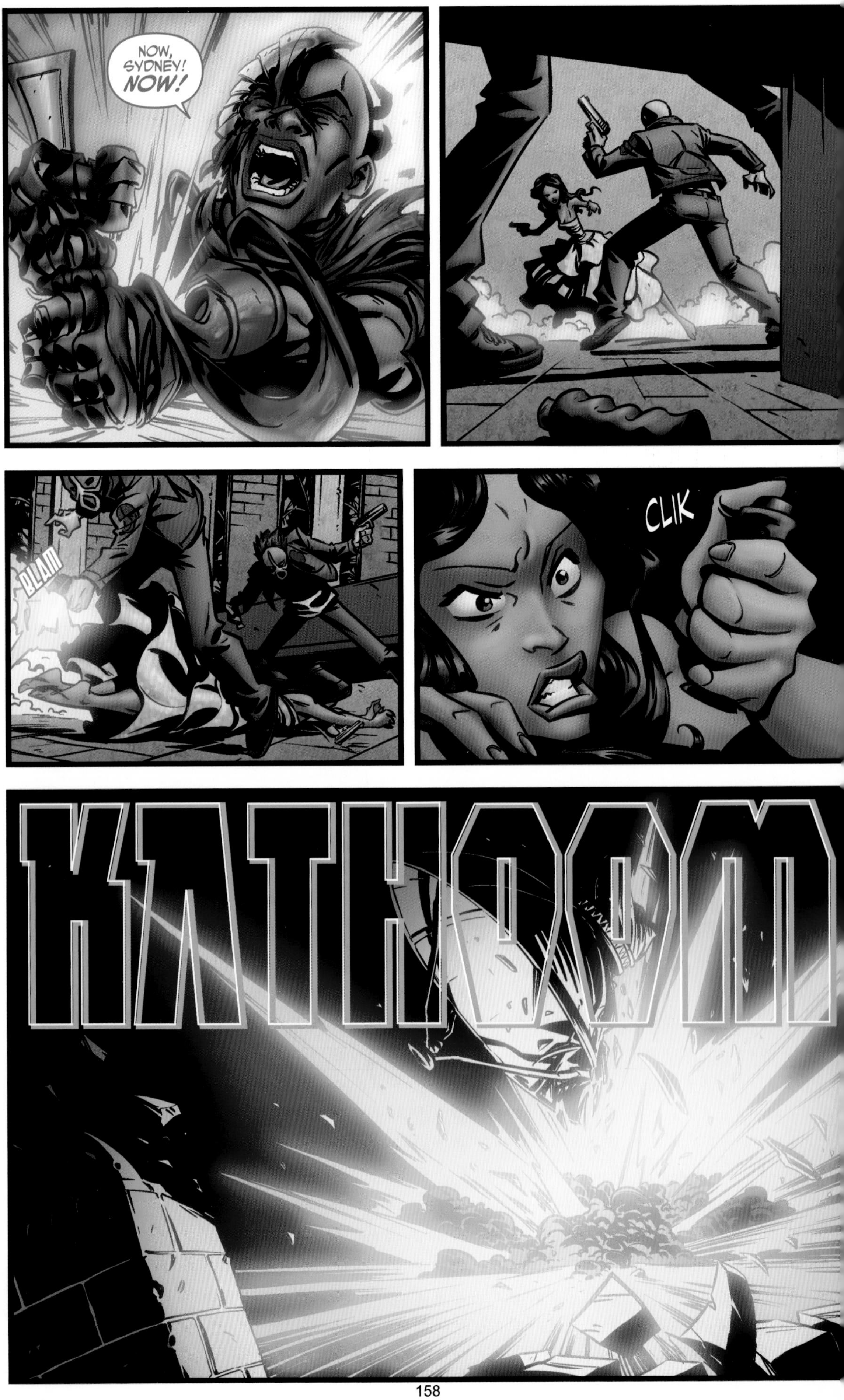
NOW, SYDNEY! NOW!
BLAM
CLIK
KATHOOM

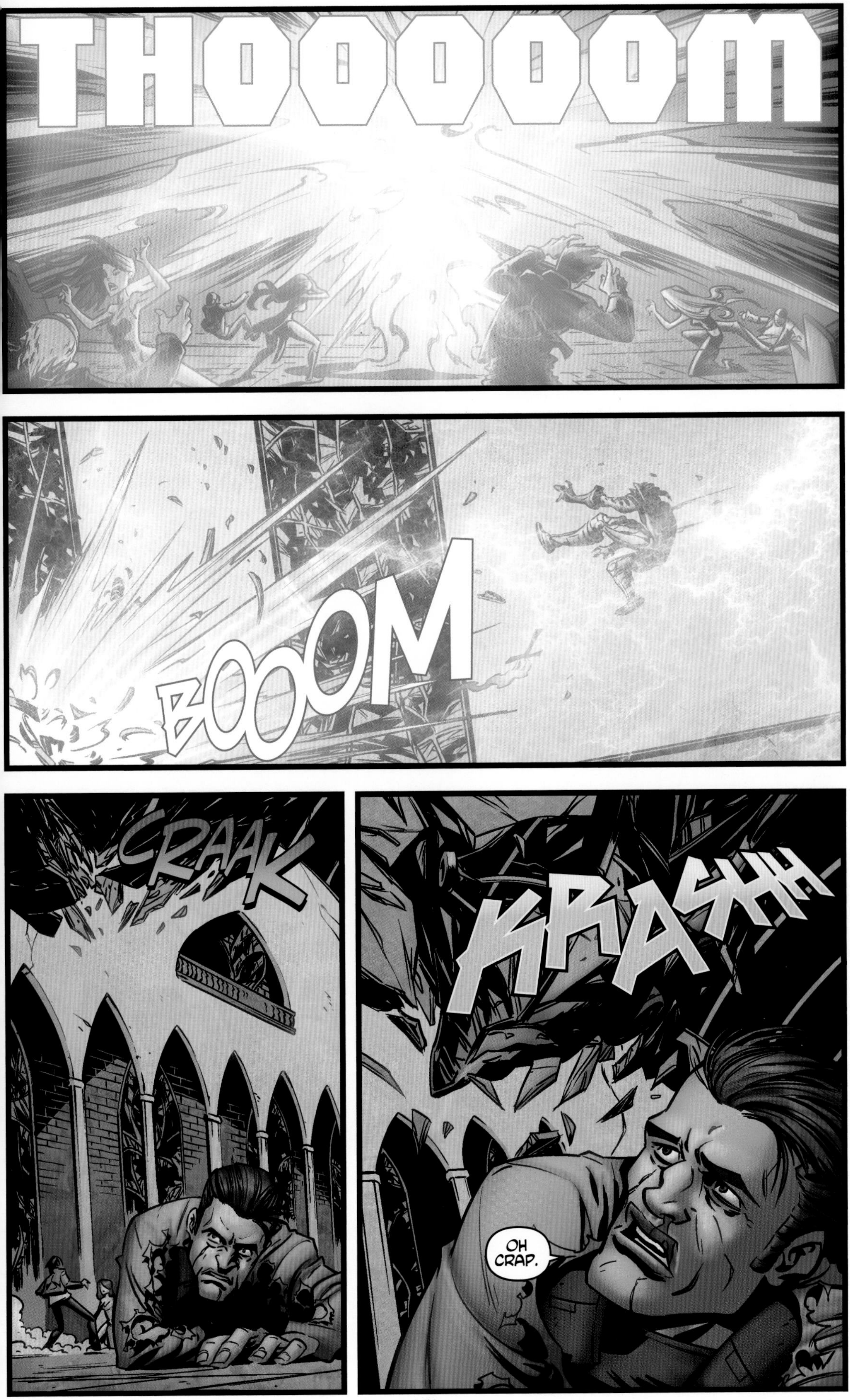
THOOOOOM
BOOOM
CRAAK
KRASHH
OH CRAP.

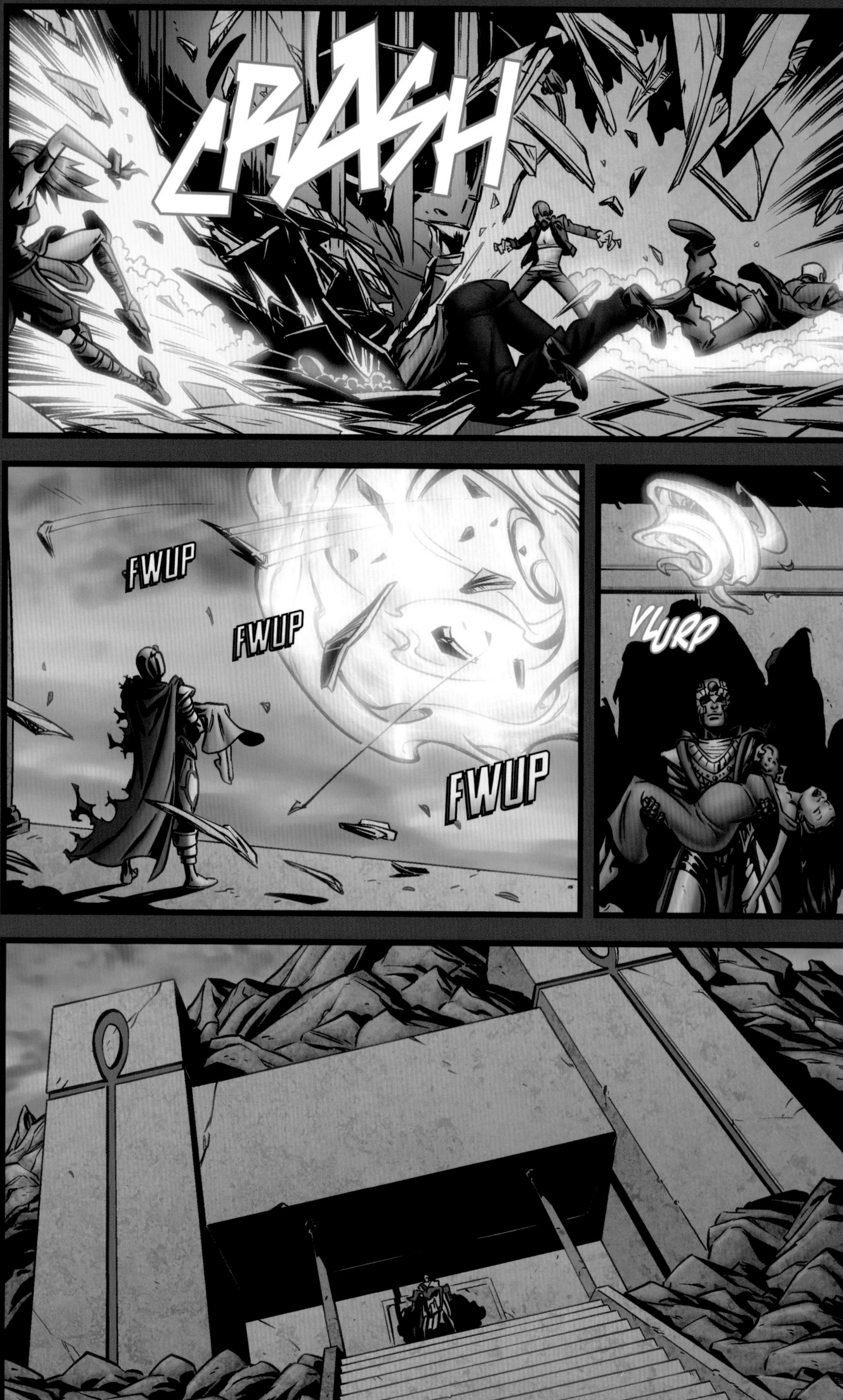
CRASH
FWUP
FWUP
FWUP
VLURP

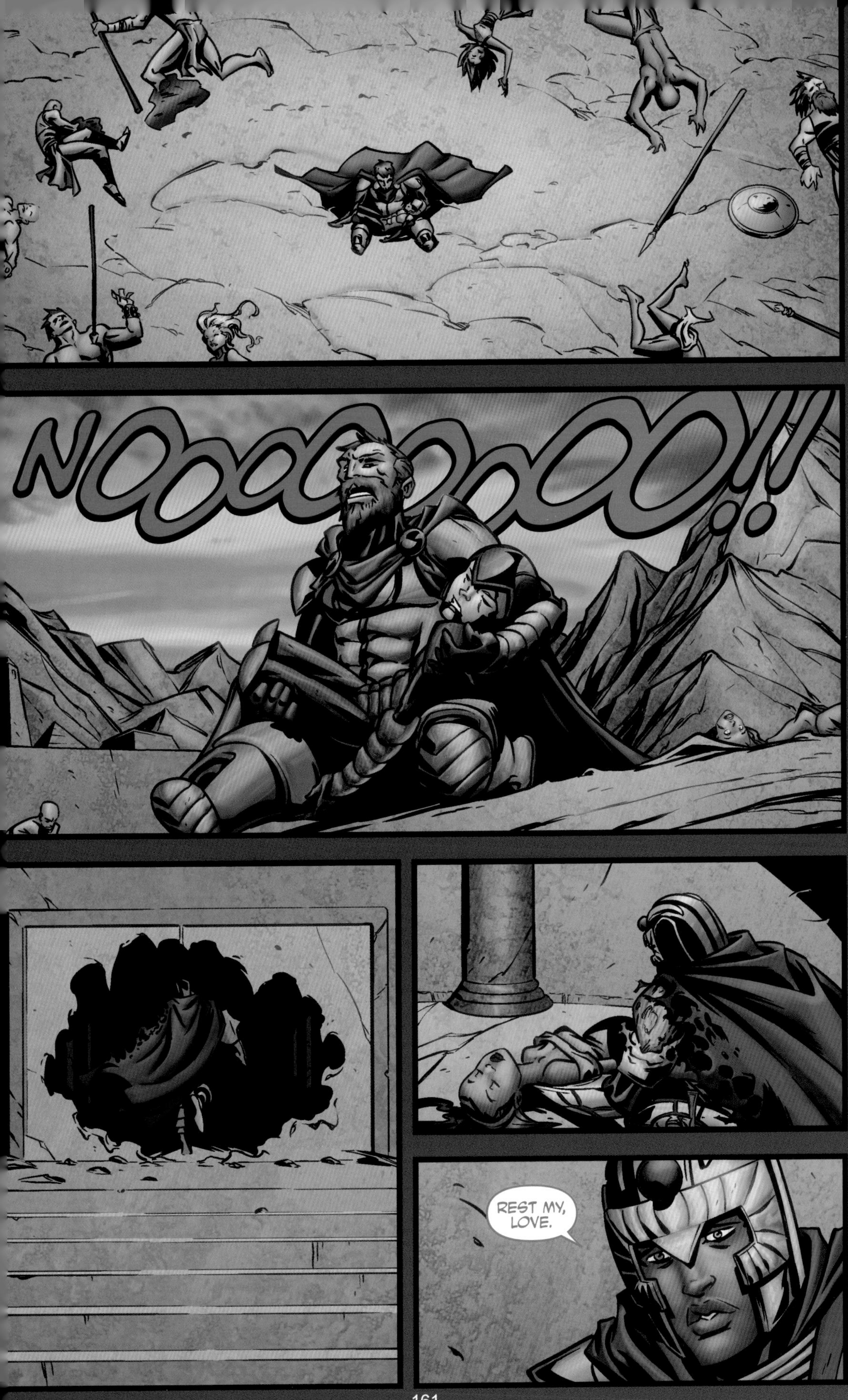
NOOOOOOO!!
REST MY, LOVE.

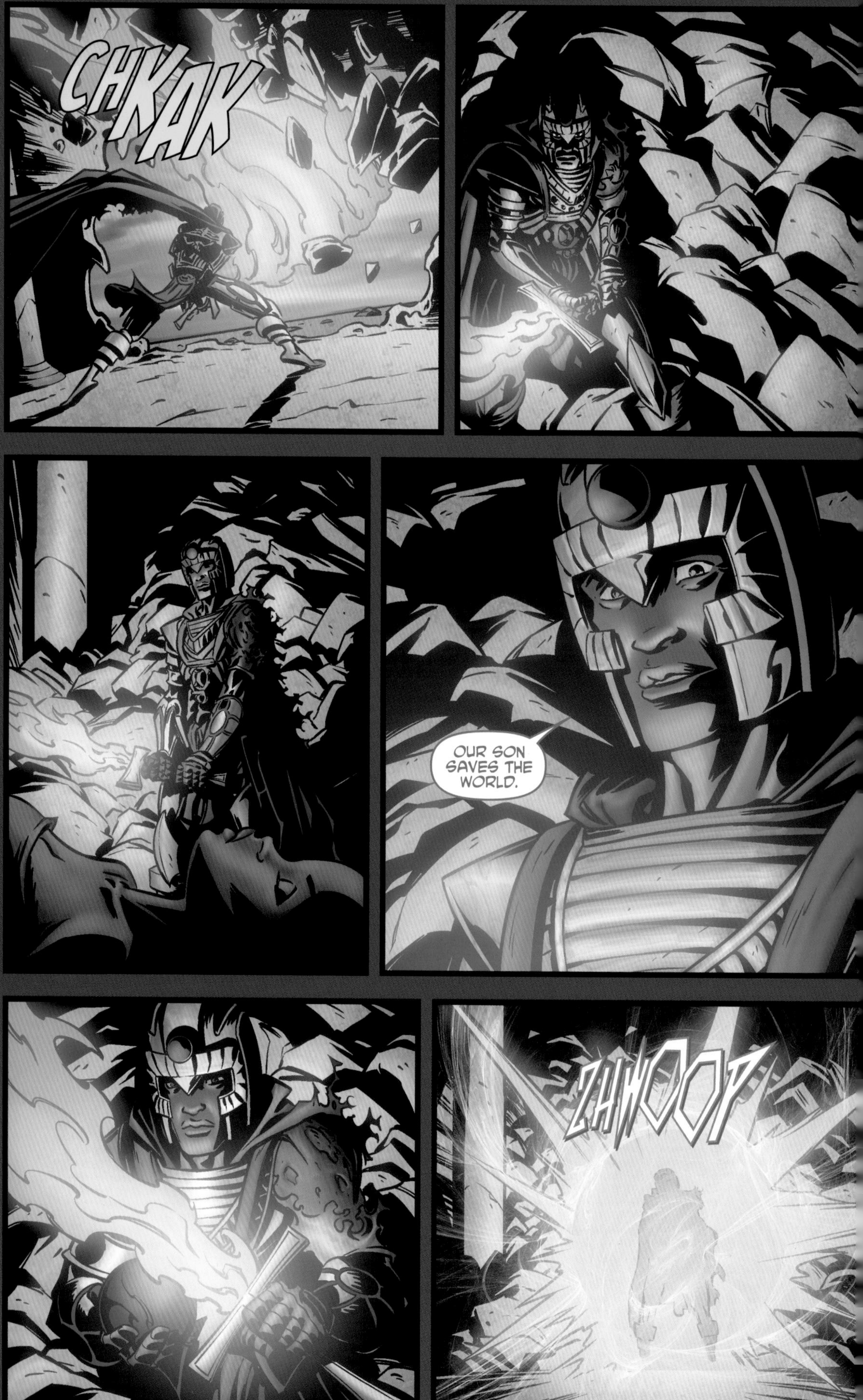

CHKAK
OUR SON SAVES THE WORLD.
ZHWOOP

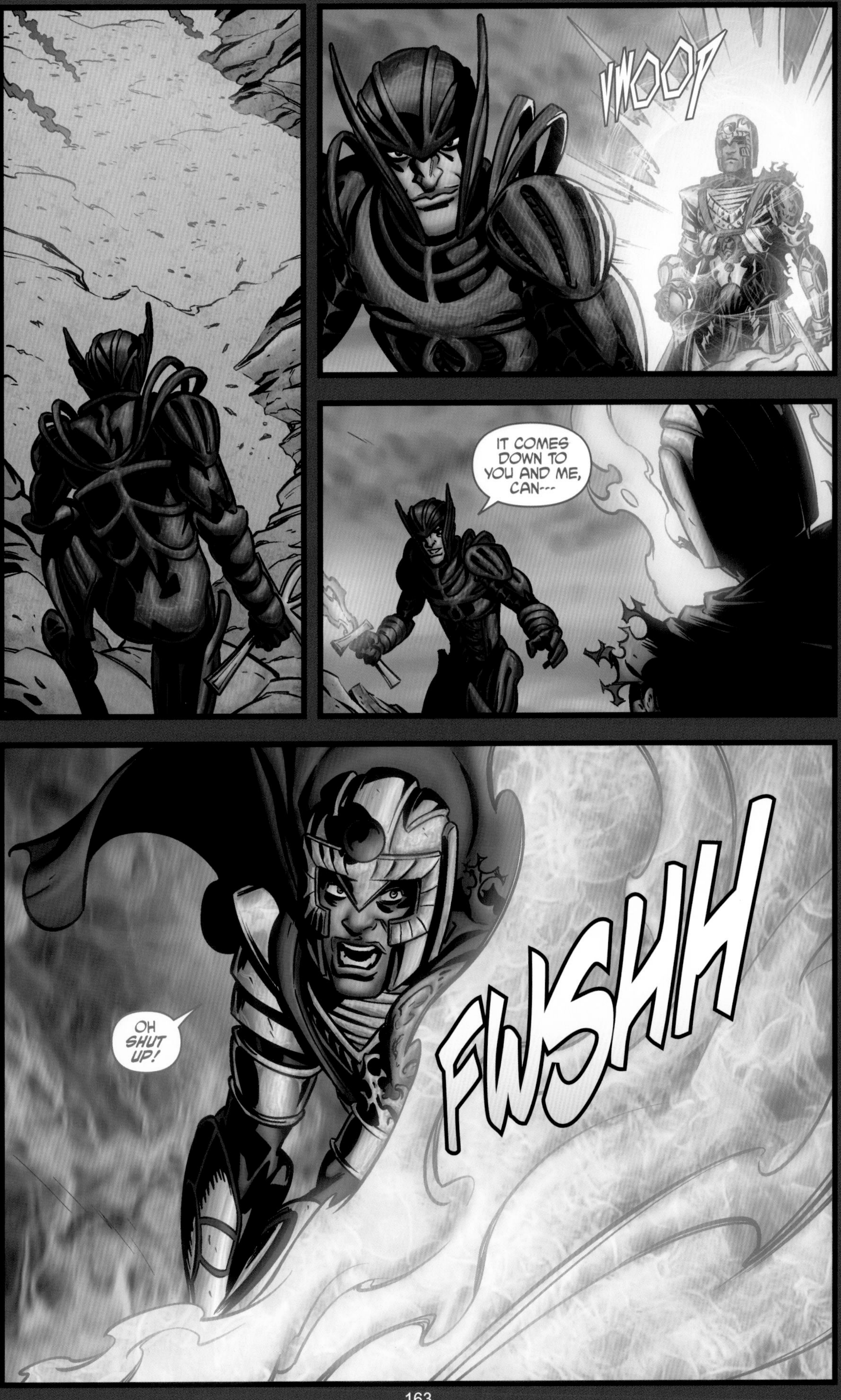
VWOOP
IT COMES DOWN TO YOU AND ME, CAN---
OH SHUT UP!
FWSHH

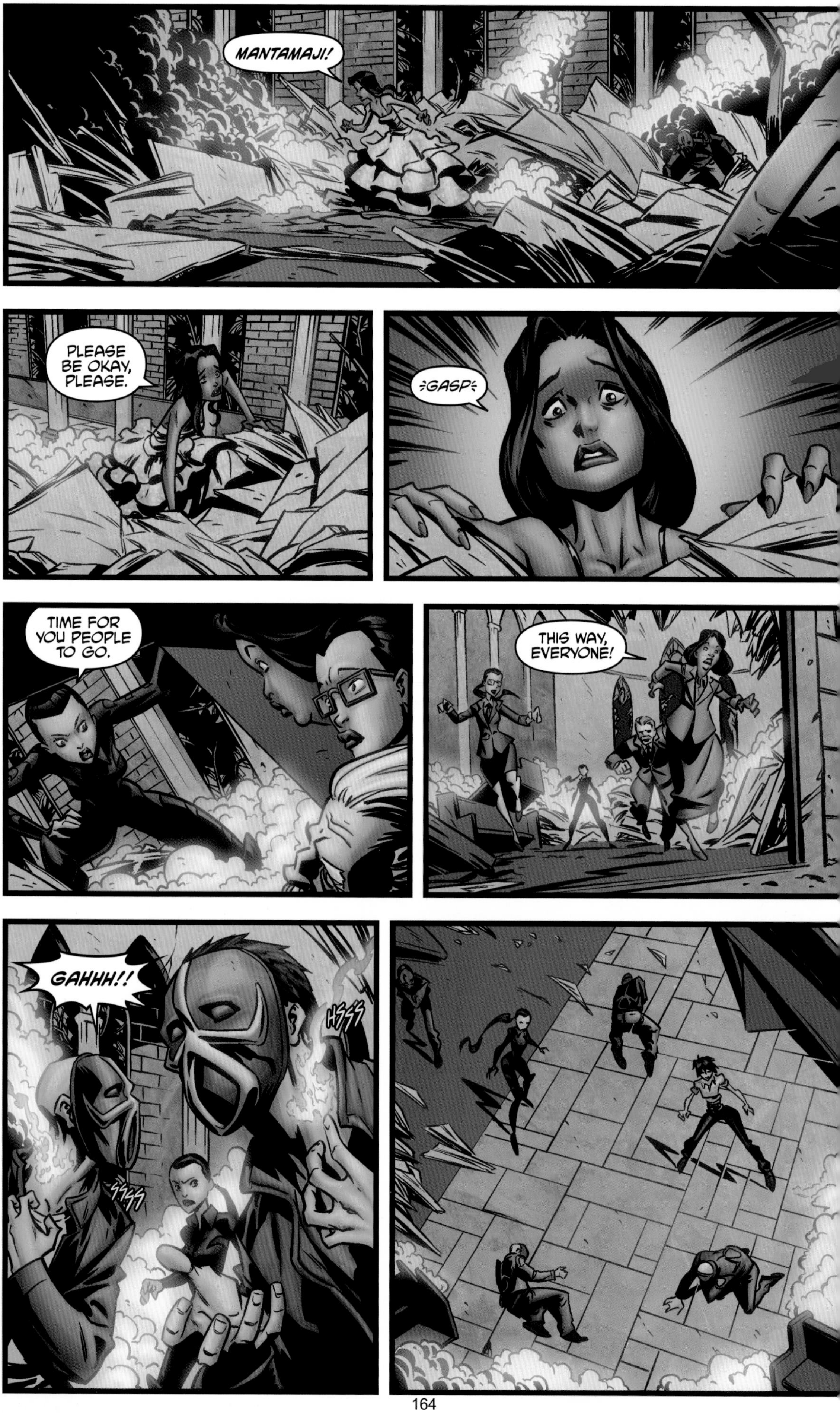
MANTAMAJI!
PLEASE BE OKAY, PLEASE.
GASP
TIME FOR YOU PEOPLE TO GO.
THIS WAY, EVERYONE!
GAHHH!!
HSSS
SSSS

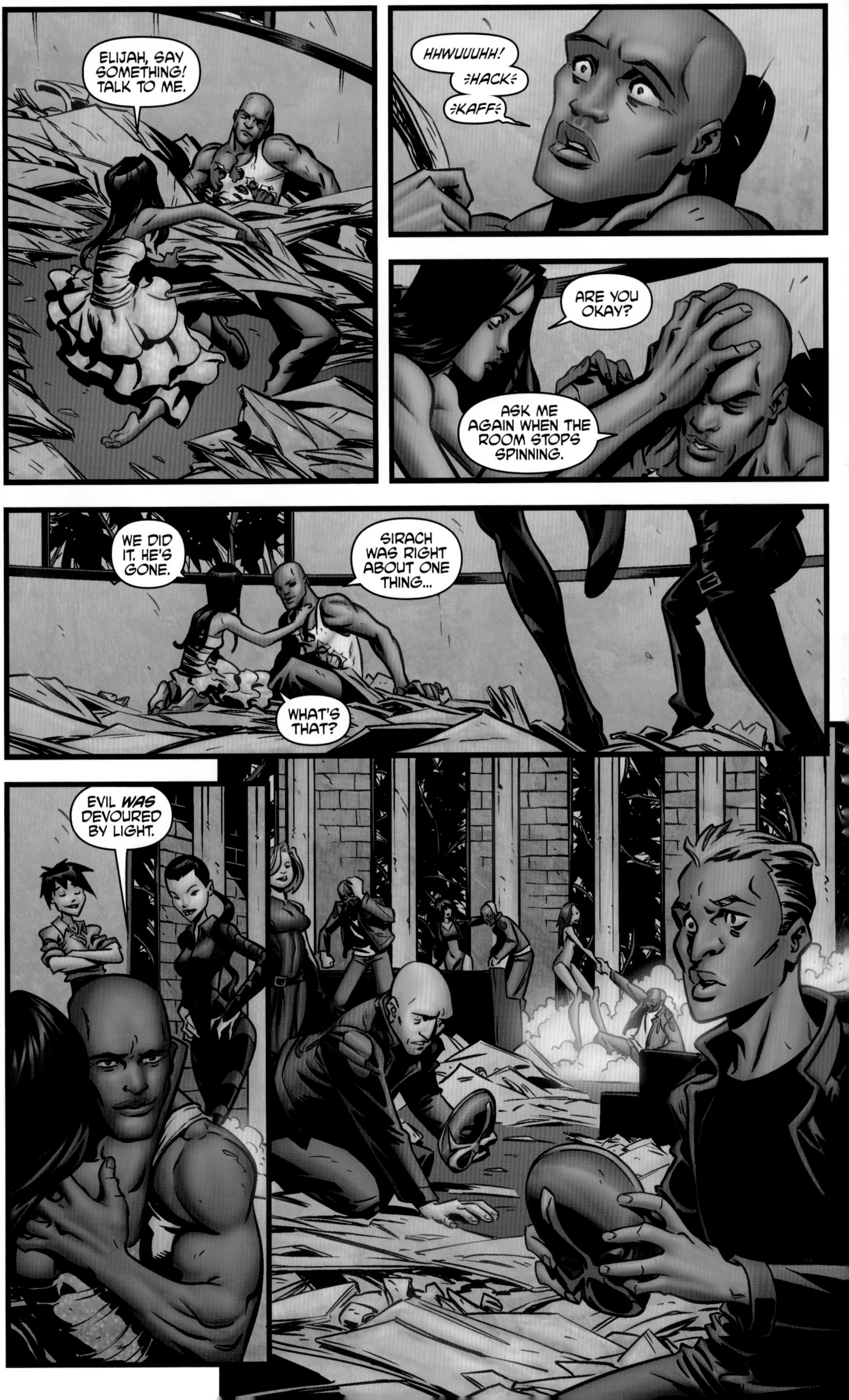
ELIJAH, SAY SOMETHING! TALK TO ME.
HHWUUUHH!
HACK
KAFF
ARE YOU OKAY?
ASK ME AGAIN WHEN THE ROOM STOPS SPINNING.
WE DID IT. HE'S GONE.
SIRACH WAS RIGHT ABOUT ONE THING...
WHAT'S THAT?
EVIL *WAS* DEVOURED BY LIGHT.

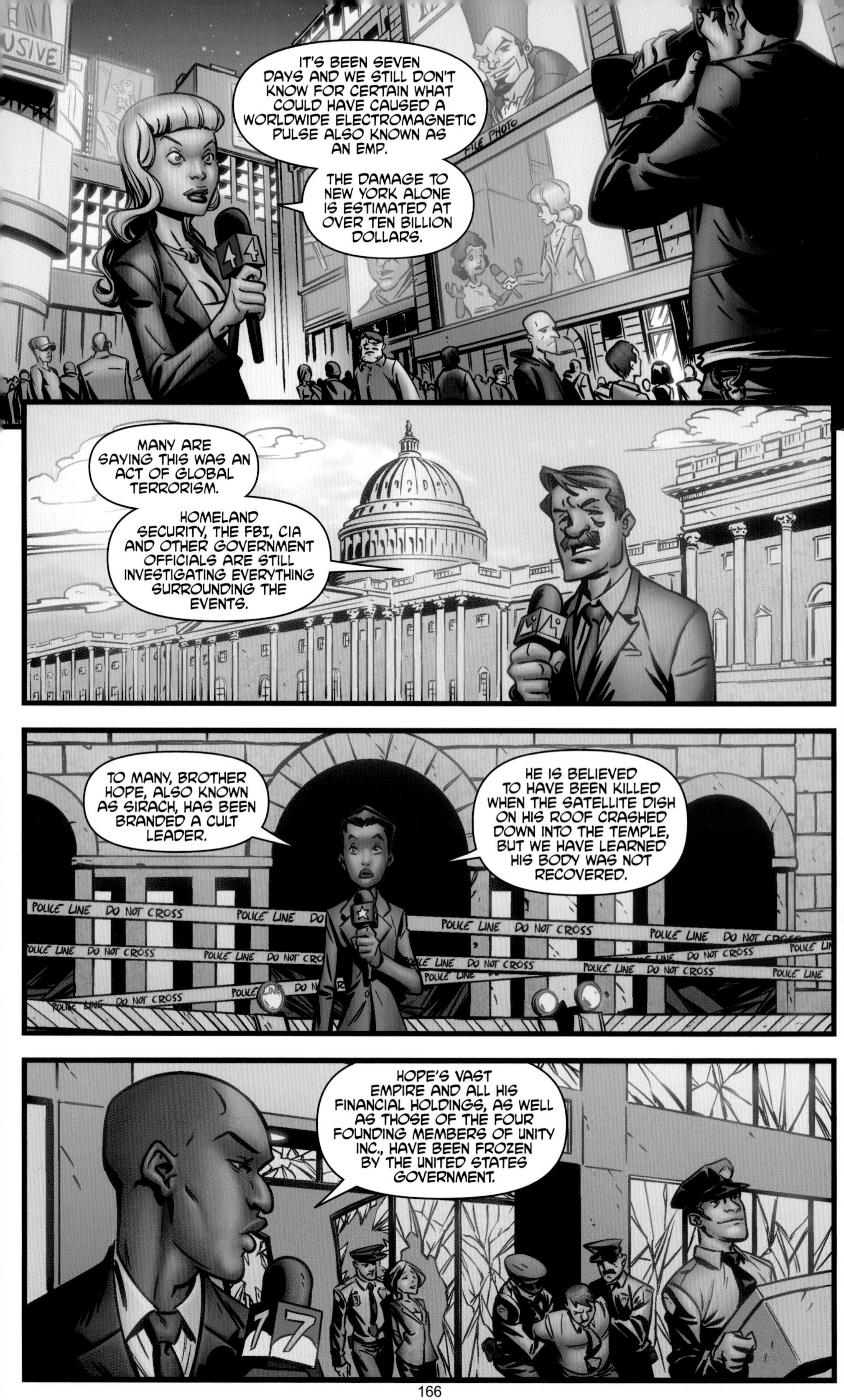
USIVE
FILE PHOTO
IT'S BEEN SEVEN DAYS AND WE STILL DON'T KNOW FOR CERTAIN WHAT COULD HAVE CAUSED A WORLDWIDE ELECTROMAGNETIC PULSE ALSO KNOWN AS AN EMP.
THE DAMAGE TO NEW YORK ALONE IS ESTIMATED AT OVER TEN BILLION DOLLARS.
MANY ARE SAYING THIS WAS AN ACT OF GLOBAL TERRORISM.
HOMELAND SECURITY, THE FBI, CIA AND OTHER GOVERNMENT OFFICIALS ARE STILL INVESTIGATING EVERYTHING SURROUNDING THE EVENTS.
TO MANY, BROTHER HOPE, ALSO KNOWN AS SIRACH, HAS BEEN BRANDED A CULT LEADER.
HE IS BELIEVED TO HAVE BEEN KILLED WHEN THE SATELLITE DISH ON HIS ROOF CRASHED DOWN INTO THE TEMPLE, BUT WE HAVE LEARNED HIS BODY WAS NOT RECOVERED.
POLICE LINE DO NOT CROSS
HOPE'S VAST EMPIRE AND ALL HIS FINANCIAL HOLDINGS, AS WELL AS THOSE OF THE FOUR FOUNDING MEMBERS OF UNITY INC., HAVE BEEN FROZEN BY THE UNITED STATES GOVERNMENT.
17

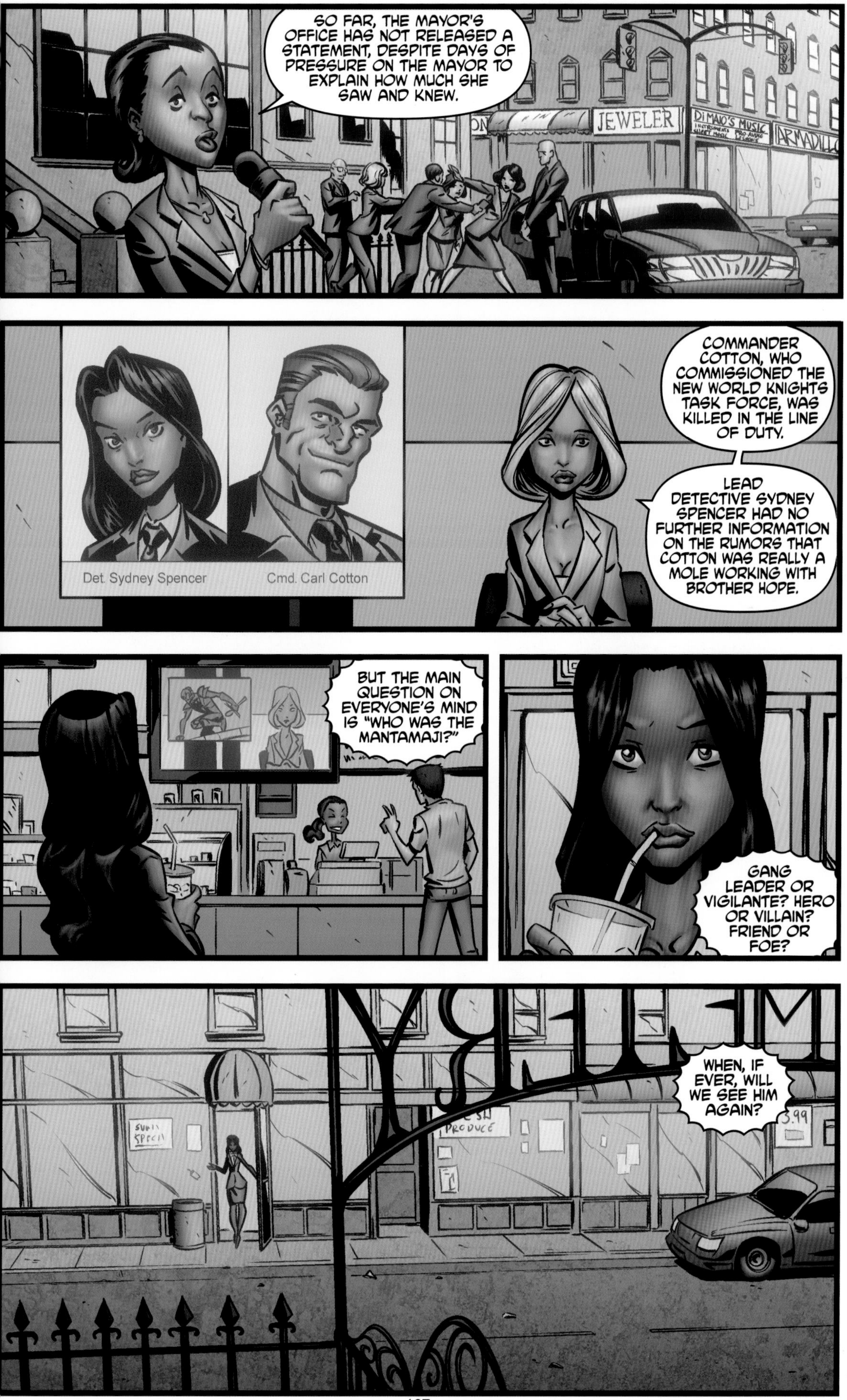
SO FAR, THE MAYOR'S OFFICE HAS NOT RELEASED A STATEMENT, DESPITE DAYS OF PRESSURE ON THE MAYOR TO EXPLAIN HOW MUCH SHE SAW AND KNEW.
JEWELER
DIMAIO'S MUSIC
ARMADILLO
Det. Sydney Spencer
Cmd. Carl Cotton
COMMANDER COTTON, WHO COMMISSIONED THE NEW WORLD KNIGHTS TASK FORCE, WAS KILLED IN THE LINE OF DUTY.
LEAD DETECTIVE SYDNEY SPENCER HAD NO FURTHER INFORMATION ON THE RUMORS THAT COTTON WAS REALLY A MOLE WORKING WITH BROTHER HOPE.
BUT THE MAIN QUESTION ON EVERYONE'S MIND IS "WHO WAS THE MANTAMAJI?"
GANG LEADER OR VIGILANTE? HERO OR VILLAIN? FRIEND OR FOE?
WHEN, IF EVER, WILL WE SEE HIM AGAIN?
PRODUCE
3.99

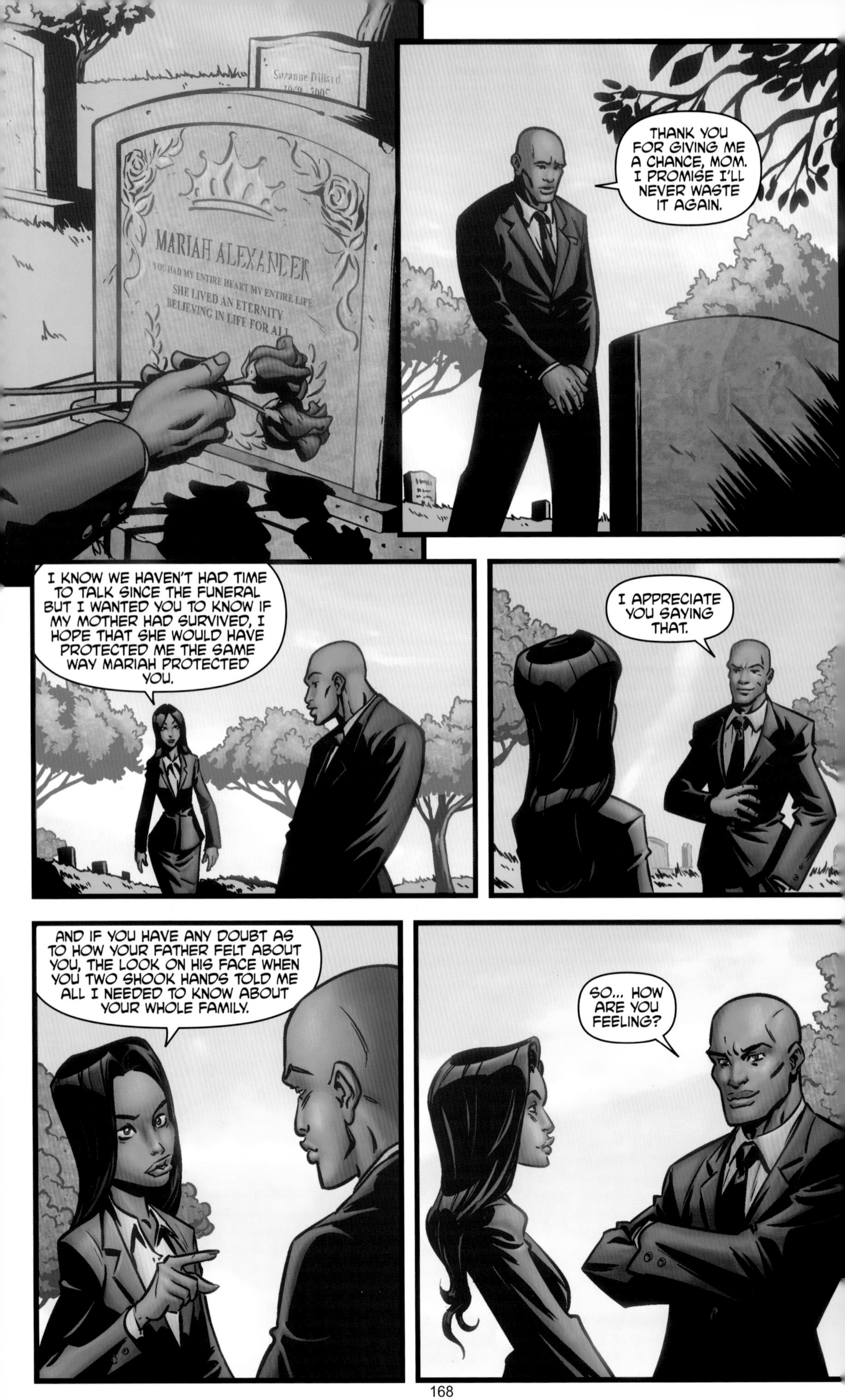
Suzanne Dillard
MARIAH ALEXANDER
YOU HAD MY ENTIRE HEART MY ENTIRE LIFE
SHE LIVED AN ETERNITY
BELIEVING IN LIFE FOR ALL
THANK YOU FOR GIVING ME A CHANCE, MOM. I PROMISE I'LL NEVER WASTE IT AGAIN.
I KNOW WE HAVEN'T HAD TIME TO TALK SINCE THE FUNERAL BUT I WANTED YOU TO KNOW IF MY MOTHER HAD SURVIVED, I HOPE THAT SHE WOULD HAVE PROTECTED ME THE SAME WAY MARIAH PROTECTED YOU.
I APPRECIATE YOU SAYING THAT.
AND IF YOU HAVE ANY DOUBT AS TO HOW YOUR FATHER FELT ABOUT YOU, THE LOOK ON HIS FACE WHEN YOU TWO SHOOK HANDS TOLD ME ALL I NEEDED TO KNOW ABOUT YOUR WHOLE FAMILY.
SO... HOW ARE YOU FEELING?

IF YOU'RE ASKING IF I'VE BEEN ABLE TO LIGHT UP AGAIN. I HAVEN'T. CORNERSTONE SAID IT WAS FROM THE STRESS OF THE SITUATION—MAYBE A ONE-TIME THING. THERE'S NO WAY TO KNOW IF IT'LL EVER HAPPEN AGAIN.

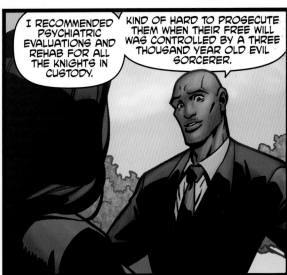

I RECOMMENDED PSYCHIATRIC EVALUATIONS AND REHAB FOR ALL THE KNIGHTS IN CUSTODY.

KIND OF HARD TO PROSECUTE THEM WHEN THEIR FREE WILL WAS CONTROLLED BY A THREE THOUSAND YEAR OLD EVIL SORCERER.

HOW IS IT GOING WITH ALL THE APPEALS BY THE MOB BOSSES THE KNIGHTS PUT IN JAIL?

NOT GOOD, THEY WERE FRAMED SO THEY ARE GETTING OFF, BUT WE WILL GET THEM AGAIN.

ON THE BRIGHT SIDE, NOBODY SEEMS TO KNOW WHO THE MANTAMAJI WAS, SO I GUESS YOU'RE IN THE CLEAR.

YOU SEE, THAT'S THE BAD THING ABOUT BEING A HERO. IT'S A THANKLESS JOB.

MAYBE THAT'S YOUR CUE TO RIDE OFF INTO THE SUNSET, HERO.

ONLY IF YOU RIDE WITH ME.

I'M SORRY I DIDN'T TELL YOU THE TRUTH.

I'M SORRY *I* DIDN'T TELL YOU THE TRUTH.

YOU WERE TRYING TO PROTECT ME.

YOU WERE AFRAID I WOULDN'T UNDERSTAND.

NO, I WAS FIGHTING TO KEEP CONTROL OF THE FAKE LIFE I HAD CREATED. I JUST DIDN'T REALIZE IT'S WHAT WE DO WITH WHAT WE HAVE THAT TRULY DEFINES WHO WE ARE.

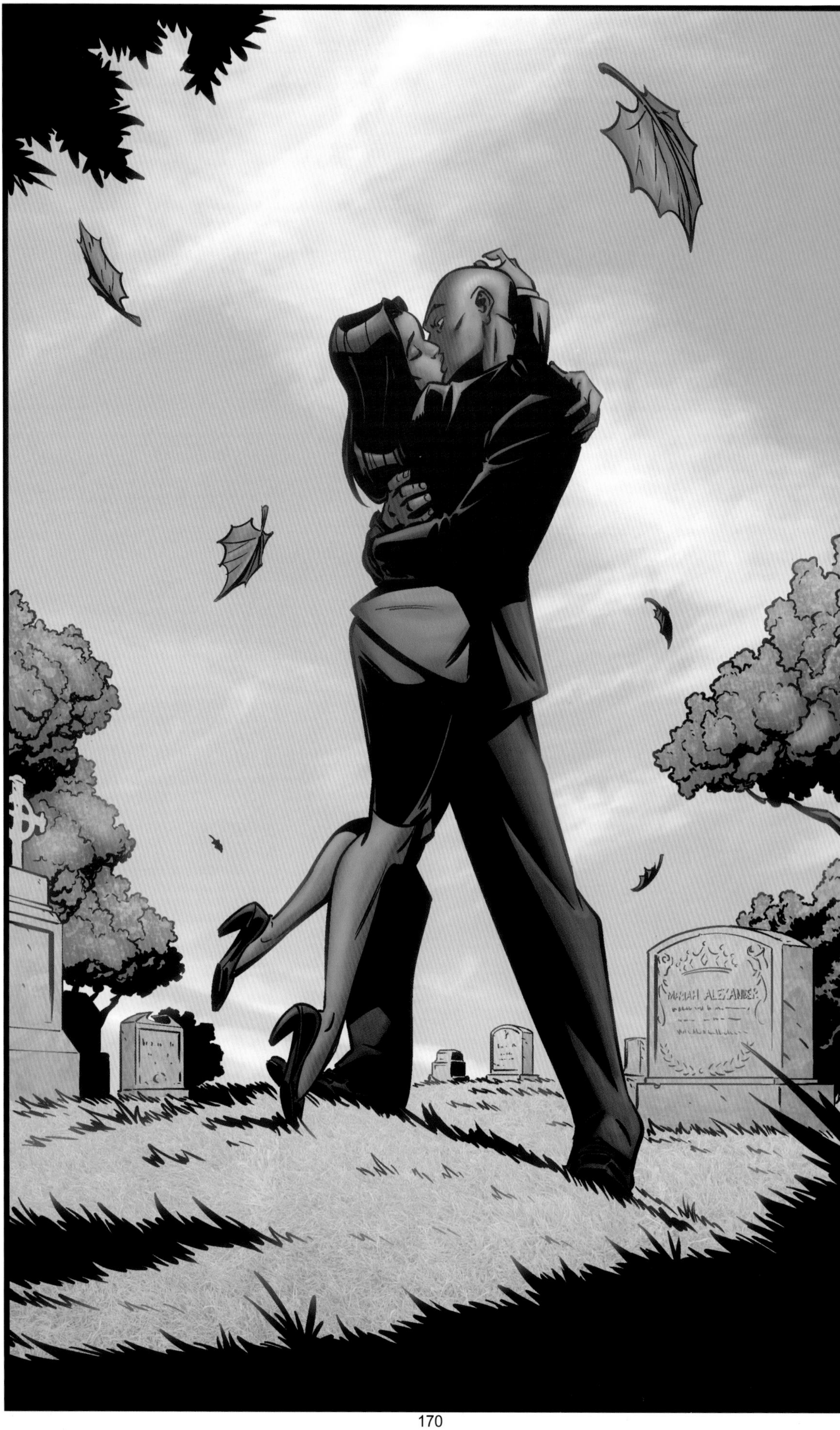
MARIAH ALEXANDER

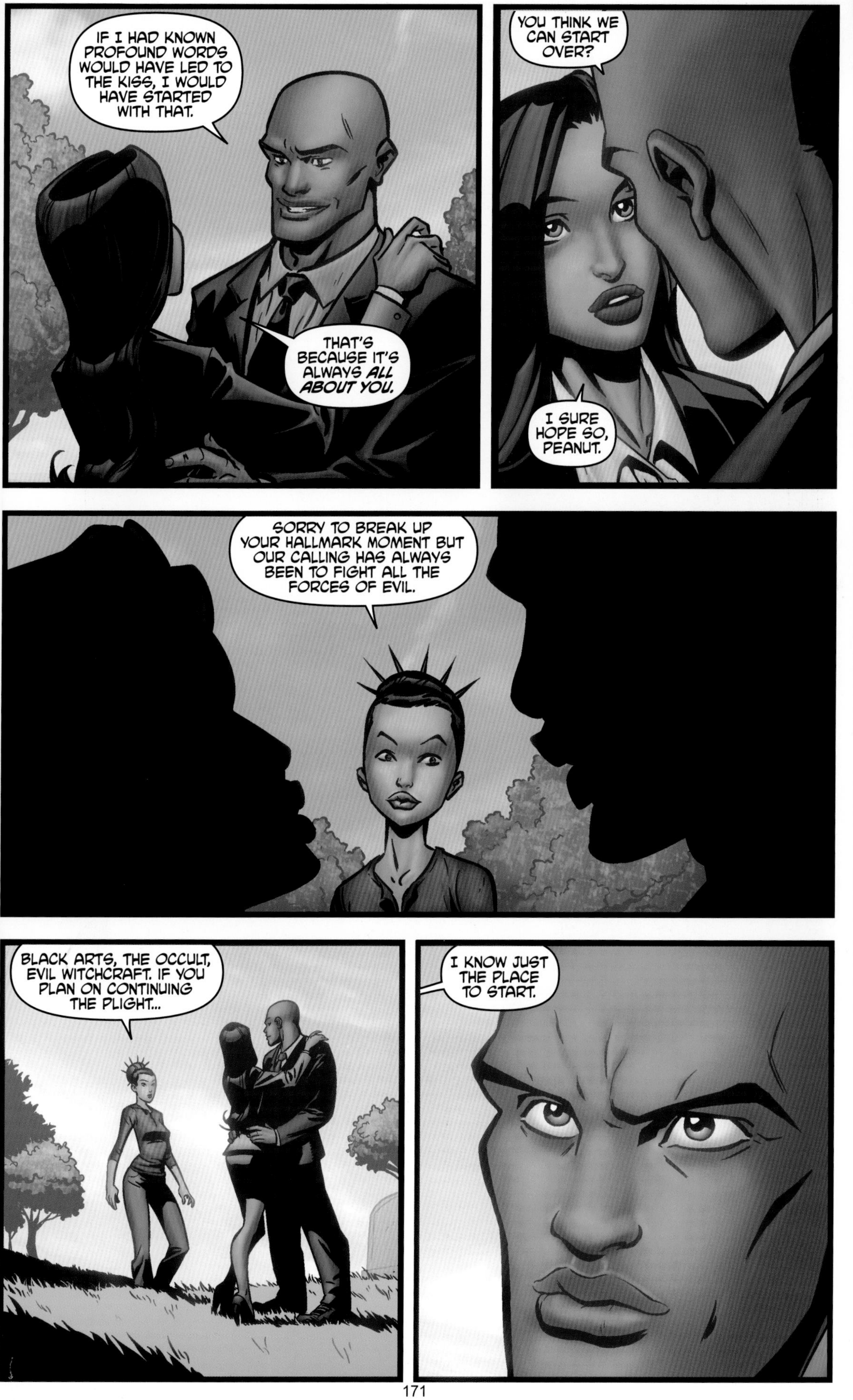
IF I HAD KNOWN PROFOUND WORDS WOULD HAVE LED TO THE KISS, I WOULD HAVE STARTED WITH THAT.
THAT'S BECAUSE IT'S ALWAYS *ALL ABOUT YOU.*
YOU THINK WE CAN START OVER?
I SURE HOPE SO, PEANUT.
SORRY TO BREAK UP YOUR HALLMARK MOMENT BUT OUR CALLING HAS ALWAYS BEEN TO FIGHT ALL THE FORCES OF EVIL.
BLACK ARTS, THE OCCULT, EVIL WITCHCRAFT. IF YOU PLAN ON CONTINUING THE PLIGHT...
I KNOW JUST THE PLACE TO START.

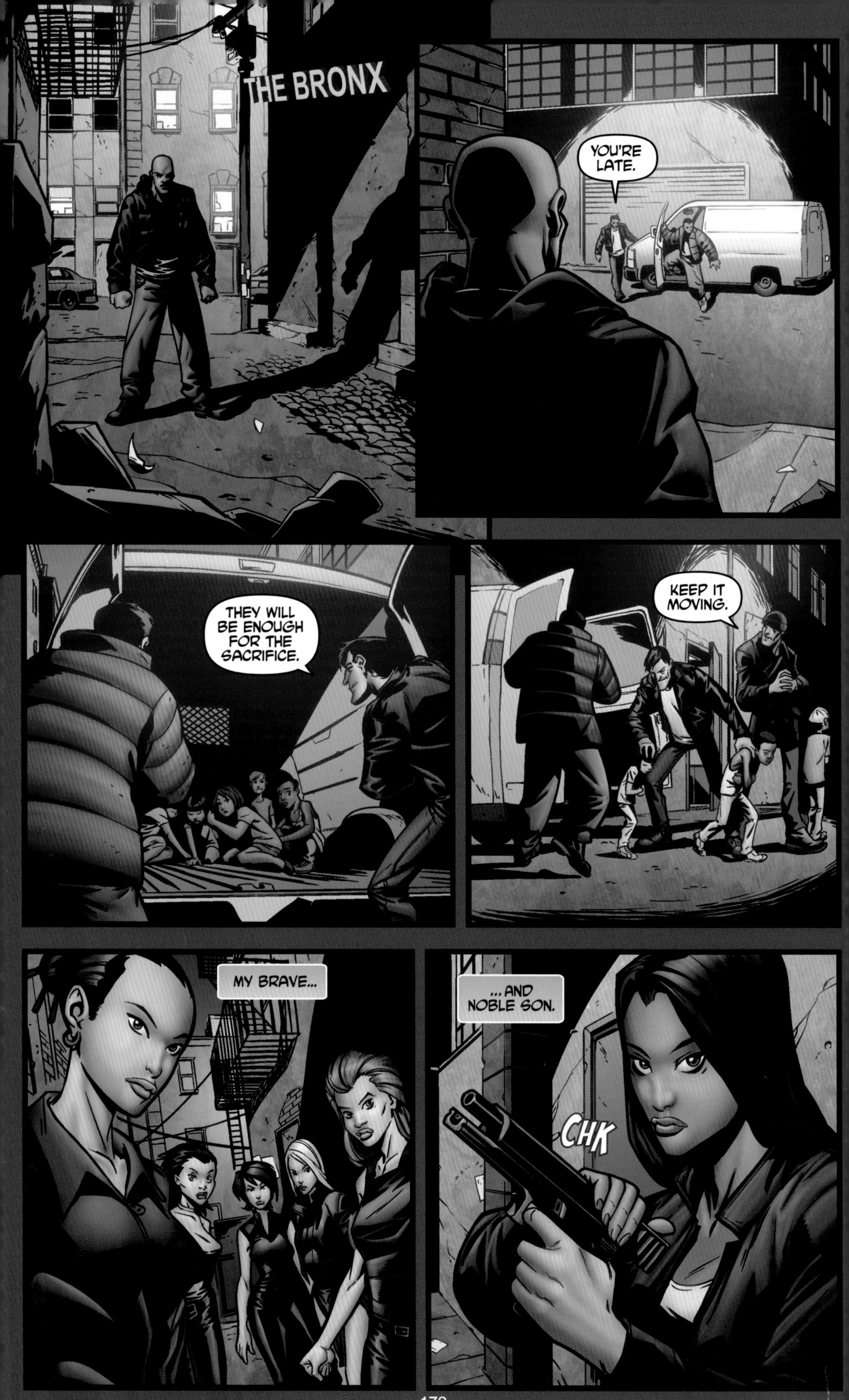
THE BRONX
YOU'RE LATE.
THEY WILL BE ENOUGH FOR THE SACRIFICE.
KEEP IT MOVING.
MY BRAVE...
...AND NOBLE SON.
CHK

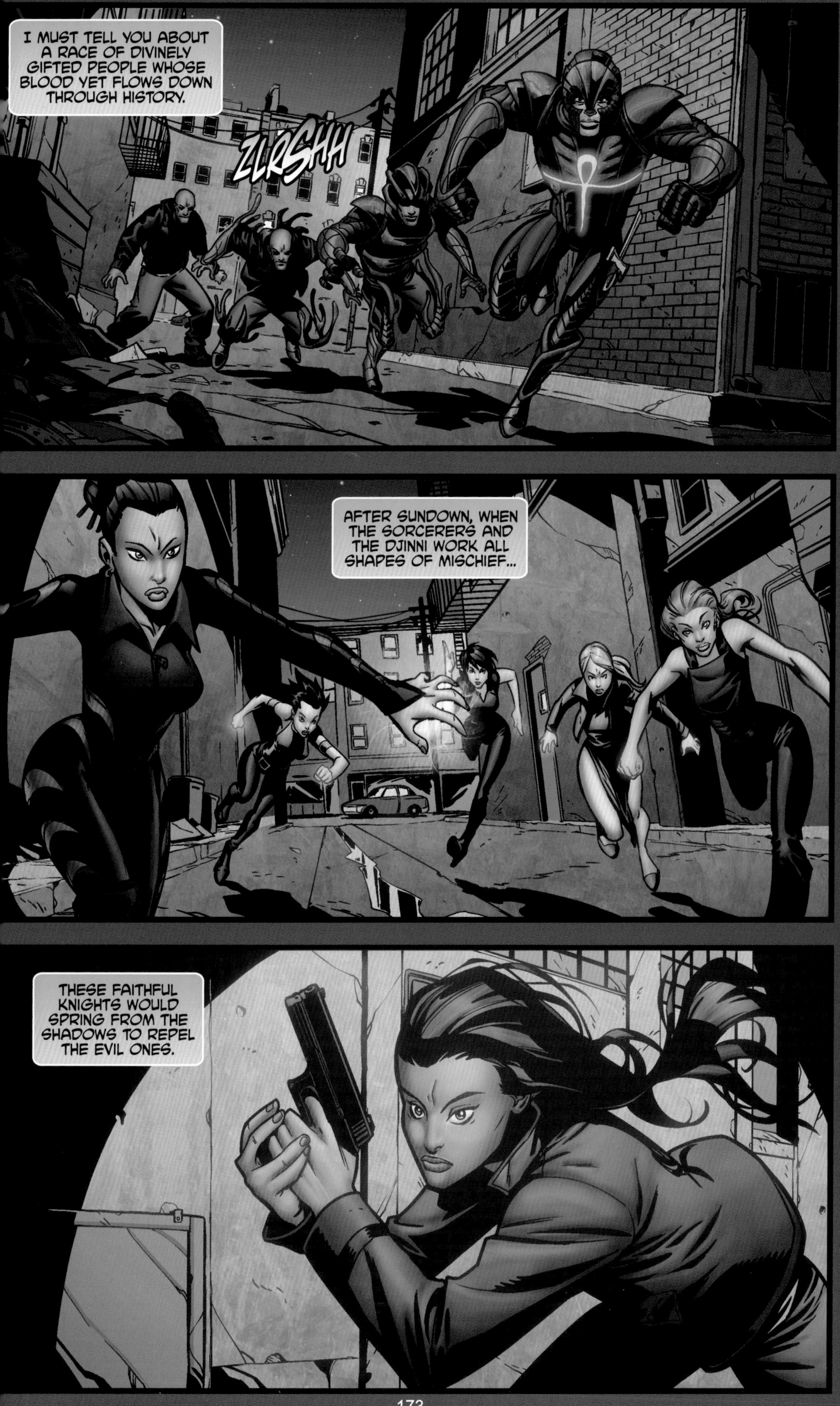
I MUST TELL YOU ABOUT A RACE OF DIVINELY GIFTED PEOPLE WHOSE BLOOD YET FLOWS DOWN THROUGH HISTORY.
ZLRSHH
AFTER SUNDOWN, WHEN THE SORCERERS AND THE DJINNI WORK ALL SHAPES OF MISCHIEF...
THESE FAITHFUL KNIGHTS WOULD SPRING FROM THE SHADOWS TO REPEL THE EVIL ONES.

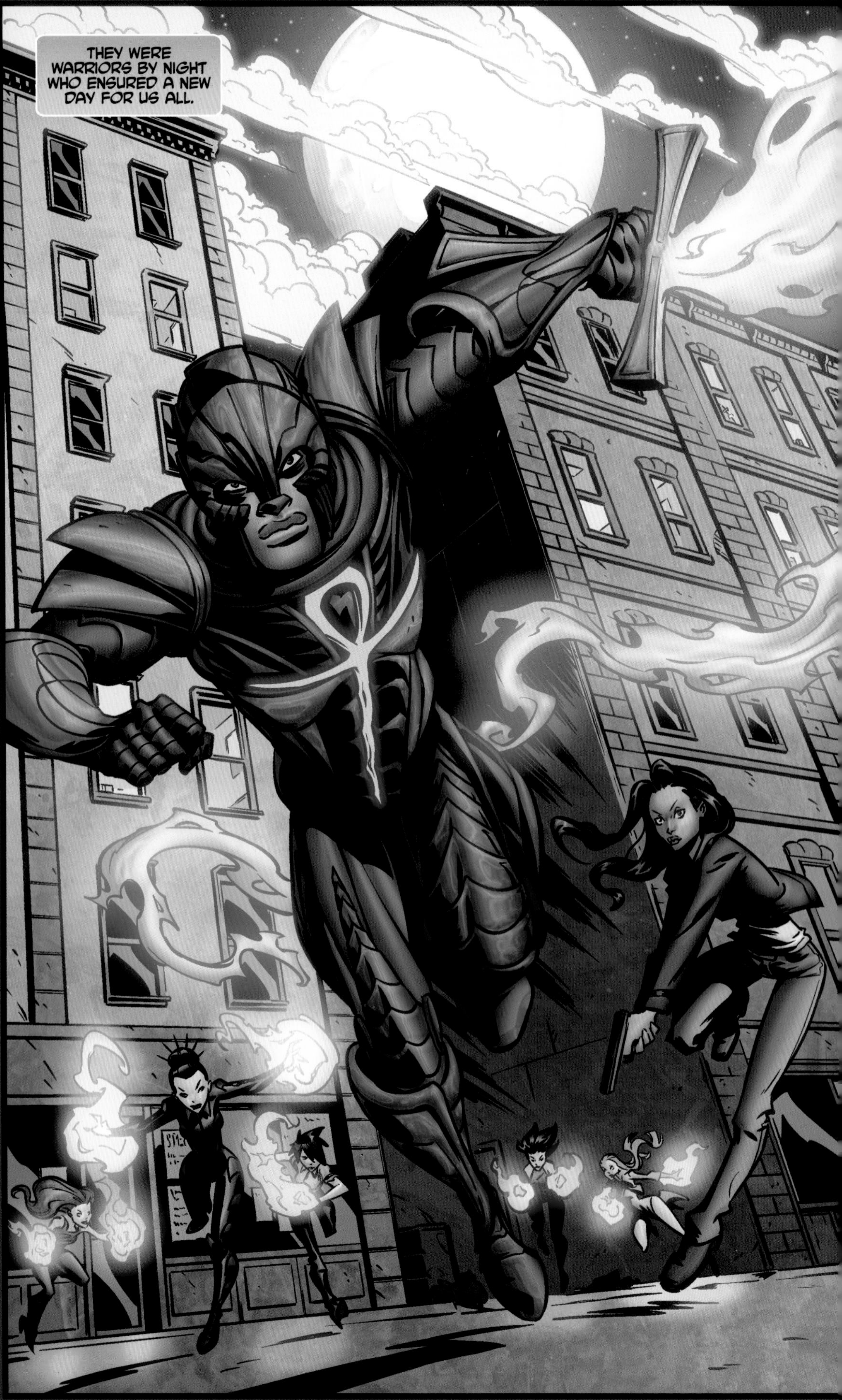
THEY WERE WARRIORS BY NIGHT WHO ENSURED A NEW DAY FOR US ALL.

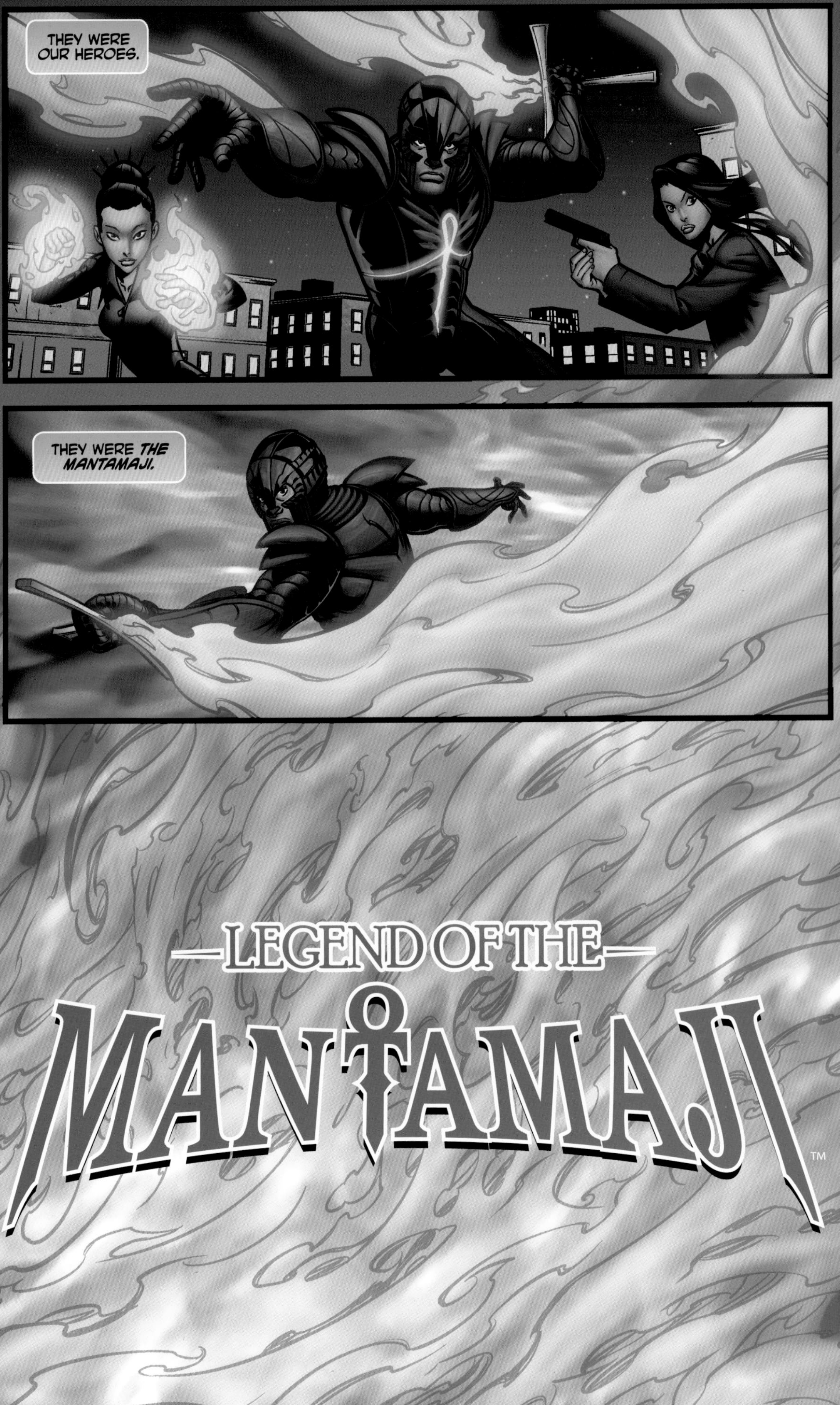
THEY WERE OUR HEROES.
THEY WERE *THE MANTAMAJI.*
LEGEND OF THE
MANTAMAJI™

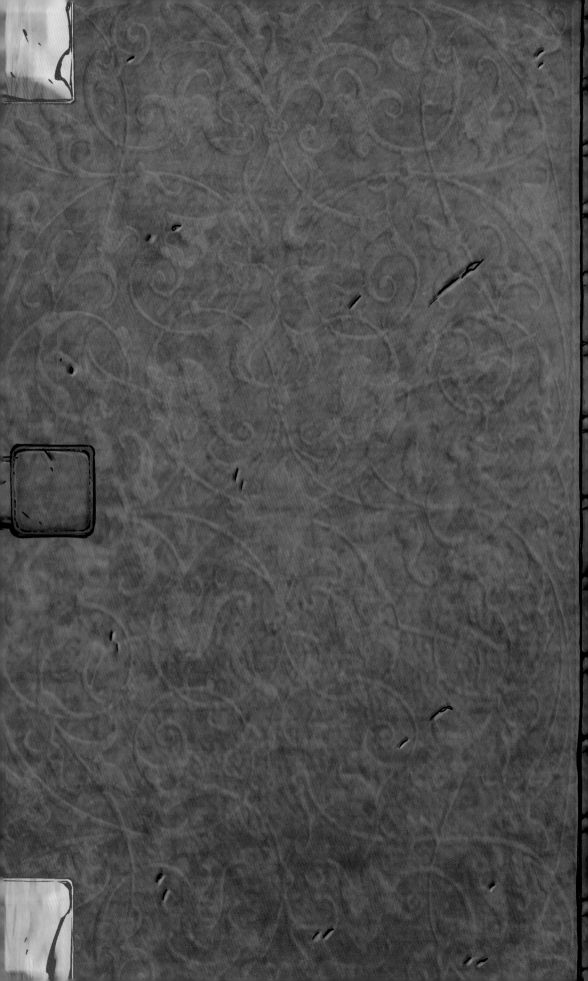

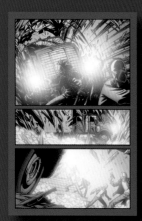

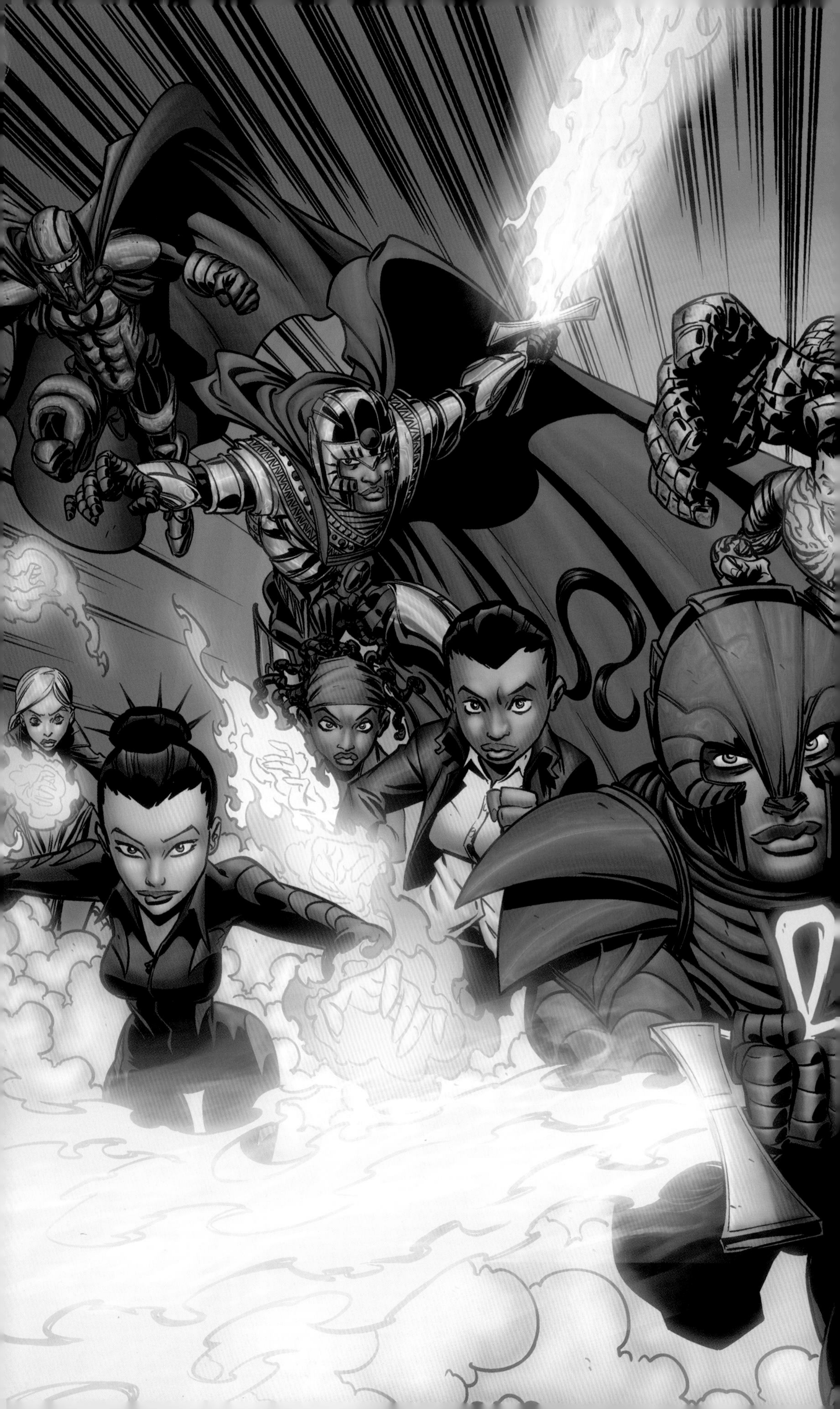

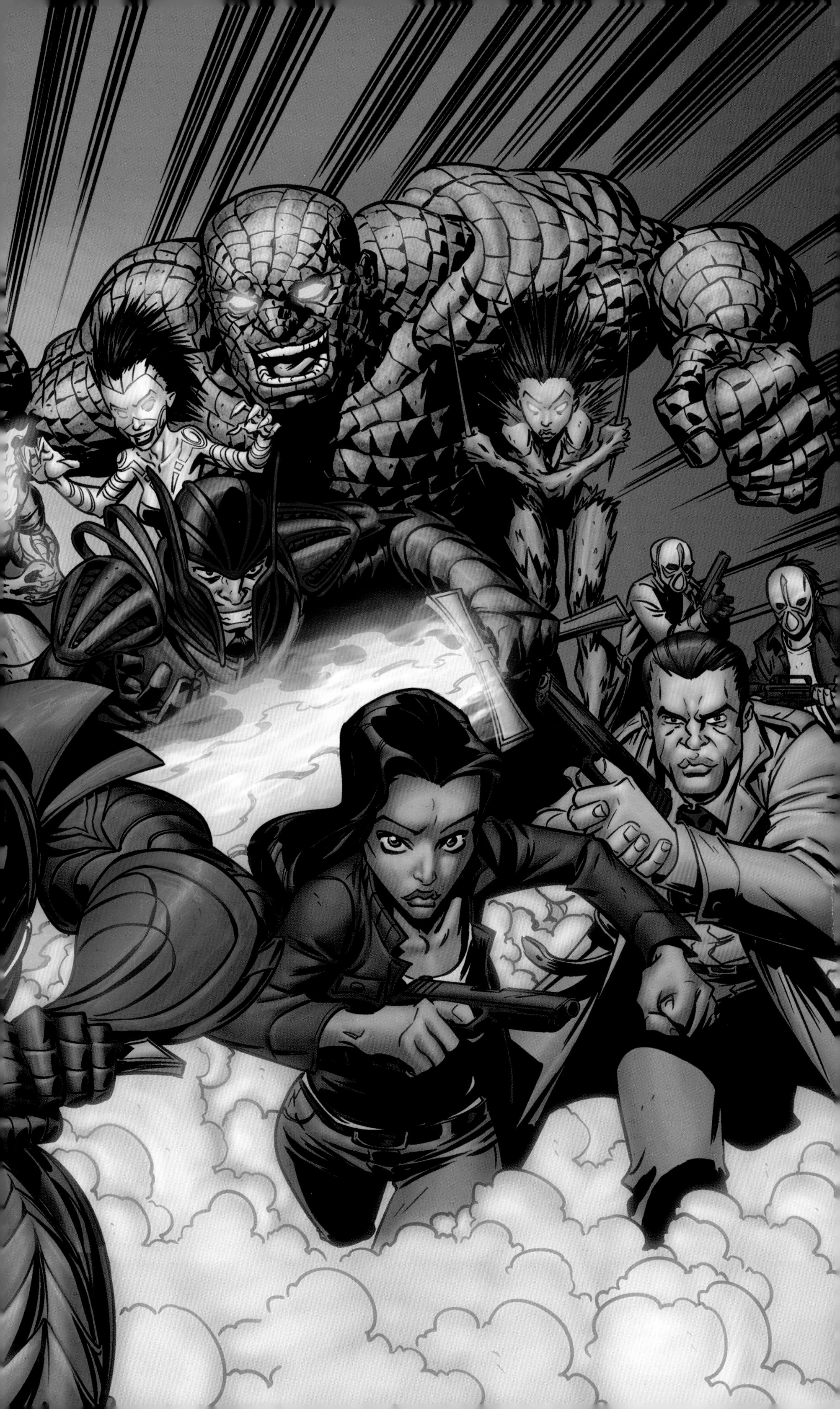

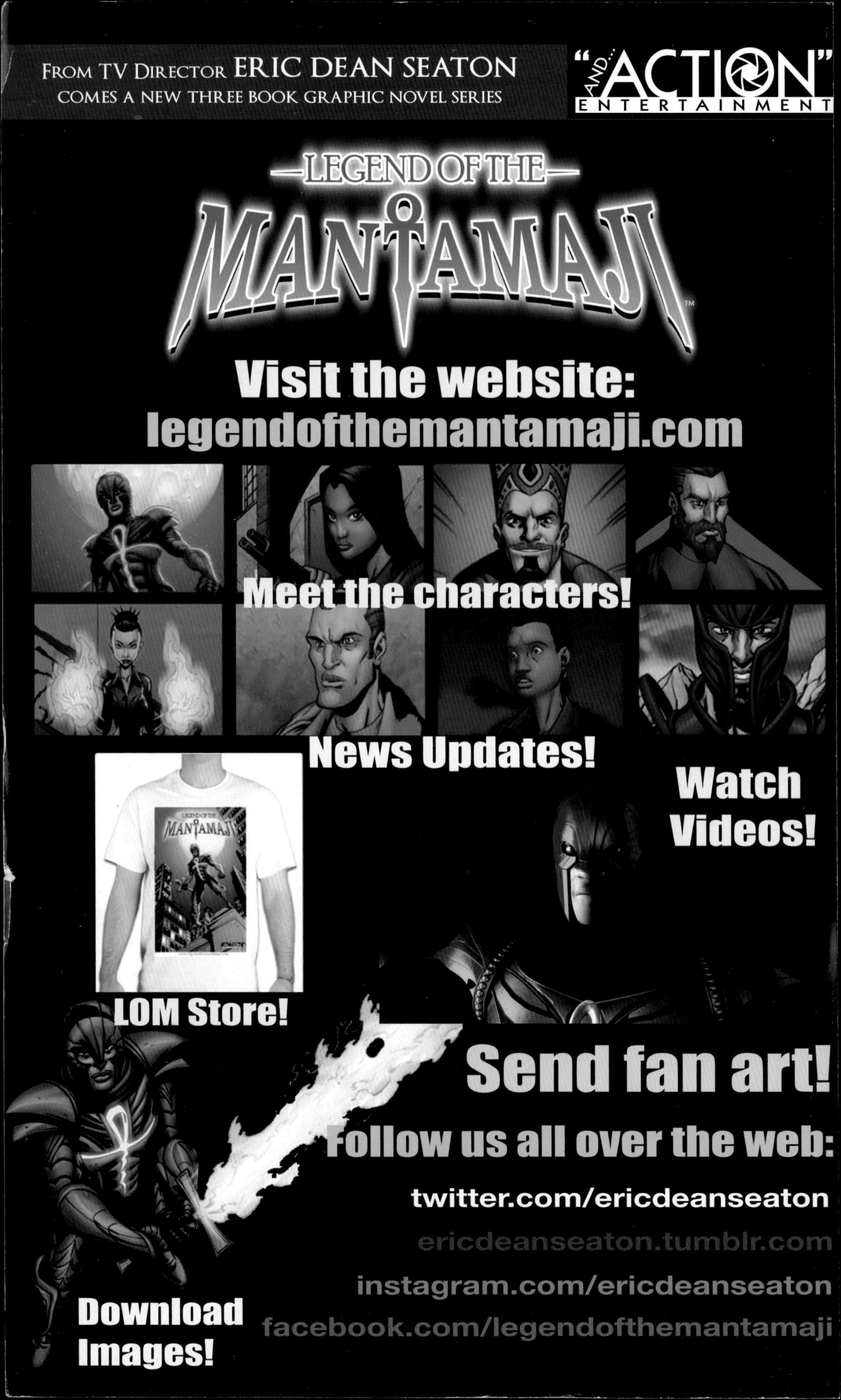

From TV Director ERIC DEAN SEATON
COMES A NEW THREE BOOK GRAPHIC NOVEL SERIES
"AND... ACTION" ENTERTAINMENT
LEGEND OF THE MANTAMAJI™
Visit the website:
legendofthemantamaji.com
Meet the characters!
News Updates!
Watch Videos!
LOM Store!
Send fan art!
Follow us all over the web:
twitter.com/ericdeanseaton
ericdeanseaton.tumblr.com
instagram.com/ericdeanseaton
facebook.com/legendofthemantamaji
Download Images!